THE HUMAN RIGHTS REVOLUTION

NATIONAL HISTORY CENTER

REINTERPRETING HISTORY
Wm. Roger Louis, *series editor*

The series Reinterpreting History is dedicated to the historian's craft of challenging assumptions, examining new evidence, and placing topics of significance in historiographical context. Historiography is the art of conveying the ways in which the interpretation of history changes over time. The vigorous and systematic revision of history is at the heart of the discipline.

Reinterpreting History is an initiative of the National History Center, which was created by the American Historical Association in 2002 to advance historical knowledge and to convey to the public at large the historical context of present-day issues.

Making Sense of the Vietnam Wars: Local, National, and Transnational Perspectives ■ EDITED BY Mark Philip Bradley and Marilyn B. Young

Atlantic History: A Critical Appraisal ■ EDITED BY Jack P. Greene and Philip D. Morgan

The Human Rights Revolution: An International History ■ EDITED BY Akira Iriye, Petra Goedde, and William I. Hitchcock

THE HUMAN RIGHTS REVOLUTION

An International History

EDITED BY

Akira Iriye, Petra Goedde, and
William I. Hitchcock

OXFORD

UNIVERSITY PRESS

OXFORD
UNIVERSITY PRESS

Oxford University Press, Inc., publishes works that further
Oxford University's objective of excellence
in research, scholarship, and education.

Oxford   New York
Auckland   Cape Town   Dar es Salaam   Hong Kong   Karachi
Kuala Lumpur   Madrid   Melbourne   Mexico City   Nairobi
New Delhi   Shanghai   Taipei   Toronto

With offices in
Argentina   Austria   Brazil   Chile   Czech Republic   France   Greece
Guatemala   Hungary   Italy   Japan   Poland   Portugal   Singapore
South Korea   Switzerland   Thailand   Turkey   Ukraine   Vietnam

Published by Oxford University Press, Inc.
198 Madison Avenue, New York, NY 10016

www.oup.com

Oxford is a registered trademark of Oxford University Press

Library of Congress Cataloging-in-Publication Data
The human rights revolution : an international history / edited by
Akira Iriye, Petra Goedde, and William I. Hitchcock.
p.   cm. — (Reinterpreting history)
Includes index.
ISBN 978-0-19-533313-8 — ISBN 978-0-19-533314-5 (pbk.)
1. Human rights—History.
2. Human rights—Political aspects—History.
I. Iriye, Akira. II. Goedde, Petra, 1964– III. Hitchcock, William I.
JC571.H775 2012
323.09—dc23   2011017618

1 3 5 7 9 8 6 4 2

Printed in the United States of America
on acid-free paper

To the Memory of Kenneth J. Cmiel

CONTENTS

PREFACE

This book, like the field of human rights, has been a long time in gestation. It began as a series of papers delivered to the 2004 meeting of the American Historical Association (AHA) in Washington, D.C. Akira Iriye chaired a panel on the topic "Writing the Global History of Human Rights" that featured contributions by Mark Bradley, Kenneth Cmiel, Alexis Dudden, and Atina Grossmann. The original idea had been to use these essays as a nucleus of a volume on new trends in historiography as part of the Oxford series on *Reinterpreting History*. Yet the project was dealt a blow by the sudden death of Ken Cmiel, whose energy and leadership in this evolving field has been missed by his friends, colleagues, and peers across the discipline. He had done a great deal to place this field on the agenda of historians, and many of the essays in the collection have their origins in his seminal writings. The volume is dedicated to his memory.

In late 2008, William Hitchcock and Petra Goedde co-chaired a conference at Temple University on "Human Rights as International History." The event was held, in part, to mark the sixtieth anniversary of the Universal Declaration of Human Rights and also to gather together work in the field by a new generation of scholars whose fresh arguments and new archival discoveries helped transform human rights scholarship. We are grateful to the International History Workshop and the History Department at Temple for the support we received in hosting that gathering.

Susan Ferber, our always creative and indefatigable editor, saw that by combining the essays from the AHA panel and the Temple event, we had the makings of an outstanding "state of the field" volume. Susan earned our profound gratitude for keeping this project going and prodding us to bring it to fruition, even when it seemed it might not quite make it to the finish line. She is a visionary editor, and we all feel enormously proud of the volume she has done so much to create.

Akira Iriye
Petra Goedde
William I. Hitchcock

CONTRIBUTORS

ALLIDA BLACK manages the Women's Political Participation Program of the National Democratic Institute for International Affairs. She is also Research Professor of History and International Affairs at the George Washington University, where she chairs the Eleanor Roosevelt Project Advisory Board. She has written widely on Eleanor Roosevelt, women's human rights, and women's political engagement. She has coordinated (and is continuing to organize) mentoring and policy workshops on women's human rights for the United Nations, the Department of State, and a variety of nongovernmental organizations. She is the recipient of the George Washington University Millennium Medal, two honorary doctorates, and several community service and human rights awards.

CARL J. BON TEMPO is Assistant Professor of History at SUNY Albany. He is the author of *Americans at the Gate: The United States and Refugees during the Cold War* (2008). He currently is working on a history of human rights politics in the United States after the 1970s.

ELIZABETH BORGWARDT is a Fellow at the Stanford Center for Advanced Study in the Behavioral Sciences for 2010–11. A historian and lawyer, she will serve as the Richard and Ann Pozen Visiting Professor of Human Rights at the University of Chicago in 2012. She is Associate Professor of History and Law (by courtesy) at Washington University in St. Louis.

MARK PHILIP BRADLEY is Professor of History at the University of Chicago. He is completing a book-length monograph that explores the place of the United States in the global human rights imagination of the twentieth century.

KENNETH CMIEL was Professor of History and the director of the University of Iowa Center for Human Rights until he died suddenly in 2006. He taught intellectual history and the history of human rights at the University of Iowa since 1987. He is the author of *Democratic Eloquence: The Fight over Popular Speech in Nineteenth-Century America* (1990), based on his Allan Nevins Prize–winning dissertation, "A Home of Another Kind: One

Chicago Orphanage and the Tangle of Child Welfare" (1995) and numerous articles on intellectual and human rights history.

G. DANIEL COHEN is Associate Professor of History at Rice University. He specializes in the history of refugees, forced displacement, and human rights law in twentieth-century Europe. His articles on these topics appeared in various journals including *The Journal of Contemporary History*, *Immigrants and Minorities* and *Geneses*. Cohen is the author of *In War's Wake: Europe's Displaced Persons in the Postwar Order* (2011).

ALEXIS DUDDEN is Professor of History at the University of Connecticut where she also directs the program in humanitarian research study. She is author most recently of *Troubled Apologies Among Japan, Korea, and the United States* (2008) as well as numerous articles and Internet essays. She is currently writing a book about nationalism and the law of the sea in Northeast Asia.

PETRA GOEDDE is Associate Professor of History at Temple University. Her research interests are in U.S. foreign relations, and transnational, culture, and gender history. She is the author of *GIs and Germans* (2003) and articles on U.S. foreign relations and the globalization of American culture. Her current projects include a history of global culture since 1945 and a book-length study of the global discourse on peace during the cold war.

ATINA GROSSMANN is Professor of History in the Faculty of Humanities and Social Sciences at the Cooper Union in New York City where she teaches Modern German and European History, and Gender Studies. Publications include *Reforming Sex: The German Movement for Birth Control and Abortion Reform, 1920–1950* (1995) and co-edited volumes on *Crimes of War: Guilt and Denial in the Twentieth Century* (2002) and *After the Nazi Racial State: Difference and Democracy in Germany and Europe* (2009), as well as articles on gender and modernity in interwar Germany and history and memory in postwar Germany. Her book *Jews, Germans, and Allies: Close Encounters in Occupied Germany* (2007, in German, 2011) was awarded the George L. Mosse Prize of the American Historical Association. She is beginning a research project on transnational Jewish refugee stories, "Soviet Central Asia, Iran, and India: Sites of Refuge and Relief for European Jews during World War II."

WILLIAM I. HITCHCOCK is a Professor of History at the University of Virginia. He has taught at Temple University, Wellesley College, and Yale University. He took his PhD at Yale under Paul Kennedy in 1994 and has authored a number of books on Europe and trans-Atlantic relations. His most recent book, *The Bitter Road to Freedom: A New History of the Liberation of Europe* (2008), won the 2009 George Louis Beer Prize from the American Historical Association, and was a finalist for the Pulitzer Prize.

AKIRA IRIYE is Professor of History Emeritus at Harvard University. He is the author of many books on U.S. foreign relations and global history, among them the *Dictionary of Transnational History*, co-edited with Pierre Yves Saunier, (2009) and *Global Community* (2002).

BARBARA KEYS is a historian at the University of Melbourne. She is finishing a book manuscript on the roots of the U.S. turn toward human rights in foreign policy in the 1970s and is starting a project on global anti-torture campaigns from the 1960s through the 1980s.

SAMUEL MOYN is Professor of History at Columbia University, where he has taught since 2001. His most recent book is *The Last Utopia: Human Rights in History* (2010).

PAUL RUBINSON is Assistant Professor of History at Bridgewater State University. His article "Crucified on a Cross of Atoms: Scientists, Politics, and the Test Ban" appeared in *Diplomatic History* in April 2011. Before earning his PhD from the University of Texas at Austin, he served as a Smith-Richardson Foundation Predoctoral Fellow at International Security Studies, Yale University. He is currently working on a book manuscript titled *Containing Science: The U.S. National Security State and Scientists' Challenge to Nuclear Weapons during the Cold War*.

BRAD SIMPSON is Assistant Professor of History and international affairs at Princeton University and the author of *Economists with Guns: Authoritarian Development and U.S.-Indonesian Relations* (2008). He is currently writing a history of the idea self-determination, exploring its political, cultural, and legal descent through post-1945 international politics, and a history of U.S.-Indonesian international relations during the reign of General Suharto (1966–1998).

KELLY J. SHANNON is Assistant Professor of History at the University of Alaska, Anchorage. She received her PhD in history from Temple University in 2010. Her current book project explores the integration of women's rights concerns into U.S. foreign policy toward the Islamic world since the late 1970s.

SARAH B. SNYDER, Lecturer in International History at University College London, specializes in the Cold War, human rights activism, and United States human rights policy. She is the author of *Human Rights Activism and the End of the Cold War: A Transnational History of the Helsinki Network*, as well as articles in *Cold War History, Diplomacy and Statecraft, Journal of American Studies,* and *Journal of Transatlantic Studies.* She received her PhD from Georgetown University.

THE HUMAN RIGHTS REVOLUTION

INTRODUCTION

Human Rights as History

AKIRA IRIYE AND PETRA GOEDDE

Human rights have a long history, yet their tenure as a historical subject is surprisingly short. Classic works in world history such as William McNeill's *A World History* (1967) or J. M. Roberts's *History of the World* (1976) discussed slavery, discrimination against women, wartime atrocities, and other violations of individual and group rights. They did not, however, employ the term *human rights* even though it had entered the international political lexicon long before.[1] The absence of human rights history in these works suggests that even in an era of increased rights consciousness, historians did not consider human rights a useful category of analysis.

As detailed in Kenneth Cmiel's landmark historiographical essay, first published in 2004 and reprinted in this volume, this neglect was common until the 1990s, when interest in human rights history surged.[2] Since then, historians have explored the history of human rights both in its theoretical and in its concrete political, legal, social, and cultural manifestations. They have increasingly concentrated on how the universal language of human rights has been applied and negotiated in local social and political settings. They also began to see, as Cmiel suggested, human rights as integral to the history of globalization without losing sight of their local manifestations.[3] The essays in this volume bear testimony to the expansion of the field in intellectual, political, and international history. Human rights as a historical subfield has come into its own.

Even though scholars trace human rights discourses to the early Enlightenment debates on natural rights among thinkers such as David Hume, Adam Smith, Thomas Hobbes, and John Locke and to documents such as the 1789 American Bill of Rights and the French Declaration of the Rights of Man and Citizen, the transnational realization of a human rights agenda long remained elusive.[4] Human rights campaigns surfaced in different political and social contexts throughout the nineteenth century, among them the campaign against slavery, the women's rights movement, and the fight for workers' rights. The first Geneva Convention, ratified by twelve nations in 1864, established the right to humane treatment for captured and wounded enemy soldiers.[5] The often brutal colonial regimes of the late nineteenth century and the genocides and wars of the first half of the twentieth century, however, dispelled any illusion that these rights manifestations led to a more just and humane world.[6] Although Woodrow Wilson advocated a system of international laws to regulate relations among nations after World War I, he neglected to add human rights to his Fourteen Points. The main locus of advocacy for human rights thus lay with nongovernmental groups, such as the French Ligue des droits de l'homme, founded in 1898, to protect minorities as a result of the anti-Semitic Dreyfus affair.[7]

The concept of human rights stayed on the margins of high-level international politics throughout World War II. To be sure, Franklin Delano Roosevelt included the defense of human rights in his State of the Union address in January 1941 and repeated the pledge in the Allied powers' statement of war aims on New Year's Day 1942.[8] However, human rights were not included in the Atlantic Charter of August 1941. In January 1942, the Declaration of the United Nations (at the time the name of the alliance of forces against the Axis powers) vowed to "preserve human rights and justice in their own lands as well as in other lands," but there was no further elaboration on what these rights were or how they should be enforced.[9] The UN Charter, signed on June 26, 1945, in San Francisco, also enshrined in its preamble "faith in fundamental human rights, in the dignity and worth of the human person, in the equal rights of men and women and of nations large and small" but remained vague regarding the definition and extent of human rights.[10] It was not until December 10, 1948, that the UN General Assembly ratified the first-ever global declaration of human rights.[11]

The principal author of the Universal Declaration of Human Rights (UDHR) was John Peters Humphrey, a Canadian legal scholar and first director of the Human Rights Division of the United Nations Secretariat. The French jurist René Cassin, a member of the Human Rights Commission, gave it its distinctive structure: articles 1–2 laid out the general principles of human rights, followed by individual rights (articles 3–11); rights of individuals in relation to groups (articles 12–17); spiritual, public, and political rights (articles 18–21); and economic, social, and cultural rights (articles 22–27). Articles 28–30 placed the rights within the broader context of limits, duties, and order.[12] Clean and orderly as the organization of the Declaration was, it could not mask the ambiguities in the wording that led almost immediately to contestations over the meaning of such concepts as freedom and self-determination, as well as the proper relationship among individual, community, and states' rights. Moreover, it lacked any provision for the enforcement of these rights.

Scholars and practitioners of international law dominated the field of human rights literature from the 1930s to the 1960s, among them Arnold McNair, Hersch Lauterpacht, and Egon Schwelb.[13] Rarely did their concerns intersect with those of international relations historians. One of the most distinguished works in international relations history published in the 1930s, William Langer's *The Diplomacy of Imperialism*, dealt extensively with decision-makers and diplomacy at the turn of the twentieth century, but paid little, if any, attention to the objects of that "diplomacy of imperialism." Langer did not even address minority rights, an issue of utmost urgency in the 1930s as Jews and other minorities in Europe struggled to escape Nazi persecution.[14] Even if Langer had been eschewing presentism, he must have been aware that during the age of imperialism massive migrations were taking place, not just across the Atlantic but also across the Indian and Pacific oceans, bringing different races and ethnic groups into closer contact than ever before. Samuel Flagg Bemis's work on U.S.-Latin American relations, published during the war, addressed Nazi racism but did not identify Nazi Germany's atrocities as human rights violations.[15] Dorothy Borg's *American Policy and the Chinese Revolution*, published shortly after the end of World War II as the UN commission drafted the human rights declaration, was likewise silent on race and other human rights issues.[16] In short, as human rights advocates in legal and political circles shifted attention from collective to individual rights, historians remained concerned primarily with great power relations and the nation-state.

Postwar diplomatic historians, in particular, showed utmost skepticism toward the idealistic wave of rights talk. They preferred what they called a "realist" perspective, privileging matters of national security and power politics over issues of human rights and internationalism. George Kennan, Robert E. Osgood, and Henry Kissinger, among others, focused on questions of military and political power rather than ideals and values.[17] The revisionists who challenged them, among them Charles Beard, Charles Tansill, and William Appleman Williams, were equally reluctant to consider ideas, values, and rights, and instead advanced an economic interpretation of international relations.[18]

As human rights became a major concern in international politics in the 1960s and 1970s in the aftermath of decolonization, during the civil rights movement and the Vietnam War, it, for the first time, also became a subject of historical inquiry. Among the early works addressing human rights questions were histories of the Holocaust, which proliferated after the 1961 trial in Israel of Adolf Eichmann, one of the major architects of the Nazi extermination of the Jews.[19] Nonetheless, Holocaust literature remained a genre apart from both human rights and international relations literature. The burgeoning rights scholarship of the 1960s and 1970s focused on social issues, such as women's rights, minority rights, gay and lesbian rights, and ethnic rights. The foreign relations literature began to address issues of race, gender, culture, and ideology in the 1970s, yet explicit works on human rights within the international context remained rare.[20]

Until the end of the Cold War, the disjuncture between the intensity of human rights advocacy and the neglect of historical exploration of human rights persisted. Only since then have area specialists focused on the history of human rights abuses in particular national contexts, while international historians have explored particular aspects of human rights, including women's rights and minority rights, as part of state-to-state relations or in conjunction with international nongovernmental organizations.[21] Contributions by historians to the prominent journal *Human Rights Quarterly* have steadily increased over the past decade, though law and political science articles still dominate. By the same token, legal and political experts, as well as human rights activists, have begun to recognize the importance of placing their work in historical perspective.[22]

Since 1945, human rights have been defined and redefined according to political needs, moral imperatives, and local contexts. Any historical treatment of human rights has to take account of a series of political contestations that occurred at multiple levels. Human rights advocates have disagreed with one another and with political leaders how to define human rights and whether certain rights should take precedence over others. They argued over the universality of human rights and debated the appropriate mechanisms of enforcement. These contestations make it impossible to construct a linear narrative of progress over the past six decades. But that should not lead to the assumption that no progress occurred at all even though human rights are as embattled today as they were sixty years ago. The history of human rights is local and global, particular and universal, and, above all, it is a history of both advances and setbacks.

The battle over how to define human rights in the postwar period almost immediately became entangled in the Cold War struggle between East and West. It included transnational debates about racial discrimination, decolonization, self-determination, infringements on free speech, and economic and social inequalities. Anti-communists in the United States and Western Europe charged that communism itself represented a violation of human rights because it deprived those under its rule of fundamental rights, namely, freedom of expression, freedom of movement, and religious and political freedoms. The Soviets, in turn, branded the capitalist system of the West as a human rights violation against the working poor, because it fostered economic exploitation. In addition, the West's legacy of imperialism, they charged, violated the right to self-determination of the people in the global South. And most devastating to the United States' reputation in the non-Western world, the Soviet Union charged the United States with violating the rights of its African American minority. Human rights thus became defined and redefined in the service of the rhetorical Cold War battle between the two superpowers.

Political debates over the definition of human rights also became part of the struggle for decolonization. States that recently won independence from colonial powers or were struggling to gain independence had a deep political stake in defining human rights first and foremost as the right to self-determination. Delegates at the 1955 Bandung Conference, where African and Asian nations sought closer economic and political cooperation and a common strategy to fight colonialism and imperialism, officially declared self-determination as the "first" right, implicitly privileging collective over individual rights. However, in an open letter to the conference delegates, Mahmoud Aboul Fath, Egyptian journalist and publisher, warned not to lose sight of individual human rights, among them the right to free speech. Fath drew on personal experience: Gamal Abdel Nasser, Egypt's nationalist leader, had forced Fath into exile after his newspaper published articles sharply critical of his policies.[23] In his letter, Fath implored delegates to adhere to the standards laid out in the Human Rights Declaration. "The violation of human rights," he warned, "is certainly bad and intolerable when committed by imperialists against peoples on whom they force their authority, but it is also worse and more obnoxious [when] committed by a few nationals against their own people."[24] Fath's statement alluded to the conflicted attitude of many Third World nationalists toward human rights. They needed to assert the right to self-determination as a collective human right to gain independence but saw little political utility in individual rights. But was self-determination, in fact, a human right? The legal scholar A. W. Brian Simpson did not think so. His definition of human rights encompassed only individual rights and excluded the collective rights of peoples and nations.[25] However, even though the UN Declaration did not include a specific reference to self-determination, it did address collective rights in addition to individual rights. Both were of critical importance for the creation of a just postcolonial world.

Even among those who championed both collective and individual rights, disputes arose regarding whether the attainment of certain rights should take precedence over others. When the architects of the UN Declaration distinguished between economic-social and civil-political rights by organizing them in different subsections, they did not intend to create a hierarchy of rights, nor did they see these rights in competition with one another. In practice, however, hierarchies of rights emerged in different political, economic, and social settings.[26] Newly independent states in the global South often placed a higher value on social and economic rights, such as rights to housing, food, clothing, education, and medical care, as well as the collective right to self-determination, while rights advocates in the industrialized world invested more energy and activism in the realization of civil and political rights, such as freedom of expression and suffrage. The North–South clash over human rights priorities erupted unexpectedly at the first UN International Women's Year Conference in Mexico City in 1975. The United Nations had created an official venue where government representatives congregated and an unofficial one, called the Tribune, where nongovernmental women's organizations met. At the Tribune meeting, Western and non-Western feminists clashed over which rights demanded greater attention. Non-Western feminists argued that attention to economic rights, including support for development, needed to come before attention to the attainment of gender equality. The clash over priorities exposed the gulf that still separated feminists in different parts of the world.[27]

By the 1970s, women's rights, environmental rights (for instance, the right to clean water and clean air), and ethnic equality became part of the global human rights discourse. This expansion of the human rights agenda challenged the principle of national sovereignty the UN had steadfastly defended since its inception. If discrimination against women in the workplace or air pollution counted as human rights violations, then corporations, interest groups, and even national governments would become vulnerable to United Nations sanctions. These groups thus undertook a concerted effort to limit the further expansion of the human rights agenda, as well as the UN's ability to interfere in domestic affairs.

They encountered new activist groups that focused increasingly on the plight of individuals in local and national communities. One of these was Amnesty International, founded in 1961 by the British lawyer and labor activist Peter Benenson.[28] Amnesty International's initial mission was to secure the release of political prisoners through letter-writing campaigns and public pressure on law enforcement agencies and governments. Though its success rate remained sketchy in the ensuing decade, the organization rapidly grew into an international network, expanding its mandate to include women's rights, children's rights, and the rights of refugees and torture victims. In the era of 1960s social and political protest movements, the organization's idealistic public profile and grassroots practices found a receptive audience in the West.[29]

By focusing on the plight of individuals, Amnesty International tried to remain politically neutral, much to the dismay of those who believed that the human rights abuses in some regimes could not and should not be separated from their political context.[30] The organization went so far as to advise local branches to seek adoption of political prisoners in equal proportion from Western countries, the communist world, and the Third World, so as not to seem to take sides in the Cold War conflict. Furthermore, it showed a marked preference for cases with sensationalist potential because they promised greater publicity. Critics charged that this method detracted from human rights violations that deserved equal or greater attention.[31]

The effort to elevate human rights concerns above the level of the Cold War rivalry was visible in the Helsinki Accords of 1975 as well. The accords concluded the multiyear Conference on Security and Cooperation in Europe (CSCE), whose participants included Eastern and Western European states, as well as Canada and the United States. Eastern European governments had asked for the meeting to gain Western recognition of the existing postwar borders. In return for the acceptance of the territorial status quo, Western Europeans demanded the inclusion of specific human rights clauses in the final agreement.[32] Those clauses included "respect [for] human rights and fundamental freedoms, including the freedom of thought, conscience, religion or belief, for all without distinction as to race, sex, language or religion," and "equal rights and self-determination of peoples."[33] The accords led to the creation of Helsinki watch groups, nongovernmental organizations that monitored compliance by all signatories, and encouraged Eastern European dissidents to challenge their governments on civil and political rights.[34] These human rights dissidents became instrumental in bringing down the communist regimes in 1989.[35]

The Helsinki Accords also reaffirmed the universality of human rights, a second area of contestation in the postwar period. Cultural differences in the interpretation of human rights had been the subject of some debate during the drafting of the Declaration. Yet the mostly white Euro-American commission quickly rejected suggestions to interpret or enforce human rights differently in different parts of the world. The commission did, in fact, so-licit the views of a few prominent non-Western intellectuals before it final-ized the wording of the Declaration. Mahatma Gandhi, at the time arguably the Third World's most revered spiritual leader, declared that he preferred an emphasis on duties rather than rights. He explained that "the very right to live accrues to us only when we do the duty of citizenship of the world." Instead of a universal declaration of rights, he proposed "to define the duties of Man and Woman and correlate every right to some corresponding duty to be first performed. Every other right can be shown to be a usurpation hardly worth fighting for." The Chinese philosopher Chung-Shu Lo concurred: he stated that in Chinese social and political discourse rights were enshrined within the language of duties to one's neighbor.[36] Gandhi and Lo did not challenge human rights' claim to universality. Their reservations concerned the framing of the rights discourse, not its substance.

The universal language of human rights initially served well the needs of Asians and Africans as they struggled for independence from colonial powers. They were able to claim for themselves the same right to self-determination, sovereignty, and free political expression as afforded the original signers of the Human Rights Declaration. In fact, during this early phase of the human rights era, it was the Western colonial powers rather than the Third World representatives who made a case for cultural relativism. In the early 1950s, Belgium, Great Britain, France, and other Western powers eager to hold onto their overseas possessions argued for an exemption clause for colonial territories. Couched in terms of cul-tural difference, this justification was a thinly veiled expression of racial discrimination. Advocates of the exemption clause argued that giving colonial subjects equal rights would endanger the public order.[37] They were, as yet, unprepared, the argument went, to handle responsibly the freedoms granted in the Universal Declaration.

For Africans and Asians, rejection of the political system of colonial governance went hand in hand with the rejection of the cultural system of human rights relativism. Their advocacy for universal human rights found expression not only at the Bandung Conference but also in other docu-ments of the global anticolonial struggle. The African National Congress, for instance, drew heavily on the language of human rights in its 1955 for-mulation of the Freedom Charter.[38] Individual rights, the charter declared, long the prerogative of the white minority population in South Africa, should be extended to all citizens of South Africa, regardless of skin color. It took thirty-five years for those rights to become enshrined in the South African constitution.

One of the unintended consequences of the post-1960s emphasis on multiculturalism, and the attendant cultural turn in academic fields such as anthropology, sociology, literature, and history, was the revival of the cultural-relativism argument of the late 1950s. This time, however, it served the interests of the heirs of those who had earlier fought against it. In the 1990s, some African and Asian government representatives began to chip away at the increasingly expansive definition of human rights. They particularly objected to the inclusion of gender equality and tolerance of homosexuality, and sometimes the right to free speech, declaring them incompatible with non-Western traditions and social customs. For instance, when, in 1991, the United Nations Human Development Program included in its newly created Human Freedom Index a country's treatment of homosexuals, several states objected vigorously. Kofi Awoonor, Ghana's ambassador to the UN, claimed that freedom itself was a "value-laden concept that finds expression in different shapes and forms from society to society." Awonoor, who was also the spokesperson for the Group of 77 in the UN, derided the index as a product "of a particular scholar representing a particular culture seen by many in recent history as linked to the oppression and exploitation of a vast part of our world."[39] In many parts of the world, discussion of rights relating to sexual orientation, reproduction, and gender remained highly contested, making it difficult for women to have their rights recognized.

The defense of cultural relativism widened to what became known as the "Asian values" controversy, which dominated the 1993 UN Human Rights Conference in Vienna. Eager to justify their own authoritarianism, several countries, including China, Iran, Syria, Singapore, and Malaysia, assailed the UDHR as an instrument of Western imperialism. They demanded instead the primacy of the right to national sovereignty over universal claims of human rights.[40] At a regional meeting of Asian countries at Bangkok the previous spring, Asian delegates stressed the cultural specificity of regional applications of human rights and emphasized national self-determination and sovereignty as key human rights. Article 8 of the Bangkok Declaration contended that "while human rights are universal in nature, they must be considered in the context of a dynamic and evolving process of international norm-setting, bearing in mind the significance of national and regional particularities and various historical, cultural and religious backgrounds."[41]

Asian human rights organizations and leading intellectuals who met at the same time in Bangkok and Vienna immediately challenged the official position. They rejected the cultural-relativism argument and declared instead that "universal human rights are rooted in many cultures," and that because "human rights are of universal concern and are universal in value, the advocacy of human rights cannot be considered to be an encroachment upon national sovereignty."[42] Asian human rights organizations were very much aware of how their governments exploited the debates over cultural relativism to justify human rights abuses. While they acknowledged that cultural differences existed, they argued that universal human rights as defined in the 1948 UDHR applied to all cultures. The Asian NGOs scored a major victory in Vienna with the approval of the creation of the post of a UN Commissioner for Human Rights, a measure opposed by Asian governments because of the potential for further "Western" interference in their internal affairs.[43]

Asian intellectuals mounted perhaps the strongest challenge to the Asian values argument by questioning the existence of a single Asian culture whose values were different from the "West." One of them, the Indian economist Amartya Sen dismissed the argument made by Singapore's Lee Kuan Yew and China's Li Peng that Asian cultures had greater appreciation for authoritarian rule and less appreciation for individual freedoms and civil rights because authoritarianism had produced economic progress in Asia.[44] Since authoritarianism long preceded economic progress, Sen countered, the origins of that success must lay elsewhere. In addition, he pointed to specific Asian religious and cultural ideas, notably Buddhism, that promoted civic and personal independence over blind obedience to authority. Conversely, he pointed to evidence in Western philosophical and intellectual texts of a deep appreciation and valorization of authoritarianism. Sen's interpretation of human rights embedded cultural particularities within the framework of human rights universalism.

A final area of contestation occurred on the subject of enforcement. Neither the UN Charter nor the Universal Declaration of Human Rights offered a road map for the enforcement of human rights in international, national, and local contexts. The 1949 Geneva Conventions, too, had to rely on the will and ability of participating nations to enforce adherence. The conventions consisted of a set of four treaties that provided a detailed body of rules concerning the humane treatment of prisoners and victims of war.[45] The lack of an enforcement provision was deliberate: no support existed for granting the United Nations the power to interfere in the sovereignty of its member states (see Article 2 of the UN Charter), thus giving significant leeway to national and regional bodies to either devise a mechanism for the enforcement of human rights or to treat it with indifference.[46] The United Nations formulated the ideals but was unwilling to give them teeth. Regional treaties and conventions went much further in this respect, which led to an uneven application of human rights principles around the world.

UN member states only gradually developed enforcement mechanisms often mediated through supplemental continental human rights declarations. The first and most powerful such manifestation came from the Council of Europe, which created the European Convention for the Protection of Human Rights and Fundamental Freedoms (ECHR). Enacted in 1953, it guaranteed adherence of all member states to a human rights code and created an international court, the European Court of Human Rights, to adjudicate violations of human rights in Europe.[47] However, the fourteen signatories of the convention made adherence voluntary. Acceptance of individual petitions was voluntary as well, leaving much of the power of jurisdiction still in the hands of participating states.[48]

Even when U.S. President Jimmy Carter made human rights a cornerstone of his foreign policy agenda in 1977, Cold War considerations restricted his ability to put pressure on many repressive regimes.[49] Carter's failure to apply human rights principles consistently to his foreign policy together with the reemergence of Cold War tensions in the late 1970s undermined again the enforcement of human rights in international relations. To be sure, his successor, Ronald Reagan, liberally employed human rights rhetoric to denounce the Soviet Union, but did little to enforce human rights around the world.

In 1979, Latin American states followed the European model with the Inter-American Court of Human Rights. The court created the enforcement mechanisms lacking in the American Declaration of the Rights and Duties of Man, signed more than three decades earlier in April 1948. The court operated under the auspices of the Organization of American States (OAS), a regional foreign policy body created in 1948 to coordinate relations between American states and the rest of the world.[50] The African Court on Human and Peoples' Rights was established in Arusha, Tanzania, in 2004. The court was authorized to enforce the provisions laid down in the 1981 African Charter on Human and Peoples' Rights.[51] Asia, to date, does not have a regional convention on human rights or a judicial body to enforce human rights laws, leaving the interpretation and enforcement of human rights to individual states.

The first global effort to enforce human rights laws came only after the end of the Cold War in the 1990s, when the United Nations set up ad hoc courts to deal with war criminals in the former Yugoslavia and Rwanda. In 1993, the United Nations Security Council established the International Criminal Tribunal for the former Yugoslavia (ICTY) to try individuals accused of human rights violations in that territory since 1991. Defendants included the former Serbian Prime Minister Slobodan Milošević, former President of the Serbian Republic of Bosnia-Herzegovina, Radovan Karadžić, and former Bosnian Serb military leader Ratko Mladić.[52]

In 1994, the UN Security Council established the International Criminal Tribunal for Rwanda (ICTR), a similar ad hoc court to bring to justice perpetrators of the genocide there. The court heard several dozen cases over the next decade and a half and is scheduled to complete its work in 2012. Among its most prominent defendants were Rwanda's interim Prime Minister Jean Kambanda and Jean-Paul Akayesu, mayor of the town of Tabe where Hutu militants systematically rounded up and killed Tutsis. Both Kambanda and Akayesu received life sentences.[53] Even though the United Nations was gradually developing the mechanisms to bring to justice human rights violators in Yugoslavia and Rwanda, countless other offenders in Sri Lanka, Indonesia, Somalia, and elsewhere went untried. In 1998, UN member states agreed to create the International Criminal Court (ICC) as an institution separate from the United Nations, but working in close cooperation with it. By the end of 2010, 114 states had signed on to the court, including most European countries. Notable exceptions included the United States and Israel. The court's jurisdiction is limited to the prosecution of nationals whose governments belong to the court and in cases where "the investigating or prosecuting State is unwilling or unable to genuinely carry out the investigation or prosecution."[54]

By the beginning of the twenty-first century, disputes over definition, universality, and enforcement of human rights remained unresolved. In fact, disagreement intensified in the aftermath of the September 2001 terrorist attacks on the World Trade Center in New York and the Pentagon in Washington, DC, which claimed almost three thousand lives. The Bush administration justified its pursuit of Al Qaeda terrorists first in Afghanistan, then in Iraq in part by pointing to the Taliban's and Saddam Hussein's human rights violations. The revelation of the torture and physical abuse of prisoners in American custody at the Abu Ghraib prison in Iraq, however, brought charges of human rights abuses against the United States itself.[55] Legal advisers' efforts to justify abusive interrogation techniques such as waterboarding caused a domestic and international uproar. The incident gravely damaged the reputation of the United States as a champion of universal human rights.[56] As the U.S. government became entangled in its own rhetorical battle over what constituted torture, human rights violations, most hidden from public view, remained endemic and systematic in many parts of the world.

The evolution of human rights discourse and activism cannot be separated from political, economic, and cultural globalization.[57] Globalization allowed human rights advocates to move beyond the primacy of the nation-state, though it by no means eliminated the state as a source and a target of activism. Globalization has contributed to the fragmentation of national and international communities by linking the local to the global. It has elevated the importance of new means of communication and information technology. Though imperfect and uneven, global human rights networks broadcast eyewitness testimony and visual images of human rights abuses, thus engaging a global audience in the campaign against perpetrators.[58] Those efforts have not created an international consensus on the meaning and extent of the human rights regime, however. To the contrary, multiple groups and political constituencies continue to battle over how to define human rights, and these groups often operate in the interest of political expediency rather than moral principle. As a result, the understanding of human rights in the early twenty-first century is possibly more fragmented than ever before.

The essays in this volume examine human rights issues with respect to both political utility and moral principle. They showcase the theoretical and philosophical debates about the meaning of human rights, as well as the practical implications of the emergence of human rights as a political cause in the service of varied international political agendas. Because of the latter, the United States figures prominently in many of the essays. Americans, both governmental and nongovernmental actors, played a significant role in shaping the international human rights discourse. These essays show the multiple and, at times, contradictory facets of those discourses over the past sixty years. Kenneth Cmiel's chapter analyzes the historiography of human rights through 2004. He identified two major approaches: the exploration of the evolution of the language and meaning of human rights, and the history of human rights activism. For Cmiel, human rights history was inseparable from the processes of globalization, and he encouraged scholars to further explore human rights from a variety of perspectives. The essays that follow demonstrate the richness of those new perspectives both in the early postwar period, when states, organizations, and individuals struggled to make sense of the language and scope of human rights, and since the 1960s, when human rights campaigns turned global.

Focusing on the moment in 1945 when human rights first took center stage in the international arena, Daniel Cohen dispels the popular myth of the close link between the Holocaust and the birth of the human rights regime. Even though several key architects of the Declaration were profoundly and personally affected by the German mass murder of Jews, they did not invoke the Holocaust in the drafting of the document. Instead, Cohen argues, the UDHR and other human rights documents set the stage for the

later memorialization of the Holocaust. He regards the human rights revolution as the first instance of philosemitism in the postwar period.

Elizabeth Borgwardt and William Hitchcock explore the meaning and
substance of two key human rights texts, the Nuremberg Principles and the
Geneva Conventions. Like Cohen, they argue that each document's meaning
and significance expanded over time. Borgwardt shows that the Nuremberg
Principles were originally aspirational and highly contested but became
inscribed in the international legal system through a process of "thickening."
The principles became constitutionalized through their codification in a
variety of national and regional statutes, as well as through their application
in domestic and regional disputes over human rights. Hitchcock reveals a
similar trajectory for the Geneva Conventions. Like the Nuremberg Principles, the Geneva Conventions had to rely on states and courts to apply them.
Hitchcock argues that the human rights principles enshrined in the Geneva
Conventions grew in stature, to a point where even the most powerful
nations found themselves bound by them. Even if in its original provisions
the conventions included scant directive as to the mechanisms of enforcement, by the twenty-first century those mechanisms were firmly in place.

Atina Grossmann moves the theoretical discussion of human rights
ideals to the material level of human survival. In the context of postwar
Germany, where Jewish survivors of the Holocaust competed with German
nationals for food allocation, Grossmann argues that material aid was not
just a means to physical survival but became an emotional and ideational
symbol of one's status as war victim and human being. She explains that
basic human rights like food and shelter took on political meaning and
remained hotly contested in the immediate postwar period. Allida Black
provides a bridge to the globalization of human rights by documenting the
long and arduous struggle of getting women's rights recognized as human
rights in the United Nations. Black traces the campaign for women's rights
from the early days of the Human Rights Commission under the leadership
of Eleanor Roosevelt to the 1995 UN World Conference on Women in Beijing. Black demonstrates the fine line women's advocates walked between
working toward their objectives within the system and establishing separate
institutions.

Focusing on the global implications of the human rights discourse since
the 1960s, Samuel Moyn explores the nexus between decolonization and
human rights rhetoric. He argues that human rights rose in the era when the
Allies were stepping back from earlier promises of collective self-
determination in which colonized peoples were more directly interested. As
decolonization proceeded and their influence in the UN General Assembly

grew, the "new states" that arose on the ruins of the empire made self-determination the first human right, implying a fully decolonized world and supporting antiracist and developmental agendas, rather than the individual protections that international human rights eventually connoted. Moyn concludes that while in theory there was no need to champion collective over individual rights, in practice that was often the case. Brad Simpson reveals another dimension of the treachery of hierarchies via a case study of human rights violations in East Timor in the 1970s. As Indonesia placated the Carter administration with a steady trickle of releases of political prisoners, it engaged in massive human rights violations in its struggle to absorb East Timor, a former Portuguese colony that had declared independence in 1975. Simpson's analysis demonstrates that privileging either individual or collective human rights could not produce a viable human rights regime. He also shows that definitions of self-determination remained hotly contested in the 1970s and resulted not only in competing claims to the "first right" of self-determination but also to human rights abuses in support of that right of self-determination.

Barbara Keys provides another case study from the late 1960s, the international campaign to end torture in Greece. She illustrates how Amnesty International's documentation of torture in Greece helped fuel an embrace of international human rights as a new cause for American liberals disillusioned by the Vietnam War—a cause that gave special prominence to integrity-of-the-person abuses, such as torture, while neglecting other abuses. The human rights "boom" is typically traced to the 1970s, but Keys shows that its origins and its preoccupation with torture lay, in part, in the 1960s campaign against the Greek junta. Liberals embraced the anti-torture campaign because it allowed them to bypass the traditional political fault lines of the Cold War. The conservative flipside to the liberal campaign against torture is the subject of Carl Bon Tempo's essay. He examines the 1970s human rights campaign of Freedom House, an American bipartisan foreign-policy think tank founded in 1941. Unlike Keys's political liberals, who welcomed the chance to escape the Cold War focus on anti-communism, Freedom House members capitalized on it by offering a distinctly conservative vision of human rights activism that focused on infractions of free speech and free movement in the communist world.

The next two essays offer two perspectives on the human rights discourse with respect to the Soviet Union. Paul Rubinson focuses on a group of prominent U.S. scientists that, until the late 1970s, attempted to bypass Cold War divisions and politics in the interest of global scientific endeavors. However, the imprisonment of scientists who were engaged in the Soviet dissident movement compelled them to become human rights activists on behalf of their Soviet colleagues. Sarah Snyder puts the spotlight on the remarkable transformation of international human rights politics under Gorbachev. She credits the human rights watch groups that emerged in the aftermath of the Helsinki Accords with prompting the Gorbachev regime to change its approach to human rights in the Soviet Union. Her essay demonstrates the important interplay between NGOs and high-level diplomacy in the final years of the Cold War. Both Snyder and Rubinson reveal the central role nongovernmental groups played in advancing the human rights agenda.

Kelly Shannon, like the previous two contributors, reveals the growing power of NGOs in international relations in her explorations of the international campaign during the 1980s and 1990s against female genital mutilation (FGM). That campaign illustrates the expansion of the idea of human rights to include women's rights, the growing importance of individual rights vis-à-vis the demands of state sovereignty, and the growing strength of human rights universalism over cultural relativism. Though the road to success was fraught with conflicts, even among feminists, Shannon argues that at least in principle, if not in enforcement, by the beginning of the twenty-first century the international community was condemning FGM as a violation of human rights.

Alexis Dudden's essay takes stock of the history of human rights discourse refracted through the lens of memorialization. She discusses the competing motivations attached to the politics of apology that proliferated dramatically in the 1990s. Using Japan as a case study, Dudden argues that victims demanded an official apology to make their past suffering visible, and thus part of the historical record. The Japanese government, in contrast, offered apologies as a political tool to contain the same past. The former see apology as a starting point for coming to terms with the past, the latter see it as an end point for their accountability. The Japanese case most starkly illustrates the political capital invested in the human rights dialogue at the end of the twentieth century.

Mark Bradley completes the collection with an assessment of sixty years under the Universal Declaration of Human Rights. He suggests that we need to set aside the skepticism and triumphalism of human rights history to concentrate on moments of—in Lynn Hunt's words—"jumps and discontinuities." He illustrates these jumps and discontinuities by focusing on human rights moments in the 1940s, 1970s, and 1990s.

Kenneth Cmiel, at the end of his essay in this book, struck a tone of uncertainty about the future of both human rights activism and the fate of future scholarship. "Only time will tell," he surmised, if the enthusiasm about human rights of the 1990s will be undermined by a new cynicism prevalent in the aftermath of 9/11, the same way "the Cold War and decolonization undermined the previous decade's enthusiasm and stopped the nascent drive for international human rights law in its tracks for the next fifty years." We might not be able to accurately predict the fate of human rights in the world in the coming decades, but, as this volume shows, human rights as a field of historical inquiry is alive and well, and thriving and expanding as never before. The hope remains that in the future the practice of human rights will expand as well.

NOTES

1. William H. McNeill, *A World History* (New York: Oxford University Press, 1967); J. M. Roberts, *History of the World* (New York: Knopf, 1976).

2. See Kenneth Cmiel, "The Recent History of Human Rights," *American Historical Review* 109, no. 1 (February 2004): 117–35. Reprinted in this volume.

3. Among the works to appear since Cmiel's historiographical survey are Elizabeth Borgwardt, *A New Deal for the World: America's Vision of Human Rights* (Cambridge, MA: Harvard University Press, 2005); Mary E. Stuckey, *Jimmy Carter, Human Rights, and the National Agenda* (College Station: Texas A&M University Press, 2009); Roland Burke, *Decolonization and the Evolution of International Human Rights* (Philadelphia: University of Pennsylvania Press, 2010); Samuel Moyn, *The Last Utopia: Human Rights in History* (Cambridge, MA: Belknap, Harvard, 2010). *Human Rights Quarterly*, the leading journal on human rights scholarship has a heavy emphasis on law and policy, though it has increased its publication of articles by historians. For historical articles see Roland Burke, "'The Compelling Dialogue of Freedom': Human Rights at the Bandung Conference," *Human Rights Quarterly* 28, no. 4 (2006): 947–65; Charles Rhéaume, "Western Scientists' Reaction to Andrei Sakharov's Human Rights Struggle in the Soviet Union, 1968–1989," *Human Rights Quarterly* 30, no. 1 (2008): 1–20; Paige Arthur, "How 'Transitions' Reshaped Human Rights: A Conceptual History of Transitional Justice," *Human Rights Quarterly* 31, no. 2 (2009): 321–67.

4. See Lynn Hunt, *Inventing Human Rights: A History* (New York: Norton, 2007); see also Lynn Hunt, ed. *The French Revolution and Human Rights: A Brief Documentary History* (Boston: Bedford, 1996).

5. Paul Gordon Lauren, *The Evolution of International Human Rights: Visions Seen,* 2nd ed. (Philadelphia: University of Pennsylvania Press, 2003), 37–70.

6. See, for instances, the cruel colonial Belgian regime in the Congo, the subject of Adam Hochschild's book *King Leopold's Ghost: A Story of Greed, Terror, and Heroism in Colonial Africa* (Boston: Houghton Mifflin, 1998).

7. Lauren, *The Evolution of Human Rights*, 73. See also William Irvine, *Between Justice and Politics: The Ligue des droits de l'homme, 1898-1945* (Stanford, CA: Stanford University Press, 2007).

8. Jan Herman Burgers, "The Road to San Francisco: The Revival of the Human Rights Idea in the Twentieth Century," *Human Rights Quarterly* 14, no. 4 (November 1992): 448. Elizabeth Borgwardt, *A New Deal for the World: America's Vision for Human Rights* (Cambridge, MA: Harvard University Press, 2005).

9. Mark Mazower, "The Strange Triumph of Human Rights, 1933–1950," *The Historical Journal* 47, no. 2 (June 2004): 385.

10. For the full text of the Charter of the United Nations see the UN website, http://www.un.org/en/documents/charter/index.shtml.

11. For a full text of the Universal Declaration of Human Rights see the UN website, http://www.un.org/en/documents/udhr/.

12. Mary Ann Glendon, *A World Made New: Eleanor Roosevelt and the Universal Declaration of Human Rights* (New York: Random House, 2001), 174.

13. Hersch Lauterpacht, *International Law and Human Rights* (New York: F. A. Praeger, 1950); Arnold McNair, *The Development of International Justice: Two Lectures Delivered at the Law Center of New York University in December, 1953* (New York: New York University Press, 1954). Egon Schwelb, *Human Rights and the International Community: The Roots and Growth of the Universal Declaration of Human Rights, 1948–1963* (Chicago: Quadrangle Books, 1964). Later works include A. W. Brian Simpson, *Human Rights and the End of Empire: Britain and the Genesis of the European Convention* (New York: Oxford University Press, 2001); Geoffrey Robertson, *Crimes Against Humanity: The Struggle for Global Justice* (New York: The New Press, 2000). Among works by political scientists (and political activists) were William Korey, *The Key to Human Rights Implementation* (New York: Carnegie Endowment for International Peace, 1968); Richard Pierre Claude, *Comparative Human Rights* (Baltimore, MD: Johns Hopkins University Press, 1976). Claude became the founding editor of *Universal Human Rights*, later renamed *Human Rights Quarterly*. See also Moyn, *The Last Utopia*, 182–86.

14. William H. Langer, *The Diplomacy of Imperialism* (New York: Knopf, 1935).

15. Samuel Flagg Bemis, *The Latin American Policy of the United States* (New York: Harcourt, Brace and Co., 1943).

16. Dorothy Borg, *America's Policy and the Chinese Revolution, 1925–1928* (New York: Octagon Books, 1947).

17. See for instance, George Kennan, *American Diplomacy, 1900–1950* (Chicago: University of Chicago Press, 1951); Robert Endicott Osgood, *Ideals and Self-Interest in American Foreign Relations in America's Foreign Relations: The Great Transformation of the Twentieth Century* (Chicago: University of Chicago Press, 1953); Henry Kissinger, *Diplomacy* (New York: Simon & Schuster, 1995).

18. Charles A. Beard, *President Roosevelt and the Coming of the War, 1941: A Study in Appearances and Realities* (Hamden, CT: Archon Books, 1948); Charles Callan Tansill, *Back Door to War: The Roosevelt Foreign Policy 1933–1941*

(Chicago: H. Regnery Co, 1952); William Appleman Williams, *The Tragedy of American Diplomacy* (Cleveland, OH: World Pub. Co., 1959, repr. Dell, 1962).

19. See, for instance, Hannah Arendt, *Eichmann in Jerusalem: A Report on the Banality of Evil* (New York: Viking, 1963); Raul Hilberg, *The Destruction of the European Jews* (1961; repr. Chicago: Quadrangle Books, 1967); Jehuda Bauer, *The Holocaust in Historical Perspective* (Seattle: University of Washington Press, 1978).

20. Among them Michael Hunt, *Ideology and U.S. Foreign Policy* (New Haven, CT: Yale University Press, 1987); Akira Iriye, *Power and Culture: The Japanese-American War, 1941–1945* (Cambridge, MA: Harvard University Press, 1981); John Dower, *War Without Mercy: Race and Power in the Pacific War* (New York: Pantheon, 1986); Cynthia Enloe, *Bananas, Beaches & Bases: Making Feminist Sense of International Politics* (London: Pandora, 1989). Gaddis Smith wrote about human rights as part of his analysis of Jimmy Carter's foreign policy in *Morality, Reason, and Power: American Diplomacy in the Carter Years* (New York: Hill and Wang, 1986).

21. See for example H. Gordon Skilling, *Charter 77 and Human Rights in Czechoslovakia* (London: George Allen & Unwin, 1981); Rosemary Foot, *Rights Beyond Borders: The Global Community and the Struggle over Human Rights in China* (New York: Oxford University Press, 2000); Lauren, *The Evolution of International Human Rights*; Glendon, *A World Made New*.

22. One of the first contributions to the history of human rights was by the political scientist M. Glen Johnson, "Historical Perspectives on Human Rights and U.S. Foreign Policy," *Universal Human Rights* 2, no. 3 (July–September 1980): 1–18.

23. According to a 1954 article in *Time* magazine, Aboul Fath and his brother Hussein's opposition to Nasserist politics stemmed at least in part from business interests rather than concerns over free speech. See "The Press; Egyptian Uproar," *Time*, May 17, 1954.

24. Mahmoud Aboul Fath, letter to Bandung Delegates (April 13, 1955), cited in Roland Burke, "'The Compelling Dialogue of Freedom': Human Rights at the Bandung Conference," *Human Rights Quarterly* 28, no. 4 (2006): 951. See also Burke *Decolonization and the Evolution of Human Rights*.

25. A. W. Brian Simpson, *Human Rights and the End of Empire: Britain and the Genesis of the European Convention* (New York: Oxford University Press, 2001), 300–301. See also Moyn, *The Last Utopia*, 84–89; Jan Eckel, "Utopie der Moral, Kalkül der Macht: Menschenrechte in der globalen Politik seit 1945," *Archiv für Sozialgeschichte* 49 (2009): 451; See also Burke, *Decolonization and the Evolution of Human Rights*, 35–38. For the issue of minority rights after World War I see Mazower, "The Strange Triumph of Human Rights," 382.

26. See Moyn, *The Last Utopia*.

27. Christa Wichterich, "Strategische Verschwisterung, multiple Feminismen und die Glokalisierung von Frauenbewegungen," in *Frauenbewegungen weltweit: Aufbrüche, Kontinuitäten, Veränderungen,* Hg., Ilse Lenz, Michiko Mae, Karin Klose (Opladen: Leske + Budrich, 2000), 257–58. See also Jocelyn Olcott "Cold

War Conflicts and Cheap Cabaret: Sexual Politics at the 1975 United Nations International Women's Year Conference" *Gender and History* 22, no. 3 (November 2010): 733–54.

28. Tom Buchanan, "The Truth Will Set You Free! The Making of Amnesty International," *Journal of Contemporary History* 37, no. 4 (2002): 575–97.

29. Jonathan Power, *Amnesty International: The Human Rights Story* (New York: Pergamon Press, 1981); Kirsten Sellars, *The Rise and Rise of Human Rights* (Stroud: Sutton Publishing Ltd, 2002), 97–113; Stephen Hopgood, *Keepers of the Flame: Understanding Amnesty International* (Ithaca, NY: Cornell University Press, 2006).

30. Sellars, *The Rise and Rise of Human Rights*, 97. Sellars argues that despite the official insistence on political neutrality, the leadership was at times strongly partisan in favor of British positions. See also Hopgood, *Keepers of the Flame*, 4–6.

31. Eckel, "Utopie der Moral, Kalkül der Macht," 460–61.

32. William Korey, *The Promises We Keep: Human Rights, the Helsinki Process, and American Foreign Policy* (New York: St. Martin's Press, 1993), 5–9.

33. For a full text of the Helsinki Accords see University of Minnesota Human Rights Library, *The Final Act of the Conference on Secuirty and Cooperation in Europe*, August 1, 19755, 14 I.L.M. 1292 (Helsinki Declaration); Accessed at http://www1.umn.edu/humanrts/osce/basics/finact75.htm.

34. William Korey, *NGOs and the Universal Declaration of Human Rights: "A Curious Grapevine"* (New York: St. Martin's Press, 1998), 242–43.

35. Those dissidents included Andrei Sakharov, Aleksandr Solzhenitsyn, and Vaclav Havel. For more detail see Daniel C. Thomas, *The Helsinki Effect: International Norms, Human Rights and the Demise of Communism* (Princeton, NJ: Princeton University Press, 2001).

36. Mohandas Gandhi, "Letter addressed to the Director-General of UNESCO," and Chung-Shu Lo, "Human Rights in the Chinese Tradition," cited in Glendon, *A World Made New*, 75.

37. Burke, "The Compelling Dialogue of Freedom," 962; Burke, *Decolonization and the Evolution of International Human Rights*, 40.

38. "The Freedom Charter," reprinted in *Third World Quarterly* 9, no. 2 (April 1987): 672–77.

39. Kofi Awoonor, "Statement by H.E. Dr. Kofi Awoonor, Ambassador and Permanent Representative of Ghana and Chairman of the Group of 77 in the General Debate of the UNDP Governing Council, June 11th, 1991" (New York: The Group of 77, 1992), 2, cited in Russel Lawrence Barsh, "Measuring Human Rights: Problems of Methodology and Purpose," *Human Rights Quarterly* 15, no. 1 (February 1993): 87–88. For a powerful critique of the use of cultural relativism in Iran see Reza Afshari, *Human Rights in Iran: The Abuse of Cultural Relativism* (Philadelphia: University of Pennsylvania Press, 2001), 1–13.

40. See the report on the opening day by Elaine Sciolino, "U.S. Rejects Notion that Human Rights Vary by Culture," *New York Times,* June 15, 1993.

41. Asian Cultural Forum on Development, *Our Voice: Bangkok NGO Declaration on Human Rights* (Bangkok, 1993). The African meeting was held in Tunis in November 1992 and stressed the primacy of development as a human right. The Latin American meeting took place in January 1993 and confirmed the universality of human rights. Only the Asian meeting in Bangkok produced controversy. The declaration is reprinted in Asian Cultural Forum on Development, *Our Voice*, 244.

42. Ibid., 199.

43. William Korey, *NGOs and the Universal Declaration of Human Rights*, 273–306. For the full text of the Vienna Declaration and Programme of Action (VDPA) see United Nations General Assembly, Distr. General A/Conf.157/23, 12 July 1993, World Conference on Human Rights, accessed online at http://www.unhchr.ch/huridocda/huridoca.nsf/(Symbol)/A.CONF.157.23.En?OpenDocument (accessed June 3, 2009).

44. Amartya Sen, "Human Rights and Asian Values: What Kee Kuan Yew and Le Peng Don't Understand about Asia," *New Republic*, July 14, 1997, 1–9.

45. For a full text of the Geneva Conventions of 1949 see the website of the International Committee of the Red Cross (ICRC) at http://www.icrc.org/ihl.nsf/INTRO?OpenView.

46. Mark Mazower, *No Enchanted Palace: The End of Empire and the Ideological Origins of the United Nations* (Princeton, NJ: Princeton University Press, 2009), 8.

47. Simpson, *Human Rights and the End of Empire*.

48. Helen Keller and Alex Stone Sweet, eds., *A Europe of Rights: The Impact of the ECHR on National Legal Systems* (New York: Oxford University Press, 2008), 5–11.

49. Gaddis Smith, *Morality, Reason, and Power: American Diplomacy in the Carter Years* (New York: Hill and Wang, 1986). See also Stuckey, *Jimmy Carter, Human Rights, and the National Agenda*.

50. Anna P. Schreiber, *The Inter-American Commission on Human Rights* (Leiden, Sijthoff, 1970); J. Scott Davidson, *The Inter-American Human Rights System* (Brookfield, VT: Dartmouth Publishing Co., 1997). See also Eckel, "Utopie der Moral," 449–50.

51. Frans Viljoen, *International Human Rights in Africa* (Oxford: Oxford University Press, 2007.

52. Samantha Power, *"A Problem from Hell": America and the Age of Genocide* (New York: Basic Books, 2002), 326, 475–76.

53. Ibid., 484–86.

54. See the ICC's official website at http://www.icc-cpi.int/.

55. For a detailed account of the Abu Ghraib case see Seymour M. Hersh, "Torture at Abu Ghraib," "Chain of Command," and "The Gray Zone," all in *The New Yorker*, May 10, 2004, 42; May 17, 2004, 38; May 24, 2004, 38.

56. Jane Mayer, "The Memo: How an Internal Effort to Ban the Abuse and Torture of Detainees was Thwarted," *The New Yorker*, February 27, 2006, 32.

57. Kenneth Cmiel, "Review Essay: The Recent History of Human Rights," *American Historical Review* 109, no. 1 (February 2004): 130.

58. For the importance of communication see Kenneth Cmiel, "The Emergence of Human Rights Politics in the United States," *Journal of American History* 86, no. 3 (December 1999): 1231–50.

PART I

The Human Rights Revolution

1

THE RECENT HISTORY OF HUMAN RIGHTS

KENNETH CMIEL

Few political agendas have seen such a rapid and dramatic growth as that of "human rights." Prior to the 1940s, the term was rarely used. There was no sustained international movement in its name. There were no nongovernmental organizations (NGOs) with a global reach to defend its principles. There was no international law crafted to protect our human rights.[1] By the 1990s, however, you couldn't escape it. The better-known Western organizations—the International Commission of Jurists, Amnesty International, and Human Rights Watch—roamed the globe looking for infractions. NATO prosecuted a war in the name of "human rights." Less well known to Europeans and North Americans were the hundreds of NGOs outside Europe and the United States defining themselves as human rights agencies, almost all of them with birth dates no earlier than 1985. Rigoberta Menchú now presides over the Fundación Rigoberta Menchú Tum, a peace organization located in Mexico that campaigns in the name of human rights, particularly for indigenous peoples. It is one of many such organizations in Latin America.[2] In 1993, when a number of Asian governments tried to derail the Vienna United Nations Conference on Human Rights, calling for recognition of special "Asian values" and a reconsideration of the Universal Declaration of Human Rights, 180 Asian NGOs gathered, produced a counterdocument, and proved a formidable political force in opposition to their governments.[3] In Africa, in the early 1990s, a string of regimes vowed to democratize and respect human rights. Numerous local monitoring groups sprang up to try to keep track of some very unstable situations.[4]

It was not only that activism spread around the globe. The human rights agenda expanded as well. There was new attention to international justice, most famously in the effort to bring bloody dictators to trial. Slobodan

Milošević in the dock is the result. "Women's rights are human rights, too," a call dating from the 1980s, expanded the agendas of human rights organizations in another way. Indigenous people's rights, children's rights, the right to health, even economic and social rights—none were on the table in 1970 as "human rights" claims. All, in one way or another, were part of the discussion by the end of the century.[5]

Yet what does all this add up to? The 1990s have been a sadly fitting end to the bloody twentieth century. Rwanda, Kosovo, East Timor, Iraq, the West Bank—take your pick. Who would argue the decade has been as wonderfully pacific as the heady talk in 1989 of the "end of history" or the "new world order" had predicted? What good did the expanded human rights agenda do for Afghani women under the Taliban, for the unemployed of Argentina, for the mentally ill now incarcerated in American jails, for the Kurds in Iraq or Turkey? Governments continued to be as duplicitous as always, ritually mouthing slogans they ignored when convenient. The contradiction begs for explanation: Why does all the energy and effort going into human rights activism produce such decidedly meager results? How could the rhetoric of human rights be so globally pervasive while the politics of human rights is so utterly weak?

Given all the human rights activism of the decade, it is not surprising that historians have, in a small way, joined the march. In 1994, Amnesty International sponsored a series of lectures by historians on the interplay between history and human rights. Patrick Collinson, Carlo Ginzburg, Emmanuel Le Roy Ladurie, Robert Darnton, Elizabeth Fox-Genovese, and Ian Kershaw were among the luminaries who contributed.[6] "Human rights" was the theme of the 1997 American Historical Association convention in New York. In the past few years, a number of books have appeared attempting to historicize the subject. While university-based historians such as Paul Lauren, Lynn Hunt, and Jeffrey Wasserstrom have addressed the subject, journalists, legal scholars, political activists, and political scientists have still done far more of this history writing. The field remains refreshingly inchoate.

Historians have been, at least in the twentieth century, for the most part particularists. They want to know in great depth the local scene they survey. And in the recent past, this has meant, more often than not, a sort of reflexive cultural relativism. Talk of universal rights was suspect, with the odors of cultural imperialism and simple-minded rationalism vaguely hanging about it. It took the end of the Cold War and the chatter about globalization to move some historians to the subject. It should be no surprise that the shift in history was paralleled by a similar shift among anthropologists.[7] But this has left, for both groups, a strain between their traditional respect for the local and renewed interest in the global. How to manage this is slippery indeed.

One important trend in the recent scholarship has been to explore the history and nuances of the human rights idiom. Centering on language raises its own problems. On the one hand, it seems unduly restricting to limit oneself to analyzing claims explicitly made in the name of "the rights of man" or "human rights." Much of the activism for social justice had taken place without using the idiom of human rights. Does one exclude from this story the drive to make the workplace safe, for example, if done in the name of "social justice" instead of "human rights"? On the other hand, analysis done in the name of the "rights of man" can be wildly anachronistic, akin to talking about auto repair in the sixteenth century. Mohandas Gandhi, for one, is mentioned in several of the books discussed here as a friend of human rights. Yet Gandhi generally disliked "rights-talk" of all kinds, associating it with the self-indulgence of the modern age. This was one way he differed from the Indian Congress Party, whose UN representatives were active supporters of human rights work at that time. Gandhi preferred to frame his rhetoric in terms of "duties" and kept his distance from 1940s human rights campaigns.[8]

It should be no surprise that these two tendencies are but a version of the universal/particular divide. The expansive approach can wind up equating "human rights" with anything "good." Buddha and Jesus now become human rights activists. This sort of thing can get soggy fast. The other method, however, potentially crabs us to those places where some magic words—*rights of man, human rights, derechos humanos, renquan*—were actually being uttered.

There are no definitive answers here. Rather, historians need to make informed choices, making clear to themselves and their readers what they are, and are not, trying to do. With this caution in mind, attention to the history of human rights talk can yield a lot. Ahistoric claims about human rights are still rampant among activists, lawyers, and political theorists. Grand assertions and abstract arguments made in the name of human rights continue to flourish, with charges of cultural imperialism and defenses of cultural relativism predictably coming in response. Historians have the opportunity to tug this discussion to a more sophisticated level by refusing to see the particularist/universal divide as the last word. One way of doing this is by attending to the nuances of political language in different cultural settings. And some recent historians are doing just that.

Claims about natural rights, the rights of man, or human rights were but one aspect of the larger expansion of rights-talk in the last three centuries. On the subject of human rights, there are some fine starting points. Burns

Weston's essay in the *Encyclopedia Britannica* is a gem, a panoramic sweep through four centuries of intellectual history.[9] Such an overview, however, as good as it is, still remains only a starting point.

In recent years, some attention to the subject has come about as historians of the early modern Euro world try to move beyond what was called the "republican synthesis." This interpretive frame, most notably associated with J. G. A. Pocock, understood much seventeenth- and eighteenth-century political life as suspicious of modernity. Virtue was the core civic value; commerce, self-interest, and individual rights were suspect. But as this interpretation has lost adherents, it has also created new interest in early modern natural rights, especially in the Anglo-American world. Knud Haakonssen has published an extraordinarily rich study of early modern natural law theory, demonstrating the gradual shift from duties to rights in seventeenth- and eighteenth-century ethics and philosophy.[10] Haakonssen begins his *Natural Law and Moral Philosophy* with seventeenth-century thinkers, Hugo Grotius, Thomas Hobbes, and Samuel Pufendorf. Most of the book is given to a detailed analysis of the ideas of Scottish moral philosophers. Francis Hutcheson, David Hume, Adam Smith, Thomas Reid, Dugald Stewart, and James Mill each gets a chapter. He closes the book with a discussion of the U.S. revolution.

According to Haakonssen, American revolutionary rhetoric was dominated by the European tradition that viewed natural rights as flowing out of natural law. There was a natural order to the world, and duties were more important than rights. Rights did exist, even inalienable rights, but they were "logically subordinate." For Haakonssen, the 1970s and 1980s debates over liberal versus republican interpretations of the American Revolution missed the point. It wasn't a question of "rights" versus "virtue." Talk of subjective rights disconnected from natural law was not common coin until the nine teenth century. At the time of the revolution, according to Haakonssen, natural rights were "derivative from the duties imposed by natural law."[11]

Haakonssen is brilliant discussing European moral philosophers. What he says about the American Revolution is intriguing but less convincing. He has to cover far too much far too quickly, quite different from the chapters on individual Scottish thinkers. In his discussion of the revolution, there are too many paragraphs making assertions about the American perspective that have no footnotes. The author has to do some overly complicated explaining to justify why the Americans spoke so insistently about "rights" instead of "duties." Such passages are not history, they are the modern philosopher reconstructing the past as it logically should have been. This criticism, how ever, is not meant to diminish the overall power of this book.

Haakonssen's is the most sophisticated discussion of natural rights philosophy in this generation, a truly formidable achievement.

A different rendering of natural rights can be found in the work of Michael Zuckert. Zuckert has written a substantial body of work in the 1990s attacking the republican synthesis.[12] Unlike Haakonssen, however, Zuckert defends, with great verve and tenacity, the idea that the revolution was Lockean and modern. Unlike Haakonssen, he dismisses the notion that Lockean natural rights were derived from natural law duties. And whereas Haakonssen diminished the importance of the social contract in his reading of eighteenth-century natural rights thinking, Zuckert continues to highlight it. The United States was, according to Zuckert, the "natural rights republic."

Zuckert does a fine job of showing how pervasive natural rights talk was during the revolution. The most excessive claims of Pocock or Gordon Wood about the classical republican origins of the revolution have not stood up particularly well. Zuckert's analysis of the Declaration of Independence is similarly convincing. From the start, the American Revolution was about protecting natural rights. He is less persuasive, however, when arguing that core revolutionary thought stemmed from John Locke. There were multiple places, as Haakonssen shows, where natural rights ideas might grow. Moreover, as good as Zuckert's analysis of political ideas is, the politics is largely missing. Zuckert's revolutionaries are political philosophers, not politicians.

Both Haakonssen and Zuckert excel at the analysis of political ideas. They are well worth reading, some of the best work trying to rethink early modern political thought after the death of the republican synthesis. But their work will no doubt will leave many historians cold, looking too much like old-fashioned intellectual history. The relation of political ideology to European political theory is very important to these authors. Race and gender, however, are largely absent. The pursuit of interest is ignored. The grime of past politics, so dear to historians, is missing.

A different strain of the new work on natural rights is looking at how claims about human rights were deployed in specific historic settings, unpacking what political stakes at any given moment were attached to the rhetoric.[13] Lynn Hunt's collection of documents about the rights of man during the French Revolution is a good example.[14] The 1789 Declaration of the Rights of Man and Citizen is a landmark in the history of human rights discussions. Hunt brings together documents going back to the 1750s but principally dating from 1789 to 1794, all debating the implications of theories of natural rights. The 1789 declaration becomes just one stopping point in a vibrant, ongoing, and sometimes vicious debate. On the heels of the declaration's adoption, fights erupted about its implications for black Haitian slaves, French women, and Calvinists and Jews living in France. Hunt presents documents on each of these disputes. Not surprisingly, the results were checkered. Jews became French citizens in 1791, slavery ended in Haiti in 1794, but women, in 1793, were explicitly denied the right to form political clubs. Within a decade, Napoleon Bonaparte revived slavery in the colonies, confirmed women's second-class status, but left Jewish citizenship untouched. Talk of the rights of man, according to Hunt, "helped push the Revolution into radical directions, but it did not by itself afford a permanent foundation for rule."[15]

It is not only *who* gets rights that matters. As important are *what* rights are on the table. That too has a history. There is the obvious—there is no right to social security in the French declaration of 1789. The UN's 1948 Universal Declaration of Human Rights, however, includes it. But Hunt does more, noting the different ways that rights were clustered together. Distinctions between civil and political rights, she observes, were commonplace and of crucial importance in the eighteenth century. Civil rights include such classic freedoms as the rights to own property, to not be thrown in jail without proper arrest and trial, to be treated equally before the law. Political rights, on the other hand, include voting, serving on juries, and holding office. Such a distinction, important in the eighteenth and nineteenth centuries, is not one that makes much sense to us. The mid-twentieth-century events we call the "Civil Rights Movement" had at its core the drive to extend to African Americans the right to vote—a preeminently political right. The international human rights community today conventionally distinguishes between "civil and political rights" as one grouping and "economic, social, and cultural rights" as another. This linking of the "civil" and political" is relatively new. It was the distinction between them that was crucial in the eighteenth and nineteenth centuries, a distinction with real consequences. Women, for example, would get the right to own property in the 1800s but not the right to vote. The civil versus political divide was routinely cited for this. Understanding the ways that rights have been clustered together over time, when tied to close attention to political ramifications, is still one more way for historians usefully to unpack the history of rights-talk.

If Hunt's collection tells us how to do it, Paul Lauren's *Evolution of International Human Rights* shows some of the pitfalls of not attending to the nuances of the rhetoric. Lauren's book is the best single overview of modern human rights activism thus far. It is especially informative on the politics of the 1940s. And Lauren deserves our thanks for being the first scholar to address systematically the issues of color and empire in relation to human rights activism. He shows that human rights idioms were used by African Americans in the United States, blacks in South Africa, and anticolonial activists in Asia and Africa.

Lauren's work allows us to recognize that the divide between "civil and political rights" and "economic, social and cultural rights," now written into conventional wisdom, itself betrays the Western origins of the contemporary human rights movement. A third set of ideas, revolving around the notion of the "self-determination of peoples," was also part of the mid-century human rights debates.[16] The trouble was, Westerners did not agree that this was a fundamental human right. In 1946, the Nigerian activist Mbonu Ojike would state, "The right to rule oneself is a natural right." The year before, Ho Chi Minh declared independence for Vietnam quoting the "inalienable rights" of Thomas Jefferson's Declaration of Independence. In 1952, Asian, African, and Latin American nations, over the objections of Western nations, officially made respect for the "self-determination of peoples" part of the UN's human rights program. In the Western nations, however, opposition persisted, even as formal colonialism was folding. As Michael Ignatieff has recently pointed out, Isaiah Berlin's famous essay "Positive and Negative Freedom," first delivered as an Oxford lecture in 1958, was in part an expression of skepticism about Third World nationalism. About the same time, the French jurist René Cassin, who would later win a Nobel Prize for his work drafting the Universal Declaration of Human Rights, was complaining that the whole UN human rights program had gone off track thanks to the "Arab states" forcing "self-determination" onto the agenda. In 1962, the British historian Maurice Cranston, in a widely read book on human rights, argued that self-determination did not really belong on the list.[17]

Lauren is right to see anticolonialism as a key strain ignored by other historians. Yet he does not distinguish it from other visions, a practice more confusing than enlightening. Whatever different things historians make of Ho Chi Minh, it is safe to say he was no Jeffersonian democrat, and not even an Eleanor Rooseveltian New Dealer. In Lauren's account, however, any such distinctions are either passingly mentioned or ignored. For Lauren, Ho as well as Eleanor contributed to an emerging human rights vision. Citing Frantz Fanon's *Wretched of the Earth* as an anticolonial human rights document, as Lauren does, without noting Fanon's celebration of revolutionary violence and his general indifference to "bourgeois" civil liberties, is just plain misleading.[18] It ignores absolutely crucial distinctions in outlook. Political language can tell us a lot, but only if we treat it seriously.

More attention to political discourse, however, will no doubt destroy the shibboleth that rights-talk has had no life outside the West. Political claims made in the name of "natural rights," or "the rights of man" did first surface in Western Europe during the seventeenth and eighteenth centuries. During the nineteenth century, this debate spread to Asia, Africa, and Latin America. We still have only scattered bits of this history.[19]

The work of Stephen Angle and Marina Svensson shows what can be done. Each wrote excellent individual books on human rights debates in China, and they collaborated on a collection of documents.[20] Angle's book is a classic intellectual history, especially good at unpacking the layered meanings of *quan*, a word traditionally meaning "power" or "authority" but around the turn of the twentieth century beginning to be used for "rights." His close readings of key translations of mid-nineteenth-century texts in international law (where rights-talk first explicitly enters Chinese debate) reveal how complicated translations of key terms can be. Angle is also good at relating the complexities of neo-Confucian thinking to an emerging discussion of "rights." Svensson, more attuned to the concrete political contexts of ideological claims, pursues the twentieth-century debate about *renquan*, the term now generally translated as "human rights." Svensson demolishes the assumption that no one discussed human rights in China before the UN's Universal Declaration of Human Rights.

The *Chinese Human Rights Reader*, their collective work, makes the same point. It is a compendium of primary sources in China on renquan. The documents cover the entire twentieth century, contextualized by the editors' informative commentary. Their sources show, first of all, that debates about "human rights" emerged in China during the 1890s and connected to a larger reassessment of Confucian pieties in the face of Chinese humiliations vis-à-vis the West. Throughout the last century, party ideologists, lawyers, and independent intellectuals debated the concept. Nationalist Guomindang (GMD) intellectuals from the 1920s such as Zhou Fohai explicitly contrasted Sun Yat-sen's call for "people's rights" (*minquan*) with the French Revolution's "rights of man" (*renquan*). Only those loyal to the nation, in their estimation, deserved rights. In the 1940s, certain intellectuals who worked with Chiang Kai-shek defended the notion of human rights, although Chiang did not.[21] In the 1920s and 1940s, activists, trying to push the GMD to respect its citizens more, mounted "human rights" campaigns. A short-lived magazine called *Human Rights* (*Renquan*) was published in China in 1925. Chinese communists, similarly, in the last sixty years, have had more than one position on the subject. At different times, they have denounced human rights talk as a bourgeois ruse, used the idiom strategically, made halting and brief gestures to respect civil and political rights, and argued that the true core of human rights was economic and social rights.[22]

Notions of human rights have been a part of China's ideological battles, not only in the 1990s but for the whole twentieth century. It impoverishes these debates, Angle and Svensson argue, to reduce them to Western parasitism. The "discussion of rights in China," they write, "has long been motivated by indigenous concerns, rather than imposed from without, and it has been interpretive and critical, rather than passive and imitative."[23]

If careful attention to the idiom can lead to new insights, so too can examination of how the absence of the idiom has mattered. In 1993, the United Nations expanded the definition of "war crimes" to include systematic rape. Historians Atina Grossmann and Elizabeth Heineman have recently written on what it meant *not* to have this definition of war crimes in the 1940s.[24] There was, they note, brutal and widespread rape of German women by Soviet military personnel in 1945. But, as Grossmann first observed, unlike what some have argued, this was not "silenced" at the time. Quite the contrary: U.S. and British army officers discussed the rapes as a problem of venereal disease, all the occupying armies discussed the abortion issues raised (huge numbers of raped German women wanted abortions), and the women themselves passed around survival stories to each other. Even German communists openly worried that the rapes hindered efforts to recruit Germans to the Communist Party. Heineman adds that discussion of the rapes allowed Germans to construct the image of themselves as innocent victims of the war. This was not silence. But the terms mattered. Amid all the talk, never at the time were the rapes discussed as a crime against humanity. Rape was not part of the Nuremberg indictment. Nor was there any international outcry against Soviet behavior. "Cold War-era references to the Soviet rapes," Heineman observes, "explained them in political, national, or even racial terms—and not as gendered acts."[25] Nor, I would add, as human rights violations. It took the women's movement of the 1970s and 1980s to change the way the discussion took place.

The language of human rights is fluid. The term has meant widely different things at different points in time. It may be too much to say that "human rights" is an empty signifier, but given the range of usages over time—the phrase can mean diametrically opposed things—that seems to be a useful starting point. Hunt, Angle, Svensson, and Grossmann demonstrate that historians of human rights can do much to further our understanding of global political discourse by not taking the term for granted; by carefully attending to its different uses; and by locating those uses in local, political contexts. It is precisely in not treating assertions of "human rights" in hushed, reverential tones that the best possibilities lie.

These historians refuse to be tripped up by any universal/local divide. Rather, they are writing the local histories of universal claims. Such claims —specifically attached to human rights discourse—have become one way that peoples around the world now interact with each other. In this sense, human rights talk communicates across cultures in ways similar to money, statistics, pidgin English, or a discussion of soccer. Such idioms are important, at times extraordinarily important, but they are also expressively thin. We do successfully communicate with them, but only in a rough and ready way.

But if human rights have become one of the *linguae francae* of a globalized world, this certainly does not mean that local cultures are irrelevant. If human rights talk is a thin communicator across cultures, it also gathers thicker meaning within cultures. Hunt, Angle, Svensson, and Grossmann explore how this universalistic idiom acquires local meanings that are fought over and evolve through time. And they are exploring this with a sharp eye on the specific political stakes involved at any given moment. It is the careful and constant interplay between local and global, between specific political settings and grand political claims that promises to contribute to knowledge.[26]

If the talk is everywhere, though, why are human rights politics so weak? Here we shift from political language to the history of activism. This is the other area where much recent work has been done, especially looking at the 1940s to the present. The last sixty years has really made for a remarkable shift.

International activism in the name of some shared basic rights has not had a distinguished history. The liberal revolutions of the eighteenth and early nineteenth centuries took place within the frame of the nation-state. While intellectuals such as Tom Paine and Immanuel Kant dreamed of moving international affairs beyond the "Westphalian system" devoted to respecting the autonomy of sovereign states, the French Declaration of the Rights of Man and Citizen and the American Declaration of Independence both announced universal rights that were to be protected by national states. In other words, as far as the international community was concerned, nations could still do what they wanted inside their borders. This presumption does not appear to have been dramatically challenged until the 1940s, when international law against genocide was written and when it was proclaimed that the world community needed to monitor basic human rights.

To be sure, Gary Jonathan Bass, in *Stay the Hand of Vengeance*, his excellent history of war crimes tribunals, shows that the British wanted to try Napoleon in 1815. (The Prussians wanted to shoot him.) Bass also recounts the efforts to try Kaiser Wilhelm in 1919 for war crimes. But both cases make the point about the weakness of humanitarian law before the 1940s. Neither of these trials actually happened. Napoleon was shipped to Elba; the Dutch would not hand over the kaiser. Nuremberg marked the first "successful" war crimes trial.[27]

If you think of "human rights activism" in another way—as efforts to make claims across borders in the name of basic rights—this activism has been intermittently strong but not sustained. The international campaign against slavery, scattered attempts in the 1880s and 1890s to regulate the Ottoman Empire's treatment of Christians, the birth of the international women's movement are all examples.[28] But so much was left undone. There was no international outcry or organizations devoted to the slaughter of Indians in the United States, no important transnational NGOs fighting pogroms against Jews in Russia. There was no real organized international opposition to European empire, or important groups of activists devoted to securing former slaves their rights in the United States.

Adam Hochschild's powerful account of international activism against the slaughter of African workers in the Congo under the colonial regime of King Leopold of Belgium underscores the point. The leader of the campaign was Edmund Dean Morel, an employee of a Liverpool shipping line, who, shortly after 1900, became outraged at the wanton cruelty and stunning, murderous disregard for life that Belgian overlords exhibited toward their African subjects. Horrific brutality, outright starvation, inhuman workloads—all were astoundingly commonplace. Hochschild recounts the tireless efforts of Morel and his associates to bring these horrors to the attention of the Western public. Morel developed ties throughout Europe and the United States. Hochschild accurately sees Morel's work as the bridge between the international antislavery activism of the mid-nineteenth century and the human rights work of the present.

Still, the limitations stand out. Morel focused on the Congo alone, refusing to expand his crusade to other locales. He was not against empire in general and, Hochschild notes, "ignored his own country's use of forced labor." Moreover, his Congo Reform Association disbanded in 1913 after a series of Belgian reforms seemed to put the colony on a more "humane" imperial path. Morel's campaign was a bridge, but—limited to a specific issue and fading from existence after ostensibly accomplishing its end—it looks more like a smaller version of earlier transnational antislavery efforts than contemporary human rights activism.[29]

There were other scattered campaigns to protect basic rights. In France, the Ligue des droits de l'homme was founded in 1898 and remained active until the mid-1930s.[30] In South America, the Liga Argentina por los Derechos del Hombre dates from 1937.[31] A few Russian, Latin American, and West European international lawyers tried to put human rights on the table during the 1920s, one example of the internationalism of the day. This internationalism took varied forms, cultural and political, but in general it was a weak current, overwhelmed by the aggressive 1930s nationalism of Italy, Germany, and Japan, and politically weaker than the Western isolationist or appeasement hope that staying away from fights would keep them from erupting.[32]

Nor was the League of Nations really committed to human rights in the 1940s sense of the term. The international lawyers who have tried their hand at human rights history—Mary Ann Glendon, Geoffrey Robertson, A. W. Brian Simpson—each makes this point with varying detail, as does historian Paul Lauren.[33] The League was interested in protecting the rights of minority groups, not individuals. Racial minorities outside of Europe were left to fend for themselves. The League's devotion to the principle of self-determination, similarly, was also designed to protect the rights of groups, not individuals.

In the 1940s, however, "the focus on minority rights was supplanted by an emphasis on human rights."[34] Much of the recent work on the history of human rights activism underscores the importance of that decade. Mary Ann Glendon's account of Eleanor Roosevelt's work drafting the Universal Declaration of Human Rights is one of the best of the recent books. A. W. Brian Simpson, the distinguished legal historian, has written a massive book on Britain's role in framing the 1950 European Convention on Human Rights, the starting point of today's European Court of Human Rights. The heart of Paul Lauren's *Evolution of International Human Rights* is the four chapters recounting the interwar years and the 1940s. Samantha Power's *Problem from Hell: America in the Age of Genocide* provides the first glimpse of Raphael Lemkin's career in the 1940s—Lemkin being the Polish Jew who coined the term "genocide" in 1944, drafted the UN Convention on Genocide two years later, and devoted enormous energy in the next decade to keeping the world focused on the subject. These accounts are drawing the first substantive portrait of 1940s human rights activism.[35]

These accounts suggest the range of political actors involved. Liberal reformers and social democrats were at the forefront—Eleanor Roosevelt of the United States, René Cassin of France. Yet deeply conservative men and women played a role. Winston Churchill fought at the end of the decade to have the European Commission devise the European Convention on Human Rights. Glendon rightly gives Charles Habib Malik, the Lebanese diplomat, a prominent place in drafting the Universal Declaration of Human Rights. Malik was a conservative spirit who ended his career as a hero to certain Christian intellectuals in the United States.[36] Yet he played a major role in drafting the Universal Declaration and shepherding it through the United Nations.

This activism was also designed to build international law, and the new United Nations was at the heart of it. The Nuremberg Principles were meant to be the start of something much grander. The Universal Declaration of Human Rights was the first step. That set of principles was supposed to be quickly turned into binding international law. The Genocide Convention, adopted by the General Assembly the day before it adopted the Universal Declaration, was similarly supposed to matter.

Yet the world waited until the 1990s for the next major international tribunal charging someone with crimes against humanity. The Cold War and fights between Western and Third World nations undermined the human rights élan of the 1940s. The second important period scholars are reviewing is the 1970s, when there was an explosion of interest in human rights. The exponential growth of Amnesty International (which was founded in 1961), as well as the birth of Human Rights Watch in New York, the Mothers of the Plaza de Mayo in Buenos Aires, and the Helsinki Watch Groups in the Soviet Union and Eastern Europe—these are stories starting to be told.[37]

New transnational communication networks became extremely important. This activism, in other words, was part of the emergence of late twentieth-century globalization, a point not mentioned in enough of the historiography. And the center of the activism shifted. NGOs rather than the UN were the focal point. The 1970s activists were less interested in international law and more invested in publicizing cruel behavior to shame perpetrators into change. Nor were the new human rights campaigns truly part of a mass movement. Rather, they depended on small numbers of very well-educated people in Latin America or Eastern Europe connecting with activists in New York, London, Paris, and Geneva and getting their stories into venues such as *Le Monde,* the *New York Times*, or the BBC. Regional treaties such as the Helsinki agreements, or national legislation like the Jackson-Vanik Amendment in the United States, were far more important than international law crafted at the UN. In fact, relations between the UN and the Western human rights NGOs steadily worsened during the 1970s.[38]

The agenda also shrank from the 1940s. The "self-determination of peoples" remained off the radar screen of the Western NGOs, a principal source of the tension with UN representatives. But, just as important, the general 1940s liberal or social democratic emphasis on civil and political rights *and* economic rights was lost. The major Western human rights organizations, Amnesty International in London, Human Rights Watch in New York, the International Commission of Jurists in Geneva, all devoted themselves solely to combating appalling abuses of civil and political rights around the globe.

Finally, a third wave of activism dates from the late 1980s but gathered real steam in the 1990s. Being so recent, far less is written on it. Still, some things can be said. The agenda of Western human rights activists expanded to include health rights, women's rights, economic justice, and indigenous people's rights. Go to Amnesty International's website today and you will find current campaigns touching a much wider set of concerns than in the 1970s. There has also been a renewed interest in international law. The end of the Cold War turned human rights activists back to the United Nations. The idea of trying tyrants marked a return to a 1940s concern. Expansions of the UN court system via bodies such as the International Criminal Tribunal for the former Yugoslavia or a permanent International Criminal Court were examples of this drive.

This third, most recent wave of activism has also seen an explosion of new human rights NGOs outside the West. They have a huge range of agendas. They often exist on shoestring budgets. Very little systematic research has been done on these organizations. Whether they are financially driven by Western European or U.S. sources is not known. (Some are, but we don't know if this is usual.) How they matter, if at all, has not had enough attention.

If the new literature suggests three waves of activism since the 1940s, it also reveals three competing attitudes of the historians to this activism. First, there is the "it's getting better" story: the world now pays increasing attention to the violation of rights. International law is expanding. Dictators can be prosecuted. The last half of the century, according to Michael Ignatieff, has engineered a "rights revolution." Some of the breezier accounts aimed at a popular audience treat the subject this way.[39] It turns up in other, more substantial work as well, though, such as that of Ignatieff.[40]

How do these writers deal with Kosovo or Rwanda? How do they account for the United States sidestepping the UN convention on landmines or its opposition to the new International Criminal Court? Some simply ignore the dirty work of the world and sing with true Panglossian cheer. Others, more subtly, suggest that the expansion of human rights talk and the prominence of human rights NGOs is a sign of better things to come. The increasing stature of Amnesty International, according to political scientists Ann Marie Clark and Kathryn Sikkink, means that new norms are winding their way into government practice.[41] The historian Rosemary Foot has penned one of the best renderings of this point of view. Her *Rights beyond Borders* is an excellent account of China's engagement with human rights issues during the 1980s and 1990s. Foot argues that China's increasing participation in human rights debates will push the regime to better standards whether it really wants to or not.[42] I remain skeptical. More human rights NGOs do not necessarily mean that fewer people are being detained or tortured. China's participation in UN human rights venues is just as much a means of deflecting international criticism as it is moving to a more humane plateau, a point Marina Svensson notes in her account.[43] Foot is absolutely right to suggest that the emergence of a "human rights regime" in the last decades of the twentieth century throws something new into international relations. But the determination of the Chinese regime to stamp out opposition; the vacillating weakness of the UN Commission on Human Rights; the salivating desire of capital in Europe, Japan, and the United States to have new markets in China; and the lack of political will, international stature, and policy consistency in the one dominant superpower left, the United States, all militate against the view that the future will see a better record on human rights in China.

The second sensibility in this historical writing sees human rights politics as paradoxical. Jeffrey Wasserstrom, Marilyn Young, Joan Wallach Scott, and Alice Bullard all explore the dual nature of human rights discourse. Robert Darnton discusses the ironies of censorship by comparing late eighteenth-century France and 1980s East Germany. Lynn Hunt sees the very origins of human rights as mired in paradox. Human rights idioms grant rights to some but take them away from others.[44]

To be sure, this is a large category. Paradox can be charged in very different ways. Some who write in this vein are fairly skeptical of human rights ideas—Scott and Bullard. Others, however—Darnton and Wasserstrom—are quite sympathetic. Whatever these differences, however, the common focus on the irony and paradox of human rights is a change from historians' earlier disregard of the subject. "Paradox" is not exactly cultural relativism, where each autonomous culture is judged according to internal standards. Nor is it Karl Marx's critique of the French Declaration of the Rights of Man, where the falseness of the universal claims corrupted the whole project. The very point of "paradox" is that inherent problems do not destroy the idiom. As Marilyn Young shrewdly notes, paradox is not contradiction.[45] Rather, paradox calls for the persistent negotiation between claim and practice. There is no ultimate resolution, but we must go on. In her contribution to *Human Rights and Revolutions*, Bullard starkly states the point of view with a far more critical edge than some others would adopt: "The language of human rights appears particularly ill suited to situations of radical cultural difference, yet this essay does not seek to relativize human rights or standards for their evaluation."[46]

Yet even for those historians more sympathetic to human rights claims, the emphasis on paradox tends to leave little space for progress. The stories these historians tell are full of bad or unintended consequences liberally mixing with the most noble words and deeds. As Wasserstrom notes in a very fine essay, activists have painted human rights ideas as straightforward and simple while they are "complex and often internally contradictory."[47]

These historians may be right about the paradoxical nature of human rights claims in the past two centuries. Yet it is not surprising that this sensibility is the one found among academic historians, that tribe with "only paradoxes to offer."[48] "Paradox" and his good pal "Irony" are peculiarly intellectual conceits, the right pitch for academics but not well tuned for success in the political world. Don't political movements need passion more than complexity? When has paradox spurred anyone to heroism? The Czech novelist Milan Kundera has one of his characters in *Immortality* archly remark that those who preach paradox are "the brilliant allies of their own gravediggers."[49] It is a point worth pondering. If human rights talk is a practice riddled with paradox, that does not bode well for its future. Put another way, the success and plausibility of the paradoxical sensibility among intellectuals could very well be a sign of a more general retreat from human rights claims in the world.[50]

The third sensibility in recent historical writing is angrier, defined by a wrenching chasm between the glowing words or strenuous activism and the very slim real results. These writers do not think the ideals are paradoxical. They do not want to tarry with ironies. Rather, they focus on the horrible failure to protect basic rights in the modern world. The journalism of David Rieff exemplifies this attitude, as does the work of Adam Hochschild.[51] Samantha Power's spectacular book on the history of the United States and genocide, *A Problem from Hell*, provides a powerful example. Power, a journalist who has moved over to the Carr Center for Human Rights at Harvard, has written the most moving history yet of the human rights activism of the twentieth century. She portrays, from the 1940s to the present, the continued refusal of the United States meaningfully to come to terms with genocide. Unlike so much of the human rights history written in the past decade, Power emphasizes the lessons that have not been learned, the continued evasions of U.S. politicians, and the depressing record of the international community.

The strength of Power's account comes from her devoting as much ink to atrocity as to activism. Most of the other history discussed here centers differently—on the expanding networks of human rights activists or the evolving regime of international law.[52] Power, though, portrays both Raphael Lemkin's drive to write law against genocide *and* Saddam Hussein's gassing of his own citizens. She traces both Senator William Proxmire's dogged efforts to have the United States ratify the Convention on Genocide *and*, in one of the best chapters of her book, the absolutely contortion-like efforts of the Clinton administration to avoid confronting the genocide in Rwanda. Only when we have more accounts that, like Power's, take into account human rights abuses and evasions will we get a better assessment of what all the activism has actually accomplished.

There has not been enough systematic work on the history of brutality. To be sure, the Holocaust in particular and genocide in general are regular subjects of inquiry.[53] Certain atrocities, such as the Rape of Nanjing, also are studied.[54] Books such as Norman Naimark's work on ethnic cleansing or Anne Applebaum's on the Soviet Gulag surface.[55] In general, work on state violence is growing. But there are still huge gaps. The history of modern torture in all its variety and particularity remains underdeveloped.[56] We don't have a good history of disappearances. There have been individual studies of rape as a wartime practice but no real effort to connect them. Nor is there any good historical introduction to the issue of female genital mutilation, or any systematic, comparative survey of what sorts of violence colonial rulers perpetrated on native populations in the nineteenth and twentieth centuries. These are depressing topics, to be sure. But they deserve the same scholarly attention that genocide gets. While occasionally things are written about particular atrocities and practices, conceptual integration does not usually happen. As Mark Mazower recently argued, once this work gets done, historians will need to move away from images of state violence derived from Hitler's Germany or Stalin's Soviet Union. There is too much complexity in the history of violence that these models cannot accommodate.[57]

The recent wave of history writing has told us much about what human rights activists have been doing. It is starting to turn the noble, yet slippery phrase into something that can be historically unpacked. But all this history has basically been written from inside—by journalists, lawyers, and scholars who were contributing to the human rights activism of the 1990s. And precisely because everyone writing this history is inside the club, very little of this work is asking the hard questions—what if all the activism didn't really matter? What if all the brutality that human beings do to each other continues? Amnesty International began its international campaign against torture in 1973. Recent work suggests that torture is just as prevalent today.[58] What if claims made in the name of universal rights are not the best way to protect people?

In the 1840s, that is exactly what the radical Karl Marx was suggesting. In the 1940s, that is exactly what Hans Morgenthau, the conservative theoretician of political realism, and Melville Herskovits, the liberal cultural relativist, were arguing.[59] All three were concerned about world peace, although each had a different way to get there: a violent lurch to the next stage of history, an ongoing balance of power, an increased respect for cultural difference. But, despite their very different sensibilities, all three were equally skeptical that some regime of liberal international law would do the trick. All found the universalistic claims masking a dangerous hubris. If the history of human rights starts to get written from a variety of perspectives, we will be in a better position to develop a more realistic balance sheet of its successes and failures.

After 9/11, there has been an outpouring of commentary on the danger that the human rights era is over.[60] A few accounts are now surfacing—both journalistic and scholarly arguing that the wave of recent activism has not been very successful at all.[61] The optimism that underscored so much of the 1990s writing now appears to be past. This has happened before, in the 1950s, for example, when the Cold War and decolonization undermined the previous decade's enthusiasm and stopped the nascent drive for international human rights law in its tracks for the next fifty years. Only time will tell if something similar is going on right now. The answer will ultimately help us see if the recent writing on the history of human rights represents a footnote to fin-de-siècle fantasies or a true start to a new way of being in the world.

NOTES

Reprinted from *American Historical Review* 109, no. 1 (Feb 2004): 117–35. By permission of the University of Chicago Press.

1. On this background, see A. W. Brian Simpson, *Human Rights and the End of Empire* (New York: Oxford University Press, 2001), 91–156; J. H. Burgers, "The Road to San Francisco: The Revival of the Human Rights Idea in the Twentieth Century," *Human Rights Quarterly* 14 (1992): 447–77.

2. On the general growth of human rights NGOs in Latin America and the Caribbean, see Edward Cleary, *The Struggle for Human Rights in Latin America* (Westport, CT: Praeger, 1997), 61–68.

3. On the debate over this conference, and the recent growth of human rights NGOs in Asia, see William Korey, *NGOs and the Universal Declaration of Human Rights: A Curious Grapevine* (New York: Palgrave Macmillan, 1998), 472–91. For statements by the Asian NGOs themselves, see Asian Cultural Forum on Development, *Our Voice: Bangkok NGO Declaration on Human Rights* (Bangkok: Asian Cultural Forum on Development, 1993).

4. To take just one example, note the Committee for the Defence of Human Rights (CDHR), based in Lagos, Nigeria. Created in 1989 after a union organizer was tossed into prison, the CDHR kept active through the 1990s, publishing annual reports of the human rights situation in Nigeria. The University of Minnesota Human Rights Library reported in 1993 that the group had over two thousand members in nineteen states in Nigeria, and listed it as one of thirteen Nigerian human rights groups then active. See the University of Minnesota Human Rights Library, "The Status of Human Rights Organizations in Sub-Saharan Africa: Nigeria," viewed February 16, 2003, http://www1.umn.edu/humanrts/africa/nigeria.htm.

5. Cheris Kramarae and Dale Spender, eds., *Routledge International Encyclopedia of Women: Global Women's Issues and Knowledge* (New York: Routledge, 2000); Charlotte Bunch and Samantha Frost, "Women's Human Rights: An Introduction"; Elisabeth Friedman, "Women's Human Rights: The Emergence of a Movement," in *Women's Rights, Human Rights: International Feminist Perspectives*, ed. Julie Peters and Andrea Wolper (New York: Routledge, 1995); Arvonne Fraser, "Becoming Human: The Origins and Development of Women's Human Rights," *Human Rights Quarterly* 21 (1999): 853–906; Judith Zinsser, "From Mexico to Copenhagen to Nairobi: The United Nations Decade for Women, 1975–1985," *Journal of World History* 13 (2002): 139–68; Saba Bahar, "Human Rights Are Women's Right: Amnesty International and the Family," in *Global Feminisms Since 1945*, ed. Bonnie G. Smith (New York: Routledge, 2000), 265–89; Mallika Dutt, "Some Reflections on United States Women of Color and the United Nations Fourth World Conference on Women and the NGO Forum in Beijing, China," in *Global Feminisms Since 1945*, Smith, 305–13; Temma Kaplan, "Women's Rights as Human Rights: Grassroots Women Redefine Citizenship in a Global Context," in *Women's Rights and Human Rights: International Historical Perspectives*, ed. Patricia Grimshaw, Katie Holmes, and Marilyn Lake (New York: Palgrave, 2001), 290–308; Henry Minde, "The Making of an International Movement of Indigenous Peoples," *Scandinavian Journal of History* 21 (1996): 221–46; Kay Warren, *Indigenous Movements and Their Critics: Pan-Maya Activism in Guatemala* (Princeton, NJ: Princeton University Press, 1998), *passim*; Stephen P. Marks, "The Evolving Field of Health and Human Rights: Issues and Methods," *Journal of Law, Medicine and Ethics* 30 (2002): 742–43.

6. Olwen Hufton, ed., *Historical Change and Human Rights: The Oxford Amnesty Lectures, 1994* (New York: Basic Books, 1995).

7. Karen Engle, "From Skepticism to Embrace: Human Rights and the American Anthropological Association, 1947–1999," *Human Rights Quarterly* 23 (August 2001): 536–59.

8. Gandhi expressed his distrust of rights-talk as early as 1910 in *Hind Swaraj*. See M. K. Gandhi, *Hind Swaraj and Other Writings*, Anthony J. Parel, ed. (New York: Cambridge University Press, 1997), 81–82. In the 1940s, he expressed his skepticism about human rights projects to both H. G. Wells and a UNESCO symposium that asked for his comments on the proposed Universal Declaration of Human Rights. In both cases, he urged people to think about their "duties" instead of "rights." See Gandhi to Wells, undated, H. G. Wells Papers, Folder G-22, Rarebook and Special Collections Library, University of Illinois, Champaign-Urbana; Jacques Maritain, et al., *Human Rights: Comments and Interpretations* (New York: Colum bia University Press, 1949), 18.

9. *Encyclopedia Britannica Online*, s.v. "Human Rights" (by Burns Weston), http://www.britannica.com/ (accessed January 22, 2003).

10. Knud Haakonssen, *Natural Law and Moral Philosophy: From Grotius to the Scottish Enlightenment* (New York: Cambridge University Press, 1996).

11. Ibid., 326, 328.

12. Michael Zuckert, *Natural Rights and the New Republicanism* (Princeton, NJ: Princeton University Press, 1994); Zuckert, *The Natural Rights Republic* (Notre Dame, IN: University of Notre Dame Press, 1996); Zuckert, *Launching Liberalism: On Lockean Political Philosophy* (Lawrence: University Press of Kansas, 2002).

13. See Dale Van Kley, ed., *The French Idea of Freedom: The Old Regime and the Declaration of Rights of 1789* (Stanford, CA: Stanford University Press, 1994); Michael Lacey and Knud Haakonssen, eds., *A Culture of Rights: The Bill of Rights in Philosophy, Politics, and Law—1791 and 1991* (New York: Cambridge University Press, 1991).

14. Lynn Hunt, ed., *The French Revolution and Human Rights: A Brief Documentary History* (Boston: Bedford, 1996). For other recent collections dealing with French documents, see Christine Fauré, ed., *Les déclarations des droits de l'homme Du débat 1789–1793 au préamble de 1946* (Paris: Payot, 1989). For a recent history directly on the subject, see Ladan Boroumand, *La guerre des principes: Les assembliées révolutionnaires face aux droits de l'homme et à la souveraineté de la nation* (Paris: Éditions de l'École des hautes Études en Sciences Sociales, 1999).

15. Hunt, *French Revolution and Human Rights*, 18.

16. The International Covenant on Civil and Political Rights and the International Covenant on Economic, Social and Cultural Rights, adopted by the United Nations in 1966, *each* contain the right to self-determination as the first article. The right was given prominence of place, in other words, but did not fit easily into the categories that by then were conventionally used to organize human rights discussions.

17. Mbonu Ojike, *My Africa* (New York: John Day Company, 1946), 261; Ho Chi Minh, "Declaration of Independence of the Democratic Republic of Vietnam," in Ho Chi Minh, *Selected Writings: 1920–1969* (Hanoi: Foreign Language Publishing House, 1973), 53–56; on the UN resolutions of 1952, see United Nations,

General Assembly, *Official Records, Sixth Session, Plenary Meeting* (February 5, 1952), 519; UN General Assembly, *Official Records, Sixth Session, Supplement no. 20*, "Inclusion in International Covenants on Human Rights of an Article Relating to the Right of Peoples to Self-Determination" (February 5, 1952), 36–37; Michael Ignatieff, *Isaiah Berlin: A Life* (New York: Viking, 1998), 227; Marc Agi, *René Cassin: Fantassin des droits de l'homme* (Paris: Plon, 1979), 244–48; Maurice Cranston, *Human Rights To-day* (London: Ampersand, 1962), 65–72. For another critique from a prominent Western social scientist of the time, see Rupert Emerson, *Self-Determination Revisited in the Era of Decolonization* (Cambridge, MA: Center for International Affairs, Harvard University, 1964).

18. Paul Gordon Lauren, *The Evolution of International Human Rights: Visions Seen* (Philadelphia: University of Pennsylvania Press, 1998), 251.

19. For a recent foray into this topic, see Robert H. Taylor, ed., *The Idea of Freedom in Asia and Africa* (Stanford, CA: Stanford University Press, 2002).

20. Stephen Angle, *Human Rights and Chinese Thought: A Cross-Cultural Inquiry* (New York: Cambridge University Press, 2002); Marina Svensson, *Debating Human Rights in China: A Conceptual and Political History* (Lanham, MD: Rowman & Littlefield, 2002); Stephen C. Angle and Marina Svensson, eds., *The Chinese Human Rights Reader: Documents and Commentary, 1900–2000* (Armonk, NY: M.E. Sharpe, 2001).

21. Among the defenders was Peng-chun Chang, who served on the drafting committee of the Universal Declaration of Human Rights. For Chiang Kai-shek's opposition, see Chiang Kai-shek, *China's Destiny*, trans. Wang Chung-hui (New York: Macmillan, 1947), 207–8.

22. Angle and Svensson, *Chinese Human Rights Reader*, passim.

23. Ibid., xiii.

24. Atina Grossmann, "A Question of Silence: The Rape of German Women by Occupation Soldiers," in *West Germany under Construction: Politics, Society, and Culture in the Adenauer Era*, ed. Robert G. Moeller (Ann Arbor: University of Michigan Press, 1997), 33–52; Grossmann, "The Difficulty of Historicizing Rape and Sexual Violence: Victims, Resisters, and Liberators in World War II" (unpublished paper). Also see Elizabeth Heineman, "The Hour of the Woman: Memories of Germany's 'Crisis Years' and West German National Identity," *AHR* 101 (April 1996): 364–74.

25. Heineman, "Hour of the Woman," 370.

26. On the concepts of "thick" and "thin" in human rights talk, see Michael Walzer, *Thick and Thin: Moral Argument at Home and Abroad* (Notre Dame, IN: University of Notre Dame Press, 1994); Kenneth Cmiel, "The Emergence of Human Rights Politics in the United States," *Journal of American History* 86 (December 1999): 1249–50; Angle, *Human Rights and Chinese Thought*, 11–15.

27. Gary Jonathan Bass, *Stay the Hand of Vengeance: The Politics of War Crimes Tribunals* (Princeton, NJ: Princeton University Press, 2000); on war crimes trials, also see Howard Ball, *Prosecuting War Crimes and Genocide: The*

Twentieth-Century Experience (Lawrence: University Press of Kansas, 1999); and Devin Pendas, "'I Didn't Know What Auschwitz Was': The Frankfurt Auschwitz Trial and the German Press, 1963–65," *Yale Journal of Law and the Humanities* 12 (Summer 2000): 397–446. On the related topic of transitions to democracy, see Carla Hesse and Robert Post, eds., *Human Rights in Political Transitions: Gettysburg to Bosnia* (New York: Zone Books, 1999).

28. Audrey Fisch, *American Slaves in Victorian England: Abolitionist Politics in Popular Literature and Culture* (New York: Cambridge University Press, 2000); Alan Rice and Martin Crawford, eds., *Liberating Sojourn: Frederick Douglass and Transatlantic Reform* (Athens: University of Georgia Press, 1999); Nitza Berkovitch, *From Motherhood to Citizenship: Women's Rights and International Organizations* (Baltimore, MD: Johns Hopkins University Press, 1999); Leila J. Rupp, *Worlds of Women: The Making of an International Women's Movement* (Princeton, NJ: Princeton University Press, 1997).

29. Adam Hochschild, *King Leopold's Ghost: A Story of Greed, Terror, and Heroism in Colonial Africa* (New York: Houghton Mifflin, 1998), 210.

30. Emmanuel Naquet, "Entre justice et patrie: La ligue des droits de l'homme et la grande guerre," *Movement social* 183 (1998): 93–109; "La Ligue française des droits de l'homme et la L.I.D.U., son homologue italienne, organisation d'exiles antifascistes dans l'entre-deux-guerres," *Movement social* 183 (1998): 119–34; Wendy Perry, "Remembering Dreyfus: The Ligue des Droits de l'Homme and the Making of the Modern French Human Rights Movement" (PhD diss., University of North Carolina, Chapel Hill, 1999).

31. The Liga was founded in 1937. It had many Communist Party ties, although it was not formally connected with the party. It is now "a pluralist organization of the Left in Argentina." Louis Bickford, "Human Rights Archives and Research on Historical Memory," *Latin American Research Review* 35 (2000): 173; for general background on the organization, see Alfredo Welsh, *Tiempos de ira, tiempos de esperanza: 50 años de vida política a través de la Liga Argentina por los Derechos del Hombre* (Buenos Aires: R. Cedeño, 1984).

32. Lauren, *Evolution of International Human Rights*, 91, 110–14; Burgers, "Road to San Francisco"; Simpson, *Human Rights and the End of Empire*, 151–54. For more general background to the internationalism of the era, see Akira Iriye, *Cultural Internationalism and World Order* (Baltimore, MD: Johns Hopkins University Press, 1997).

33. Mary Ann Glendon, *A World Made New: Eleanor Roosevelt and the Universal Declaration of Human Rights* (New York: Random House, 2001), 9–10; Geoffrey Robertson, *Crimes against Humanity: The Struggle for Global Justice* (New York: New Press, 2000), 21; Simpson, *Human Rights and the End of Empire*, 121–49; Lauren is especially good on the racial limits of League policy, see *Evolution of International Human Rights*, 98–103.

34. Stephen D. Krasner, *Sovereignty: Organized Hypocrisy* (Princeton, NJ: Princeton University Press, 1999), 105. For a particularly clear 1940s statement of the opposition between the concept of self-determination and the notion of human rights, see Morris D. Waldman, "A Bill of Rights for All Nations," *New York Times*, November 19, 1944.

35. Other works on the 1940s include Johannes Morsink, *The Universal Declaration of Human Rights: Origins, Drafting and Intent* (Philadelphia: University of Pennsylvania Press, 1999); Arieh Kochavi, *Prelude to Nuremberg: Allied War Crimes Policy and the Question of Punishment* (Chapel Hill: University of North Carolina Press, 1998); Carol Anderson's excellent *Eyes off the Prize: The United Nations and the African American Struggle for Human Rights, 1944–1955* (New York: Cambridge University Press, 2003); Kenneth Cmiel, "Human Rights, Freedom of Information, and the Origins of Third World Solidarity," in *Truth Claims: Representation and Human Rights*, ed. Mark Bradley and Patrice Petro (New Brunswick, NJ: Rutgers University Press, 2002), 107–30; Marilyn Lake, "From Self-Determination via Protection to Equality via Non-Discrimination: Defining Women's Rights at the League of Nations and the United Nations," in Grimshaw, Holmes, and Lake, *Women's Rights and Human Rights,* 254–71; Elizabeth Borgwardt, "An Intellectual History of the Atlantic Charter: Ideas, Institutions, and Human Rights in American Diplomacy, 1941–1946" (PhD diss., Stanford University, 2002).

36. In the early 1960s, Malik began publishing books in the United States with religious publishers. *A Christian Critique of the University* (Downers Grove, IL: InterVarsity Press, 1982), which condemned the godless turn in higher education and was published by a prominent evangelical press, and is still read in the United States.

37. Cmiel, "Emergence of Human Rights Politics in the United States"; Jeri Laber, *The Courage of Strangers: Coming of Age with the Human Rights Movement* (New York: Public Affairs, 2002); Daniel Thomas, *The Helsinki Effect: International Norms, Human Rights, and the Demise of Communism* (Princeton, NJ: Princeton University Press, 2001); Iain Guest, *Behind the Disappearances: Argentina's Dirty War against Human Rights and the United Nations* (Philadelphia: University of Pennsylvania Press, 1990); Marguerite Guzman Bouvard, *Revolutionizing Motherhood: The Mothers of the Plaza de Mayo* (Wilmington, DE: Scholarly Resources, 1994); Charles Rhéaume, "Science et droits de l'homme: Le soutien international à Sakharov" (PhD diss., McGill University, 1999). Two useful books that range from the 1940s through the 1990s but contain much on the 1970s activism are Korey, *NGOs and the Universal Declaration of Human Rights*, and Howard Tolley, *The International Commission of Jurists: Global Advocates for Human Rights* (Philadelphia: University of Pennsylvania Press, 1995).

38. Jack Donnelly, "Recent Trends in U.N. Human Rights Activity: Description and Polemic," *International Organization* 35 (Autumn 1981): 633–55; Howard Tolley, *The U.N. Commission on Human Rights* (Boulder, CO: Westview Press, 1987).

39. Jonathan Power, *Like Water on Stone: The Story of Amnesty International* (Boston: Northeastern University Press, 2001); Robert Drinan, S.J., *The Mobilization of Shame: A World View of Human Rights* (New Haven, CT: Yale University Press, 2001); Kirsten Sellars, *The Rise and Rise of Human Rights* (Thrupp, UK: Sutton, 2002); Linda Rabben, *Fierce Legion of Friends: A History of Human Rights Campaigns and Campaigners* (Madison: University of Wisconsin Press, 2002).

40. See Lauren's *Evolution of International Human Rights*, esp. 241–98; Michael Ignatieff, *The Rights Revolution* (Toronto, 2000); but for a more recent, and more skeptical, assessment, see Ignatieff, "Is the Human Rights Era Ending?" *New York Times*, February 5, 2002.

41. This strain of optimism comes from international relations theory known as "constructivism," which challenges both neo-realist and neo-liberal understandings of the international order. Recent constructivist scholarship has emphasized the ability of human rights NGOs to alter the behavior of states. At times, this literature reads modestly—human rights NGOs can have successes. At other moments, however, these writers lean toward arguing that human rights NGOs have the power to significantly rearrange the international system. For examples, see Ann Marie Clark, *Diplomacy of Conscience: Amnesty International and Changing Human Rights Norms* (Princeton: Princeton University Press, 2001); Margaret Keck and Kathryn Sikkink, *Activists beyond Borders: Advocacy Networks in International Politics* (Ithaca, NY: Cornell University Press, 1998); Thomas Risse-Kappen, et al., eds., *The Power of Human Rights: International Norms and Domestic Change* (New York: Cambridge University Press, 1999); Thomas, *Helsinki Effect*.

42. Rosemary Foot, *Rights beyond Borders: The Global Community and the Struggle over Human Rights in China* (Oxford: Oxford University Press, 2000), 250–73.

43. Svensson, *Debating Human Rights in China*, 266.

44. Jeffrey N. Wasserstrom, Lynn Hunt, and Marilyn Young, eds., *Human Rights and Revolutions* (Lanham, MD: Rowman & Littlefield, 2000); Joan Wallach Scott, *Only Paradoxes to Offer: French Feminists and the Rights of Man* (Cambridge, MA: Harvard University Press, 1996); Robert Darnton, "Censorship, A Comparative View: France, 1789–East Germany, 1989," in *Historical Change and Human Rights*, 101–30. For Hunt, see her essay in *Human Rights and Revolutions*, "The Paradoxical Origins of Human Rights," 3–17.

45. Marilyn Young, preface to *Human Rights and Revolutions*, vii.

46. Alice Bullard, "Paris 1871/New Caledonia 1878: Human Rights and the Managerial State," in *Human Rights and Revolutions*, 95.

47. Jeffrey N. Wasserstrom, "Chinese Revolutions and Contemporary Paradox," in *Human Rights and Revolutions*, 20.

48. Scott, *Only Paradoxes to Offer*.

49. Milan Kundera, *Immortality*, transl. Peter Kussi (New York: Grove Weidenfeld, 1991), 122.

50. Lynn Hunt's contribution to *Human Rights and Revolutions* tells a deeply paradoxical story. Yet her commentary in her collection of documents, *The French Revolution and Human Rights*, gives a much more optimistic reading of human rights history. See *French Revolution and Human Rights*, 3, 18–19. Does it matter that the collection of documents is meant for an undergraduate audience while Hunt's contribution to *Human Rights and Revolutions* is intended for a largely academic readership?

51. David Rieff, *A Bed for the Night: Humanitarianism in Crisis* (New York: Simon & Schuster, 2002); Hochschild, *King Leopold's Ghost.*

52. Other exceptions include a number of the essays in *Human Rights and Revolutions.*

53. For a recent overview, see Eric D. Weitz, *A Century of Genocide: Utopias of Race and Nation* (Princeton, NJ: Princeton University Press, 2003).

54. Daqing Yang, "Convergence or Divergence? Recent Historical Writings on the Rape of Nanjing," *AHR* 104 (June 1999): 842–65.

55. Norman M. Naimark, *Fires of Hatred: Ethnic Cleansing in Twentieth-Century Europe* (Cambridge, MA: Harvard University Press, 2001); Anne Applebaum, *Gulag: A History* (New York, 2003).

56. For some of the best work recently done, see Edward Peters, *Torture*, 2nd ed. (Philadelphia: University of Pennsylvania Press, 1996); Daius Rejali, *Torture and Modernity: Self, Society, and State in Modem Iran* (Boulder, CO: Westview Press, 1994); Rejali, "Electric Torture Instruments: Innovation and Diffusion in Torture Methods: A Case Study" (unpublished paper, 1998); Rejali, "Studying a Practice: An Inquiry into Lapidation," *Critique* 18 (Spring 2001): 67–100.

57. Mark Mazower, "Violence and the State in the Twentieth Century," *AHR* 107 (October 2002): 1158–78.

58. Amnesty International, *A Glimpse of Hell: Reports on Torture Worldwide* (London: Cassell, 1996); Bertil Dunér, ed., *An End to Torture: Strategies for Its Eradication* (London: Zed Books, 1998).

59. Karl Marx, "On the Jewish Question," in Marx, *The Early Texts*, ed. D. McLellan (Oxford: Blackwell 1971); for Morgenthau criticizing the drive for "an international bill of rights," see Hans Joachim Morgenthau, *Scientific Man vs. Power Politics* (Chicago: University of Chicago Press, 1946), 106; for Morgenthau's critique of international law, see Morgenthau, *Politics among Nations: The Struggle for Power and Peace* (New York: A.A. Knopf, 1948), 209–42; for the Herskovits position, see American Anthropological Association, "Statement on Human Rights," *American Anthropologist* 49 (1947): 539–41.

60. Ignatieff, "Is the Human Rights Era Ending?"; Peter Maass, "How America's Friends Really Fight Terrorism," *New Republic*, November 11, 2002, 18–21; "Does the Western World Still Take Human Rights Seriously?" *Lancet*, no. 358 (November 24, 2001): 1741; David Lubin, "The War on Terrorism and the End of Human Rights," *Philosophy and Public Policy Quarterly* 22 (Summer 2002): 9–14; Jacques Julliard, "La défaite du droit d'ingerence," *Le nouvel observateur*, no. 2027 (September 11–17, 2003): 9.

61. Rieff, *Bed for the Night*; Oona Hathaway, "Do Human Rights Treaties Make a Difference?" *Yale Law Journal* 111 (June 2002): 1870–2042.

2

THE HOLOCAUST AND THE "HUMAN RIGHTS REVOLUTION"

A Reassessment

G. DANIEL COHEN

Speaking at the tribune of the United Nations in June 2004, the former Secretary-General Kofi Anan explicitly linked the Holocaust to the emergence of modern human rights: "Worldwide revulsion at this terrible genocide was the driving force behind the Universal Declaration of Human Rights."[1] Reactions to the mass murder of European Jews, intimated the Ghanaian diplomat, promoted the diffusion of human rights norms in the postwar era. This statement certainly conveyed noble intentions. "A human rights agenda that fails to address anti-Semitism," Anan rightly reminded his audience, "denies its own history." Yet the causality between the Holocaust and the expansion of human rights inferred in this address also echoed a widespread assumption: at the end of the Second World War, the shocking discovery of the Jewish genocide allegedly added a moral core to international politics. Accordingly, the various human rights instruments designed under the umbrella of the United Nations and the Council of Europe in the late 1940s—the Universal Declaration of Human Rights (1948), the Genocide Convention (1948), the European Convention on Human Rights (1950), and the Geneva Convention on Refugees (1951)— exemplified a deliberate rejection of "barbarous acts which have outraged the conscience of mankind," the Holocaust chiefly among them.[2] The official websites of the United Nations and the European Union are not the only propagators of this foundational narrative. Numerous historians of human rights have also contended that the first international guarantees aimed at sheltering individuals from abusive states predominantly stemmed from Holocaust awareness, even if detailed knowledge of Nazi genocidal intentions and actions was still decades away. Although the 1948 Universal Declaration of Human Rights (UDHR) has multiple origins, one of its premier commentators argued, "none of them match the Holocaust in importance." Consequently, the liberal-individualist overtones of the "Magna Carta for Mankind" did not merely resurrect Enlightenment principles but also affirmed "deep truths rediscovered in the midst of the Holocaust and put on paper again shortly thereafter."[3] For Paul G. Lauren, what ultimately tipped the scale in favor of human rights after the Second World War was the "unimagined destruction of human life in the genocide of the Holocaust's 'Final Solution' that exceeded all previously known bounds."[4] Michael Ignatieff offered more abstract wording; in his opinion, the postwar preoccupation with human rights was a radical attempt at creating "firewalls against barbarism" and symbolized a "war-weary generation's reflection on European nihilism and its consequences."[5] Yet even when not overtly named, the Holocaust ranks particularly high among the explanatory factors currently advanced to elucidate the outbreak of the so-called human rights revolution.[6]

This "Holocaust-centric" interpretation has not always prevailed. The first pamphlet on human rights issued by the United Nations in 1950 devoted only a few lines to Nazi anti-Semitic violence. What first and foremost stirred the "conscience of the free world" after the Second World War, explained the UN Department of Public Information, was the "absolute power of the state" and the "disappearance of political freedom" under fascism and Nazism.[7] Similarly, legal commentaries on the UDHR written during the early Cold War era hardly singled out the Nazi genocide as the progeny of human rights law. Although published by the World Jewish Congress to commemorate the tenth anniversary of the Declaration, Nehemiah Robinson's pioneering study limited itself to a general observation: "the war initiated by the Axis in violation of the most elementary rules of civilized behavior" was the document's main source of inspiration.[8] Five years later, another commentator succinctly added that "the savage campaign of extermination directed against the members of the Jewish race" ranged among the crimes which the Declaration sought to banish.[9] Since the late 1960s, however, the central place occupied by the Holocaust in the remembrance of the Second World War has reshaped our perception of the origins of modern human rights. Now elevated to the rank of iconic "breach of civilization," the Holocaust is today equally portrayed as a "civilizer of nations": the epitome of twentieth-century suffering that purportedly fostered the internationalization of human rights and the humanization of international law.[10] As one author summarized, "the horror of the Holocaust would shape new international humanitarian law for decades to come."[11] Implicit in this view is that immediate memories of the Jewish catastrophe rescued the postwar human rights project from its numerous shortcomings. Despite the persistence of racial segregation in the United States, of European rule in the colonial world, and of the gulag system in the Soviet Union, widespread outrage at Nazi genocidal policies infused substance and moral energy into the emerging human rights regime. The legacy of the Holocaust thus solidly "lies at the heart of the moral consensus on human rights that was born in the 1940s and has expanded ever since."[12]

Remarkably, few historians have weighed the merits of this popular claim. The recent emergence of "human rights history" has generated important research on the diplomatic, political or cultural foundations of human rights but has left the specific question of "Holocaust causality" largely unaddressed. To the extent that an historical debate exists over the main factors accounting for the expansion (or invisibility) of human rights after 1945, it chiefly revolves around the role successively played by American hegemony, anticolonialism, détente, Eastern European dissidence, Jimmy Carter's foreign policy, or post-1989 globalization. Another dividing line separates historians who attribute the postwar resonance of human rights to the top-down protections envisioned in the late 1940s from others who now locate in the 1970s the soaring phase of the "last utopia."[13]A question generally shunned by historians, the precise impact of the Holocaust on the articulation of human rights principles has been predominantly investigated by sociologists and legal scholars focused on the post–Cold War period. As the human rights impulse finally "burst free into an interconnected world that seemed made for it," expansive memories of the Holocaust elicited a new "cosmopolitan morality"; dramatized other abuses of human dignity; and heavily impinged on the conduct of international justice and humanitarian interventions.[14] While illuminating the role played by Holocaust memorialization in the production of contemporary moral and legal norms, these studies reassert what has become the conventional story of origin: "The horrors of the Holocaust formed the background against which human rights norms and a host of other UN conventions initially established their legitimacy."[15]

Historians have nonetheless started to challenge the ideational premises of this "Holocaust-centric" thesis. More interested in Great Powers politics than in the idealism of individual "visionaries," Brian Simpson and Mark Mazower have belittled the significance of the "human rights revolution" as a corrective to the Final Solution. Admittedly, the 1948 Genocide Convention was passed in response to the "European Holocaust." But throughout the second half of the 1940s, the permanent concern of the Great Powers—and of the British government in particular—remained first and foremost the safeguard of sovereignty against external interventions in national and colonial affairs. At best a "pious exhalation of hot air," the nonbinding Universal Declaration was perfectly suited to secure this goal. The human rights regime thus originated in "complicated interrelationships between individuals, institutions, and governments, with their varied ideological commitments and perceptions of reality, history and self-interest."[16] For Mark Mazower, the "strange triumph" of human rights reflected a widespread international desire to finish off the moribund interwar system of minority rights in favor of individual rights abstract enough to be safely embraced. Designed at a time when colonized nations did not yet belong to the United Nations, the human rights framework intentionally blocked the full-fledged recognition of self-determination and only offered weak protections to endangered minority groups. Rather than a radical shift in moral standards, the "human rights revolution" reinforced the sovereign prerogatives of nation-states.[17] From this perspective, therefore, what had yet to be called the Holocaust hardly functioned as a driving force toward a moral world: polite invocations aside, the legacy of the Final Solution remained peripheral to the formation of the human rights system. Since there was no Holocaust-consciousness in the immediate postwar era, stated Samuel Moyn in a thought-provoking study, "human rights could not have been a response to the Nazi genocide. Unrelated to the Holocaust or at times explicitly silent on Nazi murderous anti-Semitism, Christian-personalist and conservative thought strongly inspired the turn to human rights after 1945.[18]

This essay strikes a middle ground between these polarized interpretations. The dominant ideational school of thought plausibly asserts that the Holocaust weighed upon the dawn of the "age of rights," but this argument warrants qualification. The United Nations human rights project did not miraculously rise "from the ashes of the Holocaust," as a self-congratulatory Kofi Anan proclaimed. Even if politically marginal until the outbreak of the Second World War, the idea of individual rights enshrined in international law was incubated in Western Europe and the United States in the first half of the twentieth century. At the end of the Second World War, the seven nonbinding and hortatory mentions of human rights in the United Nations Charter undoubtedly installed this rhetoric at the core of the new world order. But in June 1945, this first international evocation of human rights was not a reaction to the Final Solution. A few weeks removed from the liberation of Europe, participants in the San Francisco conference did not yet "grasp the full scale of the horrors perpetrated by the Nazis."[19] Often described as the imperfect but pathbreaking beginning of the "human rights revolution," the United Nations Charter bore little relation to the Nazi assault on European Jewry. Six months later, the massive documentary evidence produced in the course of the Nuremberg Trials (November 1945–October 1946) nonetheless brought the Holocaust into closer proximity with the human rights project. The first distinctive international effort "outside of Jewish circles to grasp the awful significance of the murder of European Jews," the proceedings of the International Military Tribunal also played a pivotal role in the subsequent drafting of human rights instruments.[20] Elicited in part by this wealth of information, references to the Holocaust are traceable, among others, in the UDHR and the Genocide Convention. They generally intermingled with the denunciation of other German atrocities and served to broadly magnify Nazi inhumanity. But the language of international human rights did not encourage historical amnesia: the human rights regime established under the auspices of the United Nations universalized the Holocaust without negating its historical significance. While in postwar Europe the Jewish catastrophe was expediently blurred within a narrative of national or antifascist martyrdom, it was both memorialized and naturalized in international law.

On the other end, skeptical authors offer essential cautionary tales for historians too easily seduced by the idealist pronouncements of celebrated human rights pioneers. The political scientist Andrew Moravcsik warned that when engaged in the study of human rights regimes, "scholars should not jump too easy to the conclusion . . . that altruism must motivate the establishment of morally attractive international norms."[21] The UN General Assembly could solemnly proclaim, as it did on the passing of the 1948 Genocide Convention, that "in this field relating to the sacred right of existence of human groups, we are proclaiming the supremacy of international law."[22] But in the context of the nascent Cold War, recently countered Mark Mazower and Samuel Moyn, "international law could no longer claim a position over politics."[23] Their harsh dismissal of the "revolution" obscures, however, the triggering effect of the Holocaust on the formulation of human rights, irrespective of their shape or immediate effectiveness. The turn to individual rights characteristic of the 1940s may well have served to hinder third-party interference in the Great Powers' affairs, legitimate ethnic cleansing and population transfers, or prevent self-determination in the colonies. Yet the individualization of international law, even if devoid of rigorous mechanisms of enforceability, was also a response to Nazi genocidal actions and to the plight of Jewish survivors in displaced persons camps. That Great Power politics obstructed the implementation of human rights and narrowed their scope should not mask this referential dimension.

Despite its flaws, the "human rights revolution" constituted the first *inter-national* site of Holocaust remembrance.

The place occupied by the genocide in the writings of three influential Jewish jurists aggrieved by Nazi violence exemplifies the simultaneous centrality and invisibility of the Holocaust in postwar human rights discourse. Hersch Lauterpacht, the Galician-born legal scholar who during and after the Second World War forcefully endorsed individual rights as the foundation of international law, lost his parents and siblings in the Holocaust. René Cassin, the premier French drafter of the 1948 Universal Declaration, never saw twenty-nine relatives, including his sister, return from Vichy-condoned deportation. Raphael Lemkin, the tireless crusader for the criminalization of genocide, miraculously escaped his native Poland before the Nazis murdered forty-nine members of his family in the Warsaw ghetto, in concentration camps, and during death marches.[24] Yet, in their respective and divergent efforts to promote human rights after the war, Lauterpacht and Cassin remained silent about the Holocaust. According to an attentive reader of Lauterpacht's postwar writings, the Cambridge scholar alluded to the Final Solution only once, in a footnote.[25] In keeping with French public discourse in the aftermath of the Liberation, René Cassin never addressed "Nazi barbarism" in specific Jewish terms. Although an open advocate of Jewish rights and (like Lauterpacht) a sympathizer of Zionism, Cassin preferred to evoke the "atrocities of the Second World War," "Nazi aggression," or the "revolting and monstrous acts" perpetrated by the Axis to stress the historical timeliness of the Declaration. Raphael Lemkin was, of course, much more explicit about the annihilation of European Jews. His landmark *Axis Rule in Occupied Europe*, published in 1944, presciently grasped the gravity of the Holocaust. Lemkin's subsequent campaign for the Genocide Convention, however, did not exclusively stem from the Jewish catastrophe. The lone crusader was also deeply affected by the ruthless destruction of Poland, as well as greatly influenced by Johann Gottfried Herder's thought on the singularity of world cultures and the crucial need to protect them. In unpublished research conducted in the last years of his life, Lemkin also extended the concept of genocide to settler colonialism. Although Lemkin was more vocal than Lauterpacht and Cassin about the Holocaust, his concern for the "essential foundations of the life of a national group" transcended the exclusive realm of Jewish history.[26]

Important doctrinal and political differences separated Lauterpacht, Cassin, and Lemkin from one other. Lauterpacht was a strict "neo-Grotian" with grave legalistic focus on the individualization of international law. A French republican and World War One veteran, Cassin was a more flexible individualist who sought the inclusion of social rights and the protection of the human "personality" into the human rights regime whose birth he oversaw.[27] At odds with legal individualism, Lemkin's single-issue campaign for the recognition of genocide revivified the dwindling legacy of interwar minority rights. These three Jewish jurists nonetheless conveyed the experience of the Holocaust through the formulation and codification of human rights. Above all, they sought to extract universality from the singular Jewish tragedy. The Holocaust, in their mind, violated humanity as a whole; whether through individual or collective rights, the most urgent form of redress was to challenge the "Leviathan State" as an entity beyond the reach of law. Staunch individualists like Lauterpacht regretted that the attack against state sovereignty was significantly weakened by the impossibility for individual citizens to petition the United Nations against abusing states. Contrary to Lauterpacht, Cassin pinned his hopes on the future compliance of nation-states with the new moral standards vibrantly proclaimed by the Declaration. More interested in the protection of collective rights than in the promotion of individual rights, Lemkin advocated the international criminalization of genocide and the adoption of uniform domestic laws prohibiting this offense. All, nevertheless, crucially imported the Holocaust into their own conceptions of international law.[28]

Recent commentators on the Universal Declaration found a similar disposition among the multiple diplomats, NGO representatives, and United Nations spokesmen who took part in drafting the document from January 1947 to December 1948. Johannes Morsink regards nearly every article of the Declaration as an expression of outrage at the Holocaust. In his opinion, articles on personal security, legal rights, democratic governmental procedures, citizenship, and asylum mirror the experience of the Final Solution. According to Morsink, recent historical research retroactively confirms the "impetus of the Holocaust behind the acceptance of the entire range of rights in the Declaration."[29] A closer examination reveals, however, a more ambivalent picture.[30] If the finalized language of the Declaration can be easily opposed to Nazi crimes, it does not always call the Holocaust to mind. "All human beings are born free and equal in dignity and rights" (Article 1) may well have alluded to "the unity of the human race as opposed to the theories like those of Hitler," as Cassin himself argued, but this article also resurrected the late eighteenth-century rhetoric of the Atlantic revolutions. Article 2 on the universal enjoyment of "the rights and freedoms set forth in the Declaration" counteracted Nazi claims of racial supremacy but also nominally challenged European rule in the colonial world. The "right to life, liberty and security of persons" guaranteed in Article 3 alluded to the Nazi euthanasia program, which subsequent research identified as the preparatory phase of the Final Solution. Cassin again stressed the necessity of such a provision when he reminded the General Assembly that "when Germany began to violate these principles in 1933 . . . the nations of the world did not intervene." But Charles Malik, the Lebanese rapporteur of the Commission of Human Rights and a former student of Martin Heidegger, championed the "right to life" as a way to safeguard "bodily integrity from the moment of conception." Representatives of women's organizations logically countered that such a provision could impede the passing of "advanced legislation" favorable to abortion, thereby taking the debate further away from Nazi euthanasia. In Article 4, "No one shall be held in slavery of servitude" surely implied a condemnation of Nazi slave labor—not incidentally voiced during the deliberations by a Polish delegate—but also covered the Nazi treatment of prisoners of war and more generally the trafficking of women and children.[31] The prohibition of "torture, cruel and degrading treatment or punishment" (Article 5) pertained in part to Nazi medical experiments performed on concentration camp inmates or more generally to the "medieval methods . . . practiced in the recent past by the Nazis and Fascists" but also encompassed other forms of corporal violations.[32]

The series of legal rights spelled out by the Declaration appear more specifically related to the origins of the Final Solution. Article 6 on the "right to recognition everywhere as a person before the law" derived from the exclusion of German Jews from the juridical realm prior to their physical elimination. The World Jewish Congress (WJC), one of the most active consultative organizations at the United Nations, successfully reminded the drafters that Hitler "annulled every human right by law . . . up to the point of mass murder of six million Jews and innumerable other victims in Germany and the whole of Europe." The WJC also scored a victory in amending Article 7, guaranteeing universal equality before the law. Because the initial assault on German Jews was paradoxically mounted through legal means, "this equality [before the law] must be protected by prohibiting incitement against discrimination."[33] More important, the WJC and other advocates of ex post facto prosecution demanded the retroactivity of crimes against humanity perpetrated under the Nazi regime. The first draft of Article 11 presented by the Commission of Human Rights had initially proposed—in conformity with Anglo-American principles— that no law should be retroactive. This language prevented the prosecution of crimes not punishable under German law at the time they were committed. But the Declaration ultimately recognized the retroactivity of international law: even if committed with impunity under Nazi law, any offense subsequently defined as crimes against humanity by the Nuremberg and Tokyo tribunals was considered punishable.[34] Article 13 on the "right to leave a country" was undoubtedly inspired by the Jewish refugee crisis of the late 1930s, even if it was complemented by "the right to return to one's country," applauded, among others, by representatives of Arab governments in support of Palestinian refugees. Article 14 ("Everyone has the right to seek and enjoy in other countries asylum from persecution") was stripped of the more daring "right to be granted asylum," which was dear, in particular, to René Cassin and the World Jewish Congress. But this first international recognition of the right to *seek* asylum sought to prevent another "abandonment of the Jews" or other disenfranchised communities in the future. Article 15 on "the right of everyone to a nationality" also evoked the predicament of Central European Jewish refugees on the eve of the Second World War. The second part of this article—"No one shall be arbitrarily deprived of his nationality"—explicitly referred to the wholesale denationalization of Jews under Nazi law.

The social, economic, and cultural rights proclaimed in the second half of the Universal Declaration are much more difficult to link to Nazism, let alone to the Holocaust. The right "to marry and found a family" (Article 16) obviously had little to do with the Final Solution. Nazi marriage laws, as Cassin reminded, forbade unions between Aryans and non-Aryans, but during the drafting process the debate chiefly revolved around the definition of consent and on the equality of men and women in contracting marriage. Evidently, the "right to social security" (Article 22) and "the right to work and form labor unions" (Article 23) expressed liberal, social-democratic and communist concerns, even if it was occasionally claimed that the international recognition of these rights "would make the return of fascism impossible." Finally, the right to a "peaceful international order" (Article 28), the duty to exercise rights and freedoms according to "the principles of the United Nations" (Article 29), and the warning sent to states against the performance of acts "aimed at the destruction of any of the rights and freedoms set forth herein" (Article 30) sought to establish the Declaration as an international code of conduct. But overall, precise references to the Holocaust in this general appeal to humanity are scarcer than assumed in the idealist literature. This relative invisibility did not however amount to oblivion: the Declaration did honor to Jewish suffering by processing its singularity into a universalistic vision, to the ample satisfaction of postwar Jewish organizations.[35] The Holocaust was therefore simultaneously visible and absent from early human rights rhetoric and sufficiently reconciled particular memories with universal rights.

Passed by the UN General Assembly on December 9, 1948, the Convention on the Prevention and Punishment of the Crime of Genocide bore in its very title a more tangible relation to the Holocaust. Yet like the UDHR adopted in Paris one day later, it significantly broadened the legacy of the Jewish tragedy. Here again, the writings of the World Jewish Congress jurist Nehemiah Robinson—the first legal commentator on the Genocide Convention—serve as a reliable yardstick to gauge the level of "Holocaust-centrism" in the emergence of postwar human rights.[36] For Robinson, the "Nazi war of aggression and the crimes against the Jews and other nationalities demonstrated clearly the necessity of international action to punish the perpetrators of the mass destruction of peoples." The United Nations Department of Public Information concurred with this rationale: "In modern times, this crime of crimes was practiced on a larger scale by Nazi Germany . . . to destroy millions of Jews, Slavs and almost all the gypsies of occupied Europe."[37] These statements faithfully conveyed Lemkin's cosmopolitan goal of outlawing all forms of group destruction. They were also historically sound, as well as historiographically prescient. As Timothy Snyder demonstrated in his study of mass murder in wartime Eastern Europe, the Final Solution was originally only one of the exterminatory projects to be implemented after a victorious war against the Soviet Union. Contrary to their expectations, the Germans were unable to eliminate some fifty million people as envisioned in Generalplan Ost. They nonetheless intentionally starved one million people in the siege of Leningrad, provoked famines in Ukrainian cities, and allowed three million Soviet POWs to perish.[38] This plurality of murderous practices prompted the Soviet delegation at the United Nations to demand the recognition of an "organic connection" between the concept of genocide and Nazi eliminationist violence. This proposal was ultimately rejected on the grounds that a strict correlation between the Genocide Convention and Nazism would impede its applicability in the future. Its core articles, however, clearly mirrored various instances of planned mass murder in wartime Eastern Europe: all recognize the Holocaust as an ideal-type for the crime of genocide while acknowledging other patterns of collective annihilation. The Genocide Convention has often been criticized for its deliberate omission of "cultural genocide" (due to American and European lack of enthusiasm for the group rights of minorities and colonial peoples); and for its disregard of "political genocide" (due to Soviet fears of retroactive incrimination and the opposition of NGOs such as the World Jewish Congress reluctant to downgrade genocide to a struggle of states for predominance). As part of the United Nations weak preventative system, the Genocide Convention has also been blamed for failing to protect minorities from massive violence during and after the Cold War. But more than any other United Nations instrument, the Genocide Convention availed the Holocaust as a referential "crime of crimes" for postwar human rights activists.

In this regard, the European Convention of Human Rights (ECHR) adopted in 1950 by the Council of Europe presents a sharply different case. Rooted in the politics of European integration and Cold War diplomacy, the ECHR sought to stabilize Western European liberal democracies—or as one of its promoters explained, "generalize social democracy"—against the threats of domestic communist parties and Soviet hegemony on the Continent. Its overall goal was to cement a consensus on the political importance of individual liberty in Europe through common standards of human rights. Initially crafted by a group of elite jurists, including the former French resister and Christian-Democrat politician Pierre-Henri Teitgen, the Conservative British lawyer and former prosecutor at the Nuremberg Trials David Maxwell Fyfe, and the Belgian legal scholar and pan-European Fernand Dehousse, the ECHR "was not simply a continuation of the UN system but also a pragmatic reaction to it."[39] Indeed, the distinctive feature of the first regional human rights covenant signed in the postwar era was its juridical enforceability. In addition to a catalog of rights, reminiscent of those proclaimed in the Universal Declaration, the ECHR allowed the right of individual petition to a European Court of Human Rights enabling citizens to mount a legal challenge against their own state. Although few governments initially accepted this daring but optional supranational provision, the ECHR drastically improved on the limited declarative purpose of UN instruments.

Holocaust memories did not, however, impinge upon the birth of the European human rights system. The rich scholarship on the origins of the ECHR is noticeably silent on any link between the Final Solution and the European covenant.[40] Among the forefathers of ECHR, surmises Andrew Moravcsik, "some Jewish parliamentarians and law professors were also prominent and may have been influenced by their experiences and beliefs."[41] One reason accounting for the absence of Holocaust invocations in the preparation of the ECHR lies in its limited number of articles, eighteen overall. Designed with enforceability in mind, the ECHR purposely restricted the amount of rights which individual claimants could take to court. This economical scope contrasted with the expansive rhetoric of the Universal Declaration and its larger array of rights potentially related to the Holocaust. Promoters of the ECHR—at times, like Fernand Dehousse, also key actors in the drafting process of human rights at the United Nations—benefited therefore from a set of ready-made articles already debated at length under the auspices of the world organization. Their main task was instead to produce a list of basic binding rights and imagine methods of implementation.

Yet redundancy with the Universal Declaration does not fully explain the absence of specific mentions of the Holocaust in the ECHR. Sponsored by overtly anticommunist politicians to prevent the resurgence of dictatorship and foster consensus politics and economic integration in Western Europe, the European Convention was first and foremost "antitotalitarian" in nature. Echoing the Atlanticist rhetoric of NATO founders, Robert Schuman recognized in the ECHR "the foundations on which to base the defense of human personality against all tyrannies and against all forms of totalitarianism."[42] From this perspective, the Holocaust disappeared into a broader campaign to salvage democracy from the threat of authoritarianism. The legacy of Nazi political violence remained, of course, linked to this antitotalitarian agenda. "Democracies do not become Nazi countries in one day," declared the French promoter of the European Convention Pierre-Henri Teitgen. "One by one, freedoms are suppressed, in one sphere after another. And then, when everything is in order, the Führer is installed and the evolution continues even to the oven of the crematorium." This "progressive corruption," warned Teitgen, inexorably led to "Buchenwald and Dachau."[43] A Europeanist politician with impeccable resistance credentials, Teitgen naturally pointed to these two symbolic sites of *political* deportation to champion the idea of an enforceable European system of human rights guarantees. The iconic incarnation of "*l'univers concentrationnaire*" in early French memories of the Second World War, "Buchenwald and Dachau" conjured up memories of the ruthless treatment of predominantly non-Jewish resisters and political prisoners and absorbed the Final Solution into indiscriminate evocations of Nazi evil. As sociologists Daniel Levy and Natan Sznaider have shown, the Holocaust has played a central role in the fashioning of a common European cultural memory since the end of the Cold War.[44] In the immediate postwar period, however, it was devoid of explicit historical significance within the European segment of the "human rights revolution."

In July 1951, the Geneva Convention on the Status of Refugees capped off several years of intense activity in the field of human rights law. Like the ECHR, the Refugee Convention was strongly influenced by the Cold War climate. Its individualized definition of refugees as persons in flight with a "well-founded fear of being persecuted for reasons of race, religion, nationality, membership of a particular social group or political opinion" directly pertained to escapees and dissidents from Iron Curtain countries. "The drafters thought mainly of the refugees from Eastern Europe," commented a jurist who took part in the deliberations, "and they had no doubt that these refugees fulfilled the definition they had adopted."[45] Moreover, temporal and geographical restrictions attached to the Refugee Convention initially favored European asylum seekers so as to permanently solve the lingering postwar displacement problem on the Continent and offer advantageous conditions to future anticommunist exiles. "In a Manichean political world," wrote a refugee expert, "recognizing persecution and identifying perpetrators caused no headaches and the grant of asylum was generally used to reaffirm the failures of Communism and the benevolence of the West."[46] The 1951 Refugee Convention should not however be reduced to Cold War strategy. It also introduced for the first time a healthy dose of enforceability into the UN human rights project. As an American advisor observed at the time, "it is a curious paradox that out of a postwar clean up job, out of the wreck of the refugee's fundamental freedoms, there had arisen the first widespread and binding international agreement for the advancement of human rights."[47] The commitment of contracting states to honor the provisions of the Refugee Convention directly stemmed from one of the most tragic features of the Jewish refugee crisis before and during the Second World War. Like the Universal Declaration, the Refugee Convention did not formally recognize the right "to be granted" asylum. Yet it guaranteed unprecedented and legally binding protections against the arbitrary deportation of aliens: "No country shall expel or return a refugee in any manner whatsoever to the frontiers of territories where his life or freedom would be threatened," stipulates the landmark and still-effective Article 33. Several other articles among the long list of individual rights embedded in the Refugee Convention similarly read like retroactive atonement for the German-Jewish refugee tragedy: the right to exercise liberal professions or the right to freedom of movement within a host country—related to the travails experienced a decade earlier by the "scum of the earth." Substantially shaped by the Jewish "pariahs" of the 1930s, the figure of the refugee finally reconciled the declarative "human rights revolution" with enforcement and implementation. In the emphatic words of United Nations officials, the "Magna Carta for Refugees" elicited a "new level of world morality" and stood as "the most international code of ethics yet devised for refugees."[48]

Even more so than their interwar predecessors, postwar Jewish refugees also left their mark on the human rights project. The quarter-million Jewish displaced persons (DPs), predominantly regrouped between 1945 and 1949 in the American occupation zone of occupied Germany, formed the most conspicuous group of Holocaust survivors in the postwar period. Their central role in the political and diplomatic struggle that led to the partition of

Palestine and the creation of the State of Israel has been amply documented. The "Surviving Remnant," however, also exerted considerable influence on one of the most emblematic human rights figures of the 1940s. Eleanor Roosevelt's "conversion" to human rights owes much indeed to her personal encounters with Jewish displaced persons in Germany. In December 1945, President Franklin Roosevelt's widow's unexpected appointment to the U.S. delegation at the first session of the UN General Assembly in London gave her ample opportunity to grapple with issues with which she had long taken a keen interest, such as "refugees, relief, and rehabilitation and human rights."[49] There she faced a hard Soviet stance on the question of non-Jewish anticommunist displaced persons who the USSR wanted to repatriate. "The battle is on about the refugee resolution," she wrote in her diary on January 9, 1946."[50] A decisive trip to the DP camps of Germany added a crucial Jewish dimension to her concern for refugee rights in particular and human rights in general. Between February 13 and 16, she toured four refugee camps in the American and French occupation zones. A visit to a DP camp for non-Jewish Polish and Baltic refugees left her with mixed feelings of sadness and hope. She was, however, particularly shocked by her discovery of Zeilsheim, a Jewish camp near Frankfurt. There she "felt all the time . . . a kind of spiritual uprooting, a kind of being lost."[51] A few weeks before her appointment as chairperson of the UN Commission of Human Rights, her first exposure to the desolate world of Holocaust survivors convinced her of the urgency of an international human rights infrastructure. "Even in the worst days of the Depression," she told a Jewish audience upon her return to the United States, "the people came to one and said 'We want our government to know . . .' Nobody has that right in a displaced persons camp."[52] In Zeilsheim, she also realized that the rehabilitation of refugees did not simply entail material improvement but was also a civic and political process: "What is important is rehabilitation [of the person] . . . the sooner those people can be taken where they can become citizens and feel that they are actually building a new life, the better it will be for the whole world."[53] Among Jewish survivors, she vividly sensed "a kind of desperation about the dignity of the individual" and "the crumbling of the thing that gives most of us a sense of security," thereby announcing some of the main themes of the Universal Declaration.

Eleanor Roosevelt's compassionate feelings for the "Surviving Remnant," part of her growing sensitivity to Jews and Judaism since the late 1930s, did not merely pave the way for her advocacy of human rights at the United Nations.[54] "In the mud of Zeilsheim," she recalled later with reference to the State of Israel, "I knew for the first time what that small land meant to so many, many people." At the beginning of the 1950s, her deep sympathy for Jewish nationhood—then an exceptional foray into the dangerous waters of collective rights—had evolved into a wider belief in "the Universal Validity of Man's Right to Self-Determination."[55] In a speech delivered on this topic at the UN General Assembly in December 1952, Roosevelt cautiously refrained from advocating immediate decolonization. "Self-determination as applied to non-self governing territories," she declared, "was a much more complicated matter." In the midst of the Cold War, she insisted that self-determination should also apply to the captive nations of Eastern Europe overrun "by a conqueror and subjected to his dictatorial control." Despite these qualifications, Eleanor Roosevelt now branded self-determination as a "universal human right" for the benefit of all peoples around the world. Initially restricted to the urgent predicament of Jewish refugees, self-determination had expanded into a soft, noncommittal but universal value. As Mark Mazower convincingly argued, the establishment of the State of Israel by the United Nations was a first step toward the global expansion of the principle of national self-determination in the 1950s and 1960s.[56] From her early sympathies for Jewish nationhood to her later affirmation of self-determination as a universal human rights, Eleanor Roosevelt's rhetorical evolution paralleled this Holocaust-inspired political path.

"Prior to World War Two," wrote the United Nations war crimes investigator Richard Goldstone, "the subjects of international law were not individuals but nations. Individual human beings had no standing. But the Holocaust changed that."[57] The former chief prosecutor of United Nations International Tribunals referred to the Nuremberg judgment recognized by the United Nations as universal jurisdiction as early as 1946. Revived in the 1990s when the United Nations finally confronted instances of mass murder in Yugoslavia and Rwanda, the concept of crimes against humanity had become instrumental to redress contemporary genocidal acts. The Holocaust is also firmly rooted today within international law thanks to a "memory of judgment" gradually accrued through the successive trials of Nazi perpetrators. In the late 1940s, however, the impact of the Holocaust on the emergence of human rights was more diffuse. Alongside other German crimes, a blend of precise and abstract references to the destruction of European Jewry informed the drafting of human rights documents. But in sharp contrast with the first Holocaust "memory regime" (1945 to the 1960s), often criticized for its repressiveness and silence, the "revolution" offered an incomparable channel of communicability. "Human rights talk," in other words, amounted to the first significant instance of "Holocaust-talk" in a non-Jewish environment. This unique forum of discussion was facilitated by the desire of Jewish human rights actors to incorporate Holocaust legacies in a liberal cosmopolitan democracy (this time however at the risk of self-repression). For René Cassin, the overall achievement of the Universal Declaration was its ability to redress the "monstrous acts" of the past while offering the world a "monument of positive progress" directed to the future.[58] For the consultative NGOs involved in the drafting of human rights, the main flaw of the United Nations' instruments was not their insufficient references to the Holocaust but their weak enforceability.[59] Loosely "Holocaust-centric" without violating Jewish memories, the postwar human rights project facilitated the appearance of philosemitism in postwar international politics.

NOTES

1. See Kofi Anan's statement of June 21, 2004, at the UN website, http://www.un.org/News/ossg/sg/stories/statments_search_full.asp?statID=54.

2. Preamble of the 1948 Universal Declaration on Human Rights.

3. Johannes Morsink, *The Universal Declaration of Human Rights. Origins, Drafting and Intent* (Philadelphia: University of Pennsylvania Press, 1999), 37–38.

4. Paul Gordon Lauren, *The Evolution of International Human Rights. Visions Seen* (Philadelphia: University of Pennsylvania Press, 1998), 291.

5. Michael Ignatieff, *Human Rights as Politics and Idolatry* (Princeton, NJ: Princeton University Press, 2001), 5.

6. Although several activists in the 1940s used the term "revolution" to describe the emergence of international human rights, this contested expression only gained currency in the post-Cold War era.

7. UN Department of Public Information, *These Rights and Freedoms* (New York: United Nations, July 1950), 2.

8. Nehemiah Robinson, *The Universal Declaration of Human Rights; Its Origins, Significance, Application and Interpretation* (New York: Institute for Jewish Affairs, 1958), xix.

9. Ambert Verdoodt, *Naissance et signification de la Déclaration Universelle des Droits de l'Homme* (Louvain-Paris, 1964), 37.

10. Thomas Buergenthal, "International Law and the Holocaust" in *Holocaust Restitution. Perspectives on the Litigation and its Legacy*, ed. Michael Bazyler and Roger P. Alford (New York: New York University Press, 2006), 17–30.

11. Micheline R. Ishay, *The History of Human Rights. From Ancient Times to the Globalization Era* (Berkeley: University of California Press, 2004), 241.

12. Morsink, *The Universal Declaration of Human Rights*, 36.

13. Samuel Moyn, *The Last Utopia. Human Rights in History* (Cambridge, MA: Harvard University Press, 2010).

14. Daniel Levy and Natan Sznaider, "The Institutionalization of Cosmopolitan Morality," *Journal of Human Rights* 3, no. 2 (June 2004): 143–57. Mark Osiel, *Mass Atrocity, Collective Memory, and the Law* (New Brunswick, NJ: Transactions Publisher, 1999); Lawrence Douglass, *The Memory of Judgment: Making Law and History in the Trials of the Holocaust* (New Haven, CT: Yale University Press, 2001).

15. Levy and Sznaider, "The Institutionalization of Cosmopolitan Morality," 149.

16. A. W. Brian Simpson, *Human Rights and the End of Empire: Britain and the Genesis of the European Convention* (Oxford: Oxford University Press, 2001), vii.

17. Mark Mazower, "The Strange Triumph of Human Rights, 1933–1950," *The Historical Journal* 47, no. 2 (2004): 379–98; *No Enchanted Palace. The End of Empire and the Ideological Origins of the United Nations* (Princeton, NJ: Princeton University Press, 2009), 130.

18. Moyn, *The Last Utopia*, 6; See also Samuel Moyn's essay on Gerhard Ritter's human rights conservatism: "The First Historian of Human Rights," *American Historical Review* 116, No. 1 (February 2011), 58–79.

19. J. H. Burgers, "The Road to San Francisco: The Trajectory of the Human Rights Idea in the Twentieth Century," *Human Rights Quarterly* 14 (1992): 447–77.

20. Michael Marrus, *The Nuremberg War Crimes Trial 1945–46: A Documentary History* (Boston: Bedford Books, 1997), 254.

21. Andrew Moravcsik, "The Origins of Human Rights Regime: Democratic Delegation in Postwar Europe" *International Organization* 54, no. 2 (Spring 2000): 217–52.

22. UN, *These Rights and Freedoms*, 125–26.

23. Mazower, *No Enchanted Palace*, 131. Moyn, *The Last Utopia*, 187.

24. To that list can be added the Lithuanian-born brothers Jacob and Nehemiah Robinson, two eminent jurists closely involved with human rights at the United Nations on behalf of the World Jewish Congress.

25. Martti Koskenniemi, "Hersch Lauterpacht (1897–1960)," in *Jurists Uprooted: German-speaking Émigré Lawyers in Twentieth-century Britain*, ed. Jack Beatson and Reinhard Zimmermann (Oxford: Oxford University Press, 2004), 601–61, 644.

26. See, among others, John Cooper, *Raphael Lemkin and the Struggle for the Genocide Convention* (New York: Palgrave MacMillan, 2008); John Docker, "Are Settler Colonies Inherently Genocidal? Re-Reading Lemkin" in *Empire, Colony, Genocide*, ed. A. Dirk Moses (New York: Berghahn Books, 2008), 81–101; Samantha Power, *"A Problem from Hell": America and the Age of Genocide* (New York: Basic Books, 2002), 18–60.

27. On the French origins of Cassin's human rights ideas see Jay Winter, *Dreams of Peace and Freedoms: Utopian Moments in the Twentieth Century* (New Haven, CT: Yale University Press, 2006), 99–120.

28. For a comparative view of Lemkin and Lauterpacht see Ana Filipa Vrdoljak, "Human Rights and Genocide: The Work of Lauterpacht and Lemkin in Modern International Law," *European Journal of International Law* 20, no. 4 (2009).

29. Morsink, *The Universal Declaration of Human Rights*, 40.

30. The following section derives from Robinson, *The Universal Declaration of Human Rights*; Verdoodt, *Naissance et signification*; and UN, *These Rights and Freedoms*.

31. UN, *These Rights and Freedoms*, 25. Verdoodt, *Naissance et signification*, 105.

32. Robinson, *The Universal Declaration of Human Rights*, 106. yes correct book.

33. Nehemiah Robinson, *The United Nations and the World Jewish Congress* (New York: Institute of Jewish Affairs, 1955), 69–74.

34. Ibid.

35. Michael Galchinsky, *Jews and Human Rights: Dancing at Three Weddings* (Lanham, MD: Rowman & Littlefield, 2008), 29–41.

36. Nehemiah Robinson, *The Genocide Convention: A Commentary* (New York: Institute of Jewish Affairs, 1960).

37. UN, *These Rights and Freedoms*, 124.

38. Timothy Snyder, *Bloodlands. Europe Between Hitler and Stalin* (New York: Basic Books, 2010).

39. Moravcsik, *The Origins of Human Rights Regime*, 234.

40. A. H. Robertson and J. G. Merrils, *Human Rights in Europe: A Study of the European Convention on Human Rights*, 3rd. ed. (Manchester: Manchester University Press, 1993); Simpson, *Human Rights and the End of Empires*; Mikael Rask Madsen, "From Cold War Instrument to Supreme European Court: The European Court of Human Rights at the Crossroads of International and National Law and Politics," *Law & Social Inquiry* 32, no. 1:137–59; Tom Buchanan, "Human Rights, The Memory of War and the Making of 'European' Identity" in *Europeanization in the Twentieth Century. Historical Approaches*, ed. Martin Conway and Kiran Klaus Patel (New York: Palgrave Macmillan, 2010), 157–171.

41. Moravcsik, *The Origins of Human Rights Regime*, 235.

42. Cited in Robertson and Merrils, *Human Rights in Europe*, 5.

43. Ibid, 4.

44. Daniel Levy and Natan Sznaider, "Memory Unbound: The Holocaust and the Formation of Cosmopolitan Memory," *European Journal of Social Theory* 5, no. 1 (2002): 87–106.

45. Paul Weis cited in Ivor C. Jackson, *The Refugee Concept in Group Situations* (The Hague: Martinus Nijhoff Publishers, 1999), 79.

46. Gil Loescher, "The UNHCR at Fifty," in *Problems of Protection: The UNHCR, Refugees, and Human Rights*, ed. N. Steiner, M. Gibney, and G. Loescher (New York: Routledge, 2003), 7.

47. L. K. Hyde, *The United States and the United Nations: Promoting the Public Welfare 1945–1955* (New York: Carnegie Endowment for International Peace, 1960), 79.

48. UN Department of Public Information, *Magna Carta for Refugees* (New York: United Nations, 1953), 3.

49. Allida M. Black, ed., *The Eleanor Roosevelt Papers: The Human Rights Years, 1945–1948*, vol. 1 (New York: Thompson Gale, 2007), 172.

50. Ibid., 230.

51. Ibid., 255.

52. Ibid.

53. Ibid., 258.

54. Michelle Mart, "Eleanor Roosevelt, Liberalism, and Israel," *Shofar: An Interdisciplinary Journal of Jewish Studies* 24, no. 3 (2006): 58–89; Mary Ann Glendon, *A World Made New: Eleanor Roosevelt and the Universal Declaration of Human Rights* (New York, Random House), 2002.

55. U.S. Department of State, "The Universal Validity of Man's Right to Self-Determination" *Bulletin* 27, no. 702 (December 8, 1952): 917–19. Reproduced in *What I Hope to Leave Behind: The Essential Essays of Eleanor Roosevelt*, ed. Allida Black (New York: Carlson Publishing, 1995), 603–7.

56. Mazower, *No Enchanted Palace*, 25.

57. Richard Goldstone, *For Humanity: Reflections of a War Crimes Investigator* (New Haven, CT: Yale University Press, 2000), 75.

58. Cited in Verdoodt, *Naissance et signification*, xi.

59. Galchinsky, *Jews and Human Rights*, 40–41.

3

"CONSTITUTIONALIZING" HUMAN RIGHTS

The Rise and Rise of the Nuremberg Principles

ELIZABETH BORGWARDT

The seven so-called Nuremberg Principles marked an attempt to begin the codification process around issues of individual responsibility, the role of superior orders, and the relationship of domestic to international law in the wake of World War II. These principles also spelled out the so-called Nuremberg offenses of individual responsibility for crimes against peace, war crimes, and crimes against humanity as punishable offenses under international law beyond the context of the war.

The Nuremberg Principles affect how military manuals are drafted to train soldiers; under what circumstances political leaders might be called to account for impunity; and the way we conceptualize international justice, "shrinking alternatives," in the words of one commentator, to respond to mass atrocities with judicial proceedings. Even more broadly, the Nuremberg Principles reinforce the idea of a direct relationship between violations of human dignity and some set of supranational legal norms, not dependent on the intervening layer of a possibly repressive sovereign state. The "thickening" of such a relationship is a key component of our contemporary conception of international human rights.[1]

In an American context, the Nuremberg Principles have served as a site of contestation between "inward-facing" and "outward-facing" visions of the U.S. Constitution, according to international legal scholar Noah Feldman's framing. The Nuremberg Principles—and related UN human rights instruments such as the Universal Declaration of Human Rights (1948) and the Genocide Convention (1948)—arguably lost what this chapter calls the "Bricker Amendment battle" in domestic American politics in the late 1940s and early 1950s, and indeed throughout much of the Cold War era. Yet these same principles, viewed as part of a longer historical trajectory, seem to be winning a larger war over the legitimacy of a more expansive vision of rule of law ideals.[2]

"It deserves to be studied and weighed by the best legal minds the world over"

A recent book entitled *Human Rights at the UN: The Political History of Universal Justice* does not mention the Nuremberg Principles, and it only touches on the Nuremberg Trials once in passing. Similarly, historian of modern Europe Tony Judt spends barely two pages each on Nuremberg and human rights respectively in his masterful *Postwar*—an 878-page book featuring a very textured and nuanced treatment of issues of guilt and responsibility. Former U.S. secretary of state Henry Kissinger—understandably rather less preoccupied by questions of guilt and responsibility—similarly does not mention Nuremberg at all, much less the Nuremberg Principles, in a detailed meditation on geopolitics focusing on the twentieth century.[3]

Yet, on another level, the Nuremberg Principles are so familiar they are regularly invoked to the point of being taken for granted in legal and even popular cultures, especially in the West (including Latin America). A casual reference to the principles features in a Doonesbury cartoon; Bertrand Russell and Jean-Paul Sartre staged a set of public hearings formally named the "International War Crimes Tribunal," based on the Nuremberg Principles to discuss U.S. accountability for Vietnam-era atrocities, which continued through a second set of hearings on human rights violations in Brazil, Chile, and Uruguay. After about 1990, the City of Nürnberg itself decided to embrace—and to seek to shape—the idea of a Nuremberg legacy. It recently designated itself a "city of Peace and Human Rights," even as it placed its famous Courtroom 600 on display as part of a museum exhibition.[4]

What Nuremberg is "about" now is arguably the norms embodied in the Nuremberg Principles—yet commentators have often noted how these issues were not really the focus of the trials in real time. If we were able to shake Nuremberg Chief Prosecutor Robert H. Jackson awake in the middle of the night and question him about the pith of these proceedings as they were unfolding, our sleepy Supreme Court justice would most likely have murmured, "it's about aggression—the outlawry of aggressive war." Nuremberg's real-time headlines did not lead with crimes against humanity and certainly not with genocide, a locution coined before the trial's charter was negotiated but not widely absorbed as a mental construct until years later.[5] Similarly, while individual responsibility was on one level an organizing concept of the International Military Tribunal (IMT)—why have a trial at all, rather than some more collective form of accountability?—the defendants were also selected for their capacity to serve as exemplars of various "guilty" sectors of German politics and society, such as the army, navy, general staff, media, the professions, and wartime industry.[6]

Nor were the Nuremberg Principles codified in an international instrument in the way originally envisioned by the UN General Assembly. UN accounts of the genesis of the "Principles" project reprint some 1946 correspondence between the American judge at Nuremberg, former U.S. Attorney General Francis Biddle, and President Harry Truman, where Biddle indicated that "the time has now come to set about drafting a code of international criminal law," and that part of this proposal should include the United Nations formally "reaffirm[ing] the principles of the Nürnberg Charter in the context of a general codification of offenses against the peace and security of mankind." Truman replied that "the setting up of such a code" would be "an enormous undertaking, but it deserves to be studied and weighed by the best legal minds the world over," before confirming that the UN was the appropriate forum and that he approved of the description and scope of the endeavor.[7]

In 1947 the General Assembly approved a resolution calling for the drafting of a convention "incorporating the principles of international law recognized by the Charter of the Nuremberg Tribunal and sanctioned by the judgment of that tribunal," looking toward "a detailed draft plan of general codification of offenses against the peace and security of mankind."[8] These projects were housed with a working group called the Committee on the Progressive Development of International Law and its Codification under the auspices of the Sixth Committee of the General Assembly (the Legal Affairs Committee), before that group recommended expanding its membership and mandate more formally, reconstituting itself as the International Law Commission (ILC).[9] Manley O. Hudson of Harvard Law School served as chair of the fifteen-member ILC, and the group framed its approach as a "compromise between the codification of international law through official conventions, as had been tried under the auspices of the League of Nations, and codification through the unofficial scientific restatement of positive law," meaning experts getting together, debating and writing reports, and then agreeing on what they think the state of the law is, an approach that had proved especially popular—and singularly ineffectual—in the interwar era.[10]

The ILC's ultimate vision was the elusive goal of "codification," a process discussed in the Statute of the International Court of Justice under the traditional heading "sources of international law." International law may be created by a variety of processes, listed in order of perceived legitimacy as explicit agreements among sovereign states—i.e., by means of treaties and conventions—or in several other less favored ways, such as through recognized international custom; or, even more amorphously, the "general principles of law recognized by civilized nations"; and, least favored of all, "the teachings of the most highly qualified publicists of the various nations," listed explicitly as a "subsidiary means for the determination of rules of law." In short, the ILC saw itself as synthesizing these generative sources in an ambitious bootstrapping measure, using a group of experts to generate a draft convention (treaty) to which sovereign states would then adhere.[11]

As with the earlier Nuremberg Trials, the centerpiece of this program was the outlawing of aggressive war, driven by "the conviction crystallized in the minds of thinking people" that "war is a crime against the human race," along with the perhaps wishful assessment that "the public opinion of the world has been clamoring for the establishment, in one form or another, of an international jurisdiction competent to deal with international crimes."[12] As the politics of the surrounding Cold War context heated up with the advent of the "police action" in Korea, however, the atmosphere surrounding the codification of the Nuremberg Principles cooled off. Ostensibly because they could not agree on a working definition of aggression, the ILC shunted the resulting draft convention aside as "not ripe" for reconsideration until 1980, and the text was not presented for a formal "second reading" by the ILC until 1996.[13]

It was, of course, nothing new to see powerful countries failing to sign up for binding international provisions to be invoked against themselves—although many did eventually include Nuremberg-related standards in their domestic laws and military manuals.[14] As Nuremberg slipped into the past, it quickly came to be reframed as a Cold War set-piece, with one of the most lyrical passages of Robert H. Jackson's opening statement becoming one of the most derided for hypocrisy: "We must never forget that the record on which we judge these defendants today is the record on which history will judge us tomorrow. To pass these defendants a poisoned chalice is to put it to our own lips as well."[15]

How can a set of norms fail and succeed at the same time? How can legal ideas be said to have become "constitutionalized"—achieving the status of a body of fundamental principles—when they fall short of the status of ordinary law? More specifically, how did the thirteen trials in the ruins of the medieval city of Nürnberg—which the essayist Rebecca West had dismissed as a "citadel of boredom"—become the Nuremberg of the iconic Spencer

Tracy peroration, as somehow emblematic of the "value of a single human being" under the rule of law?[16]

Cold War Considerations: "To slow the State Department in its mad pursuit for a World Bill of Rights"

As noted, the Nuremberg Principles highlighted the ideas that individuals and states have obligations under international law and that the demands of international law may take precedence over national laws. The Nuremberg Principles also asserted that the Nuremberg crimes had transcended the status of treaty law and had entered the generally applicable realm of laws that are universally valid whether or not a particular state has agreed to them.[17]

The historian Richard Overy observed that "what is striking about the summer of 1945 is . . . that so much was achieved in the chaos of post-war Europe in building the foundations for contemporary international law on war crimes, and contemporary conventions on human rights."[18] He goes on to cite the 1998 creation of the International Criminal Court as a "direct descendant of the Nuremberg Military Tribunal," along with the European Convention on Human Rights, and the Genocide Convention. These treaties, declarations, conventions, and institutions were meant to work together, to "produce" international justice in an almost mechanistic way. Indeed, American internationalists—many of them former New Dealers—would often speak about the workings of the United Nations using mechanical imagery, perhaps as a way of depoliticizing the underlying implications for national sovereignty and emphasizing the role of "experts" in institutional design.[19]

Early postwar public pronouncements by the U.S. State Department embed the development of what they unblinkingly termed a "world rule of law" ideology in fairly straightforward institutional terms. A State Department pamphlet from 1949 on the UN and international organization states plainly that a major goal of the postwar international order was "the establishment of the method and precedents of a world rule of law in which disputes among nations would be resolved just as most disputes among individuals are resolved today—through recourse to a proper and established court of justice." After explaining that "the United Nations exists today as a living organization accurately reflecting the aspirations, the difficulties, and the immaturities of our world society," the pamphlet goes on to assert, just a tad defensively, that "the United Nations is not, and never was intended, to be a super-state. It is not a world government in the sense that the member states have assigned their sovereignty to a central body."[20]

But even this carefully hedged language dredged up some venerable American anxieties, complete with rhetoric reminiscent of the interwar era "World Court" battles and even the ratification debates over the League of Nations. A number of activist domestic groups in the U.S.–whom their opponents tended to label "isolationist" but who generally preferred the moniker "nationalist"—came to believe that "America has been caught in a noose which can only be removed by a constitutional amendment."[21] Such an amendment was necessary because "the American people want to make certain that no treaty or executive agreement will be effective to deny or abridge their fundamental rights. Also, they do not want their basic human rights to be supervised or controlled by international agencies over which they have no control."[22]

This "noose" was any kind of multilateral treaty such as the Genocide Convention, the UN Human Rights Covenants, or the 1949 revisions to the Geneva Conventions, but also included looser, normative commitments such as the Universal Declaration of Human Rights or, indeed, the Nuremberg Principles themselves.[23]

One result of this unilateralist agitation was the Bricker Amendment controversy of 1951–53. The text of the proposed amendment underwent various mutations, but the debate centered on the possibility of amending Article 6 of the U.S. Constitution to ensure that no treaty could alter domestic law unless Congress passed supplemental enabling legislation—an extremely cumbersome process—to close what proponents called "a loophole in the Constitution through which our fundamental rights might be lost."[24]

John W. Bricker, a Republican senator from Ohio who had served as Thomas E. Dewey's vice presidential running mate in 1944, launched the campaign for his eponymous amendment by asserting that "my purpose in offering this resolution is to bury the so-called covenant on human rights so deep that no one holding high public office will ever dare to attempt its resurrection." More informally, he asserted that his proposed amendment would "slow the State Department in its mad pursuit for a World Bill of Rights."[25]

Even though the Bricker Amendment ultimately failed, when it was first introduced it had sixty-one co-sponsors, including forty-four of the forty-seven Republicans in the Senate and was only two votes shy of the necessary two-thirds majority. The ferment around this proposed amendment put a tremendous amount of pressure on President Dwight D. Eisenhower—a group called "Vigilant Women for the Bricker Amendment" collected half a million signatures on behalf of the amendment within a few months, for example. In seeking to short-circuit Senate support for the Bricker Amendment, Eisenhower sent Secretary of State John Foster Dulles to assure the Senate Judiciary Committee that an Eisenhower administration would never even submit a number of human-rights-related covenants—notably the Genocide Convention—to the Senate for ratification. Such human rights treaties would "commit one part of the world to impose its particular social and moral standards upon another part of the world community, which has different standards," as Dulles explained in his testimony, and would represent "a device to circumvent" the provisions of the U.S. Constitution relating to issues that were "essentially matters of domestic concern."[26]

International relations scholar Natalie Hevener Kaufman was still able to assert in the 1990s that "during the Bricker Amendment debates, human rights treaties were effectively branded as dangerous to the American way of life and cast into a senatorial limbo from which they have never been released."[27] Such an analysis fits with a traditional "rise and fall" narrative about the U.S. reception of various kinds of multilateral initiatives over the course of the entire postwar era: American multilateralism may have won certain battles—such as the struggle over the Bricker Amendment—but nevertheless lost the wider war. Perhaps the U.S. "unsigning" of the ICC statute under the George W. Bush administration was an emblematic moment, or even more recent expressions of unilateralist anxiety such as the "Bill of Federalism" movement, a set of ten constitutional amendments proposed by Tea Party theorist Randy Barnett.[28]

A deep fear and mistrust of multilateralist initiatives, particularly those originating in the United Nations, underpinned much of the emotional support that the proposed Bricker Amendment received from American conservatives. Their disillusionment with the UN was embedded in a wider Cold War story taking in the 1949 defeat of Jiang Jieshi (Chiang Kai-shek) and the attendant "loss" of China to communism; the successful Soviet explosion of a nuclear device in September 1950; the conviction of State Department official Alger Hiss for perjury, also in 1950; and fears aroused by North Korean successes in the Korean conflict. The Truman administration's strategy for garnering Senate approval of the Marshall Plan, initiated in 1947, had also explicitly involved playing up conservatives' fears of the Soviet threat, as well as further inflaming public anxieties.[29]

A strong supporter of the Bricker Amendment, Senator Everett M. Dirksen, Republican of Illinois, told the press in 1953: "We are in a new era of international organization. They [the UN] are grinding out treaties like so many eager beavers which have an effect upon the rights of American citizens." Frank Holman, president of the American Bar Association in 1948, argued:

> The Internationalists in this country and elsewhere really proposed to use the
> United Nations and the treaty process as a lawmaking process to change the
> domestic laws and even the Government of the United States and to establish
> a World Government along socialistic lines.[30]

This fear of putative multilateralist penetration as "socialistic"—either Soviet inspired or perhaps projecting the revolutionary values of what only the
year before came to be labeled the Third World—offers the explanatory
engine that gives Secretary Dulles's comments, quoted earlier, their power
and traction.[31]

Another way to tell this same story would be as part of a narrative with a
much longer term trajectory in the history of U.S. foreign relations, that is,
authority and influence in the realm of diplomacy gravitating toward the
executive branch and moving away from the legislative. Eisenhower quickly
determined that the Bricker Amendment would have to be either rejected
outright or drastically modified, fearing it would "hamstring" the president's conduct of foreign policy in a nuclear age, remarking at one point
that "this whole damn thing is senseless and plain damaging to the prestige
of the United States."[32] The president reportedly observed to his press secretary that "if it's true that when you die the things that bothered you most
are engraved on your skull, I am sure I'll have there the mud and dirt of
France. . . . and the name of Senator Bricker."[33] Another map for the Bricker
Amendment controversy is the way a vigilant executive drew lines to stop a
perceived encroachment by the legislative branch. Eisenhower was focused
on protecting executive prerogatives in the realm of foreign affairs; it was
merely an extra irritant that the Bricker initiatives originated in the unilateralist wing of the president's party.

Yet another domestic dimension to this controversy, ably demonstrated
by historians Carol Anderson, Penny von Eschen, and others, is the way the
Bricker story may also be framed as a story of domestic racial politics.
Amendment supporters argued that ratification of various proposed United
Nations' covenants on human rights, labor, and genocide would force on
American society socialized medicine, mandatory unionization, and, espe-
cially, racial desegregation and accountability for racialized violence. In
ABA President Holman's memorable formulation:

> I pointed out that if, in driving me from the airport, [a white driver] had un-
> fortunately run over a Negro child running out into the street in front of him,
> what would have been a local offense under a charge of gross negligence or
> involuntary manslaughter would, under the Genocide Convention, because of

the racial differential, not be a local crime but an international crime and that [the driver] could be transported some place overseas for trial where he would not have any of the protections of the Bill of Rights to wit: presumption of innocence, trial by jury, etc.[34]

While it is hard to know where to begin in debunking the various inaccuracies in the preceding statement, one starting point might be the text of the Genocide Convention, which requires intent to destroy a definable group "as such."[35] The larger point is that from the perspective of these unilateralist critics, international norms and institutions for transnational governance were threatening to intrude into the "domestic" sphere in both traditional senses of that term: domestic as in not international, and domestic as in private realms of conduct that should be insulated from international or other official scrutiny.

In addition to the race-related angle, this dimension of unilateralist outrage had a gendered aspect to it, as well. For example, Senate testimony offered in favor of the Bricker Amendment by W. L. McGrath, president of the Williamson Heater Company of Cincinnati and a representative of the U.S. Chamber of Commerce at the International Labor Organization, noted with alarm how international agencies could use treaties as a device to institute "socialistic legislation" relating to issues such as maternity benefits, benefits for illegitimate children, or even time off for nursing mothers. Describing a debate he had witnessed at the ILO over this latter issue, McGrath reported that "labor and employer delegates from all over the world, debated the question as to whether a woman nursing her baby, on time paid for by the employer, should do so in a single period of one hour per day, or two periods of one-half hour each."[36]

Even on paper and at a remove of almost sixty years, we can still hear the disdain in his voice as he sneered, "on this great international point the representatives of the United States Government appeared neutral," before concluding that the Bricker Amendment was necessary because "nobody could have dreamed that proposed international treaties could ever be devised which would include subject matter such as is now included in the ILO conventions," provisions which in another publication he termed "socialist gobledegook."[37] Aside from the truly mind-boggling ignorance about infant care exhibited by the underlying debate, the tone in the Senate also tells us something about the anxiety over perceived violations of privatized spaces previously dominated by (male) employers and legislators.

And there is arguably a fourth way to analyze the Bricker Amendment episode, in addition to the Cold War story, the executive authority story, and the race-and-gender stories outlined previously. We might also fold in a narrative about Supreme Court jurisprudence, or more specifically, the congressional response to an era of anxiety over the constitutional role of treaties as analyzed by the U.S. Supreme Court, initiated by the ruling in *Missouri v. Holland* (1920) and not assuaged until *Reid v. Covert* (1957). *Missouri v. Holland* had interpreted Article 6 of the Constitution as upholding the federal government's ability to regulate certain activities that would otherwise fall within the jurisdiction of the states. The case involved a treaty that the U.S. State Department had negotiated with Great Britain protecting flocks of migratory birds flying south from Canada.[38] Expansive language in Justice Holmes's opinion in *Missouri v. Holland* struck fear into conservatives of various stripes, not exclusively unilateralists but also those who we would now call strict constructionists.

In explaining why such a treaty necessarily implied the supremacy of the federal government's ability to make treaties over competing concerns about states' rights under the Tenth Amendment, Holmes offered his famous statement about a "living Constitution":

> [W]hen we are dealing with words that are also a constituent act, like the Constitution of the United States, we must realize that they have called into life a being the development of which could not have been foreseen completely by the most gifted of its begetters.[39]

Even now, it is hard to imagine a more succinct statement of how norms might over time become "constitutionalized." Contemporaneous critics were also alert to these implications. While one Bricker Amendment supporter complained that the Holmes opinion left the Tenth Amendment "dead as a dodo," Bricker explained that the "major problem is not how to protect States' Rights as such, but how to protect all purely domestic matters, Federal and State, from the consuming ambition of the United Nations and its specialized agencies to regulate those matters by treaty."[40]

The 1957 Supreme Court holding in *Reid v. Covert* quieted some of these concerns. There the Court held that agreements with foreign powers could not abrogate the Bill of Rights, and that "no agreement with a foreign nation can confer power on the Congress, or on any other branch of government, which is free from the restraints of the Constitution," in Justice Black's plurality opinion. In *Reid*, the decision reversed the conviction of an American civilian on an overseas military base who had been convicted by a military tribunal of murdering her husband, a member of the U.S. armed forces. A treaty or an executive agreement could not deprive Covert of her right to a jury trial.

The Court's decision in *Reid* undercut the Bricker position that a constitutional amendment was necessary to protect the Constitution from being gutted by executive agreements and treaties—quite intentionally, according to some correspondence between Justices Black and Felix Frankfurter.[41]

This last retelling offers an important corrective to persistent attempts to separate Supreme Court jurisprudence from an artificially delineated realm of "politics." At a minimum, these four different narrative strands of the Bricker story all support the assertion that domestic politics was the key determinant whether multilateralist initiatives stood or fell in this initial postwar phase of U.S. history, with the further refinement that the viability of postwar human-rights-related proposals was inversely correlated with the virulence of domestic Cold War preoccupations. Such a framing also offers a twist on some political science literature highlighting the tendency of liberal states to seek to project their own domestic legal norms and to take in circumstances when international legal norms and ideals are able to percolate into domestic political debates, along with the backlash such perceived threats then generate.

"Constitutionalizing" Human Rights Ideas

"The relationship between the Nuremberg process and modern war crimes tribunals is not a one-way street," in the assessment of defense attorney Guénaël Mettraux of the International Criminal Tribunal for the former Yugoslavia. This added dimension of change over time is where the "rise and rise" dimension comes in most clearly—Mettraux elaborates on how "the Nuremberg Trial has itself grown in stature and significance, both historically and legally, with the advent of its modern successors."[42] So too with the resulting Nuremberg Principles: what was, in many ways, perceived as a dubious and controversial set of innovations has become, over the ensuing decades, a touchstone in the development of human rights ideas and institutions. This assessment offers a kind of international version of Barry Friedman's recent analysis about how the meaning of the U.S. Constitution evolves as part of a "dialogue" with American public opinion that is processed through another conclave of elites, the U.S. Supreme Court.[43]

Human rights norms are becoming constitutionalized because they percolate through specific institutions in concrete, operational ways, such as the way the Nuremberg Principles are being "adopted in the constitutive documents of all modern international criminal tribunals," as Mettraux elaborates. Such institutions have "generative power," in Cardozo's language, in the most basic sense of constituting something new.[44] This includes expressions at regional levels; for example, the European Union has developed a treaty regime at its core that trumps later laws deemed to be inconsistent, even when duly enacted by member states.[45]

This "institutionalizing" level also includes incorporation into domestic law. Democratic theorist Seyla Benhabib calls these domestic processes "jurisgenerative politics," where the transparency of democratic states allows citizens to become increasingly convinced of the independent validity of human-rights-related norms.[46] One example is that the criteria related to medical experimentation stemming from one of the twelve subsequent Nuremberg Trials (the "Doctors' Trial") became codified internationally and then adopted nationally, in a variety of environments, as the Nuremberg Code, both in domestic legislation and as part of the Code of Research Ethics of the American Medical Association.[47] Again, the key distinction is not so much domestic versus international, or written versus unwritten, as it is institutionalized versus aspirational, or in the terms of some strands of social theory, "thick" versus "thin."[48]

This "thickening" process can accommodate, but goes beyond, models of the migration of human rights norms outward from the center to the periphery and is best analyzed in the burgeoning scholarship on the growth of the European Union. Comparative constitutionalist Vicki C. Jackson discusses how states such as New Zealand and the United Kingdom are incorporating "legal norms drawn from transnational or international sources" by means of statutes, due to systemic changes in what she calls "the global sociology of law."[49]

The charters of the international institutions of the 1940s, notably Nuremberg but also the United Nations and Bretton Woods charters, did indeed serve to thicken international politics somewhat, in the sense of jumping ideas about international justice across a realm of thin precepts to one of thicker rules, in part by injecting a strengthened sense of community standards and even a mild enforceability into the international realm. Not that an international community was constituted that is somehow like a national community writ large; the idea is much more diluted. The afterlife of the Nuremberg idea and the subsequent career of the Nuremberg Principles is nevertheless emblematic of what international relations specialist Andrew Hurrell calls "the greatly increased normative ambition of international society" in the postwar era.[50]

The Nuremberg moment was a turning point in what Hurrell calls "the marked, and normatively highly significant, shift towards individual criminal responsibility for grave human rights violations." Institutionally, the clearest offspring of the Nuremberg-related lineage are the various ad hoc international courts and tribunals, most notably the tribunals established for the former Yugoslavia (ICTY) and Rwanda (ICTR) and the creation of the International Criminal Court; but also in the increased number of domestic trials, such as trials in Spain for human rights abuses in Latin America. This lineage also arguably includes processes that do not involve assigning individual criminal responsibility but nevertheless address issues of accountability, transparency, and due process that are clearly recognizable as Nuremberg inspired.[51]

These various multilateral instruments were also "words that are also a constituent act," in the terms of the Holmes quotation from *Missouri v. Holland*. Moreover, the developing legitimacy of these norms—what legal theorist Gerald Neuman calls their "suprapositive status"—seems to be consolidating over time, even as the so-called international bill of rights remains emphatically unincorporated.[52] Despite the pronounced lack of enthusiasm in official U.S. circles, we do indeed seem to be moving from amorphous human rights norms about dignity toward a more concrete corpus of human rights law about accountability, in a perhaps unexpected challenge to received ideas about American exceptionalism.

NOTES

The author thanks Akira Iriye, William Hitchcock, Petra Goedde, and Susan Ferber for their patience, tact, and guidance. Thanks also to the Legal History Colloquium at Harvard Law School; the workshop on "Transatlanticism: The Impact of Lawmakers and Judges" at the Heidelberg Center for American Studies; the conference on "Decline of the West? The Fate of the Atlantic Community after the Cold War" at the University of Pennsylvania; the Mershon Center for International Security at Ohio State University; co-panelists from a panel on "Sovereignty and Citizenship at War" at the 2009 meeting of the American Historical Association; and co-panelists on a roundtable on "Historical Attitudes of the United States Toward International Law" at the American Branch of the International Law Association. Special thanks to Manfred Berg, John Harlan Cohen, Andrea Friedman, Philipp Gassert, Peter Hahn, Robert McMahon, Jed Shugerman, Jim Sparrow, and Kara Swanson for invitations to speak; Daniel Cohen, Michael Geyer, Daniel Hamilton, the late Tony Judt, Linda Kerber, Samuel Moyn, Gerald Neuman, Harry Scheiber, Jonathan Simon, David Tanenhaus, Lori Watt, and Lora Wildenthal for various opportunities to present new work or helpful comments on the broader project from which I draw this material.

1. Guénaël Mettraux, "Judicial Inheritance: The Value and Significance of the Nuremberg Trial to Contemporary War Crimes Tribunals," in *Perspectives on the Nuremberg Trial*, ed. Mettraux (Oxford: Oxford University Press, 2008), 599–614, at 603; see generally, Norbert Ehrenfreund, *The Nuremberg Legacy: How the Nazi*

War Crimes Trials Changed the Course of History (New York: Palgrave Macmillan, 2007). Ehrenfreund points out, importantly, that when the "legacies of Nuremberg" are broadened to include the twelve subsequent Nuremberg Trials, additional legacies include an influential medical code of conduct and the groundwork for current human-rights-related responsibilities of large corporations.

2. Noah Feldman, "When Judges Make Foreign Policy," *New York Times Sunday Magazine*, September 28, 2008, 50–57; 66–70; UN General Assembly, Universal Declaration of Human Rights, UN GA Res. 217A(3), A/810, 71, adopted December 10, 1948; UN General Assembly, Third Session Part 1, Official Records, Convention on the Prevention and Punishment of the Crime of Genocide, UN GA Resolution 260A(III), A/810, 1948, entered into force January 12, 1951; ratified by the U.S. Senate February 19, 1986, and entered into force for the United States February 23, 1989.

3. Roger Normand and Sarah Zaidi, *Human Rights at the UN: The Political History of Universal Justice* (Bloomington: Indiana University Press, 2008); Tony Judt, *Postwar: A History of Europe since 1945* (New York: Penguin Press, 2005); Henry Kissinger, *Diplomacy* (New York: Simon & Schuster, 1995).

4. Gary Trudeau's *Doonesbury*, August 16, 2008. I thank Kara Swenson of Harvard Law School for calling the Doonesbury strip to my attention, at http://www.gocomics.com/doonesbury (accessed February 14, 2010); John Duffet, ed., *Against the Crime of Silence: The Proceedings of the Russell Tribunal* (New York: Russell Peace Foundation, 1968); "Memorium Nürnberger Prozesse: Projekt zür Schaffung einer Erinnerungsstätte im Justizgebäude Nürnberg," *Museen der Stadt Nürnberg*, May 29, 2008.

5. Commentators who should know better sometimes assert that the term *genocide* was not mentioned at Nuremberg, despite the efforts of Polish jurist and coiner of the neologism Raphael Lemkin as a sometime consultant at the IMT. The term *genocide* did not feature in the trial's charter, as noted, but it was mentioned in the IMT's rambling sixty-seven-page indictment, which sought to apply the various "counts" in the charter to each individual defendant. The point is not so much to gainsay the not quite accurate assessment that genocide went unmentioned at Nuremberg, but rather to highlight that even though the concept was at least preliminarily in place and even deployed in 1945, it was not "processed" on a meaningful level until well after the flagship trial was over. Indictment in International Military Tribunal, *Trial of the Major War Criminals, Official Text*, 42 vols. (Nuremberg: Secretariat of the International Military Tribunal under the jurisdiction of the Allied Control Authority for Germany, 1947) (IMT) 1, 27–92. See generally, "The Challenge of the Unprecedented—Raphael Lemkin and the Concept of Genocide," *Jahrbuch des Simon-Dubnow Instituts* 4 (2005): 397–42.

6. The twelve subsequent trials run by the Americans from 1946–49, indicting an additional 185 defendants arranged by thematic groups (industrialists, doctors, judges, etc.), served as a kind of mop-up operation on this score. American prosecutors were particularly frustrated by their inability to prosecute a representative of the

Krupp concern as part of the main trial, due to their having erroneously indicted the ailing Krupp patriarch, rather than the son. Telford Taylor, *Final Report to the Secretary of the Army on the Nuernberg War Crimes Trials Under Control Council No.10* (Washington, DC: GPO, August 15, 1949). On the Krupp debacle, see Airey Neave, "Memorandum for the General Secretary of the International Military Tribunal," October 24, 1945, PRO, United Kingdom National Archives, LCO 2 2982 x/ LO6978.

7. Correspondence quoted in UN, report by Jean Spiropolous, Special Rapporteur, A/CN.4/25, April 26, 1950, 255–56.

8. UN General Assembly, Official Records, 177 (II) November 21, 1947; A/ CN.4/3; ILC 129–30.

9. The memorandum arguing most forcefully for this expansion was by committee member Donnedieu de Vabres, who had also served as France's representative on the Nuremberg Tribunal.

10. UN, International Law Commission, "Summary Records of the First Session, Opening Remarks by Mr. Kerno, Assistant Secretary-General in Charge of Legal Affairs, April 12, 1949," *Yearbook of the International Law Commission 1949*, 9; pre-1945 examples of such expert conclaves and the dates of some of their statements regarding international criminal jurisdiction include the Advisory Committee of Jurists (1920), the International Law Association (1922), the Inter-Parliamentary Union (1925), the International Association of Penal Law (1926), the committee of experts contributing to the Geneva Conventions for the Prevention and Punishment of Terrorism and for the Creation of an International Criminal Court (1937), the London International Assembly (1941), the International Commission for Penal Reconstruction and Development (1942), and of course, the United Nations War Crimes Commission (1943).

11. Article 38(1), Statute of the International Court of Justice, annexed to the United Nations Charter of June 26, 1945.

12. UN General Assembly, "Question of International Criminal Jurisdiction," report by Ricardo J. Alfaro, A/CN.4/15, March 3, 1950, 2, 15. For a recent analysis on how American public opinion in particular was actually much more internationalist in the interwar era than widely believed, see Trygve Throntveit, "Related States: Pragmatism, Progressivism, and Internationalism in American Thought and Politics" (PhD diss., Harvard University, 2008).

13. The draft convention is widely held to have influenced the 1998 Rome Statute of the International Criminal Court. Kai Ambos, "General Principles of International Law in the Rome Statute," *Criminal Law Forum* 10, no. 1 (March 1999): 1–32; Rosemary Rayfuse, "The Draft Code of Crimes against the Peace and Security of Mankind: Eating Disorders at the International Law Commission," *Criminal Law Forum* 8, no. 1 (February 1997): 43–87.

14. On Nuremberg standards in domestic laws, see, for example, Canadian Criminal Code sec. 6.1.91; Michele Jacquart, "La notion de crime contre l'Humanité en droit international contemporain et en droit canadien," 21 *Revue Générale de*

Droit (1990): 607; for Britain, see *Report of the War Crimes Inquiry*, Cmnd. 744 (1989), which served as the basis for the House of Commons War Crimes Bill of May 2, 1991. See also the *Australian War Crimes Amendment Act 1988*, assented to January 25, 1989 (amending the War Crimes Act of 1945).

15. Opening Statement of U.S. Chief Prosecutor Robert H. Jackson, November 21, 1945, IMT 5:371ff; video available on YouTube at www.youtube.com/watch?v=L50OZSeA (accessed February 14, 2010). On the Cold War dimensions of the main trial, see Francine Hirsch, "The Soviets at Nuremberg: International Law, Propaganda, and the Making of the Postwar Order," *American Historical Review* 113, no. 3 (June 2008): 701–30.

16. See Gerald Stourzh, "Constitution: Changing Meanings of the Term from the Early Seventeenth to the Late Eighteenth Century," in *Conceptual Change and the Constitution*, ed. Terence Ball and J. G. A. Pocock (Lawrence: University Press of Kansas, 1988) and reprinted in *From Vienna to Chicago and Back: Essays on Intellectual and Political Thought in Europe and America* (Chicago: University of Chicago Press, 2008), 96–97; Rebecca West, articles from *The New Yorker* reprinted in *A Train of Powder* (London: Macmillan, 1955), 13–14. For the speech voiced by Spencer Tracy on the meaning of the Nuremberg Trials, see the film *Judgment at Nuremberg* produced and directed by Stanley Kramer, written by Abby Mann (United Artists, December 1961).

17. UN, International Law Commission, Nuremberg Principles, A/CN.4/Ser. A/1950/Add.1, *Yearbook of the International Law Commission 1951*, vol. 2; UN, "Formulation of the Nuremberg Principles," report by Jean Siropoulos, A/CN.4/22, April 12, 1950.

18. Richard Overy, "The Nuremberg Trials: International Law in the Making," in *From Nuremberg to the Hague: The Future of International Criminal Justice*, ed. Geoffrey Wawro and Philippe Sands (Cambridge: Cambridge University Press, 2003). For the opposite perspective, see Samuel Moyn, *The Last Utopia: Human Rights in History* (Cambridge, MA: Harvard University Press, 2010).

19. Overy, "Nuremberg Trials" in *From Nuremberg to the Hague*, Wawro and Sands; Convention for the Protection of Human Rights and Fundamental Freedoms, initially 1950, as amended and with additional protocols, available online from the Human Rights Education Association at http://www.hrea.org/erc/Library/hrdocs/coe/echr.html (accessed February 14, 2010); UN GA, Convention on the Prevention and Punishment of the Crime of Genocide.

20. U.S. Department of State, *The United Nations: Four Years of Achievement*, Department of State Publication 3624, International Organization and Conference Series III, 36 (Washington, DC: GPO, September 1949), 13; 1–2.

21. Frank E. Holman, speech to the Tacoma Council of World Affairs, 1951.

22. Ibid. See also Senate Subcommittee on the Judiciary, *Treaties and Executive Agreements* 1953, 11; see generally Natalie Hevener Kaufman, *Human Rights Treaties and the Senate: A History of Opposition* (Chapel Hill: University of North Carolina Press, 1990); Duane Tananbaum, *The Bricker Amendment Controversy: A*

Test of Eisenhower's Political Leadership (Ithaca, NY: Cornell University Press, 1988); Frank E. Holman, *Story of the "Bricker" Amendment* (New York: Committee for Constitutional Government, Inc., 1954).

23. The United States did not ratify the International Covenant on Civil and Political Rights until 1992; it has never ratified the International Covenant on Economic, Social, and Cultural Rights. While the United States ratified the1949 revisions to the Geneva Conventions in 1955, it did not adopt conforming legislation until 1996, and as noted earlier, did not ratify the Genocide Convention until 1988. See University of Minnesota Human Rights Library, Ratification of International Human Rights Treaties, http://www1.umn.edu/humanrts/research/ratification-USA.html (accessed January 15, 2011); 18 U.S.C. 2441.

24. For an excellent account of the Bricker Amendment battle as a defensive scenario of "performative sovereignty," see Mark Bradley, "The Ambiguities of Sovereignty: The United States and the Global Rights Cases of the 1940s," in *Art of the State: Sovereignty Past & Present*, ed. Douglas Howland and Luise White (Bloomington: Indiana University Press, 2008); see also Richard O. Davies, *Defender of the Old Guard: John Bricker and American Politics* (Columbus: Ohio State University Press, 1993); text of the proposed amendment in *Cong. Rec.*, 83rd Cong., 1st sess. (1953), 99, pt. 1:160.

25. S. Res. 177, 82nd Cong., 1st sess. (July 17, 1951); 97 *Cong. Rec.* 8254, 8263; Bricker to Holman, July 23, 1951, as quoted in Tananbaum, *The Bricker Amendment Controversy*, 35; see also the *New York Times*, July 18, 1951, 5.

26. Department of State, *Bulletin*, 28, no.721 (April 20, 1953), 591. See also L. H. Woolsey, "Editorial Comment: The New Policy Regarding United Nations Treaties," *American Journal of International Law* 47 no. 3 (July 1953): 449–51; Louis Henkin, "U.S. Ratification of Human Rights Conventions: The Ghost of Senator Bricker," *American Journal of International Law* 89 no. 2 (April 1995): 341–50.

27. Kaufman, *Human Rights Treaties*, 94; see also Justus D. Doenecke, *Not to the Swift: The Old Isolationists in the Cold War Era* (Lewisburg: Bucknell University Press, 1979), 236–38.

28. Edward T. Swaine, "Unsigning," Symposium on Treaties, Enforcement, and U.S. Sovereignty, *Stanford Law Review* (May 2003); Randy E. Barnett, "The Case for a Federalism Amendment," *The Wall Street Journal*, April 24, 2009, A17. Note that Amendment IV of the proposed bill echoes the Bricker Amendment; see "Bill of Federalism Project—About Us" at http://www.federalismamendment.com/about.html (accessed January 15, 2011).

29. Richard Treeland, *The Truman Doctrine and the Origins of McCarthyism* (New York: Alfred A. Knopf, 1972), 11.

30. Davies, *Defender of the Old Guard*, 154; Holman, *Story of the Bricker Amendment*, 22.

31. See the text accompanying note 27 for Dulles remarks; "Tiers monde" as a locution is generally attributed to the French demographer Alfred Sauvy, in "Trois Mondes, Une Planète," *l'Observateur* no. 118 (August 14, 1952): 14.

32. Davies, *Defender of the Old Guard*, 155.

33. Diary of Eisenhower Press Secretary James Hagerty as quoted in Tananbaum, *The Bricker Amendment Controversy*, 151.

34. Anderson, *Eyes Off the Prize*; Penny Von Eschen, *Race against Empire: Black Americans and Anticolonialism, 1937–1957* (Ithaca, NY: Cornell University Press, 1997); Frank E. Holman, *The Life and Career of a Western Lawyer, 1886–1961* (Baltimore, MD: Port City Press, 1963), 570.

35. See Convention on the Prevention and Punishment of the Crime of Genocide cited in note 2, especially the provisions in articles 2, 5, and 6 specifying that intent to destroy a group is necessary; that killings and persecutions must be deliberate; that contracting parties should in the first instance enact necessary legislation and that parties must have accepted the jurisdiction of any relevant penal tribunal; see generally William Schabas, *Genocide in International Law: The Crime of Crimes* (Cambridge: Cambridge University Press, 2000).

36. 1953 hearings as quoted in Tananbaum, *The Bricker Amendment Controversy*, 84–85.

37. Ibid. W. L. McGrath, "What Should We Do About the ILO?" *The Freeman: A Fortnightly for Individualists* 3, no. 8 (June 1, 1953): 627–28, 628. I thank Linda Kerber for encouraging me to search for a gender-related angle on this material.

38. *State of Missouri v. Holland, United States Game Warden*, 252 U.S. 416, 40 S.Ct. 382 (1920), interpreting the *Migratory Bird Treaty Act of 1918*. Diplomats from the British Foreign Office still tended to handle many dimensions of Canada's foreign relations in this era.

39. Ibid., 433.

40. 252 U.S, 433; Carl Rix to Zechariah Chafee, Jr., June 2, 1952, Chafee papers (microfilm), Reel 9, Harvard Law School; John Bricker, "The Fight for a Treaty-Control Amendment: Round One," address by Senator Bricker before the Western Regional Conference of the American Bar Association, Bricker papers, Box 110, Ohio Historical Society.

41. *Reid, Superintendent, District of Columbia Jail v. Clarice Covert*, 354 U.S. 1, 77 S.Ct. 1222 (1957); Editorial, "Trial of Civilians Abroad," *Washington Post*, June 12, 1957, A14; Memorandum, Felix Frankfurter for the Conference re: Nos 701 and 713, official transcript, 1955, June 5, 1957, Box 326, Hugo Black Papers, LOC. Yet another nail in the coffin of the Bricker rationale is offered by *José Ernesto Medellín v. Texas*, 552 U.S. 491 (2008), 128 S.Ct. 1346 where a Roberts opinion indicated that a treaty or a judgment of the International Court of Justice was not binding on the United States unless Congress has enacted statutes implementing it, or the treaty is specifically designed to be self-executing.

42. Mettraux, "Judicial Inheritance," 612.

43. Barry Friedman, *The Will of the People: How Public Opinion Has Influenced the Supreme Court and Shaped the Meaning of the Constitution* (New York: Farrar, Straus & Giroux, 2009).

44. Ibid., 609, Cardozo quoted in ibid., 610; see also Gennady M. Danilenko, "The Changing Structure of the International Community: Constitutional Implications," *Harvard International Law Journal* 32, no. 2 (Spring 1991): 353–61.

45. See, for example, Neil Walker, "Reframing EU Constitutionalism," in *Ruling the World? Constitutionalism, International Law, and Global Governance*, ed. Jeffrey L. Dunoff and Joel P. Trachtman (Cambridge: Cambridge University Press, 209), 149–77; Joseph H. H. Weiler and Marlene Wind, eds., *European Constitutionalism Beyond the State* (Cambridge: Cambridge University Press, 2003).

46. Benhabib takes the term "jurisgenerative politics" from legal theorist Robert Cover but develops it further. Seyla Benhabib, *Another Cosmopolitanism: The Berkeley Tanner Lectures* (New York: Oxford University Press, 2006), 4.

47. *United States of America v. Karl Brandt, et al.*, Trials of War Criminals before the Nuremberg Military Tribunals, November 21, 1946–August 20, 1947 (Washington DC:GPO, 1974); the ten principles of the Nuremberg Code—a code of medical ethics not to be confused with the broader Nuremberg Principles—relating to informed consent and absence of coercion, are codified at Title 45 of the Code of Federal Regulations, Public Welfare, Subtitle A, Department of Health and Human Services, Part 46, Protection of Human Subjects. In the United States, the Nuremberg Code has also been incorporated into the laws of individual states and the codes of various universities and professional associations. See "The Nuremberg Code," *Journal of the American Medical Association* 276, no. 20 (November 27, 1996): 691.

48. In the context of ethics and politics, the locution "thick and thin" is identified most recently with the thought of Michael Walzer, but is also well developed in the scholarship of Avishai Margalit, Jürgen Habermas, and, arguably, Hegel (especially his division between "ethics" and "morality"). See, for example, Michael Walzer, *Thick and Thin: Moral Argument at Home and Abroad* (Notre Dame: University of Notre Dame Press, 2004); Kenneth Cmiel, "Review Essay: The Recent History of Human Rights," *American Historical Review* 109, no. 1 (February 2004): 117–35, n.26 (reprinted in this volume); Richard Mullender, "Hegel, Human Rights, and Particularism," *Journal of Law & Society* 30, no. 4 (December 2003): 554–74; Avishai Margalit, *The Ethics of Memory* (Cambridge, MA: Harvard University Press, 2002), 7–9.

49. Vicki Jackson, *Constitutional Engagement in a Transnational Era* (New York: Oxford University Press, 2010), 2; see also Melissa Waters, "Mediating Norms and Identity: The Role of Transnational Judicial Dialogue in Creating and Enforcing International Law," *Georgetown Law Journal* 93 (2005).

50. Andrew Hurrell, *On Global Order: Power, Values, and the Constitution of International Society* (Oxford: Oxford University Press, 2008), 143. See also Gennady M. Danilenko, "International *Jus Cogens*: Issues of Law-Making," *European Journal of International Law* 2, no. 1 (1991): 42–65.

51. Hurrell, *On Global Order*, 146. See, for example, Bruce Broomhall, *International Justice and the International Criminal Court* (Oxford: Oxford University Press, 2003); Ellen Luz and Kathryn Sikkink, "The Justice Cascade: The Evolution and Impact of Human Rights Trials in Latin America," *Chicago Journal of International Law* 2, no. 1 (2001): 1–34, as well as the examples in Gerald L. Neuman, "Human Rights and Constitutional Rights: Harmony and Dissonance," *Stanford Law Review* 55 (2002): 1863–1900. On truth commissions and other nonjudicial processes see, for example, the essays in Robert I. Rotberg and Dennis Thompson, eds., *Truth v. Justice: The Morality of Truth Commissions* (Princeton, NJ: Princeton University Press, 2000), especially the essays by Sanford Levinson, "Trials, Commissions, and Investigating Committees: The Elusive Search for Norms of Due Process," 211–34; and Martha Minow, "The Hope for Healing: What Can Truth Commissions Do?" 235–60.

52. On the "suprapositive" content of human rights law, see Neuman, "Human Rights and Constitutional Rights," 1866–67. On consolidation over time, see, for example, Dieter Grimm, "The Constitution in the Process of Denationalization," *Constellations* 12, no.4 (2005): 447–63, and the syllabus designed by Michael Geyer and James Sparrow on "The History and Theory of Human Rights," Department of History, University of Chicago, especially the unit "Can Global Society be Constitutionalized?" available online at http://humanrights.uchicago.edu/curriculum.shtml (accessed January 15, 2011). On the so-called international bill of rights, the UN's Universal Declaration was the first of three human-rights-related instruments that when bundled together are sometimes referenced as an international bill of rights. See Stephen Gardbaum, "Human Rights as International Constitutional Rights," *European Journal of International Law* 19, no.4 (2008).

4

HUMAN RIGHTS AND THE LAWS OF WAR

The Geneva Conventions of 1949

WILLIAM I. HITCHCOCK

Do the Geneva Conventions of 1949—the cornerstone of international humanitarian law—belong in the history of human rights? It seems not: most surveys of human rights history neglect the Conventions entirely. Historians rarely place Geneva alongside other founding documents of the "human rights revolution" of the 1940s.[1] To be sure, historians of human rights will argue that the Geneva Conventions do not figure prominently in their work because the Conventions form part of the laws of war. The laws of war, or international humanitarian law (IHL), date back many centuries to the age of chivalry and evolved through painstaking interstate negotiation over what constitutes suitable, and unsuitable, behavior by armies on the battlefield. Originally, the laws of war, unlike the post-1945 body of human rights law, assumed no sacrosanct rights for the individual. Rather, they were concerned with restraining and codifying state power in times of war—times which are, after all, often desperate and can lead states to take drastic actions against their enemies. The aim of these laws of war has been to protect soldiers, should they become captives, from extreme brutality and punishment by enemy states and to protect civilians from depredations by enemy armed forces. In this, their ambitions are limited to the behavior of states and armies with respect to a wounded or captured soldier or a noncombatant who is unfortunate enough to be swept up in the maelstrom of war. As a consequence, they do not posit any universal individual rights inherent in human beings.

Yet this defense—that Geneva does not belong in the human rights "story"—has of late been fatally undermined. Powerful forces have combined to bring Geneva to the forefront of human rights debates. First, scholars of international humanitarian law have recently noted that during the post-1945 period, the laws of war and human rights converged. Today, legal scholars—if not historians—generally consider the Geneva Conventions as one of a series of international treaties that form part of the human rights regime, and that compel states to recognize and respect the inalienable right of individuals to exist in freedom, security, and dignity.[2] What is more, since the beginning of the "global war on terror" (GWOT) in 2001, the United States government also has been intensely preoccupied with the meaning of the Geneva Conventions and their power to bind states in their prosecution of war against shadowy global networks of terrorists. The United States has honored the Geneva Conventions only in the breach, but this breach has brought renewed attention to the text of the Conventions and placed it squarely in a global debate about human rights in the war on terror. Further, human rights activists, who have heartily criticized the United States' effort to deny Geneva protections to certain classes of prisoners, have raised the Geneva Conventions to a greater degree of visibility than ever before. Finally, the courts of the United States, most notably the U.S. Supreme Court, have taken up the question of Geneva's applicability in the war on terror. Scholars, governments, activists, and jurists, then, have pulled the Geneva Conventions from the periphery of the global human rights conversation to the center. It is time that historians follow suit.

The Geneva Conventions of 1949, which are four separate treaties combined into a single charter for the protection of wounded soldiers and sailors, prisoners of war, and civilians in war zones, might have lain largely invisible for another sixty years had it not been for the events of September 11, 2001, and the subsequent launching of the war on terror by the United States.[3] To be sure, the Geneva Conventions had been briefly controversial in the Korean War, when North Korea refused to abide by its guidelines for the treatment of captured prisoners, and also in the Vietnam War, when captured U.S. pilots were routinely tortured by the North Vietnamese forces. But the texts themselves were not at issue in these cases: the mistreatment of captured enemy soldiers was explicitly banned by the Geneva Conventions, and the argument made by North Korea and North Vietnam—that the soldiers and airmen of the United States were war criminals because they had killed civilians during combat operations—was anticipated and specially refuted in the Convention itself. The United States, indeed, reaped some degree of international propaganda value by making it plain that it adhered to the Geneva Conventions even when its enemies flaunted it. The failure of the Geneva Conventions to compel respect for its articles was lamentable and

disappointing; but at no point in the Cold War era were the articles themselves subject to serious dispute.[4]

September 11 changed everything, because it led the United States to
reconsider its position toward the Geneva Conventions: whereas previously, American leaders had publicly embraced Geneva and its strictures
against the mistreatment of captured enemy soldiers, after 9/11 the United
States came to see Geneva as an obstacle to achieving its aims in the
global war on terror, a conflict in which America's enemies were not
soldiers of a clearly recognized national military force but transnational
terrorists and their allies. To understand this shift in U.S. policy toward
an adversarial relationship to the Geneva Conventions, historians must
study the text of the Conventions, as well as their origins. Only after
knowing precisely what they say and why they say it can we track the
later efforts made by American officials to skirt, defy, or render irrelevant
the Conventions. A detailed historical analysis of the text reveals a critical link between the laws of war and human rights, and shows that
Geneva has played a vital role in introducing key "human rights" concepts about the inviolability of human beings into the laws of war. Human
rights historians, then, can find much in this convention to illuminate the
ways that human rights "travel" across legal regimes and take on weight
and power sufficient enough to compel the attention of even the world's
most powerful nations.

The origins of the Geneva Conventions reach back to the nineteenth century,
when Henry Dunant, a visionary Swiss, conceived of the idea of a humanitarian organization that could offer neutral and wholly disinterested services
to wounded soldiers. Dunant was motivated by the appalling carnage of the
Battle of Solferino (1859), which he witnessed, when thousands of wounded
French and Austrian soldiers died because of lack of water and basic medical care. Conspiring with a small number of humanitarian countrymen,
Dunant helped found the International Committee of the Red Cross (ICRC)
and, in 1864, framed the first Geneva Convention: an international agreement
for the provision of medical care to wounded soldiers regardless of their
nationality. In 1899, and again in 1906–07 at the Hague, the ICRC pressed
for new rules concerning the treatment of the wounded on land and sea, as
well as of prisoners of war. These were promulgated and blended with the
Geneva agreements, forming the body of international law in place during
the First World War. Another revision and expansion occurred in 1929, and
it was this Geneva Convention Relative to the Treatment of Prisoners of War
that applied throughout the Second World War. The 1929 agreements

focused on the rights of prisoners captured during war and the obligation of the detaining power to treat prisoners humanely during their captivity.[5]

Plainly, each of these successive agreements, from 1864 to 1929, was designed to meet deficiencies that had become apparent in the Conventions during a just-concluded war; they share a reactive, backward-looking character. Yet no amount of foresight could have anticipated the ideological foulness of the Nazi regime and the barbarism of the Japanese empire. It was the failure of the 1929 Convention to imagine a world of genocide, extermination camps, torture, mass reprisals carried out on innocent civilians, forced transfers of populations, death marches of prisoners, and other such acts of destruction that brought the ICRC to the conclusion—even while the war was still raging—that a new, comprehensive and ambitious document was needed, one that aimed to offer international protection to all peoples caught in the maelstrom of war. In February 1945, the ICRC announced its intention to begin a revision process of the POW convention and the creation of a new treaty to cover civilians in wartime. In July 1946, a meeting of national Red Cross societies began work on the process, and in April 1947, a Conference of Government Experts convened in Geneva to hammer out working drafts. These were then submitted in August 1948 to the XVII International Red Cross Conference in Stockholm, which approved the drafts and arranged for a major diplomatic conference to promulgate the final revised Geneva Conventions. That conference, attended by fifty-nine national delegations, met in Geneva from April 21 to August 12, 1949, and it was there that the final texts of the four Geneva Conventions for the Protection of War Victims were approved.

Of course, the 1949 Conventions were not wholly new. They were built upon the foundation of the 1929 text, some of which was substantially retained. For historians of human rights, what makes the most interesting reading is the text that was added during the lengthy and intriguing negotiations that took place over the period from 1946 to 1949. These were, of course, precisely the same years when the United Nations was coming into shape, when the Nuremberg Trials were held, and when the Universal Declaration on Human Rights and the Genocide Convention were being hammered out. It was a moment of innovation and idealism in the area of international law. The ICRC sought to take advantage of this propitious moment. Not only did it push for the expansion and revision of rules concerning the treatment of prisoners, but it also called for, and secured, an entirely new convention—the Fourth Convention—to be added to the three that had predated the war. This was the most ambitious component of the 1949 agreements and the most novel: it outlined protections for civilian noncombatants in war zones and defined the obligations of warring states to protect their well-being. It was this extension of the Geneva principles to civilians that marked a dramatic shift away from a narrow conception of laws of war as applicable to soldiers toward a capacious and inclusive set of international laws that would protect all peoples in wartime, whether active combatants or passive civilians. All peoples, the 1949 Conventions imply, are vulnerable in times of war; all peoples, therefore, must have recourse to some kind of protection from wanton violence, unjust punishment, and persecution.

Throughout the revision process, there emerged a fundamental conflict between those who wanted to push the "humanitarian" agenda—mostly continental European states that had endured direct German occupation, as well as the ICRC itself—and those states, especially Britain and Australia, and occasionally the United States—that were determined to do nothing that would weaken the privileges of a state to protect its national security. A good example of this tension was visible in the language of a proposed preamble to the Conventions. In the preliminary meetings of Red Cross societies in the summer of 1946, the ICRC, supported by the French delegation, proposed opening language for the revised convention that would "guarantee in all circumstances the essential rights of the individual, as well as the respect of the human dignity of all persons who, for any reason whatever, are in the hands of the enemy."[6] The signatories were to have universally embraced a ban on inhumane treatment, torture, the taking of hostages and summary execution. "Respect for the personality and dignity of human beings," the ICRC stated, "constitutes a universal principle which is binding even in the absence of any contractual undertaking."[7] But the British opposed the preamble, marking out battle lines that would continue throughout the negotiations. The British delegation saw the preamble precisely for what it was: an effort to create a blanket provision of human rights and throw it over the whole of the specific text that followed. Fighting a delaying action, the British insured that no agreement could be reached on the wording, so the idea for a soaring preamble, acknowledging the submission of the laws of war to the broader principle of sacrosanct human rights, was dropped.[8] Even so, this is a clue to the intentions of at least some of the framers: the 1949 Conventions were infused with, and guided by, a universal conception of human rights that had never before been included in the laws of war. In drawing upon the experience of a global and intolerably cruel war, the framers of the 1949 Convention pushed the laws of war outward to cover previously unprotected categories of persons and to define the rights of all persons, not just soldiers, who might find themselves at the mercy of captors or invading armies. Here is the strongest argument for placing the Geneva Conventions of 1949 alongside other documents that form "the human rights revolution" of the 1940s.

To illuminate this shift from a narrow to a broad conception of personal rights in wartime, the historian can select a number of key debates from the revision process of 1946–1949. In particular, three questions debated during the redrafting of the Conventions reveal the way the human rights agenda began to penetrate into the laws of war. First, what kinds of combatants should the Third (prisoner of war) Convention cover—only soldiers, or other kinds of informal militias and resistance groups, too? Second, if a person is not a POW and therefore not covered by the Third Convention, is he or she automatically covered by the Fourth Convention, the new Civilian Convention? Or is there a crack in the system into which unlawful combatants, those who are neither soldier nor civilian, might fall? And if so, what rights are they to be granted, if any? And third, do the Conventions apply in conflicts other than those between sovereign states, that is, so-called wars not of an international character? If so, what rules govern sovereign states engaged in internal or nonstate conflicts? And how might such rules impinge on national sovereignty? Each of these issues triggered difficult and drawn out debates in the late 1940s; each has at its core a tension between laws of war and human rights; and each has continued to be the subject of heated dispute in the public discourse of U.S. foreign policy since 2001.

The first issue was the most elemental to the Conventions: who is a prisoner of war? Here the Third Convention drew on language that had been included in Article 1 of the 1907 Hague agreements. "The laws, rights, and duties of war apply not only to armies, but also to militia and volunteer corps fulfilling the following conditions," that agreement declared. Protected persons must be "1. commanded by a person responsible for his subordinates; 2. have a fixed distinctive emblem recognizable at a distance; 3. carry arms openly; and 4. conduct their operations in accordance with the laws and customs of war." The 1907 agreement also granted protection to ordinary peoples who spontaneously rose up against an invader: "inhabitants of a territory which has not been occupied, who, on the approach of the enemy, spontaneously take up arms to resist the invading troops without having had time to organize themselves in accordance with Article 1, shall be regarded as belligerents if they carry arms openly and if they respect the laws and customs of war." Thus, even those involved in a popular uprising against an invader had been covered by the 1907 agreements. So clear and unambiguous were these 1907 terms that they were retained in 1929 and again in the 1949 Conventions.

Yet the new 1949 Conventions went considerably further by extending Geneva protections to long-term resistance movements—without any distinction as to the duration of the occupation. Provided that irregular resistance units had an identifiable commander, wore some sort of distinctive emblem, carried arms openly, and abided by the laws and customs of war, they too would enjoy full POW status should they fall into captivity. [GC III, 4 (2)] The extension of Geneva protection to resistance fighters was an enormously acrimonious issue during the revision process. It was driven by the experience of World War II, when the German army and security forces refused to recognize resistance fighters as legitimate combatants. They were, when caught, summarily shot, or transported to jail for harsh interrogation as a preliminary to transfer to concentration camps. French, Belgian, Danish, Dutch, Norwegian, Czech, and Polish delegates joined forces in the negotiations. Their nations had experienced German occupation and witnessed extreme brutality. They wanted resistance fighters to secure the same protections as soldiers. The Danish delegate put it this way: "in the case of modern warfare . . . warlike acts committed by civilians against the aggressor could no longer be considered illegal. Civilians who took up arms in good faith for the defense of their country" should be protected by the Conventions.[9] But an intense effort was launched by the delegation from the United Kingdom to roll back such protections. Why did Britain, a nation that had done so much to encourage armed resistance to Hitler across occupied Germany, resist the introduction of protections into the Conventions for resistance fighters?

Documents from the British War Office provide the answer. Britain had just fought (and lost) a war against Zionist "resistance" fighters (who the British called terrorists) in Palestine and was fighting a powerful anticolonial insurgency in Malaya. Predictably, British officials wanted to avoid creating protective rights for anticolonial nationalists. The British were also aware that the Soviet Union, which at Geneva was also championing the idea of protecting resistance movements, was in 1946–47 using fifth columnists across Western Europe to foment strikes, political instability, and economic chaos. The geopolitics of empire and the Cold War drove the British position. British officials felt that the proposal to protect resistance units would allow any person who opposed an occupation force—or an empire—to conduct hostile attacks on an occupying force but then seek protections as a "resistance" fighter. Any effort to offer rights to resistance units would, the British felt, encourage random violence and terrorism in the colonies. The British delegation in Geneva, however, realizing that opinion in the conference was strongly against them—and the United

States offered no help in this case—retreated to a new position: protections should be granted only to fighters of resistance movements that were really substantial and had permanent headquarters and controlled actual territory. Even this position was rejected, and in the last analysis, the British could only win a small point: resistance fighters, in order to secure POW status, must have an identifiable commander, wear some sort of distinctive emblem, carry arms openly, and abide by the laws and customs of war—a fairly low threshold.[10]

The British, driven by imperial self-interest, were looking forward to an era of colonial policing and national liberation movements, rather than backward to a time of heroic underground movements causing havoc for Hitler's forces in Europe. But the dispute is revealing: not only were formerly occupied countries in favor of extending protection to resistance movements, but the ICRC itself was pushing this agenda as a means of extending Geneva protections to as many people as possible, whatever their wartime role. The ICRC had concluded that in an era of total war and ideological mobilization, the old categories of soldier and civilian were being eroded; international law had to keep up with these realities. The ICRC made its own interest clear in the wording of GC III, Article 5: "Should any doubt arise as to whether persons, having committed a belligerent act and having fallen into the hands of the enemy, belong to any of the categories enumerated in Article 4, such persons shall enjoy the protection of the present Convention until such time as their status has been determined by a competent tribunal." This meant that the default position was that all persons suspected of hostile activity against a state must be accorded Geneva rights until their status could be determined by a tribunal. This article has compelled signatory states to treat hostile but irregular combatants that they might capture as innocent before proven guilty and to insure that they receive a fair trial. In short, the extension of POW status to resistance fighters was a crucial moment in extending the laws of war beyond traditional forms of warfare, and it opened the way to challenges of unlawful detentions by states who simply wanted to arrest potential suspects.

A second and related issue of interest to human rights historians concerns the Civilian Convention and the extent of its coverage. The Fourth Geneva Convention, entirely new in 1949, was designed to protect noncombatants "who, at a given moment and in any manner whatsoever, find themselves, in case of a conflict or occupation, in the hands of a Party to the conflict or Occupying Power of which they are not nationals." (GC IV, Article 4) That is, any civilian whose nation is occupied by a hostile power has rights—not be tortured, imprisoned, transported, raped, or in any way deliberately and unjustly harmed by the occupying power. The roots of the Civilian Convention lie obviously in the experience of German occupation of Europe and Japanese occupation of Asia, when these invading conquerors imposed barbaric and genocidal policies upon conquered peoples.

There was little dispute in the Stockholm or Geneva meetings about the importance of stipulating such protections for civilians. But there was sincere concern that enemy aliens inside the home territory of a warring state, or spies and saboteurs who might do harm to an occupying force inside a foreign country, could strike at a military target and then melt back into the civilian population, only to claim the status of protected person under the Civilian Convention. What should be done about such persons who wage war while posing as civilians? Article 5 of the Fourth Convention tries to walk a fine line between state interest and human rights. As to the first category of enemy aliens in the home territory of a given state, if "an individual protected person is definitely suspected of or engaged in activities hostile to the security of the State, such individual person shall not be entitled to claim such rights and privileges under the present Convention as would, if exercised in the favor of such individual person, be prejudicial to the security of such State." That is, on its own home territory, a state could invoke national security to apprehend suspected subversives. However, when a state was in occupation of *foreign* territory, the equation changed: "Where in occupied territory an individual protected person is detained as a spy or saboteur, or as a person under definite suspicion of activity hostile to the security of the Occupying Power, such person shall, in those cases where absolute military security so requires, be regarded as having forfeited *rights of communication* under the present Convention." This language was significant: it meant that a spy or a terrorist who was aiming to strike at the occupying forces of a combatant state could be apprehended as a legitimate security threat, but that he lost *only* the right of communication with the outside world. That is, a captured spy or terrorist could not alert his handlers of his whereabouts or the fact of his capture. Without a doubt, this was a major achievement for the delegations, like the British, who wanted to protect the rights of states to detain saboteurs or others who waged a clandestine war in occupied territory. The humanitarian states in the 1949 negotiations—France, Norway, Sweden, Denmark—conceded to the British that spies and saboteurs should not be granted all the protections afforded to civilians by the Fourth Convention. But, as the Norwegian delegate put it, even spies and saboteurs "should nevertheless be protected against criminal treatment and torture."[11] Article 5 therefore represented a crucial compromise that allowed states to apprehend and detain subversive persons. As the ICRC's director for general affairs, Jean Pictet, stated in his masterful commentaries on the Conventions, this language is "an important and regrettable concession to State expediency."[12]

Yet, the humanitarian impulse is still marked in the rest of the article's language: an enemy alien, or a spy or saboteur captured during military operations in a foreign land maintained certain basic *human* rights: "In each case," Article 5 continued, "such persons shall nevertheless be treated with humanity and, in case of trial, *shall not be deprived of the rights of fair and regular trial* prescribed by the present Convention. They shall also be granted the full rights and privileges of a protected person under the present Convention at the earliest date consistent with the security of the State or Occupying Power, as the case may be." (GC IV, Article 5) That is, even the most loathed and vulnerable captives—a spy or a terrorist—forfeited only his right to communicate with the outside world and that only temporarily. He did not forfeit a right to trial, nor could his captors treat him harshly. He must at all times be treated "with humanity." This is a far cry from the old-school laws of war, in which spies, saboteurs, or illegal combatants had no rights at all and could be executed on the spot. On the contrary, the text is perfectly clear that even guerillas have some basic rights to trial and to decent treatment, if not to full POW status. As Jean Pictet put it, "every person in enemy hands must have some status under international law . . . There is no intermediate status; nobody in enemy hands can be outside the law."[13] The point is this: the Geneva Conventions of 1949 had again worked their conjuring trick, extending rights to even the lowest of subversive bomb-throwers and opening the way to a claim that rights inhered in all peoples, even illegal combatants. The laws of war, again, were being extended to cover an ever larger community from which virtually no one was exempt.

The significance of extending protection to so many categories of people is immediately clear when one considers the issue of interrogation. Extracting time-sensitive information from a saboteur or a terrorist in wartime would seem to be a vital national security interest. Yet the Geneva Conventions, by extending Article 5 even to saboteurs and spies, effectively bans the use of "physical or moral coercion" upon anyone, no matter how useful and timely his information might be to a state at war. If soldiers as well as civilians, resistance fighters as well as spies and saboteurs, do have some basic inalienable protections—the latter giving up only their right to communication by virtue of their illegal activities—then all are, in some fashion, "protected persons" and none could be harmed in any way to extract information from them. It follows, then, that GC IV articles 27, 31 and 32, which ban torture and any physical violence upon protected persons, apply to all captives of any kind, regardless of their actual behavior on the battlefield. We would expect to find in these Conventions that the mistreatment of captive soldiers or civilians is explicitly banned; but it is amazing to see how far the family of "protected persons" has been extended by Article 5, which gave some basic protections even to captured illegal combatants. The Conventions expel no one completely from its protected community. There is no "spider hole" down which a detained person in an occupied territory can be thrown—no place a captured suspect could be imprisoned where these restrictions against coercion would not apply. Pictet made it clear that the ICRC meant these prohibitions against violence to have the widest possible meaning: "the requirement of humane treatment and the prohibition of certain acts incompatible with it are general and absolute in character . . . They are valid 'in all circumstances' and 'at all times.'" As Pictet pointed out, it is in times of war and extreme national danger that "human values appear to be in greatest danger," and therefore it is precisely then that the principle of humane treatment for all captives must be most urgently defended.[14] The agenda of the ICRC to expand rights to all peoples in wartime was clearly gaining the upper hand over the concerns of national security and raison d'état.

Nothing is so demonstrative of the far-reaching humanitarian ambitions of the ICRC than "Common Article 3," a wholly new article that was drawn up in the revision process and inserted into all four conventions with exactly the same wording. Common Article 3 treads on one of the most sacred principles of the laws of war: national sovereignty. The article asserts that certain principles of the Geneva Conventions—which were originally designed to regulate war *between* states—should also apply in cases of *internal* conflict, uprisings, or civil war. According to Article 3, in cases of "armed conflict not of an international character," certain specific provisions, especially the humane treatment of civilians, as well as captured or ill combatants, must be respected. Although the entire text of the Conventions was not made applicable to civil wars and internal conflict, "violence to life and person," "outrages upon personal dignity," and torture were explicitly banned. And if such principles applied in cases of internal conflict, then the logical implication was, of course, that this requirement to treat all people humanely applied to international war as well. As Jean Pictet pointed out, this was for the ICRC "an almost unhoped-for extension" of the basic principle of the inviolability of the human person into the laws of war.[15] How did this dramatic shift happen and what has been its significance?

The idea of extending Geneva principles to civil wars had been taken up in 1938 by the International Red Cross Conference, in an atmosphere much influenced by the atrocities committed during the Spanish Civil War, but the outbreak of the war in Europe derailed the matter until the postwar revision process of Geneva began. With the memories of Nazi atrocities still fresh in their minds, ICRC officials moved rapidly to assert the applicability of certain basic standards of humane treatment during any and all conflicts, even those conflicts that were limited to the territory of one state. The usual arguments of the sanctity of state sovereignty had been much weakened by the abuse of that privilege by the Third Reich, and so an article was drafted at the 1947 Stockholm meeting that required all High Contracting Parties to recognize the principles of the Conventions in "civil war, colonial conflicts, or wars of religion." More striking was the proposal that "the application of the Conventions shall in no wise depend on the legal status of the parties to the conflict."[16] This suggested a blanket application of Geneva to any group who might be waging a civil war or who might be the subject of an attack inside a sovereign state. It was a frontal assault on the principle of state sovereignty. Clearly, the ICRC, as it had done with the preamble, was trying to insert a universal principle—that of the inviolability of the human person, whoever he or she may be—into the laws of war.

When this text came before the delegations at Geneva in the spring of 1949, the British mounted a vigorous rebuttal. The UK delegation knew that previous "conflicts in Spain, China, Indonesia and Palestine have led to strong pressure to make the Conventions applicable to civil war. It will be almost impossible for the UK to resist this pressure." But the British felt the threshold for triggering Geneva protections for civil wars was being set far too low. Their position was that only sovereign governments should be allowed to declare when a civil war existed, for otherwise any insurgent group could claim to be fighting a civil war and so gain access to Geneva protection for its fighters. Initial draft language seemed to offer protection to any group involved in internal strife of any kind, or even two nonstate groups fighting each other. The British cabinet heaped scorn on the notion of giving treaty protection to all squabbling adversaries inside a sovereign state: "It would cover, for example . . . an armed disturbance—in a colony for example—over an unpopular tax, 'racial riots'—between Jew and Fascist for example, or between Negro and White—and so-called 'wars of religion.'" Clearly, such commitments to protect all combatants anywhere in whatever cause were "capable of misrepresentation by subversive interests, and in colonial territories in particular might successfully be used as a propaganda document to instruct the native that he owed no allegiance towards lawfully constituted authority." Extending the conventions to civil war "strikes at the very root of national sovereignty and endangers national security."[17]

The British delegation knew that it would be difficult to keep civil wars out of the Convention altogether, and so they prepared a fall-back position in which signatories would apply the "principles" of the Convention to civil wars, rather than the precise binding text of the whole treaty. In return for this concession, the British would insist on removing all references to colonial conflicts and wars of religion. After what Sir Robert Craigie, the leader of the British delegation, described as "a war of attrition" with the other states at the negotiations, the British lost the struggle to keep "wars not of an international character" out of the Conventions. But they did win a crucial point: only the principles of the Convention would be applied to civil wars. Still, those basic provisions now had to be defined in Common Article 3, and so they were:

> In the case of armed conflict not of an international character occurring in the territory of one of the High Contracting Parties, each Party to the conflict shall be bound to apply, as a minimum, the following provisions:
>
> (1) Persons taking no active part in the hostilities, including members of armed forces who have laid down their arms and those placed hors de combat by sickness, wounds, detention, or any other cause, shall in all circumstances be treated humanely, without any adverse distinction founded on race, color, religion or faith, sex, birth or wealth, or any other similar criteria. To this end the following acts are and shall remain prohibited at any time and in any place whatsoever with respect to the above-mentioned persons:
>   (a) violence to life and person, in particular murder of all kinds, mutilation, cruel treatment and torture;
>   (b) taking of hostages;
>   (c) outrages upon personal dignity, in particular, humiliating and degrading treatment;
>   (d) the passing of sentences and the carrying out of executions without previous judgment pronounced by a regularly constituted court affording all the judicial guarantees which are recognized as indispensable by civilized peoples.

The British delegation felt that this language was as good a result as they could have achieved . Sir Robert Craigie concluded that "there is little in Article 3 which could be of direct encouragement to subversive movements."[18] Yet in truth, Article 3 was a major victory for the countries that wanted to provide protections to resistance groups, civilians, and detained combatants—in short, all those peoples who had suffered so much at the hands of the Nazis. Common Article 3 opens up once darkened areas of state activity—namely, internal repression and violence against citizens—and subjects them to the bright light of international law. To be sure, Article 3 only applied certain "provisions" about humane treatment to those internal conflicts. Yet the article has commutative properties: if humane treatment must be provided to all people at all times in *civil* wars, then it logically must also be applied to all peoples in *international* conflicts as well. That is certainly how the ICRC read the meaning of Common Article 3. Jean Pictet described its expansive power succinctly: "Representing as it does the minimum which must be applied in the least determinate of conflicts, its terms must *a fortiori* be respected in the case of international conflicts proper, when all the provisions of the Convention are applicable."[19] Once again, the ICRC and its allies among the national delegations managed to graft a central principle of human rights—humane treatment for all persons at all times, everywhere—into the preeminent legal charter of the laws of war.

It is clear, then, that there is within the text of the Geneva Conventions much to interest human rights historians. This treaty is no mere guidebook for warring states: it contains assumptions about the inviolable individual rights of the human person—a sharp departure from all previous treaties defining the laws of war. But so what? Why does it matter that the laws of war, which are designed to govern state behavior in times of war, now demand that states respect the right of the individual person to be treated humanely at all times, and if he is to be judged, that he be given a fair trial by a regularly constituted court? Do these guarantees amount to a major advance for the human rights agenda?

Until 2001, human rights historians failed to consider the question at all. But since the United States government began its global war on terror in the wake of the September 11, 2001, terrorist attacks, the real character of the Geneva Conventions as a core text of the human rights revolution has been revealed. Indeed, nothing is so illustrative of the power of the Geneva Conventions than the intensity of the efforts made by the United States after 9/11 to assault this legal citadel.

Following the 9/11 attacks, the United States undertook military operations in Afghanistan (a signatory of the Geneva Conventions) to pursue and destroy both the Al Qaeda terrorists who had planned and launched the attacks, and the Afghan Taliban government that had offered sanctuary to Al Qaeda terrorists. United States forces captured a number of Al Qaeda and Taliban combatants in these operations and kept them detained both inside

Afghanistan and later at the U.S. naval facility at Guantánamo Bay, Cuba. Various human rights organizations and foreign governments pressed the United States for reassurances that such detainees would be treated according to the Geneva Conventions.[20] Of course, the United States government did not wish to provide such status to the detainees. The Counsel to the President Alberto R. Gonzales advised President George W. Bush that the Geneva Conventions did not apply to the war against Al Qaeda and the Taliban. This decision, Gonzales told the president, would "preserve flexibility" in a "new kind of war" that "renders obsolete Geneva's strict limitations of questioning of enemy prisoners." Gonzales wanted the United States military to be able "to quickly obtain information from captured terrorists." Moreover, Gonzales advised the president that denying Geneva's applicability would "substantially reduce the threat of domestic criminal prosecution under the War Crimes Act (18 U.S.C. 2441)." The Bush administration's motive was plain: to free U.S. officials to conduct interrogations of captured terrorists and to protect those same officials from the consequences of breaking the law.[21]

But the president needed a reasoned argument for why Geneva did not apply to Al Qaeda or the Taliban. A number of crucial memoranda reveal the almost frantic efforts to devise a legal rationale for denying Geneva's relevance to the war on terror. Deputy Assistant Attorney General John Yoo took the first crack at the job, producing a long memo on January 9, 2002 for the general counsel of the Department of Defense. Working in haste to provide legal cover for the long-term incarceration and probably violent interrogation of Al Qaeda terrorists and Taliban militia members, Yoo developed a multipart attack on the Geneva Conventions. It can be condensed into three lines of argument. First, Yoo posited that Geneva does not protect Al Qaeda terrorists because Al Qaeda is a nonstate actor and could not be a signatory of the treaty. Geneva only protects members of the states that have signed it, whereas Al Qaeda was merely "a violent political movement" and had no rights under Geneva. Yoo later summarized the argument this way: "the conflict with al Qaeda is not governed by the Geneva Conventions, which applies only to international conflicts between states that have signed them."[22] Second, the conflict with Al Qaeda was global, and so the language of Common Article 3–enforcing certain humane principles in "armed conflict not of an international character"–was not applicable. Third, the Taliban militia was also not covered by Geneva because the Taliban was not a recognized government, Afghanistan was a "failed state" that had lost any legitimacy, and the Taliban was closer to being a nonstate terrorist group than a government, and so not able to enjoy Geneva protection. Thus, any Al Qaeda terrorist or Taliban militia fighter in U.S. custody could not appeal to the Geneva Conventions for protection. These arguments formed the legal position promulgated by President Bush on February 7, 2002, which would guide U.S. detainee policy for the next six years.[23]

But how persuasive are these arguments? Having seen in detail how the text of the Convention was actually developed, the reader will immediately perceive that all these arguments that John Yoo mobilized had been anticipated—and neutered—by the framers of the Conventions. First, Yoo's claim that Al Qaeda terrorists do not warrant prisoner of war status is a red herring. That issue was not in dispute. Yoo tried to divert attention from the fact that Geneva offers certain protections even to those captured combatants who do not gain the privileged status of prisoner of war. As we have seen, the treaty provides minimal protection to "spies and saboteurs" who, though they might lose their rights of communication, must nevertheless be treated humanely and given a fair trial by a competent tribunal (GC IV, Art 5). Put simply, terrorists *do* have some Geneva rights.

Second, even if Al Qaeda was acting globally as a terrorist network, Common Article 3 could be read as applying to Al Qaeda precisely because Al Qadea is not a state, and therefore America's war with it is "not of an international character." This is what the United States Supreme Court decided in June 2006: Article 3 "bears its literal meaning," and is used in the Conventions "in contradistinction to a conflict between nations." To be sure, the framers had in mind civil wars when writing Common Article 3, but the Supreme Court considered that it extended to wars between a state and a nonstate actor. The Court found that "Common Article 3 . . . affords some minimal protection, falling short of full protection under the Conventions, to individuals associated with neither a signatory nor even a nonsignatory who are involved in a conflict 'in the territory of a signatory.'" And those minimal protections include a ban on torture or degrading treatment.[24]

Third, Yoo's effort to deny the Taliban militia any Geneva protection was especially weak. Yoo had claimed that the Taliban was not a recognized government, Afghanistan was a "failed state" without any legitimacy, and the Taliban was closer to being a nonstate terrorist group than a government. To declare Afghanistan a failed state, however, opened up the possibility that any warring nation could declare its enemy a "failed state" simply to avoid applying the Conventions. The Bush administration settled on an alternative strategy: to deny Taliban fighters prisoner of war status because their fighters did not abide by the specific language of GC

III Art. 4 (2): "(a) that of being commanded by a person responsible for his subordinates; (b) that of having a fixed distinctive sign recognizable at a distance; (c) that of carrying arms openly; (d) that of conducting their operations in accordance with the laws and customs of war." But this argument too was easily dispensed with because the directly preceding clause indicated that POWs were "Members of the armed forces of a Party to the conflict, as well as *members of militias or volunteer corps* forming part of such armed forces" [GC III Art. 4 (1)]. The Taliban were surely a militia and surely were members of Afghanistan's armed forces, however poorly disciplined and shabby they appeared. The language about uniforms and commanders applied to organized resistance forces and voluntary militias—the French Resistance, for example—and had been designed to regulate underground resistance activities. Any honest reading of the terms of Article 4 would allow POW status to Taliban militia fighters on the grounds that the Taliban were a part of Afghanistan's armed forces. If there were doubts about their status, Article 5 could be invoked: "Should any doubt arise as to whether persons, having committed a belligerent act and having fallen into the hands of the enemy, belong to any of the categories enumerated in Article 4, such persons shall enjoy the protection of the present Convention until such time as their status has been determined by a competent tribunal" (GC III Art. 5). And even if POW status was refused to them, then Common Article 3 was always available as a fall-back to insure that they could not be tortured or badly treated.[25]

There was, in fact, no persuasive legal argument that would allow the United States to wall off Geneva from the war on terror. Instead, Justice Department officials offered a deliberate misreading of the text in order to provide the United States the cover it desired so that members of the U.S. armed forces and intelligence services could capture, indefinitely detain, and torture persons deemed threatening to American interests. And this, we now know, is precisely what happened.[26]

For historians of human rights, what may be most significant in this tale is the evidence it presents about how the laws of war have advanced the propositions inherent in human rights law. The Geneva Conventions had developed an overlapping, reinforced set of protections for people in wartime based on the principle that individual rights matter more than the sovereignty of the state. In this, the Geneva Conventions—whose origins lay in the laws of war—has become a crucial link in those international human rights laws that defend individuals from the rapacious power of the state.

NOTES

I would like to thank Mark Bradley, Susan Ferber, Petra Goedde, and Sam Moyn for helpful comments on earlier drafts of this essay.

1. Paul Gordon Lauren, *The Evolution of International Human Rights: Visions Seen* (Philadelphia: University of Pennsylvania Press, 2003), barely mentions the Conventions, nor does Burns H. Weston's excellent survey of human rights refer to them: *Encyclopedia Britannica Online*, s.v. "Human Rights," (by Burns H. Weston), http://www.britannica.com

2. Cordula Droege, "Elective Affinities? Human Rights Law and Humanitarian Law," *International Review of the Red Cross* 871 (September 2008): 501–48; Robert Kolb, "The Relationship Between International Humanitarian Law and Human Rights Law," *International Review of the Red Cross* 324 (September 1998): 409–19; Louise Doswald-Beck and Sylvain Vité, "International Humanitarian Law and Human Rights Law," *International Review of the Red Cross* 293 (April 1993): 94–119. The only sustained historical investigation into the origins of the 1949 Geneva Conventions is Geoffrey Best, *War and Law since 1945* (Oxford: Clarendon Press, 1994), chapters 3, 4, and 5.

3. For the official text of the Geneva Conventions, see International Committee of the Red Cross website, http://www.icrc.org/Web/eng/siteeng0.nsf/htmlall/genevaconventions.

4. Except for the case of the Protocols to the Geneva Conventions, promulgated in 1977, which extended Geneva protections to fighters in national liberation movements and other irregular militant formations. The Reagan administration refused to accept this new protocol and refused to send it to the Senate for ratification. At the time of this writing, the United States still has not ratified Protocol I of the Geneva Convention.

5. On the early history: Angela Bennett, *The Geneva Convention: The Hidden Origins of the Red Cross* (UK: Sutton Publishing, 2005); Fritz Kalshoven, *Constraints on the Waging of War* (Geneva: ICRC, 1987), 7–17; Ingrid Detter de Lupis, *The Law of War* (Cambridge: Cambridge University Press, 1987), 271–93; Hilaire McCoubrey, *International Humanitarian Law: The Regulation of Armed Conflicts* (Aldershot: Dartmouth Publishing, 1990), 11–15.

6. "Report on the Work of the Preliminary Conference of National Red Cross Societies for the Study of the Conventions," Geneva July 26–August 3, 1946, Record Group [RG] 59, Entry 5210, Box 6, US State Department Records, Office of the Legal Adviser, Records Relating to the Red Cross and the Geneva Conventions, United States National Archives and Records Administration (hereafter NARA).

7. Jean S. Pictet, *Commentary on the Geneva Convention Relative to the Protection of Civilian Persons in Time of War* (Geneva: ICRC, 1958), 12–14; "Report of the United States Delegation," October 3, 1949, RG 389, Entry 437, Box 673, Provost Marshal General, Administrative Division, NARA.

8. Revised draft and comments, February 1949, FO 369/4145, UK National Archives (hereafter UKNA).

9. *Final Record of the Diplomatic Conference of Geneva of 1949*, vol. IIA (Berne: Federal Political Department, 1949), 240.

10. The UK delegation congratulated itself for this small victory in its final report. Cabinet Memorandum by Secretary of State for Foreign Affairs, "Partisans," November 25, 1949, Annex I, WO 32/13616, UKNA. In the discussions on this matter, the United States delegation sided with the Soviets and the Western Europeans, leaving the British in "a minority of one," about which the British delegation felt extreme bitterness. "Report on the Work of the War Office Members of the UK Delegation to the Diplomatic Conference at Geneva," October 1949, WO 32/13616, UKNA.

11. *Final Record*, vol. IIA, 621–22. The French and Australian delegates had a frosty exchange in which the Australian stated his view that the rights of states at war needed to be protected, while the French delegate said that "the object of the Convention was to provide for the protection of persons, not to safeguard the rights of states." Here lies the basic divide at the heart of the Convention.

12. Pictet, *Commentary*, 58.

13. Ibid., 51.

14. Ibid., 201, 205.

15. Ibid., 26.

16. "Minute for the Secretary of State," March 10, 1949, attached papers, FO 369/4143, UKNA.

17. Cabinet Meeting of Ministers, "Revision of Geneva Conventions: Application of Geneva Conventions to Civil War," March 26, 1949, WO 32/14041, UKNA.

18. Memorandum, "Extracts from Sir Robert Craigie's Report," November 25, 1949, Annex I, WO 32/13616, UKNA.

19. Pictet, *Commentary*, 38.

20. T. R. Reid, "U.S. Pressed on Detainees' Treatment; Concern Grows Abroad About Rights of Al Qaeda, Taliban Fighters Held in Cuba," *Washington Post*, January 17, 2002.

21. Alberto R. Gonzales, Counsel to the President, "Memorandum for the President," January 25, 2002, in *The Torture Papers: The Road to Abu Ghraib*, ed. Karen J. Greenberg and Joshua L. Dratel (New York: Cambridge University Press, 2005), 118–21.

22. John Yoo, "Terrorists Have No Geneva Rights," *Wall Street Journal*, May 26, 2004.

23. John Yoo, "Memorandum for William J. Haynes III, General Counsel, Department of Defense, January 9, 2002," in *Torture Papers*, Greenberg and Dratel, 38–79. Yoo's memo was supplemented by a memo from Jay S. Bybee, an assistant attorney general, dated January 22, 2002, to Alberto Gonzales, in *Torture Papers*, Greenberg and Dratel, 81–117. Yoo's arguments were adopted in President Bush's memorandum to his top national security officials, dated February 7, 2002, in *Torture Papers*, Greenberg and Dratel, 134–35.

24. *Hamdan v. Rumsfeld*, 548 U.S. 557 (2006), June 29, 2006. For analysis of the decision, see Peter J. Spiro, "Hamdan v. Rumsfeld 126 S.Ct. 2749," *American Journal of International Law* 100, no. 4 (October 2006): 888–95.

25. George H. Aldrich, "The Taliban, al Qaeda, and the Determination of Illegal Combatants," *American Journal of International Law* 96, no. 4 (October 2002): 891–98. See also "Decision Not to Regard Persons Detained in Afghanistan as POWs," *American Journal of International Law* 96, no. 2 (April 2002): 475–80; and Johannes van Aggelen, "A Response to John C. Yoo, 'The Status of Soldiers and Terrorists under the Geneva Conventions,'" *Chinese Journal of International Law* 4, no. 1 (2005): 167–81.

26. Thanks to the work of the National Security Archive, we now have extensive documentation about the torture of detainees in American hands during the war on terror. For thousands of pages of documents, see http://www.gwu.edu/~nsarchiv/torture_archive/index.htm. The ICRC report, titled "ICRC Report on the Treatment of Fourteen 'High Value Detainees' in CIA Custody," dated February 14, 2007, was published by the *New York Review of Books*. It leaves no doubt about the systematic torture that was applied to select "high-value detainees" by U.S. personnel. See http://www.nybooks.com/icrc-report.pdf.

5

GRAMS, CALORIES, AND FOOD

Languages of Victimization, Entitlement, and
Human Rights in Occupied Germany, 1945–1949

ATINA GROSSMANN

Everyone has the right to a standard of living adequate for the health and
well-being of himself and of his family, including food, clothing, housing and
medical care, and necessary social services.
—From Article 25, Section 1, of The Universal Declaration
of Human Rights, December 10, 1948

By the spring of 1945, when the Allied Military Government and the
United Nations Relief and Rehabilitation Administration (UNRRA) confronted the masses of refugees and displaced persons gathered in, or
streaming toward, occupied Germany in the wake of the Third Reich's
defeat, food—its supply, distribution, and, not least, symbolic meaning—
had been clearly established as a key political and psychological issue for
military and occupation policy. The rhetoric of Allied war aims and of
relief work posited food provision as a fundamental issue of human survival, development, and dignity. In 1943, the anthropologist Margaret
Mead cautioned American policymakers planning the future of a defeated
Nazi Germany about the importance of food rationing for establishing control over an occupied population. "Whenever a people feels that its food
supply is in the hands of an authority," she reminded them (in deceptively
gender neutral language), "it tends to regard that authority as to some
degree parental." Moreover, she added, "probably no other operation, even
the provision of hospitalization and emergency care, is so effective in
proving to an anxious and disturbed people that the powers that be are good
and have their welfare at heart."[1]

Mead's concerns about adequate food provision fit squarely into the New Deal-inflected language of human rights and social security central to the American case against fascism. Franklin Delano Roosevelt's famous Four Freedoms address to the 77th Congress on January 6, 1941, designed to prepare the nation for possible participation in World War II, asserted the primacy of a right to "freedom from want" alongside the basic freedoms of speech and worship. The Atlantic Charter, proclaimed by Churchill and Roosevelt on August 12, 1941, as they vowed to support Great Britain and the Soviet Union with Lend Lease aid, promised all states—and significantly both "victor or vanquished . . . access, on equal terms, to the trade and to the raw materials of the world which are needed for their economic prosperity." The Charter elaborated the vision articulated by Roosevelt, announcing that the peace resulting from the "final destruction of the Nazi tyranny" would "afford assurance that all the men in all the lands may live out their lives in freedom from fear and want."[2]

Indeed, the dream of establishing the United Nations organization arguably first began with an international conference focused on food. A May 1943 gathering at Hot Springs, Virginia, led to the formation of an interim international commission that became in 1945 the Food and Agriculture Organization (FAO) of the new UN.[3] In November 1943, in the midst of brutal warfare in Europe and the Pacific and in the face of the ongoing Nazi extermination project, forty nations agreed to establish UNRRA as the international agency mandated to deal with an expected massive flow (and hoped for repatriation) of displaced persons and refugees.[4] In his 1944 State of the Union address to a nation at war, FDR reiterated the principle that political and civil rights were inextricably connected to material entitlements; food was a basic inalienable human right. "A man in need is not a free man," he stated unequivocally, and warned that "people who are hungry and out of jobs are the stuff of which dictatorships are made."[5] Thus, the basic tenet that everyone had the "right to adequate food and the fundamental right of everyone to be free from hunger"—which would eventually be enshrined in the 1948 Universal Declaration of Human Rights—was integrated into Allied war aims. Between 1945 and 1948—and in many ways into the 1950s—these putative "rights" would be severely tested on the ground, in conflicts over food rations and entitlements that roiled occupied and defeated Germany.

The Politics of Rationing

As Mead predicted, in the aftermath of unconditional surrender in 1945 and the influx of millions of refugees into the Western occupation zones, differential access to food supplies or goods that could be exchanged for food became a key gauge of the occupiers' favor, and even denoted a rough classification of groups or individuals as victim, perpetrator, or bystander during the Nazi regime. For displaced refugees in a war-torn Europe without legitimate borders or national institutions, access to adequate food and disputes over the meaning of "adequate" also served as markers of Allied and international commitment to the realization of the Allies' lofty war aims. After Germany's unconditional surrender, the Allied powers—especially the U.S. Military Government—took on the ultimate responsibility for feeding the local population and the masses of refugees streaming into occupied Germany, including up to 14 million ethnic German refugees and expellees from the Eastern territories conquered by the Red Army.[6] Together with UNRRA and associated nongovernmental aid organizations, the Military Government also confronted millions of Nazi Germany's victims: prisoners of war (POWs), forced laborers, liberated concentration camp inmates (*KZNiks*), and over a quarter-million mostly Eastern European Jews who had survived the Final Solution.[7]

During the war, economist John Maynard Keynes reportedly "scoffed" that President Roosevelt's interest in food relief led him to "start with vitamins" as the "best strategy for post-war reconstruction."[8] As it turned out, vitamins, and especially calories, did become a fulcrum of wartime planning, as well as of postwar and then Cold War occupation and reconstruction politics. The calorie, as historian Nick Cullather has detailed, invented in 1896 in an "airtight chamber" in a Wesleyan University basement, became an important measure of "social and industrial efficiency" during the Progressive Era and an "instrument of power" for military planning and humanitarian relief operations during and after World War I.[9] During and especially after World War II, calories—and what they could and could not provide in terms of food and sustenance—became a measure of the Allied commitment to human "welfare" and rights noted by Mead, proclaimed by the Atlantic Charter, and finally codified in the Universal Declaration of Human Rights of 1948.

For the occupiers, questions about food supplies for displaced persons (DPs) were inextricably linked to disputes about adequate nutrition for the Germans—how much they needed and how much they deserved. Did they require just the minimum to prevent epidemics and serious social disorder or enough to actually satisfy the population? These questions were, of course, both political and practical. Food politics had become part of the "arithmetic of standards" that marked welfare state and humanitarian activism in the second half of the twentieth century. UNRRA, which was responsible for aid to "non-enemy nationals," had declared a (frequently unattainable) daily intake of about 2500–2650 calories to be adequate, the amount that the International Labor Organization of the League of Nations had set in 1935 as the global standard for the working adult.[10] Despite Allied planning based on the principle that defeated Germans should not have more food than the most hard-hit Allied nation, SHAEF (Supreme Headquarters Allied Expeditionary Forces) originally set German rations at 2000 calories, which was no less than for liberated countries such as France or Belgium. However, when local supplies, including the contents of well-stocked German military depots, ran low, official rations for the defeated were quickly reduced, initially to a low of 1000 to 1250 calories daily.[11]

Under the chaotic conditions confronted by U.S. Military Government and UNRRA at war's end, and throughout the occupation, a complex and in many ways quite novel, language of grams of fat and total daily calories, vitamins, or cigarettes and coffee allotments emerged. It calibrated new (and constantly shifting) standards of victimization and entitlement—and importantly—recognition among the many different groups present in the American occupation zone. During a period of tumult and extreme scarcity, defeated Germans and surviving Jews competed against each other, and also among themselves, for the favors of the "good parent," embodied by occupiers (coded as military and male) and international relief organizations (often represented on the ground by female social workers). Each group resented the ostensible (and in reality extremely limited) privileging of the other, maintaining that their political innocence or severe suffering entitled them to precious supplies or a higher level of rations. To extend Mead's analogy, the "parents" discriminated among their various children who in turn squabbled over who was more entitled or deprived. "'Calories' became a kind of magical concept" and rationing categories not only established daily allotments but also delineated differential degrees of victimization, criminality, or complicity, providing in visceral form a measure of "transitional justice." They worked as a "universal currency" defining standards of justice and efficiency that operated in tandem with the informal currency of coffee, cigarettes, and nylons supporting the postwar black or "gray" market barter economy.[12]

In this calculus, ration levels set by degrees of guilt and work capacity often doubly jeopardized women, even as, in a world of "surplus women" and men missing in action or prisoner of war camps, women were generally responsible for food provision and distribution. Deployed as *Trümmerfrauen* to clear the rubble, often (but certainly not always) as punishment for having been members of, or married to members of, Nazi organizations, women were also most likely to be classified as "unproductive" *Hausfrauen*, thus eligible for the lowest level ration card, dubbed the *Himmelsfahrtkarte* (ticket to heaven) because it could not provide a livable diet. At the same time, there was no clear standard for what constituted a livable diet. American occupation officers, constrained by regulations which reminded them that, "You are entering Germany, not as a liberator, but as a victor," were constantly balancing the desire not to "pamper" the Germans with the need to maintain order and prevent epidemics.[13] In an ironic reference to the erstwhile national anthem, the sometimes still irrepressible Berliner *Schnauze* lamented, "Deutschland Deutschland *ohne alles* [without everything], without butter, without fat, and even the little bit of marmalade is eaten up by the occupiers."[14] But, as Americans did not tire of pointing out, German outrage at the low level of provisioning was also influenced by the enormous quantities they had been accustomed to consuming before, and even during, the war: up to an average of 3000 calories per day, including a good deal of alcohol, much bread and potatoes, and an astonishing 106 grams of fat—always the marker of an ample diet. Even at the height of the war in 1944, with German cities under severe bombardment, the average intake stood at a generous 2000 calories a day.

Annoyed that the Soviets, following their more explicit policy of fraternization with (often newly converted) supportive "anti-fascist" elements, tried to gain political advantage with generous soup kitchens, the U.S. Commander in Berlin, Colonel Howley groused: "Where the Russians parceled out extra bits of food in return for services rendered and for general political loyalty, I distributed food to the Germans to keep them from starving on our hands. I was not, however, in favor of giving them American sirloin steaks every night." Howley, who emerged from his tour of duty a rabid anticommunist, found that Germans nevertheless reviled him as the "beast of Berlin" for his food politics.[15]

Relatively quickly, however, political considerations changed and adequate amounts—of both calories and types of foodstuffs—were increasingly likely to be set with reference to not only the recent Nazi past but also the Cold War present. The Americans (and British) had been determined to impose punitive measures on the Germans—assuring for example that their diet should at least not exceed the low standard of postwar Great Britain, which had only instituted severe rationing after the war in order to manage the immense occupation costs. But their trepidation about being outdone on both the propaganda and provisioning front by the ever more troublesome new antagonists in the East, the Soviet Union and its German communist allies, proved a powerful counterweight.[16] Notwithstanding the Red Army's record of rape and plunder as the Soviets battled their way toward and into Berlin, the Americans feared potential popular support for a Soviet occupation driven by Stalin's conciliatory vow that "the Hitlers come and go but the German Volk remains." German officials were adept at playing on anxieties that too severe a stance would turn the defeated Germans toward communism. In her famous album, *Fatherland Rest Quietly*, the photojournalist Margaret Bourke-White displayed a scarily "Aryan"-looking female "Professor Koch" (Cook) into whose mouth she put the lines that Americans imagined all Germans to be perfecting: "America must supply food, or Stalin will have an easy time."[17] Others ominously rhymed, "Our food needs must be met, otherwise Hitler we cannot forget."[18] Adequate food offered not only a bastion against "anarchy" among the displaced but also a bulwark against revanchist Nazism and now communism. American occupiers fretted that if there was "a choice between becoming a communist on 1500 calories and a believer in democracy on 1000 calories," low or decreased rations would "pave the way to a Communist Europe."[19]

These tensions later culminated in the dramatic conflicts of the Berlin Blockade and Airlift in 1948, which unfolded just as the General Assembly in New York promulgated the Universal Declaration of Human Rights, on December 10, 1948, one day after the same body had unanimously passed the Genocide Convention. During the blockade, the communists hoped to lure West Berliners into the East with promises of full shops and adequate food supplies, while the West tried to score points by airlifting tons of supplies. However, West Berliners neither yielded to Eastern propaganda nor subsisted solely on the much-heralded supplies flown in from Frankfurt's Rhine-Main air base, managing instead with a combination of Allied goods, foraging in the countryside, and furtive shopping in the East.[20]

It was just this ability of Germans, occupied but nonetheless still living in their own familiar country (a perception that extended to German expellees and refugees who were also uprooted), to supplement low rations by recourse to relatives in the countryside or the goodwill of their customary grocers or butchers that infuriated their former victims during the immediate postwar months and years. Surviving Jews were embittered by what they perceived to be grudging treatment as troublesome foreign refugees and "homeless foreigners." For them, privileged food rations were more than an urgent necessity; they also represented political recognition and an initial form of reparation. Contemporary human rights activists have argued that states have the obligation to protect and facilitate access to food supplies for those who might be disadvantaged in receiving food. In the case of occupied Germany, where there was no state authority to carry that role, the Jewish DPs expected UNRRA; the American Jewish Joint Distribution Committee (JDC, or Joint), the main Jewish relief agency; and, finally, the

Military Government, which held quasi-state responsibility, to fulfill that role. They resented the limited and, above all, unappetizing rations supplied by their American protectors and UNRRA, as well as the patronizing and bureaucratized manner in which aid was distributed by international and Jewish aid organizations.

Even in the most drab transit camps or assembly centers, Jews maintained the emphasis on holiday feasts, occasions for which they demanded and received special allotments and shipments, involving, for example, the resumption of matzo baking at the Sarotti plant in Berlin and the shipment of kosher wine from Palestine.[21] Survivors' attitudes reflected "deeply held beliefs about food as an entitlement," and hence they were even more resentful and suspicious of the minimalist rations provided by aid groups and the Military Government.[22]

Conflicts about food certainly marked and perpetuated the bitterness between Germans and Jews. In the fall of 1945, with the memory of liberation still fresh and the Nuremberg Trials about to begin, a Jewish aid organization acknowledged that "No doubt the children loitering in railway stations or wandering on the roads, suffer cruelly at the approach of winter from a total lack of food and clothing," but insisted, however, that the countryside, if not the cities, "almost everywhere [is] intact, the herds of horses, of cows, of sheep, are well fed, the barnyards are well, even very well stocked."[23] In outraged missives, representatives from American Jewish aid organizations, soldiers, and chaplains eloquently challenged the litany of complaints from Germans about the privileges in housing and food granted to Jews: "I don't wish to be depressing darling," a Jewish officer wrote to his wife in December 1945, but the stark fact was that SS and Wehrmacht prisoners and German civilians received "more calories per day than the people who really suffered under the Nazis."[24]

At the same time, Germans, often seen as undeservedly well fed by allies and Jewish survivors, for their part quickly positioned Jews as "privileged." Germans resented Jews' guaranteed access to UNRRA rations in displaced persons camps, the generosity of individual American Jewish soldiers and chaplains, and the much-envied Joint supplements, which provided not only dried food but also chocolates, coffee, and above all, the cigarettes that were central to black-market trading. To Germans—as well as to some occupiers and UNRRA officials—it looked like the sensational report submitted by President Truman's special envoy Earl Harrison decrying the terrible conditions endured by Jewish survivors in DP camps and supporting Jewish demands for autonomous all-Jewish camps, cemented Jewish survivors' position as having a "privileged status well above that of any ordinary displaced national of the United Nations."[25] But it did not feel that way to the Jewish DPs, and much of that sense of disappointment, bitterness, and lack of recognition congealed around food. Their mood was later captured in the 1950 Hollywood film *The Big Lift* by the gruff honest Sgt. Kowalski, Montgomery Clift's Polish-American (and in some ways, one suspects, a stand-in for a Jewish) GI sidekick, who says of the Berliners he is protecting from the Soviet threat, "They can't remember Dachau, Lidice, Buchenwald, Rotterdam, Warsaw. That they can't remember, but that they couldn't get meat last week, that they remember."[26]

American requisition of German homes and apartment blocks to house the increasing population of Jewish "infiltrees" from Eastern Europe seeking refuge in the American zone further inflamed German rancor. By 1947, the keen sense of unfair and arbitrary treatment by the victors led the *Deutsche Städtetag* to avail itself of the new occupier-provided rhetoric and explicitly protest such evictions as human rights violations.[27] When official rations in the British zone were reduced to 1550 calories in March 1946, German physicians were not above making comparisons to starvation conditions in concentration camps. In 1947, a particularly harsh year in which "a worldwide scarcity of foodstuffs, a hard winter, exhausted soil, and problems with the distribution system" for food exacerbated an already difficult situation, the defeated Germans responded to a reduction in rations with sporadic strikes and unabashed appeals to "international law." Local political leaders claimed that by reducing rations the Allies were violating the terms of the Atlantic Charter which, after all, pledged that the result of the "final destruction of the Nazi tyranny" would be peace, economic prosperity, and "freedom from fear and want" for both victor and vanquished. In June of that same crisis year, the German Chamber of Physicians, meeting in Bad Nauheim, appealed to the international moral conscience: "The whole people, once vigorous and healthy has been weakened by starvation, and is now utterly incapable of work and is on the verge of manifest infirmity."[28] In a pervasive "narrative of hunger and victimization," as historian Alice Weinreb aptly characterized a persistent German discourse starting with the Allied "hunger blockade" of World War I and the provisions of the Versailles Treaty and extending to territorial readjustments and Allied rationing policies after World War II, Germans fashioned themselves into victims of hunger. Their food rations were restricted by vindictive occupiers and their food supplies were looted or unfairly traded by "homeless foreigners," especially Jewish DPs, fattened up by the favor of the Americans and their access to goods supplied by international Jewish relief organizations.[29]

Undoubtedly, ordinary Germans in cities were suffering from a rationing system much more onerous than that imposed by the Nazi regime. A cartoon in the Berlin women's magazine *sie* from January 1947 from January 1947 shows a son asking his mother "cooking over an improvised stove . . . 'Mother, do we always have to eat calories? Couldn't we occasionally eat a nice piece of cake?'"[30] In general, however, even sympathetic occupation officials agreed that Germans greatly exaggerated reports of malnutrition; While German rations were indeed lower than those granted to Jewish displaced persons and officially designated "victims of fascism," the calorie counting inscribed into ration levels was deceptive.

Most Germans did not have to rely only on official rations. Unlike DPs, who, especially in the early period, were trapped in the confines of their camps, both by regulation and fear, Germans had access to nonrationed and fresh food. As "natives," or even as ethnic German refugees, they could more easily resort to contacts in the countryside or with familiar and friendly grocers. Germans were hardly suffering from famine, unimpressed and irritated occupiers noted; it was just that they were so accustomed to a substantial diet and even saw obesity as a sign of health. Disgusted by the plump women he saw in Celle (and it is interesting to note the gendered quality of complaints about German corpulence), the town adjoining Bergen Belsen KZ in the British zone, which had been essentially undamaged by the war, a British officer remarked that, "If slimness is fashionable among German women, then Celle was certainly a most unfashionable place."[31] Margaret Bourke-White also reported that "Especially the *Fräuleins*," the object of so much controversy about fraternization, were in "good shape, their teeth are the giveaway. Much better than in any German occupied country."[32]

To Jewish survivors and many Allied observers (especially, but not only, American Jewish servicemen, chaplains, and aid workers) defeated Germans still seemed relatively well-fed, well-scrubbed, and prosperous, particularly in the rural areas where many of the larger Jewish DP camps were located. This perception held despite the mass influx of ethnic German refugees from the Red Army and Soviet-occupied territory in the East into rural areas. For many Allied occupiers, the shock was not the extensive destruction of Germany (and now much discussed victimization) but how unscathed much of it still appeared. The relative comfort and the highly developed self-pity of the defeated Germans—so frequently described as "sullen"—is a strikingly consistent theme.[33] Jewish DPs deeply resented the seemingly willful misapprehension of their unique situation, expressing bitter frustration at what they came to call "the enigma of German irresponsibility."[34] If the Allies' juggling of entitlements in regard to rations angered ordinary Germans, who found themselves officially disadvantaged, Allied food policy nonetheless seemed pathetically inadequate to the survivors, given both their experience and formal status as victims.

The Political, Bureaucratic, and Emotional
Economy of Food

Food was, indeed, a politically volatile issue. But it was primarily expressed, not in the language of rights, or even entitlement or humanitarianism, but in terms of grams and calories. UNRRA files are filled with careful charts on the caloric value of foods, more meticulously broken down than in any diet book, ranging from beef carcasses (544 cal/lb) to sweets and candies (1680/lb).[35] DPs were continually subjected to nutritional studies and mass weigh-ins by (usually female) public health workers, the necessary and standard-ized corollary to medical examinations and, as a hygiene measure, dusting with the pesticide DDT.[36] DP camp Food Offices kept careful records of all foodstuffs and cigarettes delivered by the Joint, noting precisely (at least on paper) when and how many goods were received and then distributed. Long lists tracked the goods, many of them scarce and valuable, that entered the DP camps: American cigarettes, tobacco, and canned meat, followed by marmalade, sardines, powdered and condensed milk, potatoes, bread, butter, flour, fat and *Schmalz* (chicken fat), fish, powdered eggs, cocoa, some non-specified (and probably dried) vegetables, followed by—and often listed separately—precious extras such as sugar, chocolate, biscuits, salt, and coffee. Sick and pregnant residents received ration cards for half-liters of milk from the camp store.[37]

For Jewish survivors, therefore, for whom food supplies were generally—at least after the early period of chaos—adequate, especially when measured by numbers of calories, the issue became, just as Margaret Mead had sensed, one of quality rather than quantity. DPs who had access to milk and grain, and who sometimes became quite plump, wanted more than rations mea-sured by calories. Indeed, the fresh fruits and vegetables they craved and which were essential for health had only negligible caloric value. Food was, in most cases, plentiful, carbohydrate-laden and hence calorie-laden, but it was unappetizing and monotonous. The "bare essentials" were not good enough, and demands for separate kosher kitchens or ritually slaughtered meat required by Jewish dietary laws added another layer of conflict to already contentious postwar food politics. The definition of "adequate" there-fore was bitterly contested. DPs in occupied Germany demanded satisfaction according to their interpretation of "adequate." It signified precisely what FAO officials specified as adequate only many years later; namely, food that was available, culturally acceptable, able to supply "essential nutrients" such as vitamins (not just some allotted ration of calories), safe and free of toxins, and last, but certainly not least, "of good quality." A far cry from postwar notions predicated on caloric content, the human right to nutrition now requires, at least theoretically, food that tastes and looks appetizing and provides the "dietary diversity" necessary for good health.[38] It also insists that recipients (or claimants in current language) are presumed to be knowledgeable and trustworthy about their needs and that their views are respected. Again, this is quite a different perspective from the postwar context in which aid organizations were willing to grant some self-government in the interests of better and more efficient management but certainly not willing to grant the survivors an "expert voice" in their care.[39]

Clearly, food was defined according to an emotional as well as a physical and political economy. Occupied Germans viewed the DP camps as a kind of *Schlaraffenland* (wonderland) of "sugar and spam, margarine and jam, plus cigarettes and vitamized chocolate bars" ready for lucrative sale on the black market and sullenly protested the puny privileges granted to the Jewish victims.[40] Americans worried about alienating Germans by setting rations too low and giving the impression of indulging unruly displaced persons, while simultaneously laboring to assure American Jews and antifascists that they were not pandering to former Nazis. Jews often suspected that German suppliers deliberately offered them bad food or withheld good fresh, food. DPs who maneuvered to supplement their (somewhat more ample but unequal) rations were condemned and not infrequently arrested (even in at least one notorious case, killed) by German police, who were conditioned to identify Soviet POWs and DPs in general as perpetrators of food crimes and, in a continuation of specific anti-Semitic prejudices, especially viewed Jews as food speculators and black marketers.

Increasingly, survivors were seen, by defeated and occupier alike, not as victims of National Socialism, but simply as intrusive "foreigners" (*Ausländer*). The fact that within a year of the war's end, Jewish DP camps were crowded with "infiltrees" from newly communist Poland, most of whom had been repatriated from their harsh but life-saving wartime refuge in the Soviet Union and could therefore be labeled as victims of communism rather than Nazism, only reinforced these perceptions.

In 1947, in response to the difficult food situation, the heating up of the Cold War, and the shift toward reconciliation with the former enemy (in the service of anticommunism and German economic recovery), the United States replaced the hard-line Joint Chiefs of Staff Order 1067 decreeing de-Nazification and demilitarization with a much less stringent directive, and the Military Government eliminated its policy of assigning higher food rations to the victims of Nazism. Numerous policy changes in 1947 signaled an end to Jewish DPs' (relative) "golden age" of special access to American power, protection, and rations. Yet, Germans continued to openly protest what Kathryn Hulme, an adventurous young American UNRRA worker, portrayed as the continued treatment with "kid gloves" of the "prima donnas of the DP world." Jewish survivors, on the other hand, underscored the second half of her statement, stating that "perhaps they deserved the rating" and insisted on the painful inadequacies and ironies of their situation as homeless refugees or disowned former citizens in the "blood-soaked" land of their tormentors.[41] Jews protesting conditions in Föhrenwald DP Camp asserted: "They, who are guilty of our sufferings and tortures, they who robbed us of our fortunes, they must be forced to feed us during the time we are compelled to stay in this country in order to make it possible for us to regain our health."[42]

Food, its quantity, quality, and distribution, was central therefore—both practically and symbolically—to these polarized understandings of wartime and postwar experience. As the anthropologist Mead understood, food crucially defined people's sense of how much they were recognized and valued as human beings rather than as DPs, who were frequently labeled as the miserable and unwelcome "human debris" of war and genocide. For the survivors, calorically adequate food was simply never enough. Once the early supply problems were solved, DPs continued to complain—obsessively it was said—about the amounts and taste of food; it was never enough and never good enough. American white bread and the hated UNRRA green peas could not satisfy. Drawing on the psychoanalytic understandings that dominated mental health practice in the 1940s, social workers and psychologists were quick to discern unhealthy and self-destructive patterns of "reckless eating" and "excessive desire for food," especially "sweets, chocolate, coffee and pastry."[43] They perceived refugees' preoccupation with food as symptomatic of the regression to an infantile state, complete with a childlike "[in]ability to plan," "apathy . . . helplessness . . . maniac excitement . . . aimless aggression" that the dependent DP existence fostered.[44] At best, their analysis of the emotional economy of food interpreted these reactions as a displaced response to catastrophic loss. The many grievances about the quality of food, clothing, and housing were seen as both legitimate and the product of a deep and ultimately insatiable longing for care and dignity, which no amount of institutional improvements could assuage.

Food desires, relief workers concluded, were not rational. As one frustrated but understanding UNRRA pediatrician reminded her calorie-counting superiors, "people do not eat calories, but food," and that food had to be appealing.[45] "How are we going to live—on calories?" one DP bitterly asked an American visitor, and, like many observers, she realized that "Calories in the DP camps had ceased to be a heat or food unit but had become the symbol of the drab, squalid existence" of the refugees.[46]

It was the desire for food that was more appetizing and more nurturing, rather than, as most critics insisted, the drive for profit and luxuries or even the search for necessities such as fresh milk for children, that pushed people toward the black—or more properly, gray—market. DPs aimed for access to the fresh meat, fruits, and vegetables that their German neighbors were able to take off the land or acquire from friendly shopkeepers, and that occupiers and aid officials took for granted. Trade in food—often carried on among women—provided an occasion for resentment and skirmishes over entitlements, as well as a crucial site for negotiations among Jews and Germans: about revenge, guilt, and victimization, but also about how to coexist in the post-Nazi present. Ita Muskal, a young refugee from Romania, for example, recalled with some pride how at age eighteen, she became a "businesslady" and a bit of a "big shot" as a Feldafing DP camp black marketeer. On a larger scale, UNRRA officials sometimes found that German farmers were reluctant to hand over milk from their cows or other supplies, but in this gray market, Ita could go to her "best provider," a German woman with a lovely garden filled with flowers and fresh produce. She brought her cigarette wages and treasures from the camp kitchen where she worked— margarine, peanut butter, dried and canned goods such as *Haferflocken* (Quaker Oats), peas, sardines, and tuna fish—that the Germans prized and the DPs disdained. She would collect *Marks* and goods and take them to the nearby villages or into the *Bourse*—the main black market on Möhlstrasse— in Munich for serious trading. Decades later, she still vividly remembered the deep satisfaction of walking the two and half miles to a nearby village café with her cash and ordering a German pastry, just like the "businesslady" she was, or the defiant pleasure of going to the German grocer, ordering bread, salami, and buttermilk, and insisting on real Swiss cheese. The grocer wanted to sell her an inferior, smelly cheese, *Schmierkäse*, but Ita would have none of it. "Too expensive," he told her, but Ita said no, "I have money and ration cards, I want the cheese with the holes." And then she would treat herself to the short train ride home, munching her cheese on the way. When Ita took her wares all the way to Munich, she even collected real dollars from the storekeepers, using them for further luxuries such as a dress or a pair of shoes for which the skilled DP shoemakers and tailors would charge $10 in hard currency. Armed with a picture from an illustrated magazine, she could take her dollars to the shoemaker and get the shoes she wanted, just like in the German paper. And sometimes she went into Munich with her husband Sam and played the "big shot." They would go out, to the theater or circus, even to a real restaurant to eat the "Liverwurst" that she loved.[47] Such transactions provided a means of gaining agency and overcoming the (putatively childlike) dependency that characterized refugee life. Good food, whether fresh meat or vegetables, a pastry or a rich liverwurst, offered respite from packaged rations and the regimented managed life of the postwar "refugee nation."[48]

Ironically, therefore, the victims, classified as stateless refugees or "homeless foreigners" (*heimatslose Ausländer*) dependent on "handouts," were inevitably cast in the position either of "nudging" mercenary complainants or as "privileged" when they received or demanded the paltry benefits they had been granted in recognition of their past suffering. Germans, for their part, especially as the Cold War progressed, increasingly expected to be rewarded for their good (that is, docile) behavior in the present rather than punished for possible crimes in the past. This enabled them to contrast their position as citizens in their own renovating country, simply demanding their rights to the satisfaction of basic needs, with the undeserved "special pleading" and advantages of their victims. In one of the many strange reversals of the postwar years, Germans were able to make universalizing claims as "victims" in need of internationally guaranteed human rights, while Jews, whose suffering had initially offered the paradigm for a necessary human rights regime supported by the United Nations, turned to particularism to assert their own needs and rights.[49]

The Jewish struggle in occupied Germany for the "right" to sufficient and culturally meaningful food reinforced for Jewish survivors a basic lesson: to secure rights in a world of nation-states, Jews would need a nation of their own. Their vulnerable and often begrudged status as needy supplicants led surviving Jews to a growing recognition that the key to gaining human rights that were just and universal, and more than mere benefits and privileges, was a claim to nationhood and national identity. This was a central conclusion of the DP era in occupied Germany: the human rights of Jews could only be guaranteed if they, like the other signatories of the United Nations, had their own sovereign nation-state. Even Roosevelt's iconic "freedom from want" had been phrased in national terms, as creating "economic understandings which will secure to every NATION a healthy peacetime life for its inhabitants—everywhere in the world."

The experience of the Holocaust and life as displaced persons framed the demands for a nation-state within which human rights could be granted and protected. Indeed, the collective environment of the camps mitigated against the elaboration of abstract individual rights claims. Jews formulated their calls for rights differently: in political demands for entry to Palestine and a Jewish state, and for the fulfillment of concrete material needs of everyday life, like food and housing.[50] Most Jewish DPs were determined to grasp for themselves the protections of a nationalization that was, as they imagined, entirely their own and therefore able to guarantee their universal human rights.[51] European Jews had learned that the minority rights their representatives had fought for after World War I, and that the League of Nations had supposedly guaranteed, could not protect them. At the same time, they learned that citizenship of the nation-state in which they resided did not also necessarily protect them. For the exhausted and traumatized displaced Jews of occupied Europe, the dream of citizenship in a specifically Jewish nation *outside* of the Europe that had betrayed them as a novel guarantee of human rights was not much of a stretch. Moreover, given the reluctance of the United States to admit them—at least until the passage of the quite limited 1948 and the more expansive 1950 DP acts—the Zionist path also seemed the only solution to endless displacement likely to be politically viable in terms of superpower support among the United Nations.

Survivors understood on literally a gut level what the UN World Congress on Human Rights posited it in its 1993 Vienna declaration: "The right to take part in the conduct of public affairs enables people to change their food or health situation at a political level."[52] This right to have rights, to use Arendt's formulation, was precisely what the DPs and the stateless did not possess. Political agency depended on recognition as a national collective and this was a status that Jewish DPs aspired to via a passionate Zionism, which, in some ways, allowed them to act like a proto-state even while they were still displaced and in transit in occupied Germany.[53] Unlike the ethnic German refugees who were citizens of occupied Germany, and, after 1949, then citizens of an essentially (officially "semi") sovereign Federal Republic of Germany, displaced Jews could claim no political rights as citizens. For DPs, the allotment of basic benefits such as food worked as a concrete manifestation—and representation—of their human rights.

UNRRA's definition of "relief and rehabilitation" tended to separate psychological needs—which were recognized to only a limited degree—from the more immediate urgent requirements for food, medical care, and shelter. But in fact, the two were inextricably linked. In spite of the sometimes egregious— and even at the time widely publicized—inadequacies in relief efforts, immediate needs were met relatively quickly and with remarkable efficiency. Food and feeding could not, however, be disconnected from the symbolic and emotional; they were intensely political and personal. Food remained a key issue well after the initial problems of severe hunger and malnutrition had long been solved. Not only the numbers of calories but the kind and quality of food available to Germans and Jews, especially fresh meat, fruit, and vegetables (as well as proper clothing, rather than worn and faded cast-offs), often came to stand in for the highly contested recognition of relative suffering and the entitlement to human rights and dignity. The experience of Jewish survivors as displaced persons in postwar occupied Germany underlines therefore how much the universal human rights declared by the United Nations are dominated on the ground by basic economic and social human needs such as food and delimited by access to nationally defined and codified citizenship.

NOTES

Adapted from "Grams, Calories, and Food: Languages of Victimization, Entitlement, and Human Rights in Occupied Germany, 1945–1949," by Atina Grossmann, *Central European History* 44, no. 1 (March 2011): 118–48. Copyright © 2011 Conference Group for Central European History of the American Historical Association. Reprinted with the permission of Cambridge University Press.

1. Margaret Mead, "Food and Feeding in Occupied Territory," *The Public Opinion Quarterly* 7, no. 4 (Winter 1943): 618–28, 619–20.

2. For an incisive critique analyzing the limitations of this universalist vision as it developed in the postwar politics of human rights, see Mark Mazower, *No Enchanted Palace: The End of Empire and the Ideological Origins of the United Nations* (Princeton, NJ: Princeton University Press, 2009).

3. Nick Cullather, "The Foreign Policy of the Calorie," *American Historical Review* 112, no. 2 (April 2007): 23.

4. On UNRRA see Susan T. Pettiss with Lynne Taylor, *After the Shooting Stopped: the story of an UNRRA Welfare Worker in Germany 1945–1947* (Victoria, BC: Trafford Press, 2004); Francesca Wilson, *Aftermath: France, Germany, Austria, Yugoslavia 1945 and 1946* (New York: Penguin, 1947); and George Woodbridge, *UNRRA: The History of the United Nations Relief and Rehabilitation Administration*, vol. 13 (New York: Columbia University Press, 1950). On conditions in occupied Germany, see also Jessica Reinisch, "Public Health in Germany under Soviet and Allied Occupation 1943–1947" (PhD diss., University of London, 2005).

5. Elizabeth Borgwardt, *A New Deal for the World: America's Vision for Human Rights* (Cambridge, MA: Harvard University Press, 2005), 115–18, 303–4. Here Roosevelt echoed Herbert Hoover, the engineer who had organized U.S. relief operations after World War I and who had warned that "famine breeds anarchy" and Bolshevism.

Quoted in Cullather, "Foreign Policy of the Calorie," 350. See also Asbjørn Eide, "The Human Right to Adequate Food and Freedom from Hunger," FAO Corporate Document Repository, 1998 (E/CN.4/Sub.2/1987/8.

6. This is the latest estimate for ethnic German refugees, cited by Frank Biess, *H-German*, March 7, 2006, in a (highly critical) review of Dagmar Barnouw, *The War in the Empty Air: Victims, Perpetrators, and Postwar Germans* (Bloomington: Indiana University Press, 2005). Earlier estimates usually cite a figure of 12 million.

7. In addition to Jews who had survived death and labor camps, in hiding, or with partisan units, up to two hundred thousand mostly Polish Jews who had either fled or been deported to the Soviet Union joined the influx into the American zone. I discuss these complicated and confusing issues in detail in *Jews, Germans, and Allies: Close Encounters in Occupied Germany* (Princeton, NJ: Princeton University Press, 2007).

8. Borgwardt, *A New Deal for the World*, 116.

9. Cullather, "Foreign Policy of the Calorie," 340, 339.

10. Ibid., 355. It is not clear whether this "working adult" standard was intended to apply to both men and women.

11. Malcolm J. Proudfoot, *European Refugees 1939–52: A Study in Forced Population Movements* (London: Faber and Faber, 1957), 318–19. See also chapter 11 "Jewish Refugees," 172–73.

12. For further analysis of the concept, see Ruti Teitel, *Transitional Justice* (New York: Oxford University Press, 2000). On calories as a "magical concept," see Hermann Glaser, *1945. Beginn einer Zukunft: Bericht und Dokumentation* (Frankfurt/M: Fischer, 2005), 127. "Universal currency" is Cullather's term.

13. Dale Clark, "Conflicts over Planning at Staff Headquarters," in *American Experiences in Military Government in World War II*, ed. Carl J. Friedrich and Associates (New York: Rinehart and Company, 1948), "Rules for Occupation Officers," 233.

14. Quote is from "Preisausschreiben. Berlin 1945. Wie ich es erlebte," essay contest sponsored by Berlin Senate on Berliners' experiences in 1945. Rep. 240, Acc. 2651/748, Landesarchiv Berlin/. Irmgard Heidelberg had submitted her mother's diary about her experience of defeat and occupation. My discussion here draws on research about Berlin; see also Paul Steege, *Black Market, Cold War: Everyday Life in Berlin, 1946–1949* (Cambridge: Cambridge University Press, 2007).

15. Frank Howley, *Berlin Command* (New York: Putnam, 1950), 85, 87.

16. See Reinisch, "Public Health in Germany," 16 and especially ch. 6.

17. Margaret Bourke-White, *Dear Fatherland, Rest Quietly: A Report on the Collapse of Hitler's Thousand Years* (New York: Simon & Schuster, 1946), caption on photo before p. 7.

18. Grigor McClelland, *Embers of War: Letters from a Quaker Relief Worker in War-Torn Germany* (London: British Academic Press, 1997), 145.

19. Cullather, "Foreign Policy of the Calorie," quoting General Lucius Clay, 363.

20. See Steege, *Black Market, Cold War*.

21. Quarterly report, AJDC, March 1–June 1, 1946, p. 41 in YIVO Leo W Schwarz Collection (LWS) 294.1/516/R45, also in 446/R37. On food and Jewish survivors in occupied Germany, see also Grossmann, *Jews, Germans, and Allies*, esp. 174–78.

22. See Hasia Diner, *Hungering for America: Italian and Jewish Foodways in the Age of Migration* (Cambridge, MA: Harvard University Press, 2001), 147–50.

23. *Report on the Situation of the Jews in Germany* (Geneva: Union OSE, 1946), 11, 18.

24. Letter from officer stationed near Dachau, September 17, 1945. American Joint Distribution Committee Archives, New York, file 399A.

25. Proudfoot, *European Refugees*, 325. For current reflections on these vexed issues and the argument that "As opposed to other refugee groups who entered the market of international compassion in the 1940s, Jewish refugees were granted full status of political victims," see Gerard Daniel Cohen, "The Politics of Recognition: Jewish Refugees in Relief Policies and Human Rights Debates 1945–1950," *Immigrants and Minorities* 24, no. 2 (July 2006): 125–43.

26. *The Big Lift,* produced by William Perlberg for Twentieth Century Fox, directed by George Seaton (1950). Filmed on site during the Berlin Airlift.

27. For different perspectives on these German perceptions, see Ulrich Müller, *Fremde in der Nachkriegszeit. Displaced Persons-zwangsverschleppte Personen in Stuttgart und Württemberg-Baden 1945–1951* (Stuttgart: Klett-Cotta, 1990) and Susanne Dietrich and Julia Schulze-Wessel, *Zwischen Selbstorganisation und Stigmatisierung: Die Lebenswirklichkeit jüdischer Displaced Persons und die neue Gestalt des Antisemitismus in der deutschen Nachkriegsgesellschaft* (Stuttgart: Klett-Cotta, 1998). On the connections between anti-Semitism and conflicts over food, see also Frank Stern, *The Whitewashing of the Yellow Badge: Antisemitism and Philosemitism in Postwar Germany*, trans. Frank Templar (Oxford: Pergamon, 1992), 107.

28. Reinisch, "Public Health in Germany," 284. Food riots had already broken out in some areas in spring of 1946.

29. See Alice Weinreb, "Matters of Taste: Hunger, Food, and the Making of Two Germanies" (Ph.D. diss., University of Michigan, 2009), an excellent and provocative analysis of the politics and culture of food and hunger in postwar Germany.

30. Steege, *Black Market, Cold War*, 48.

31. Reinisch, "Public Health in Germany," 284–88, quote on 291.

32. Bourke-White, *Fatherland*, 33, 61.

33. This ongoing discussion has produced a flood of books in the past decade (including republished literature), articles, and films on German civilian suffering in World War II. See for example, Jörg Friedrich, *Der Brand: Deutschland im Bombenkrieg, 1940–1945* (Munich: Propyläen, 2003), American edition, *The Fire: The Bombing of Germany, 1940–1945* (New York: Columbia University Press, 2006); and Lothar Kettenacker, ed., *Ein Volk von Opfern? Die neue Debatte um den Bombenkrieg 1940–1945* (Berlin: Rowohlt, 2003). For a fine resumé of the German victimization debates ignited by the approach of the sixtieth anniversary of the war's end, see Robert G. Moeller, "Germans as Victims? Thoughts on a Post-Cold War

History of World War II's Legacies," *History and Memory* 17, no. 1/2 (Fall 2005): 147–94. For discussion of this perception of defeated Germans as "sullen" and un-regenerate, see for example, Grossmann, *Jews, Germans, and Allies*, ch.1.

34. Moses Moskowitz, "The Germans and the Jews: The Postwar Report. The Enigma of German Irresponsibility," *Commentary* 2 (1946): 7–14.

35. See for example, "Feeding," S-401 Box 7, File 1, UNRRA Archives.

36. These scenes are recorded in numerous Army and JDC (Joint) newsreels and films. See the Steven Spielberg Video and Film Archive of the United States Holocaust Memorial Museum.

37. See for example, 294.2 MK 483. Roll 61. Folder 850, *Farflegungsamt* Landsberg DP Camp, YIVO.

38. See Eide, "The Human Right to Adequate Food and Freedom from Hunger."

39. See Lawrence James Haddad and Arne Oshaug, "How Does the Human Rights Perspective Help to Shape the Food and Nutrition Policy Research Agenda?" International Food Policy research Institute, Food Consumption and Nutrition Division (FCND) Discussion Paper Nr. 56, February 1999.

40. Kathryn Hulme, *The Wild Place* (Boston: Little Brown, 1953), 211–12.

41. Ibid.

42. Notes on hunger and work strike of all 3441 Jews in Föhrenwald on November 15, 1945, DPG 294.2/584/MK483/R44, p. 36, YIVO.

43. Stefi Pedersen, "Reaching Safety," in H. B. M Murphy, *Flight and Resettlement*, with contributions by Eduard Bakis, Miriam L. Gaertner, F. F. Kino, Stefi Pedersen, Maria Pfister-Ammende, Maud Bülbring, Louise Pinsky, Sal A. Prins, Esther Ryssdal, Henri Stern, Libuse Tyhurst, Elisabeth Nagy (Paris: UNESCO, 1955), 41.

44. H. B. M. Murphy, "The Camps," in Murphy, *Flight and Resettlement*, 59. On the not dissimilar reactions of social workers to survivors who reached the United States, see Beth D. Cohen, *Case Closed: Holocaust Survivors in Postwar America* (New Brunswick, NJ: Rutgers University Press, 2007). On the role of social workers and psychologists in Europe, see Tara Zahra, "'The Psychological Marshall Plan': Displacement, Gender, and Human Rights after World War II," *Central European History* 44, no. 1:37–62 and her *Lost Children: Displaced Families and the Aftershocks of World War II in Europe* (Cambridge, MA: Harvard University Press, 2011).

45. See for example, "Feeding," S-401 Box 7, File 1, UNRRA Archives.

46. Marie Syrkin, *The State of the Jews* (Washington, DC: New Republic Books, 1980), 46.

47. Oral history interview with Elizabeth Muskal, Yonkers, New York, June 16, 2003.

48. See Daniel Cohen, "Remembering Post-War Displaced Persons: From Omission to Resurrection," in *Enlarging European Memory: Migration Movements in Historical Perspective*, ed. Mareike König and Rainer Ohliger (Ostfildern: Thorbecke Verlag, 2006), 87–97.

49. On the impact of the Jewish Holocaust experience on notions of human rights and the the Universal Declaration of Human Rights, see for example the journal *Commentary* from1945 to 1950 and *Contemporary Jewish Record* 8 (1945): 207–9. For analysis of these debates and the role of Jewish public intellectuals in them, see especially Mazower, *No Enchanted Palace*, 104–48. See also Daniel Cohen, "The 'Human Rights Revolution' at Work: Displaced Persons in Post-War Europe," in *Human Rights in the Twentieth Century*, ed. Stefan-Ludwig Hoffmann (New York: Cambridge University Press, 2010) and his new book, *Europe's Displaced Persons: Refugees in the Postwar Order* (New York: Oxford University Press, 2011); also Rainer Huhle, "'Jewish Rights are Human Rights': Jewish Contributions and Controversies in the International Establishment of Human Rights after 1945," in *Human Rights and History: A Challenge for Education*, ed. Rainer Huhle (Berlin: Foundation Remembrance, Responsibility and Future, 2010), 37–49; on claims to food see Weinreb, "Matters of Taste."

50. See the astute discussion of rights versus duties and the universal versus the particular in Kenneth Cmiel, "Review Essay: The Recent History of Human Rights," *American Historical Review* 109, no. 1 (February 2004): 117–35.

51. Hannah Arendt, *Origins of Totalitarianism* (Cleveland, OH: World Publishing Company, 1958), 269. As Mark Mazower pointed out in his "The Strange Triumph of Human Rights, 1933–1950," *Historical Journal* 47 (2004): 379–98, the Universal Declaration of Human Rights actually represented a weakening of international enforcement authority compared to the post–World War I League of Nations system of collective minority rights, but this shift to declaration without enforcement was probably the necessary price of both U.S. and Soviet support for passage.

52. See for example, Dr. Birgit Toebes, "Human Rights, Health, and Nutrition," Abraham Horwitz lecture, *ACC-SCN Monitor*, no. 18 (1999).

53. On Zionism and the DPs, see especially the fine account by Zeev Mankowitz, *Life Between Memory and Hope: The Survivors of the Holocaust in Occupied Germany* (Cambridge: Cambridge University Press, 2002). For an interesting analysis of the possible benefits of statelessness for efforts by both Jewish and non-Jewish DPs to claim political and cultural space and gain political agency in occupied Germany, see Anna Marta Holian, *Between National Socialism and Soviet Communism: Displaced Persons in Postwar Germany* (Ann Arbor: University of Michigan Press, 2011).

6

ARE WOMEN "HUMAN"?

The UN and the Struggle to Recognize Women's Rights as Human Rights

ALLIDA BLACK

At 1 a.m., December 10, 1948, representatives of the fifty-six member states of the United Nations gathered in the Palais de Chaillot to decide whether the declaration of human rights it had commissioned should be approved.[1] After four and a half hours of debate, during which delegates from thirty-four nations spoke, members of the General Assembly finally cast their votes. Drafting the declaration had been a torturous but inclusive process, spanning almost three years, involving eighty-five committee meetings, where delegates from eighteen states reviewed 168 resolutions and spent thousands of hours, debating, stonewalling, and haranguing one another on what human rights meant, who had them, what obligations states had to guarantee them, and what the United Nations should do when states did not act. After voting on each of its thirty articles, the General Assembly passed the Universal Declaration of Human Rights (UDHR) by a vote of forty-eight to zero with eight abstentions.[2]

The UDHR revolutionized human rights. It not only inspired a powerful vision of equality, security, and respect for all the world's citizens but prompted a new, bold interpretation of international law that in turn gave women a powerful tool to use in their campaign for equal political and economic rights, social status, and full citizenship.

Yet, as this article details, this was a torturous process.

Eleanor Roosevelt (ER) hoped the power of a shared body of rights could eventually trump the fears and turf battles that kept people apart. She hoped the ideals the Declaration proclaimed would goad citizens and nations to action. But, at the same time, she remained realistic about the Declaration's major limitation—its inability to force government to act. "On the whole I think it is good as a declaration of rights to which all men may aspire and we should try to achieve," she wrote the night before the General Assembly vote. "It has no legal value but should carry moral weight."[3]

Although ER saw the UN craft some legally binding safeguards before she died in 1962, it would take several decades for the Commission on the Status of Women (CSW) and their nongovernmental organization partners (NGOs) to conceptualize the women's human rights agenda, develop measurable plans of action, and secure the international covenants necessary to enforce the UN's interpretation of "fundamental human rights" and expand them to include women's rights.

Despite the intermediate steps it took to address women's political rights, the UN waited until 1972 to give serious consideration to the totality of women's rights. That year, it designated 1975 as International Women's Year and empowered the CSW to convene the first World Conference on Women. Yet it took five international conferences, the diligent, creative advocacy of both the CSW and women's NGOs, and the end of the Cold War to force the Human Rights Commission (HRC) and the UN to accept that "women's rights are human rights and human rights are women's rights."[4]

This article traces the rise of women's rights and Eleanor Roosevelt's role in it. It argues that, despite the criticism she has received from historians for not insisting that women have a separate commission within the UN, ER knew what she was doing. Her shrewd understanding of the internal workings of the UN and her fundamental, real-world interpretation of power and politics showed her that if women's voices were relegated to a commission targeted to address women's concerns, women's voices would be marginalized and the scope of their concerns confined to the traditional feminine realm. In short, ER understood that rights are initially defined by those sitting at the negotiating table, and until women held positions of power within both mainstream organizations and nongovernmental organizations challenging those mainstream bodies to respect women, change would be slow.

Eleanor Roosevelt, the Human Rights Commission, and the Universal Declaration of Human Rights

In June 1945, after much pressure from nongovernmental organizations and political activists, the United Nations Planning Conference meeting in San Francisco approved the United Nations Charter. This standard-setting call to action reaffirmed the UN's "faith in fundamental human rights, in the dignity and worth of the human person, [and] in the equal rights of men and women." It called on member states "to promote social progress and better standards of life in larger freedom" and to act either independently or in concert with the United Nations to defend these "fundamental human rights." However, although it professed and encouraged "respect for human rights and for fundamental freedoms for all without distinction as to race, sex, language, or religion" and authorized the creation of a commission to promote human rights, it did not define these rights.[5] That task initially fell to the Human Rights Commission.

ER did not expect to join the HRC, much less become its first chair. She thought she would dedicate her energies to the refugee crisis and other specific issues she would confront as US representative to the Committee on Social, Humanitarian and Cultural Concerns. Yet after her very public and very effective rebuke of Soviet repatriation policy, she suddenly found herself appointed to the yet to be convened Human Rights Commission. At the HRC's first meeting, Henri Laugier, the assistant secretary general for social affairs and convener of the nuclear commission on human rights, appointed ER chair of the formal Human Rights Commission. Within weeks, as the HRC accepted the General Assembly's request to craft an international bill of rights, the committee turned to ER to chair the subcommittee charged with drafting a human rights declaration.

Against the backdrop of an escalating Cold War, ER mediated between delegates who held conflicting beliefs on the role of government, the responsibilities of citizenship, private property, God, marriage, race, the fundamental nature of humankind, and women's economic and political status. In the process, she marshaled her unique array of tools—her daily nationally syndicated newspaper column, her monthly question and answer column, her radio show, and her national lecture tour—to convince the State Department that human rights included economic and social rights, as well as political and civil rights, and to sustain the public support necessary to shepherd the declaration through various iterations, political and diplomatic roadblocks, and an often obstreperous Department of State.[6]

Most histories of the UDHR highlight Eleanor Roosevelt's opposition to the establishment of a separate commission for women's rights and her refusal to interpret the word "brotherhood" as potentially undermining women's human rights. They argue that the woman most responsible for the UDHR's creation and adoption shortchanged women.[7]

A closer examination of ER's actions depicts a more complicated portrait—one that documents her commitment to women's rights as human rights and her firm belief that for women to exert influence on policy and protect their rights, they must be at the negotiating table rather than caucusing amongst themselves. ER believed that "women must learn to play the game as men do." They needed to develop the "banded unity" necessary to deal "with the bosses" and "deliver" votes. They must abandon "helplessness" and "incoherent anarchy" that prompted them to embrace separatism, and "learn to play the game." She insisted:

> If women believe they have a right and duty in political life today, they must learn to talk the language of men. They must not only master the phraseology, but also understand the machinery which men have built through years of practical experience. Against the men bosses there must be women bosses who can talk as equals, with the backing of a coherent organization of women voters behind them.[8]

Only then could women set the agenda and rewrite the rules.

ER's experiences with labor, women's and civil rights organizations, as well as political parties reinforced this view. As she worked to bring women and other reformers into the New York State and federal governments, she learned that to succeed she needed to find both staff support to help craft policy and exert public pressure to implement it. Her experiences with party, civil rights, labor, and women's coalitions taught her which tactics worked and which were destined to fail. By 1940, her political advice to women had evolved significantly. "It seems to me the only way for women to grow," she wrote, is that:

> Women must become more conscious of themselves as women and of their ability to function as a group. At the same time they must try to wipe from men's consciousness the need to consider them as a group or as women in their everyday activities, especially as workers in industry or the professions.[9]

Thus, by the time ER joined the UN in 1946, she not only recognized the important voice women would bring to the organization, but she also had a highly honed strategy of how best to achieve her goals.

Moreover, she strove to get more women included in the UN. As the State Department selected delegates, she worked closely with Democratic National Committee leader Gladys Tillett to get more women appointed to the U.S. delegation to the United Nations Conference. Her passion for her new role at the UN was obvious to all observers. Martha Strayer of the *Washington Daily News* noted, "Mrs. Roosevelt was interested in the organization of the United Nations more keenly than she had been in anything since the early days of the New Deal."[10] And in what would be her final press conference as First Lady, ER again reiterated her strong support for the five women's organizations scheduled to attend the San Francisco meeting and the impact they could have on the deliberations.[11]

Even FDR's sudden death did not mitigate her interest. Although family matters dictated that she remain home in Hyde Park, she confessed to a colleague that she wished she could join the U.S. delegation to the San Francisco assembly. Furthermore, she followed deliberations closely and and stayed in touch with Secretary of State Stettinius throughout the negotiations.[12]

ER even viewed her appointment to the U.S. delegation to the United Nations in December 1945 as more of a tribute to her husband and as a major step for women, rather than a recognition of her diplomatic leadership.[13] She told readers of her daily column that "being the only woman delegate from this country" made her "feel a great responsibility to . . . the women of my own country."[14] She later confessed in her autobiography that one of the reasons she worked so hard was that she knew that if she made a mistake, it would reverberate so loudly that it would give her male colleagues a potent example to use in their not-too-secret campaign to marginalize women. And when John Foster Dulles finally realized her skills and apologized for the dismissive remarks he so often made about her, she told a dear friend "against the odds, women inch forward, but I am rather too old to be carrying on the fight."[15]

ER made her opposition to a separate women's committee within the United Nations organizational structure well known to both the press and the delegates.[16] As soon as she arrived in London the following January for the General Assembly meeting, leaders of British and American women's organizations lobbied ER to support such a committee, but she did not commit because, as she told a friend, "I don't think it should be done but I must, of course, look into it."[17]

Two days later, she made her decision public, writing in "My Day":

The women evidently want to prevail on the Economic and Social Council to set up a special commission composed of women which would not be considered as a specialized agency but would have a closer relationship to the Council . . . I can quite see that a commission representing many women's organizations throughout the world might speak for a very great number of women, but I think they should be treated on the same basis as other specialized agencies. Otherwise, an infinite number of similar groups would be demanding special recognition and special privileges in their relationship to the United Nations—a situation which would result in chaos. I think we should make a very great effort to live up to the sections in the Charter which provide for complete equality. I am sorry that Governments in all parts of the world have not seen fit to send more women as delegates, alternates or advisers to the Assembly, and I think it is in these positions that the women of every nation should work to see that equality exists.[18]

The column generated such intense response among "various" women's groups that ER returned to "My Day" three days later to clarify her position:

> I myself believe the important thing is to stress the attitude taken in the very beginning of the UNO Charter, which reaffirms "faith in fundamental human rights, in the dignity and worth of the human person, in the equal rights of men and women and of nations large and small."

"This really means," she concluded, "that women should come in on an equal basis—not even as specialized groups, unless they are representing some particular objective. Their influence should be felt as delegates, alternates and advisers."[19] In short, to be effective, women must be at the table rather than outside looking in and fighting to get a seat in the back corner.

Not all of the women delegates agreed with ER. The women delegates from Brazil, Mexico, and the Dominican Republic who had convinced the San Francisco conference to include sex as a specific human rights category in the UN Charter now pressured the first General Assembly to establish a specific women's commission to link women's rights with human rights.[20] Although the assembly rejected their request for an independent body, the Economic and Social Council (ECOSOC) recommended a Sub-commission on the Status of Women within the Human Rights Commission and instructed the women to work with HRC director John Humphrey to "submit proposals, recommendations and reports to the Commission on Human Rights."[21] The women responded by urging ECOSOC to approve "four immediate tasks": the creation of a new Secretariat office on women managed by a woman director; the completion of the international comprehensive study of laws related to women, which had been initiated by the League of Nations; promotion by all UN agencies of "equal educational opportunity"; and convening a UN-sponsored worldwide conference on women's concerns.

ER, who had a nonvoting seat on the subcommission, worked to shape the group and the scope of its activities. She objected to the worldwide conference and wanted the study to be a more tightly focused document rather than a laundry list detailing every instance of discrimination women faced in the public and private spheres.[22]

Bodil Begtrup, who chaired the subcommission, objected strongly to both ER's recommendations and Humphrey's direction and launched a full-scale campaign to have ECOSOC upgrade the women's group to a free-standing commission on the status of women. When Begtrup agreed to drop the call for an international woman's conference, ER dropped her opposition to a free-standing commission. June 14, 1946, with ER and Begtrup on board, ECOSOC approved an independent Commission on the Status of Women (CSW) and instructed it to "elevate the equal rights and human rights status of women, irrespective of nationality, race, language, or religion, in order to achieve equality with men in all fields of human enterprise and to eliminate all discrimination against women in statutory law, legal maxims or rules, or in interpretation of customary law."[23]

No longer officially tied to the HRC, CSW no longer consulted regularly with that commission and expected the HRC to make consistent overtures to them. When that did not happen, CSW complained to ECOSOC about the HRC's alleged overlooking of women's issues. On December 2, 1947, ECOSOC then instructed the HRC to inform the CSW whenever women's issues were to be discussed.

Meanwhile, ER focused on increasing the number of women delegates to the UN and its regulatory agencies and crafting a declaration of human rights and mechanisms to enforce its principles. She continued to believe that the best way to handle the horrors of war, famine, prejudice, and fear inflicted on women was to present them—as well as the men in their communities—a vision of a world that could stand up to the darkness and fear of the Holocaust, the atomic bomb, the economic crisis, and discrimination generated.[24]

In June 1947, the HRC drafting subcommittee gathered in Lake Success, New York, to review the draft declaration Humphrey had prepared for their review. Politics dominated the deliberations. Britain's delegation wanted a legally binding document (presumably focusing on political and civil rights). The Soviets objected to provisions respecting civil liberties and the right to nationality and wanted economic rights discussed in greater detail. ER—concerned that the United States would not adopt a legally binding document and convinced that the world needed the UN to act quickly to offset fear and despair—urged her colleagues to draft both a human rights declaration and the human rights covenant necessary to enforce the declaration's principles.

On June 16, the Soviets switched their focus away from civil liberties to gender. Although Article 6 of the proposed draft noted that "every one is entitled to the rights and freedoms set forth in this Declaration, without distinction as to race, sex, language or religion," Article 1, the article which set the declaration's tone and defined its view of human nature, used the term "all men."[25]

Vladimir Kortesky, the Soviet delegate, objected and insisted that the phrase "all men" eliminated "half of the human species." He then urged that Article 122 of the Soviet Constitution (which "not only . . . stated that women had equal rights in all fields," but "enumerated" the "various ways" this principle could "be put into effect") be included to insure "the rights of women."[26] ER disagreed. "I have always considered myself a feminist but I really would have no objection to the use of the word as the Committee sees fit."[27]

Yet when the Lake Success draft was submitted to the full commission for consideration in Geneva that fall, Article 1 read: "All human beings are born free and equal in dignity and in rights. They are endowed with reason and conscience, and should act towards one another like brothers." How this change occurred is not clear. As the HRC debated the draft, Hansa Mehta, the delegate from India, expressed her dislike of "the wording 'all men'" and "'should act . . . like brothers'" because terms "might be interpreted to exclude women, and were out of date." Nevertheless, after debating Metha's motion, translation problems, and intent, the HRC voted to adopt "all men" and to attach a special note to Article 1 declaring that "all men" meant "all people." Meanwhile, the Secretary-General forwarded the CSW's draft of Article 1 that used "all people" instead of "all men" and "in the spirit of brotherhood" instead of "like brothers." As debate continued in subsequent sessions, the HRC embraced "all people, men and women," discounting Soviet insistence that it would be impossible to translate into Russian. Yet when the final draft reached the full Human Rights Commission for a vote, Article 1 began "all human beings." No one objected; the HRC adopted the draft and forwarded it to ECOSOC for adoption.[28]

Clearly, Eleanor Roosevelt had an encompassing interpretation of "men," "brotherhood," and "people." She believed the subsequent articles reinforced her interpretation and wanted the declaration to be as clear in other languages as it was in English. Does her position infer that she accepted "sexist implications" to the UDHR? No. It means that she did not realize the way, decades later, it would still be used to give lip service to women and their concerns.

As chair of both the Human Rights Commission and its drafting subcommittee, ER helped craft articles that began with "no one shall be" or "'everyone." She navigated increasingly intense domestic and international political turf battles to craft a declaration guaranteeing women the right to life, liberty, and security of person (Article 3); the right to be recognized as a person before the law (Article 6); the right to equal protection against any discrimination in violation of this declaration (Article 7); the right to marry and have equal rights during the marriage and "its dissolution" (Article 16); the right to own property (Article 17); the right to vote and hold elected office (Article 21); the right to equal pay for equal work (Article 23); the right to be a mother and have one's children respected and protected (Article 25); and the right to education (Article 26). Moreover, she did so anticipating and accepting the intense opposition of the American Bar Association and other prominent legal and political groups. She would spend the rest of her life—risking her life and her income—promoting the UDHR and urging the ratifications of the covenants it generated.

ER left the UN on January 3, 1953. President-elect Dwight Eisenhower, who objected to the UDHR, did not want her to continue to represent the United States on the Human Rights Commission. She spent her last day at the UN advocating for the Convention on the Political Rights of Women and making the same argument she made when she entered it—that women must vote, hold office, and represent their nations at the UN. She concluded:

> I hope that within the next few years we will find that equal suffrage has been granted to women everywhere, including two areas—Libya and Eritrea—in which the United Nations has a special interest. I hope also that in the next session of the General Assembly and in those to follow we will find the promise of this convention reflected in increasing recognition for women in high posts in all governments and as representatives in the United Nations.[29]

The Commission on the Status of Women and Nongovernmental Organizations Take the Stage

The CSW, like the UN itself, viewed human rights as new tools to use to fight traditional (i.e., political and civil) discrimination. While the UN used the UDHR as a tool to assess government's treatment of its citizens and protect activists working to build democratic governments, the CSW saw the Declaration as a major tool to combat laws that discriminated against women. Using the UDHR as its rallying point, the CSW spurred the drafting and adoption of the Convention on the Political Rights of Women (1952);

the Convention on the Nationality of Married Women (1957); and the Convention on Consent to Marriage, Minimum Age for Marriage, and Registration of Marriages (1962). In short, as Margaret Bruce, chief of the UN section on the Status of Women, noted, throughout the 1950s and early 1960s, "the most spectacular progress" in women's rights came "in the political field."

While the UN avoided controversy by focusing on traditional women's rights issues (political and civil rights), its affiliated organizations began to address violations outside the ballot box (economic, social, and cultural rights). In 1951, as the UN and the CSW worked for the right to vote and hold office, the International Labour Organization (ILO) focused on equal pay for equal work and adopted its Convention on Equal Renumeration for Men and Women Workers. Seven years later, the ILO reinforced that convention by adopting a new convention prohibiting discrimination in employment and occupation. By the end of the decade, the United Nations Educational, Scientific and Cultural Organization (UNESCO) joined the women's rights campaign by endorsing a Convention against Discrimination in Education.

Despite the progress these conventions represented, all of these actions occurred outside the Human Rights Commission and thus marginalized women's rights as issues not worthy of the commission's time and deliberation.

This began to change when the UN adopted the Covenants on Political and Civil Rights and Economic, Social and Cultural Rights on December 16, 1966. Almost twenty years after Eleanor Roosevelt and the Human Rights Commission initiated their work, the General Assembly adopted legally binding agreements authorizing the HRC to review reports detailing human rights violations, "to make general comments as it may consider appropriate," to request additional information from offending states, and to assess that state's progress in addressing the complaints against it. As dramatic a change as the covenants introduced, however, three equally dramatic limitations remained. First, the HRC could not "judge" the state's progress in addressing these issues nor make specific recommendations as to what actions states should take to address their violations. Second, the UN focused on legal rather than de facto discrimination and thus neglected discrimination that women encountered from common law, cultural practices, and other extralegal forces.[30] Third, and perhaps most important, the Covenant on Economic, Social and Cultural Rights did not authorize any agency to address its findings, could only review reports submitted to it, and respond with "recommendations of a general nature."[31]

All the while, human rights got caught in the political crossfire of the escalating Cold War. The United States and the Chinese grew increasingly mired in Vietnam, and the Soviets and Chinese challenged Western influence in the new postcolonial nations. Calls to address economic and social rights—especially the rights to food, shelter, health, and work—seemed "suspect" to many in the noncommunist West. As a result, as Charlotte Bunch notes, "human rights bodies dominated by western conceptions of human rights priorities focused on violations within the civil and political realm—the 'public' sphere." This meant that human rights policies whipsawed women. Already battling the barriers public-private spheres posed to equal treatment, "the predominance of the civil and political rights within human rights organizations eclipsed" any assessment of the barriers to equal social and economic conditions essential to full "exercise of civil and political rights and participation in public life." In short, human rights investigations into women's legal status focused on "certain areas . . . considered to be women's rights (such as family rights and the right to vote) rather than the totality of human rights protected under the Covenant."[32]

Increasingly women, inside and outside the UN, did not see women's rights and human rights as an either/or proposition. In 1963, Polish, Ghanian, and Mexican delegates to the CSW, dissatisfied with the loopholes in the covenants, began drafting a declaration that targeted this public-private dilemma. After the CSW adopted the draft, it launched a public education campaign to generate international support to force the UN to focus—albeit briefly—on the discriminatory barriers women face. Four years later, the General Assembly adopted the Declaration on the Elimination of Discrimination against Women (DEDAW) in 1967. CSW then shifted its focus to drafting a legally binding covenant—or convention—that could enforce the principles articulated in the declaration.

Outside the UN, many women who knew nothing about the CSW or its declaration began "examining the pervasiveness of sex discrimination at all levels of society and strategizing as to the most effective means to overcome it." By 1970, a new international women's movement flourished on college campuses; business and professional communities; as well as within the labor, art, and civil rights communities. Refusing to distinguish between the personal and public spheres, they insisted that "the personal is political."[33]

Yet these two groups—the CSW and the newly formed feminist organizations—worked in their own separate sectors until 1975 when five thousand women traveled to Mexico City to attend the first UN Conference on Women. Even though the CSW led the effort to have the UN designate 1975 as International Women's Year and secured UN support for the conference, it quickly became apparent that the NGO women wanted to have their say as well. After overcoming intense Cold War sparring over development and other socioeconomic policies, the conferees crafted an ambitious World Plan of Action. Declaring "women will emerge as a powerful revolutionary social force," the plan called for verifiable progress in women's literacy and civic education, women's participation in policymaking, "recognition of the economic value of women's work in the home," women's access to health education and health services, and rural women's access to the "modern rural technology" necessary to "help reduce the heavy workload of women." It also empowered the women's NGO community by urging "the promotion of women's organizations" and "the active involvement of non-governmental women's organizations" in UN efforts to secure these benchmarks.[34]

The plan's most effective planks, however, did not deal with meeting minimum metrics. It called for a UN proclamation declaring 1975–1985 to be the UN Decade for Women, UN support for additional international women's conferences in 1980 and 1985, the establishment of a UN fund dedicated to advancing women women's rights and gender equality (UNIFEM), and the drafting of a Convention to End All Forms of Discrimination against Women (CEDAW) to be presented at the 1980 conference in Copenhagen. In short, the women's demand for institutional support created the machinery that gave women the opportunity to debate, strategize, and organize.

The UN Decade for Women gave both the CSW and the women's NGO community unique venues outside their home environments where they could meet as equals, discuss strategies, debate priorities, expand their network, and develop the platform to make their concerns known. There they explored how existing human rights practices and definitions "fail to account for the ways in which already recognized human rights abuses often affect women differently because of their gender." Working together, women human rights activists and women's rights leaders encouraged each other to take "the double shift" critical to transcending the public-private sphere gap and to crafting a new lens through which to view women's lives.

By the time more than ten thousand women and men convened in Copenhagen in 1980 for the Second World Conference on Women, the new international women's movement had inspired an "explosion" of groups dedicated to improving women's lives. A far more diverse group attended the Copenhagen conference, and stark regional divisions soon surfaced around the conference's major theme—women and development. Men led most of the government delegations and did not support a gendered approach to development. Plus, women from economically privileged and powerful nations had sustained intense, painful, and, in the case of Middle Eastern nations, volatile conversations with women from nations whose economies were either dominated by Western powers or were so unstable that development meant securing enough food and wages to remain alive. Eventually some overcame political and regional differences enough to acknowledge that while gender discrimination placed intense barriers to women's economic security, other factors such as nationality, race, class, and region also played major roles in shaping women's economic lives.

Moreover, although they did not yet realize its power, by Copenhagen, women had secured the second legal tool essential to implementing their platform—CEDAW. The General Assembly had adopted CEDAW in 1979 by a vote of 130 to 0, with ten nations abstaining. At the same time, "the Assembly expressed the hope that the Convention would come into force at an early date and requested the Secretary-General to present the text of the Convention to the mid-decade World Conference of the United Nations Decade for Women."[35]

CSW's thirteen-year campaign for a legally enforceable covenant had paid off. The Copenhagen delegates now had a framework they could soon use both for examining the "human rights framework through a gender lens, and describing women's lives through a human rights framework"[36] and for protecting those who risked their lives to defend women's human rights—those who exposed the abuses women suffered, who worked with decision makers to address these issues, and who delivered essential legal and social services.[37] Indeed, CSW so realized the central importance CEDAW would have in their work that they arranged a dramatic signing ceremony in the midst of the Copenhagen conference where sixty-four states signed the convention and two presented their instruments of ratification. Women's human rights advocates embraced CEDAW with passion and efficiency and secured, in record time, the eighteen additional ratifications CEDAW needed to be enforced. By September 1981, the convention was legally enforceable.

CEDAW held the UN, governments, and human rights communities accountable to apply the Universal Declaration of Human Rights and its covenants to women and to implement the Declaration to End Discrimination Against Women. Declaring that "extensive discrimination against women continues to exist," it then defined discrimination as:

> Any distinction, exclusion or restriction made on the basis of sex which has the effect or purpose of impairing or nullifying the recognition, enjoyment or exercise by women, irrespective of their marital status, on a basis of equality

of men and women, of human rights and fundamental freedoms in the political, economic, social, cultural, civil or any other field.

Unlike previous conventions, CEDAW mandated:

> States Parties shall take in all fields, in particular in the political, social, eco-
> nomic and cultural fields, all appropriate measures, including legislation, to
> ensure the full development and advancement of women, for the purpose of
> guaranteeing them the exercise and enjoyment of human rights and funda-
> mental freedoms on a basis of equality with men.[38]

Furthermore, it required states to "condemn discrimination against
women in all its forms, agree to pursue by all appropriate means and without delay a policy of eliminating discrimination against women" by:

> Incorporating "the principle of the equality of men and women in their na-
> tional constitutions or other appropriate legislation," and ensuring "through
> law and other appropriate means, the practical realization of this principle";
>   Eliminating "all acts of discrimination against women by persons, organi-
> zations and enterprises"; and
>   Establishing tribunals and other legal bodies necessary "to ensure the
> effective protection of women against discrimination.[39]

Equally important, Part V established the CEDAW Committee, twenty-
three "experts" of "high moral standard and competence" nominated by
their governments and approved by the UN, to monitor states' behavior and
facilitate the treaty's implementation. With a committee modeled after the
Human Rights Committee and the Committee on the Elimination of Racial
Discrimination, women now had the power to assess a state's behavior and
to enforce its compliance with the CEDAW mandate.

Yet it took a little more than a decade for CEDAW's influence to be felt.
As one long-serving CEDAW Committee member noted, "for some time"
human rights organizations viewed the committee as their "poor relative."
Therefore, as the Covenant on Economic, Social and Cultural Rights also
addressed some of the concerns CEDAW addressed, the states opted to
follow its weaker enforcement protocols—that efforts to eliminate discrimination "needed only to be progressively implemented rather than 'without
delay' as Article 2" required.[40]

CSW and their NGO allies, however, refused to accept this approach
and by the time they reconvened for the Third World Conference on

Women, a vibrant transnational women's movement insisted that "women can hold their governments accountable" for the positions CEDAW detailed. In July 1985, approximately 15,000 women (2000 delegates and more than 13,000 NGO representatives from 150 nations) traveled to Nairobi to participate in 1,198 planned workshops and in another 300-plus spontaneous discussions convened by the NGO Planning Committee. Perhaps the most significant increase, however, occurred within the delegations themselves as, for the first time, governments appointed more women than men to chair their delegations.

Also unlike Copenhagen, where regional and racial differences threatened conference consensus, the Nairobi conference used "the framework of the United Nations and the goals of the UN Charter of equality, development and peace" to examine discrimination against women and women's rights. This wider framework gave women new tools to assess their progress to date and to confront those who refused to recognize their rights in the future.

As they reflected on their experiences and debated how best to advance women's security and draft the Nairobi plan of action, the Nairobi Forward-Looking Strategies, the women delegates made three significant contributions to the international women's agenda. First, women's economic security did not just depend upon eliminating discriminatory policies and customs that targeted women. Programs advancing women's economic security must also assess how nationality, region, class, and race reinforce discrimination. Second, that violence against women—whether inflicted and supported by custom (female genital mutilation), used as a weapon of war (rape), or promoted as a business venture (trafficking and sexual slavery)—undermined any effort toward peace. And, finally, in order for women to achieve full equality, governments must not only mainstream women's concerns but also establish "high-level institutional mechanisms to monitor and implement progress towards equality in all sectors."[41]

By focusing on the UDHR, the covenants, and CEDAW, the Nairobi conference "legitimized" the goals these instruments presented "as applicable to women worldwide and elaborated them to encompass women's concerns."[42] The delegates' experience with and understanding of apartheid and civil wars taught them how violence against women posed a grave "obstacle to peace." Thus, as they prepared the conference's outcome document, the Nairobi Forward-looking Strategies, the delegates not only addressed the discrimination women encountered in peacetime but also graphically detailed the specific assaults inflicted on women in wartime and called for specific measures to address these violent crimes.[43] As one Kenyan delegate recalled, "it was at the Nairobi Conference in 1985 that the domestication of CEDAW was seen as an important step towards the implementation of the rights for women."[44]

The Vienna and Beijing Conferences: Governments Join the Campaign

As no Fourth World Conference for Women was planned for 1990, the UN Decade for Women concluded with the Nairobi conference. Determined to keep the momentum going, NGOs convened local, regional, and national meetings in the following year. When in 1991 the UN announced plans for a human rights conference in Vienna and left women's rights off the conference agenda, NGOs promptly organized to secure a prominent place for women's human rights on the conference program. The Center for Women's Global Leadership convened the Global Campaign for Women's Human Rights, a coalition of regional, national, and international women's organizations determined to correct the Vienna oversight. Global Campaign members then launched a "16 Day Campaign" (the period between the UN designated International Violence Against Women Day and International Human Rights Day) to secure signatures on its petition demanding that the UN "comprehensively address women's human rights at every level" of the Vienna proceedings and recognize that "gender violence, a universal phenomenon which takes many forms across culture, race and class, as a violation of human rights requiring immediate action." By the end of 1991, more than a half-million women, representing 1000 organizations in 124 countries, signed the petition. In 1992, women secured their space on the agenda.[45]

Geraldine Ferraro, the first woman to run for vice president of the United States on a major party ticket, and chair of the U.S. delegation in Vienna, addressed the issue of violence against women in a *New York Times* editorial on June 13, 1993, the day the conference opened.

> Several years ago, women's rights advocates worldwide began to turn up at the same conventions, seminars, university settings, diplomatic receptions and refugee centers. They had many different problems. But as they listened to one another, they saw they had at least one concern in common that no international organization was talking about: violence against women. Female infanticide. Genital Mutilation. Wife murder. Sex tourism. Rape. Assault. Discrimination in health care. Barriers to political social and economic equality that make millions of women less than third-class citizens.

As they talked, the women made a global connection: these weren't scattered "women's problems," not "minor" abuses that some governments has passed to a study commission and forgotten. These women recognized that gender-based violence as a matter of fundamental human rights.

Drawing attention to "the systematic rapes" of women in the Bosnian war and the "quieter rapes" and abuses that occurred daily around the world, Ferraro declared that the Global Campaign for Women's Human Rights, an international coalition of more than 950 organizations, would "press" the Vienna conference to finally "denounce abuse of women as abuse of human rights."[46]

The women's campaign had targeted the human rights conference because it knew that a "document" generated by that body "saying something about women's human rights that will legitimize our next step." It had prepared so well that even the press called the women "here to promote women's human rights . . . the strongest and most effective lobby."[47] Their work paid off. The Vienna Declaration and Programme of Action not only addressed women's rights and domestic violence in detail (Section 1.7), it specifically linked women's rights to human rights, declaring:

The human rights of women and of the girl-child are an inalienable, integral and indivisible part of universal human rights. The full and equal participation of women in political, civil, economic, and cultural life, at the national, regional and international levels, and the eradication of all forms of discrimination on grounds of sex are priority objectives of the international community.[48]

Thus, as women prepared for the Fourth World Conference on Women to be held September 1995 in Beijing, they had secured official UN recognition of the framework they first explored in Mexico City twenty years earlier and which the United Nations Charter proclaimed in 1945.

More than forty-five thousand women and men—more than three times the record the Nairobi conference set—convened in and out of Beijing. Concerned that the thousands of activists attending the parallel NGO forum would challenge China's human rights practices, the government relocated the forum to Huariou, a remote location thirty-five miles outside Beijing. The separation energized rather than isolated the attendees and together, the official delegates and NGO activists adopted the Beijing Declaration and Platform for Action.

Yet reaching consensus involved intense negotiations. Conservative groups and the Vatican objected to including planks supporting the right to abortion and family-planning services, as well as rights related to sexuality and gender identity. Many in the U.S. Congress objected to an American delegation traveling to communist China—which had just arrested human rights activist and Chinese expatriate Harry Wu, after he reentered China, and falsely convicted him of espionage—to address women's issues and human rights. Senators Jesse Helms and Phil Gramm told the press that the conference was "shaping up as an unsanctioned festival of anti-family, anti-American sentiment." Furthermore, for the first time, the U.S. ambassador to the UN (who just happened to be a woman) and the First Lady co-chaired the U.S. delegation to the conference.

The world press—and the international women's human rights community —followed these developments closely. Hillary Clinton told her chief of staff that she wanted her remarks "to push the envelope as far as she could on behalf of women and girls." In a speech that reverberated around the world, she threw her unquestioned support behind the conference:

> For too long, the history of women has been a history of silence. Even today, there are those who are trying to silence our words. The voice of this conference and of the women at Huariou must be heard loud and clear.

After denouncing human trafficking, female genital mutilation, specific violent acts against women, and the denial of women's "right to plan their own families," she concluded:

> If there is one message that echoes forth from this conference, let it be that human rights are women's rights and women's rights are human rights, once and for all.[49]

The delegates agreed. Citing the UN Charter, the UDHR, CEDAW and other conventions, the governments signing the Beijing Declaration affirmed that "women's rights are human rights" and pledged themselves "as Governments to implement" the Platform for Action and ensure "that a gender perspective is reflected in all our policies and programmes."[50]

This 223-page Platform for Action, coupled with CEDAW and the Vienna Declaration, defined the contemporary women's human rights agenda. It identified twelve "critical areas of concern" for women (poverty, education and training, health, violence against women, women's human rights, as well as women and armed conflict, women and the economy, women in power and decision-making, governmental and UN mechanisms for the advancement of women, women and the media, women and the environment, and the girl-child) and listed objectives and recommended actions to improve women's access to rights in these areas.

The Platform, like the UDHR, is a declaration, not a covenant, and therefore carries no legal power. However, as the governments who signed the Platform pledged themselves to act, the declaration did, as it continues to do, carry great moral weight. As the Center for Women's Global Leadership notes, "it serves as a policy guide for governments, institutions, private businesses, and UN agencies, and establishes standards by which to judge policies and programs already in place." When governments adopted the Platform, they "strongly committed themselves to addressing obstacles to the advancement and empowerment of women."[51]

Beijing compelled the UN to act. Its third Millennium Development Goal directs its members to take measurable action to "promote gender equality and empower women." The Security Council adopted Resolutions 1325 on Women, Peace & Security, 1820 on Sexual Violence in Conflict, 1888 on protecting women and girls from sexual violence in armed conflict, and 1889 on monitoring efforts to enforce Resolution 1325. The UN Foundation made women and population one of its four investment priorities.

Women, from the UN's inception, have shaped and defined its human rights framework. They led the drafting of the Universal Declaration of Human Rights, insisted on covenants defining and empowering its implementation, and, in the process, gave the world a new vision. In the process, they mastered the halls of diplomacy, developed an energetic global movement, and put discrimination at bay enough to rewrite law and challenge custom. They showed the world that "human rights are too important to be negotiable."[52]

NOTES

1. The UN had fifty-eight member states in December 1948. Honduras and Yemen did not attend the December 9 session.

2. Eight Soviet-aligned nations, who wanted the vote postponed, abstained. General Assembly, 180th Plenary Meeting, Summary Report, E/777, December 9, 1948, 933–34, United Nations Organization, General Assembly Records, Wellesley College.

3. ER to Maude Gray, December 9, 1948, *The Eleanor Roosevelt Papers, Volume I: The Human Rights Years, 1945–1948*, ed. Allida Black (Farmingham, MI: Scribners, 2008).

4. Hillary Rodham Clinton, "Remarks to the 4th UN World Conference on Women," September 5, 1995, Fifth World Conference on Women, http://5wcw.org/docs/Clinton_Speech.html; and Charlotte Bunch and Samantha Frost, "Women's

Human Rights: An Introduction," Center for Women's Global Leadership, http://www.cwgl.rutgers.edu/globalcenter/whr.html (accessed June 29, 2010).

5. United Nations Charter, *Basic Documents in Human Rights,* ed. Ian Brownlie (New York: Oxford University Press, 2000), 3.

6. For examples of ER's mediation see *The Eleanor Roosevelt Papers, Volume I*; and Mary Ann Glendon, *A World Made New: Eleanor Roosevelt and the Universal Declaration of Human Rights* (New York: Random House, 2001).

7. For example see Johannes Morsink, "Women's Rights in the Universal Declaration," *Human Rights Quarterly* 13, no. 2 (May 1991): 229–56; and Roger Normand and Sarah Zaidi, *Human Rights at the UN: The Political History of Universal Justice* (Bloomington: University of Indiana Press, 2008), 277–79.

8. Eleanor Roosevelt, "Women Must Learn to Play the Game as Men Do," *Red Book Magazine*, April 1928, 78–79, 141–42.

9. Eleanor Roosevelt, "Women in Politics," in *What I Hope to Leave Behind: The Essential Writings of Eleanor Roosevelt*, ed. Allida Black (New York: Carlson Publishing, 1995), 258.

10. Martha Strayer Transcript, April 2, 1945, in *The White House Press Conferences of Eleanor Roosevelt*, ed. Maurine Beasley (New York: Garland Publishing, 1983), 213.

11. Ibid.

12. Eleanor Roosevelt, "My Day," May 31 and June 1, 1945; and Edward Stettinius to Eleanor Roosevelt, July 10 and July 26, 1945, *The Eleanor Roosevelt Papers, Vol. I*, 41–46, 59–62.

13. Eleanor Roosevelt, "My Day," December 22, 1945; *The Eleanor Roosevelt Papers, Vol. I*, 159.

14. ER also noted "I know many men are made a little uncomfortable by having women in these positions, but I think the time has come to face the fact that you have to win as many women's votes as you do men's votes and that the Democratic Party probably has more strength among women if it stands as the liberal party and the party of human rights than it has among the men." Eleanor Roosevelt to Robert Hannegan, June 3, 1945, *The Eleanor Roosevelt Papers, Vol. I*, 48.

15. ER to Joe Lash, February 13, 1946, *The Eleanor Roosevelt Papers, Vol. I*, 248–49.

16. ER's advocacy for women to be part of UN leadership drew immediate interest. She had not yet disembarked from her transatlantic voyage to the General Assembly when the press asked what she thought about the "resumption of the old status of a women's committee or of some such body." She promptly replied that she had not "heard any direct suggestion of a specific committee," but left no doubt as to where she stood on the matter. "I should think that if we could bring any question under an existing committee it would be a good idea. I do not like the multiplication of committees as long as some committees are prepared to take up the questions." Memorandum of Press Conference, January 15, 1946, *The Eleanor Roosevelt Papers, Vol. I*, 209.

17. Rather than write daily letters to her close friends, ER decided to keep a diary that her trusted assistant Malvina Thompson would distribute to the small trusted group. Eleanor Roosevelt, London Diary, January 23, 1946, *The Eleanor Roosevelt Papers, Vol. I*, 221.

18. Eleanor Roosevelt, "My Day," January 25, 1946, *The Eleanor Roosevelt Papers, Vol. I*, 223, n.13.

19. Eleanor Roosevelt, "My Day," January 28, 1946, *The Eleanor Roosevelt Papers, Vol. I*, 224, n.13.

20. Arvonne S. Frazer, "Becoming Human: The Origins and Development of Women's Human Rights," *Human Rights Quarterly* 21, no. 4 (November 1999): 886.

21. Johannes Morsink, *The Universal Declaration of Human Rights: Origins, Drafting, and Intent* (Philadelphia: University of Pennsylvania Press, 1999), 230.

22. She supported Carrie Chapman Catt's "anxious" request that an American woman "familiar with the evolution of the rights of women in the English speaking countries" be appointed and recommended Dorothy Kenyon to be that representative. Carrie Chapman Catt to ER, May 7, 1946, *The Eleanor Roosevelt Papers, Vol. I*, 305–8.

23. Margaret E. Galey, "Promoting Nondiscrimination Against Women: The UN Commission on the Status of Women," *International Studies Quarterly* 23, no. 2 (June 1979): 276.

24. In February 1946, ER not only joined the eighteen other women delegates to sign the *Women's Appeal* but used her column to publicize their "call on the Governments of the world to encourage women everywhere to take a more conscious part in national and international affairs," as well as their call "on women to come forward and share in the work of peace and reconstruction as they did in the war and resistance." While she understood "that women in various parts of the world are at different stages of participation in the life of their communities, that some of them are prevented by law from assuming the full rights of citizenship, and that they may therefore see their immediate problems somewhat differently," ER remained optimistic. She urged her fellow women delegates to tell "the women of all our countries" that that the UN offered women "an important opportunity and responsibility"—the opportunity to shape policy and the responsibility to represent women's voices. Eleanor Roosevelt, "My Day," February 8, 1946, *The Eleanor Roosevelt Papers, Vol. I*, 240, n.8.

25. The June 1947 Human Rights Commission Draft read: All men are brothers. Being endowed with reason and conscience, they are members of one family. They are free, and possess equal dignity and rights. Glendon, *A World Made New*, 281.

26. UN Economic and Social Council, *Summary Record*, June 13, 1947, E/CN.4/AC.1/SR.6.

27. Glendon, *A World Made New*, 28 and ibid.

28. Morsink, *Universal Declaration*, 199.

29. A. M. Rosenthal, "2 U.S. Mainstays Bid U.N. Farewell," *New York Times*, December 21, 1952, 1, 4.

30. Laura Reanda, "Human Rights and Women's Rights: The United Nations Approach," *Human Rights Quarterly* 3, no. 2 (May 1981): 14.

31. Ibid. 17.

32. Bunch and Frost, "Women's Human Rights: An Introduction."

33. As Arvonne Fraser correctly notes, the nascent feminist groups "paid no attention to CSW and little to international affairs." It took the "traditional NGOs who lobbied the Commission [and who] were influenced by this new movement" to bridge that gap and bring the outside activism to CSW women determined to combat the same prejudice. Fraser, "Becoming Human,"893.

34. UN, *Report of the World Conference of the International Women's Year*, Mexico City, June 19–July 2, 1975, paragraph 46, E.76.IV.1 (1976).

35. "Short History of the CEDAW Convention," at the UN website, http://www. un.org/womenwatch/daw/cedaw/history.htm (accessed June 28, 2010).

36. Bunch and Frost, "Women's Human Rights: An Introduction."

37. Felice D. Gaer, "Reality Check: Human Rights Nongovernmental Organizations Confront Governments at the United Nations," *Third World Quarterly* 16, no. 3 (September 1995): 393–95.

38. UN, *Convention to End All Forms of Discrimination Against Women*, Article 3, at the UN website, http://www.un.org/womenwatch/daw/cedaw/ (accessed June 29, 2010).

39. UNIFEM, "30 Years: The United Nations Convention to End All Forms of Discrimination Against Women," www.unifem.org/cedaw30/about_cedaw/ (accessed July 5, 2010).

40. Hanna Beate Schopp-Schilling, "Celebration: Twenty-five Years of the Work of the CEDAW Committee," July 23, 2007, at the UN website, http://www.un.org/ womenwatch/daw/cedaw/cedaw25anniversary/HBSS.pdf (accessed July 5, 2010).

41. UNIFEM, "30 Years: The United Nations Convention to End All Forms of Discrimination Against Women."

42. Margaret E. Galey, "The Nairobi Conference: The Powerless Majority," *PS* 19, no. 2 (Spring 1986): 255–65.

43. Ibid, 256.

44. Kathambi Kinoti, "An interview with Dr Jacinta Muteshi of Kenya's National Commission for Gender and Development," June 2006 in *African Women's Engagement with the UN*, Association for Women's Rights in Development, http:// www.awid.org/eng/Issues-and-Analysis/Library/African-Women-s-Engagement-with-the-UN (accessed July 5, 2010).

45. Bunch and Frost, "Women's Human Rights: An Introduction."

46. Geraldine Ferraro, "Human Rights for Women," *New York Times*, June 19, 1993.

47. Alan Riding, "Women Seize Focus at Rights Forum," *New York Times*, June 16, 1993, A3.

48. UN, *Vienna Declaration and Programme of Action*, adopted June 23, 1993, at the UN High Commissioner for Human Rights website, http://www2.ohchr.org/ english/law/vienna.htm (accessed June 29, 2010).

49. Charlotte Bunch and Niamh Reilly, "Demanding Accountability: The Global Campaign and Vienna Tribunal for Women's Human Rights," Center for Women's Global Leadership, http://www.cwgl.rutgers.edu/globalcenter/publications/demand. pdf (accessed July 5, 2010), 14.

50. *Beijing Declaration and Platform for Action*, at the UN website, http://www. un.org/womenwatch/daw/beijing/beijingdeclaration.html (accessed June 29, 2010).

51. Center for Women's Global Leadership, "Beijing +15 Overview and Regional Activities," September 18, 2009, www.cwgl.rutgers.edu/16days/kit09/beijing15.doc (accessed June 29, 2010).

52. Mary Robinson, "Acceptance of the Erasmus Prize," in *Mary Robinson: A Voice for Human Rights*, ed. Kevin Boyle (Philadelphia: University of Pennsylvania Press, 2008), 20.

PART II

The Globalization of Human Rights History

7

IMPERIALISM, SELF-DETERMINATION, AND
THE RISE OF HUMAN RIGHTS

SAMUEL MOYN

How do we answer an Indochinese or an Arab who reminds us that he has seen a lot of our arms but not much of our humanism?
—Maurice Merleau-Ponty, 1946

"All men are created equal, they are endowed by their Creator with certain unalienable rights; among these are Life, Liberty, and the pursuit of Happiness." The famous words are not—at least not directly—from a passage midway through the second paragraph of the American Declaration of Independence of 1776. Instead, they open Ho Chi Minh's Vietnamese Declaration of Independence, issued September 2, 1945, scant weeks after his country's Japanese occupiers had been brought to their knees, and before the bitter reimposition of French colonial rule, with British assistance and American connivance.[1] In fact, as far back as May, in communication with his covert American Office of Strategic Services handlers, before the common interest of defeating Japanese imperialism had dissipated, Ho had been seeking the proper first principles of anticolonialism in American history. According to the testimony of Lieutenant Dan Phelan about a conversation that month, Ho "kept asking me if I could remember the language of our Declaration. I was a normal American, I couldn't . . . The more we discussed it, the more he actually seemed to know about it than I did."[2]

The moment sums up the historical connection between anticolonialism and rights in miniature—but only if interpreted correctly. For however remembered, the eighteenth-century American Declaration had not really been about rights; it had, above all, been about achieving postcolonial sovereignty externally, not asserting rights internationally, or even internally. "The Declaration's statements regarding rights," historian David Armitage has gone so far as to assert, "were strictly subordinate to . . . claims regarding the rights of states, and were taken to be so by contemporaries, when they deigned to notice the assertion of individual rights at all." The rights talk of the Declaration only received emphasis later, not least—Armitage says—with "the advent of a global rights movement in the second half of the twentieth century."[3] But it was not to be Ho Chi Minh or other activists against empire who inaugurated that movement: after citing the Declaration's "immortal statement," he immediately continued: "In a broader sense, this now means: All the *peoples* have a right to live, to be happy and free." The utopia that still mattered most was the original American one: postcolonial, collective liberation from empire, not individual rights canonized in international law.

How does anticolonialism, which drove the most liberatory events in the last and perhaps any century, fit in the emerging historiography of "human rights"? To put it briefly, not very well. Contemporary human rights history—a brand new enterprise—has tended to be teleological and triumphalist, ignoring the plurality of reformist ideologies in plausible contention through most of the past, before a set of mysterious set of events made human rights seem natural and necessary. Almost unanimously, historians have so far adopted a celebratory attitude toward the emergence and progress of human rights, providing recent enthusiasms with uplifting backstories and differing primarily about whether to locate the true breakthrough with the Greeks or the Jews, medieval Christians or early modern philosophers, democratic revolutionaries or abolitionist heroes, American internationalists or antiracist visionaries.[4] They have been less ready to concede, in recasting world history as raw material for progressive ascent of recent beliefs, that the past is never best read as a slow preparation for the present—and that human rights, even once invented, have been only one appealing ideology among others. One might argue that what succeeds about the very best work in the field is due to the extent it gives up a teleological and triumphalist credentialing model that still overwhelmingly dominates.[5] Anticolonialism provides another valuable illustration of this conclusion—if, that is, anticolonialism is not forced into participating in the "human rights revolution" that, in fact, it avoided for historically understandable reasons (and which is a recent historiographical construction in any case).

What ought to be the most striking and sobering fact, after all, is that anticolonial activists rarely invoked the phrase "human rights" or appealed to the Universal Declaration in particular—though decolonization was exploding precisely at the moment of its passage and after.[6] In a powerful body of historiography, tales are told of seizures from below of the formal universalisms of dominant peoples, classes, and nations, and presented simply as the realization of their original, truncated forms. Laurent Dubois makes such a claim about the Haitian Revolution, and Lynn Hunt, in her book on the same era, speaks similarly of a cascading "logic of rights." The argument, also offered by Frederick Cooper in perhaps its most general form, makes a fundamental point about how promises can be moved from paper into politics.[7] This chapter explores why, in the years immediately following World War II, no such logic of rights obtained—or rather, why an earlier, more powerful cascade, the liberation of collective peoples, flooded away the possibility of its occurrence, for better or worse.

After examining the coincidence of powerful causes that explain the absence of the new human rights in anticolonialism, this chapter turns to look at how they entered into a crucial United Nations debate. The UN was the only real place where anticolonialism and human rights intersected, but the question from the beginning was which would define which, and the answer seems clear. In the end, the true lesson of anticolonialism—the agent of the greatest dissemination of sovereignty in world history, not of its qualification—is thus not about the inevitable ascent of human rights. It is about the ideological conditions in which human rights in their contemporary connotations became a plausible and globalizing doctrine after the mid-1970s. In sum, recent attempts to place anticolonialism in human rights history must first face up to an era when the human rights idea had no movement and anticolonialism, a powerful movement, used other concepts.

Of course, anticolonialism in postwar history, though it achieved almost unbelievable successes, did not come out of nowhere. Yet, unlike some First World movements that appealed to rights language, like the women's movement and (less frequently) the workers' movement, anticolonialists rarely framed their cause that way before World War II. After all, colonial subjects were presumably well aware that Western "humanism" had not been kind to them so far.[8] The Ligue des droits de l'Homme, the French civil liberties union, staged a debate on the topic of the relation of colonization to the rights of man in 1931, but the conclusions were predictably self-serving. "To bring Science to people who do not have it, to give them roads, canals, railroads, cars, telegraph, telephone, to organize public health services for them, and—last but not least—to communicate the Rights of Man to them," as one speaker proclaimed, "is a task of fraternity."[9] True, activists sometimes appealed to legal (including judicial) remedies accorded them by the domestic legal systems in which they were working; British and French law, with their hierarchical distinction between the law governing the metropole and the law governing the colony, provided legal rights, at least on paper, to all subjects of their respective empires. As an illuminating recent study of prewar Nigeria suggests, domestic civil liberties traditions could and did have the potential to be transplanted to colonial holdings and appropriated for unexpected use. But there were no human rights prior to World War II except those concretized domestically by the state, so it is unclear how serious a bridge such prewar activities could have provided, or did in fact, to allegiance to postwar human rights. There is no neglecting the sharp distinction, both conceptually and historically, between early rights or even the rights of man, on the one hand, and later human rights, on the other.[10] The former were given their meaning by a status of citizen, or at least subject, within states and empires. The latter established nothing comparable, certainly not at the time of their invention (and perhaps not since).[11]

In any case, the most critical fact is that their interwar formation left opponents of empire with a range of ideologies, few of which were naturally open to the human rights moment of the mid-1940s or needed it for inspiration or articulation. After 1918, only, or mainly, one right was to matter. Erez Manela has provided a microscopic history of how enthusiastically the promise of the self-determination of peoples was greeted in the aftermath of World War I, but its true era of triumph was to be delayed until the 1940s and after. It was Woodrow Wilson, without leaving out V. I. Lenin, who created the conditions for an anticolonialism in which international human rights—in any case not yet formulated as an idea—were not the goal, with only one outsized (and collective) right cherished over others.[12] Indeed, though anticolonialism as self-determination may have had its international origins at that older moment, the key fact is that this framing of anticolonial aspirations proved strong enough to outlast any attempt after World War II to substitute a new language of international order and legitimacy based on personal rights. Put differently, the "Wilsonian moment," though stymied in the immediate aftermath of World War I, had a second, more successful chance after World War II, and it meant that there was no remotely comparable "human rights moment" at that time. Thus, the case of the decolonizing or soon-to-decolonize world after 1945 suggests clearly that not all formal universalisms spark seizures from below of their unrealized potential. Perhaps more than on any internal logic, the history of universalistic concepts like human rights ultimately depends on how rival human actors choose to deploy them, for good or for ill.

Could things have been otherwise? The question is tantalizing, but what seems obvious is that a clearer picture of the course of Western diplomacy and its reception elsewhere makes it counterfactual and ahistorical in the extreme. The Atlantic Charter of 1941 had announced self-determination, but not human rights, as part of the Allied war aims, even if Churchill and Roosevelt differed on what that meant. For Churchill, it applied to the liberation of Hitler's empire, not empire generally, and certainly not Churchill's empire. Roosevelt had originally more generous views. "There are many kinds of Americans, of course," FDR told Churchill at a dinner in 1942, "but as a people, as a country, we're opposed to imperialism—we can't stomach it." But he came to agree with his ally by the time of his death.[13] It is clear that the Atlantic Charter, especially, did have great resonance throughout the world. But later, to the extent that anyone paid attention, human rights must have seemed like a substitute for self-determination—which the Universal Declaration crucially does not include. Ho, who initially begged his American interlocutors to live up to the Atlantic Charter's promise of self-determination rather than allow the French to return, stopped asking and never again made even declaratory rights central.[14]

Such typically neglected facts are a glaring problem for a recent body of scholarship that presents the period after 1941 as a moment when America revived or invented its best internationalist traditions, in a genuinely universalistic spirit—offering what Elizabeth Borgwardt calls the "new deal for the world" in the American construction of the postwar order. She goes so far as to label the Atlantic Charter a "human rights instrument," though it didn't include the phrase, that set the terms for all the generosity that followed; "when you state a moral principle," she concludes of the Atlantic Charter's fate in inspiring the new order of San Francisco, Nuremberg, and elsewhere, "you are stuck with it."[15] Things look somewhat different, far less heroic and certainly less stalwart, from outside the West, where the announced principle of the Atlantic Charter, self-determination, is one the Americans decided they did not have to be stuck with after all. It would have been surprising if colonized peoples had been galvanized by the new human rights, if they were really successors of and substitutes for self-determination—in the nature of a consolation prize. Contrary to historian Paul Kennedy's assumption that the Universal Declaration, at the very late date of 1948, "enjoyed enormous global attention," the idea of human rights had strikingly little global circulation compared to other concepts, including other emancipatory universalisms.[16] A fair survey shows overwhelmingly that human rights *failed* to be embedded in global ideology at the time. Across the globe the Atlantic Charter galvanized a great many, but human rights fell on deaf ears; their differential history is what matters, and it is not hard to understand why.

This is not to say that the search for the nation-state was the only actual or possible future in the anticolonialist imaginary—far from it. It is only to say that specific appeal to supranational values encapsulated in the new human rights failed to affect it decisively. Even the crucial short-term developments after the Atlantic Charter must be set against the background of a long-fermenting anticolonialism: by the time human rights came on the scene, in other words, the train had already left the station. Interestingly, for instance, Mohandas Gandhi—often represented in retrospect as a partisan of human rights—found nothing new to take from the new rhetoric. Starting long before, he could interpret *satyagraha* as designed so as to win the rights of Englishmen for all British subjects (so long as they could be corrected through their correlation with duties). Yet there is no record of Gandhi mentioning, much less celebrating, the new idea of human rights in the era after the Atlantic Charter; he responded to a UNESCO request for his version of the idea—the assumption being that he must have one—with puzzlement, and his assassination in the beginning of the year whose end would see the Universal Declaration makes the question of what he might have seen in them, and done with them, unanswerable.[17] Similarly, except for his enthusiasm for a UN petition to safeguard Indians living in South Africa, Jawaharlal Nehru—who leavened a healthy internationalist vision with realist pragmatism—hardly invoked international rights, even when he addressed the General Assembly in Paris a month before the Universal Declaration's passage.[18]

The anticolonialism of many others was similarly fully formed before the human rights rhetoric after World War II had a chance to impact it seriously. Prominent anticolonialists like Ahmed Sukarno of Indonesia and Gamal Abdel Nasser of Egypt had itineraries that never crossed the terrain of postwar human rights, with the former an alumnus of the interwar League against Imperialism and the latter preoccupied with other things on the road to his 1952 coup, not least fighting in Palestine much of the year the Universal Declaration was being finalized. Often, the origins of anticolonialist ideology were due to tiny groups, characteristically on the far left, and in student or immigrant networks in metropoles, forging diverse compromises between nationalism and internationalism. A frequent result, of course, was the fateful connection of anticolonialism and communism that so colored twentieth-century history. And while communism had its own culture of invoking rights, especially in 1934–36 and again in the immediate post–World War II moment, those who saw in communism the best choice for liberation from empire (an earlier episode of activation by Wilsonian idealism having proved a bitter disappointment) were not seriously marked by that culture in any era. The nationalist government of China participated to some extent in early human rights formulation at the UN, but its toppling spelled the end of any ideological association of China with human rights. As for Southeast Asia, the Atlantic Charter had provided renewed grounds for Wilsonian hopes, but these were quickly dashed as the British rushed to reestablish empire throughout the region in the chaotic months after Japanese defeat. The British were eventually failures in many places, but restored the French Indochinese empire *en passant* and asserted control over Malaysia by conducting a savage counterinsurgency at the precisely the moment the move toward the Universal Declaration was occurring half a world away.[19]

If anything, the continuing course of anticolonial struggles confirmed these trends, not least due to the growing force of Marxism in anticolonialist thought. At the Bandung Conference of 1955 and elsewhere, anticolonialists announced their own internationalism, but in a subaltern key that incorporated nationalism and forged ties of idealism across borders based on racial identity and African or "Afro-Oriental" subordination. Kwame Nkrumah, who as far back as 1945 had not mentioned human rights in the celebrated Declaration to the Colonial Peoples of the World of the Manchester Pan-African Congress, claimed only the "rights of all people to govern themselves."[20] The effect of Ghana's early independence on the political aspirations of other sub-Saharan Africans was determining and, above all, in the priority accorded self-determination among all other possible aims: "Seek ye first the political kingdom," in Nkrumah's famous slogan, "and everything else shall be added unto you." It was in this atmosphere that C. L. R. James's revival of the "Black Jacobins" of the French Revolution had such power, especially since—unlike later historians of Caribbean radicalism—he had managed to present Toussaint L'Ouverture and his confederates without thinking to suggest they had been human rights activists before their time. A Trotskyist, James's view of *droits de l'homme*, interestingly, seems to have been as the "wordy" promises of "eloquent phrasemakers" who, driven by the true economic motor of history to "perorate," are in the end only willing to give up the aristocracy of the skin at the point of the insurgent's gun.[21] There were exceptions, but most typically, anticolonialists followed him in these views, whether Marxist or not, and there is almost no record of anyone taking the human rights of the new United Nations seriously. When founded in 1963, the Organization of African Unity's charter made reference to human rights but subordinated them to the need "to safeguard and consolidate the hard-won independence as well as the sovereignty and territorial integrity, of our States, and to fight against neo-colonialism in all its forms."

The case of French negritude is perhaps slightly different, as some of its partisans were willing to entertain hopes in the immediate postwar period, after the Brazzaville conference, for a France that might finally include them as equals. Thus, on occasion the great French tradition of *droits de l'homme* was, even in the angriest texts, held out as perverted rather than false. "That is the great thing I hold against pseudo-humanism," Aimé Césaire, the Martinique poet, wrote in his classic *Discourse on Colonialism* of 1950, "that for too long it has diminished rights of man, that its concept of those rights has been—and still is—narrow and fragmentary, incomplete and biased and, all things considered, sordidly racist."[22] The background mattered. Historian Gary Wilder has shown that this proposal for an alternative and realized humanism developed in dialogue with the interwar project of colonial reform, and for Césaire, as for theorist of negritude (and later Senegalese president) Léopold Senghor, it did not necessarily imply colonial autonomy in the beginning.[23] The founder of negritude advocated an inspiring vision in which a return to and revival of cultural particularity would contribute to, not interfere with, a universal civilization that deserved the name. Through the 1950s, he hoped France could provide it; yet neither Césaire nor Senghor ever referred to the human rights of the international scene. Later, after Senegalese independence, the focus of Senghor's thought, like that of so many others, was the development of a noncommunist Africanist socialism. The general infiltration of Marxism into anticolonialism, which increased after the mid-1960s, did not change the exclusionary equation and a self-styled "humanism" tolerant toward violence prevailed. For French Algerian anticolonialist Frantz Fanon, it was "a question of starting a new history of Man, a history that will have regard for the sometimes prodigious thesis which Europe has put forward."[24] But human rights were not invoked as any part—much less the core principle—of that history.

But there was a final and equally important reason that the human rights announced by the Allies failed to restructure the anticolonial imagination, which is that the United Nations, far from being the forum of a new and liberatory set of principles, appeared set at first on colluding in the attempted reimposition of colonial rule after the war. "Remember that Dumbarton Oaks"—the documents of the first plans of the organization— "leaves 750,000,000 human beings outside the organization of humanity,"

African-American anticolonialist W. E. B. Du Bois commented bitterly in spring 1945.[25] As if the Atlantic Charter had never been, those documents, indeed, did not even mention self-determination (or human rights). And, in spite of trying, anticolonialists were not to succeed in shaking the organization's complicity in the attempted continuation of colonialism, as its initial formulation occurred.

There was agitation to do so, of course, especially after the United States turned to agree by the time of Yalta to the restrictive British interpretation of the Atlantic Charter; however, the high politics did not center on whether to end colonialism outright. Instead, they involved debates on the exact terms of the reinvention of the League of Nations system of mandates, the key question being whether international supervision would cover all dependent areas, or whether its supervision would have teeth. These attempts largely failed, drastically restricting the coverage of the trusteeship system and, within it, largely reinstating the weak supervisory authority of the international community of the League era. Only a tenth of colonial subjects at the height of postwar empire was under trusteeship authority; and even then, as outlined in the UN Charter's Chapters XII–XIII, the organization's main aim of preserving the peace trumped the "sacred trust" advanced countries were supposed to have in the interests of subject populations, which did not include any definite obligation to move them toward independence.[26] Compared to the Dumbarton Oaks proposals, the concept of self-determination did enter the UN Charter twice, but only in a rhetorical and subsidiary way. (Human rights also entered at this stage, if mainly ornamentally, especially in the preamble drafted by South African marshal Jan Christian Smuts— who revealingly assumed they had no implication for racial hierarchy in his country or elsewhere.)[27]

Surprisingly, anticolonialism prevailed anyway, no thanks to the United Nations processes, which it nonetheless affected so quickly that it came as a shock. It would have been impossible to predict this in 1945, or even in the brutal postwar years when the Universal Declaration's framing was a sideshow compared to the world reimposition of empire. The British suppression of insurrection in Malaysia, at the very moment of that framing, would prove a model for other countries, indeed, through the American struggle in Vietnam, but its success did not become the rule. Anticolonial victory, through force of arms or (more often) negotiated departures, did. The era of the "new states" had begun.[28]

It was mainly on the stage of UN processes that any intersection of anticolonialism and human rights occurred, which must be understood as transpiring on the former's terms and not the latter's. By the time of the 1948 vote on the Universal Declaration, fifty-eight states were UN members, a number which would grow by leaps and bounds, to the point that within a few short years an Afro-Asian bloc in the General Assembly could outvote First World powers with Soviet help and after another few years (most notably, after 1960, when sixteen African nations entered) with no help at all. In twenty years, the number of humans under some sort of colonial rule declined from 750 million to fewer than 40 million.[29] Though this transition would have been unforeseeable in 1945, by a decade later great power observers already understood that anticolonialism would have undoubted effects. After Bandung, where representatives of so many originally and still-excluded peoples attended, the likely outcome was clear. One depressed British analyst predicted that the newly independent nations would "use the success of the conference as a means of asserting the Arab/Asian point of view and of claiming that the Bandung countries were entitled to a far bigger share of the world authority (as represented by the UN) than they had when the United Nations was founded."[30]

If that entitlement meant the development or entrenchment of something called human rights, it was only in a sense subordinate—if not equivalent—to self-determination. What was perhaps remarkable is that at first there was no doctrinal or organizational connection at the UN between human rights as a project and dependent areas as a problem, with the minor exception of the trusteeship system. But the pressure—and bit by bit, the continuing accession—of the new nations changed this entirely. In an astonishingly short space of time, the UN moved from seriously considering a proposal to exempt colonial (trust and non-self-governing) territories from coverage by the draft Covenants on Human Rights to placing the right of self-determination of peoples first of all human rights in those drafts. These debates—which fundamentally transformed the whole meaning of United Nations human rights for decades—are worth following in more detail.

In October 1950, the General Assembly's Third Committee gathered to consider whether colonial powers could bind themselves to human rights in a prospective legal covenant, without fearing that this would increase the basis on which the UN could interfere in their affairs. For the Belgian representative, it was a necessary premise for moving to binding covenant, because human rights rules "presupposed a high degree of civilization, [and] were often incompatible with the ideas of peoples who had not yet reached a high degree of development. By imposing those rules on them at once, one ran the risk of destroying the very basis of their society. It would be an attempt to lead them abruptly to the point which the civilized nations of today had only reached after a lengthy period of development."[31] René

Cassin and Eleanor Roosevelt, icons of the human rights moment at the early United Nations, agreed, speaking for the French and American governments. But this proposal to keep the applicability of human rights law out of empires did not carry the day.

Meanwhile, the same year, the General Assembly approved a resolution from Afghanistan and Saudi Arabia that the Human Rights Commission explore how self-determination could be taken more seriously.[32] The idea that the right of self-determination should be injected into the substance of the covenant, though it had not figured in the Universal Declaration, caused a sensational debate, first in the Third Committee in late 1951 and then in the General Assembly's plenary session in early 1952. The Belgian delegate, Fernand Dehousse, posed his objection as a worry about the "multiplication of frontiers and barriers among nations," with self-determination an artifact of nineteenth-century economic liberalism, now overridden by "the idea of international solidarity."[33] The inclusion of self-determination, he argued, could not be used simply to score points against colonial powers. Abdul Rahman Pazhwak of Afghanistan replied angrily on this point that he and other supporters of self-determination as a right "did not want to teach anyone lessons; it was history that taught them," not least "that under the rule of Powers which regarded themselves as qualified to teach others lessons the world had known oppression, aggression and bloodshed."[34] Self-determination, Kolli Tamba of Liberia insisted, "was an essential right and stood above all other rights."[35] At the plenary session, right before the vote, the Saudi Arabian representative, Jamil Baroody, gave a long and impassioned argument for making it the first right: "The anguished cry for freedom and liberation from the foreign yoke in many parts of the world has risen to a very high pitch, so that even those who had been compelled to block their ears with the cotton wool of political expediency can no longer deny that they can hear it. [The world's people] cannot enjoy any human rights unless they are free, and it is in a document like the covenant that self-determination should be proclaimed."[36] The General Assembly approved the directive to include in the post-Declaration human rights covenants the article that "All peoples shall have the right of self-determination," where a later version remains today, as the very first article in both the chief international legal document protecting civil and political rights and the one protecting economic and social rights.[37]

Whether one celebrates or rues this fateful day, the absorption of human rights accomplished on it transformed their meaning, so as to emphasize their necessary basis in collectivity and sovereignty, as the first and most important threshold right. And while treating self-determination as a premise for excluding from consideration other rights at the United Nations forum did not have to follow logically, it typically did so in practice. But above all, it changed them conceptually, through the move to collective sovereignty that would later seem the very barrier the concept of human rights was intended to overcome. In immediate response, Clyde Eagleton, New York University international lawyer, lobbed a critique in *Foreign Affairs* entitled "Excesses of Self-Determination." "It is sad that anti-colonial resentment," he wrote, "should have distorted so noble a principle."[38] So it was that the same international lawyers ultimately to champion human rights spent most of postwar history treating them as captured and dangerous. In the 1960s Louis Henkin— Columbia University law professor who in the 1970s championed human rights, in the process helping reclaim them from their anticolonialist definition—simply denounced their postwar interpretation "as an additional weapon against colonialism although there was no suggestion that [self-determination] was a right of the individual, that the individual could claim it against an unrepresentative government, or that minorities could invoke it."[39] For the time being, however, as another critic put it, self-determination had become "a shibboleth that all must pronounce to identify themselves with the virtuous."[40] As new states joined, a third complained the UN concern with human rights became nothing "but another vehicle for advancing [the] attack on colonialism and associated forms of racial discrimination."[41]

Most obviously, the epoch-making Declaration on the Granting of Independence to Colonial Countries and Peoples of 1960 (first proposed by Nikita Khrushchev personally in that "African Year," so called because of the wave of accessions from there) confirmed the near equivalence of human rights and self-determination. "The *colonial system* . . . is now an international crime," Amilcar Cabral, Guinean scourge of Portuguese domination, exulted, in response. "Our struggle has lost its strictly national character and has moved to an international level."[42] Fatefully, this internationalization coincided with the Sharpeville massacre in South Africa, which amplified the country's stigmatization and led to a number of UN resolutions on human rights grounds.[43] This was not progress for human rights in their current sense, but evidence of their entanglement with anticolonialism and antiracism more generally. Indeed, even as Portuguese Angola also came in for immediate attention, India explicitly cited the 1960 declaration in its December 1961 invasion of Goa. In 1962, explaining how best to honor the fifteenth anniversary of the Universal Declaration, the General Assembly approved a resolution effectively identifying the celebration of the advancement of human rights with that of the attainment of independence from colonial rule, with the hope for the future realization of human rights defined as another "decisive step forward for the liberation of all peoples."[44] The Declaration on the Elimination of All Forms of Racial Discrimination was proclaimed in the same spirit the following year, with a convention following two years later, and approved the very same day as the remarkable paean to self-determination the Declaration on the Inadmissibility of Intervention in the Domestic Affairs of States and the Protection of Their Independence and Sovereignty.[45] Such declarations became focal points of—and dominant imaginative rubrics for—human rights activities at the United Nations, in a widespread alteration of institutional arrangements and in endless discussion, with South Africa and (later) Israel repeated targets of attention.[46] Postcolonial sovereignty—linked to subaltern internationalism, and thus abrogable only in an antiracist cause—had prevailed, to the point of defining what human rights, too, meant.

It is crucial to maintain clarity about the differences between the earlier forms of idealism and activism and a later and very different idealism and activism—the human rights of more recent times. The relationship is far more one of *displacement* than it is one of *realization*. Anticolonialism did not contribute to the triumph of an idealism that privileged the antitotalitarian values at the center of the explosion in the prominence of "human rights" in the 1970s and since. In fact, anticolonialism's most characteristic concern, collective national or regional or, indeed, racial liberation, found itself in the human rights movement only to the extent it could accommodate individual civil liberties, with the problem of social and economic disempowerment suppressed as an imperative until a "second generation" moment allowed for their attempted incorporation. This is not to gainsay either of two complications, the existence of a few who argued for an anticolonialism based on human rights (typically on condition of siding with the United States in its Cold War struggle for hearts and minds around the world), and strategic invocations of human rights in international forums in response to the brutal methods the colonial powers deployed in trying to maintain control, for example against French torture in the Algerian war.[47] But for better or worse, neither complication defined the historical bearing of anticolonialism. And while this chapter focused on ideology only, analogous questions would make the point even more clearly if practices, including First World sympathy, were given attention. Anticolonialism placed emphasis on totalistic struggle—nonviolent or violent—and elicited Third-Worldist engagement from its partisans in wealthy countries. It played little role in the rise of international law as the privileged steward of norms. And it did little to make publicity the essential form of moral activism, especially in a model in which mass political involvement, if there was any, occurred either through personal or small-group identification with foreign suffering or through arm's length financial contribution. Finally, it is unclear how anticolonalism, with its famous iconic leaders, could have helped spark a model of nongovernmental politics in which elite leadership took on the characteristics of bureaucracy rather than charisma.[48]

The best use of anticolonialism in the history of human rights, then, is to think about why the latter waited for so long, until living memory, to crystallize. In other words, the main rationale for returning to anticolonialism within human rights history is not to incorporate it but to discern some reasons why human rights failed to win out in the 1940s and after, but experienced a remarkable ascendancy in the later 1970s and since. As it would turn out, human rights entered First World consciousness only, and perhaps conveniently, once two interlocking events occurred.

First, the sordid nature of formal colonial rule had to be revealed for all to accept and ultimately ended once and for all. The hard fact to contemplate is that human rights experienced their triumph as a global *lingua franca* after decolonization, not during it—and because of it, perhaps, only in the sense that the loss of empire allowed for the reclamation of liberalism shorn of its depressing earlier entanglements with formal rule abroad. The last major instances of formal colonialism, in the Portuguese holdings, were finally destroyed in the mid-1970s. The simultaneous failure of its bloody, last-ditch attempt to keep southern Vietnam—not simply the moral turpitude or deviation from national traditions of that failure, as Jimmy Carter contended at the time—set the stage for America's promised turn to human rights as a foreign policy ideal. One speculative hypothesis anticolonialism allows to be advanced, then, is that only the ideological dissociation of liberalism and empire, after more than a century of long and deep connection, paved the way for the rise of human rights. Scholars still debate whether liberalism has a genetic or only contingent relationship to imperialism, but what does seem clear is that only when formal empire ended did in fact (and perhaps could in theory) a powerful internationalism based on rights come to the fore.

Second, the widespread rise of the belief that anticolonialism in its classic forms had shipwrecked as a moral and political project also mattered a great deal. This was not least because of concerns once thought legitimately placed on hold while new states consolidated power and, assuming their leaders' good intentions, attempted radical social and economic reconstructions that might matter. It meant much, especially, that the anticolonialism of self-determination bred mounting secession crises. Even one partisan of the spread of domestic liberties in the world's multiplying constitutions could concede in the mid-1960s that "autocracy, selectively applied, may be necessary in order to create the social requisites for the maintenance of human rights."[49] A decade later, that bet did not seem worth making. Harvard professor and longtime prominent proponent of self-determination Rupert Emerson decried by 1975 the emergence of "a double standard which has worked to debase the moral coinage of the Third-World countries and to lessen the appeal of the causes they advocate . . . The wholly legitimate drive against colonialism and apartheid was in some measure called into question when the new countries habitually shrugged off any concern with massive violations of human rights and dignity in their own domain."[50] In 1977, the year of greatest prominence of human rights in U.S. history so far, New York Senator Daniel Patrick Moynihan more aggressively interpreted the ideals as a response to the "cult of the Third World" that had captured human rights at the United Nations, where Moynihan served as ambassador shortly before. Western policy had failed to stand up for human rights against their perverse redefinition, Moynihan explained, because of the "tremendous investment of hope in what we saw as the small seedlings of our various great oaks and a corresponding reluctance to think, much less speak, ill of them. Then there was the trauma of Vietnam, which perhaps made it seem even more necessary that we should be approved by nations so very like the one we were despoiling."[51] Now too much time had gone by to allow Third World nations a pass—and Vietnam was over. Only in such circumstances, it would seem, could there be an opening for a move, plausible or not, from the original and most lasting American contribution of postcolonial sovereignty to its far more recent utopia. It remains today's utopia: the dream of a world of individual human rights.

NOTES

1. Ho Chi Minh, "Declaration of Independence of the Democratic Republic of Viet-Nam," in *On Revolution: Selected Writings 1920–66*, ed. Bernard B. Fall (New York: Praeger, 1967), 143.

2. Cited in Dixee R. Bartholomew-Feis, *The OSS and Ho Chi Minh: Unexpected Allies in the War against Japan* (Lawrence: University of Kansas Press, 2006), 243.

3. David Armitage, *The Declaration of Independence: A Global History* (Cambridge, MA: Harvard University Press, 2006), 17–18. Similarly, Jack Rakove says, "in writing the preamble to the Declaration, Jefferson was seeking neither to strike a blow for the equality of individuals, nor to erase the countless social differences that

the law sometimes created and often sustained. The primary form of equality that the preamble asserts is an equality among peoples, defined as self-governing communities." Rakove, "Jefferson, Rights, and the Priority of Freedom of Conscience," in *The Future of Liberal Democracy: Thomas Jefferson and the Contemporary World*, ed. Robert Fatton Jr. and R. K. Ramazani (New York: Palgrave Macmillan 2004), 51.

4. For some exemplary works, see Micheline Ishay, *The History of Human Rights: From the Stone Age to the Globalization Era* (Berkeley: University of California Press, 2004); Paul Gordon Lauren, *The Evolution of International Human Rights: Visions Seen* (Philadelphia: University of Pennsylvania Press, 2003); John M. Headley, *The Europeanization of the World: On the Origins of Human Rights and Democracy* (Princeton, NJ: Princeton University Press, 2007); Lynn Hunt, *Inventing Human Rights: A History* (New York: W. W. Norton, 2007); Adam Hochschild, *Bury the Chains: Prophets and Rebels in the Fight to Free an Empire's Slaves* (Boston: Houghton Mifflin, 2005); Jenny S. Martinez, "Antislavery Courts and the Dawn of International Human Rights Law," *Yale Law Journal* 117, no. 4 (January 2008): 550–41; Elizabeth Borgwardt, *A New Deal for the World: America's Vision for Human Rights* (Cambridge, MA: Harvard University Press, 2006); and Marilyn Lake and Henry Reynolds, *Drawing the Global Colour Line: White Men's Countries and the International Challenge of Racial Equality* (Cambridge: Cambridge University Press, 2008), chap. 14.

5. See esp. Kenneth Cmiel's "The Recent History of Human Rights," in this volume. This is the overall approach of my *The Last Utopia: Human Rights in History* (Cambridge, MA: Harvard University Press, 2010).

6. How, for example, could decolonization be described as "the greatest extension and achievement of human rights in the history of the world," if its prime movers did not frame their aims and agenda using the language? Cited in Lauren, *Evolution*, 242.

7. Laurent Dubois, *A Colony of Citizens: Revolution and Slave Emancipation in the French Caribbean, 1787–1804* (Raleigh: University of North Carolina Press 2004); Hunt, *Inventing Human Rights*.

8. Cf. Florence Bernault, "What Absence Is Made Of: Human Rights in Africa," in *Human Rights and Revolutions*, ed. Jeffrey N. Wasserstrom et al. (Lanham, MD: Rowman and Littlefield 2000), esp. 128.

9. Cited in Raoul Girardet, *L'idée coloniale en France* (Paris: La Table Ronde 1972), 183.

10. In this sense, the title of Bonny Ibhawoh, *Imperialism and Human Rights: Colonial Discourses of Rights and Liberties in African History* (Albany: State University of New York Press, 2007) is seriously misleading.

11. Compare Jane Burbank and Frederick Cooper, "Empire, droits, et citoyenneté, de 212 à 1946," *Annales E.S.C.* 63, no. 3 (May 2008): 495–531.

12. Erez Manela, *The Wilsonian Moment: Self-Determination and the International Origins of Anticolonial Nationalism* (New York: Oxford University Press, 2007).

13. On the interpretation of the Atlantic Charter by the Allies as the war continued, see Wm. Roger Louis, *Imperialism at Bay: The United States and the Decolonization of the British Empire, 1941–1945* (New York: Oxford University Press, 1978). See also Neil Smith, *American Empire: Roosevelt's Geographer and the Prelude to Globalization* (Berkeley: University of California Press 2003), ch. 13. FDR is cited in Robert Dallek, *Franklin Roosevelt and American Foreign Policy 1932–1945* (New York: Oxford University Press, 1979), 324.

14. Efforts to add self-determination to the Universal Declaration were chiefly a concern of the Soviet and Eastern bloc delegates in the UN in 1947–48 and were rejected. See Kamleshwar Das, "Some Observations Relating to the International Bill of Human Rights," *Indian Yearbook of International Affairs* 19 (1986): 12–15. For Ho, see William J. Duiker, *Ho Chi Minh: A Life* (New York, 2000), 341.

15. Borgwardt, *New Deal*, and Borgwardt, "'When You State a Moral Principle, You Are Stuck With It': The 1941 Atlantic Charter as a Human Rights Instrument," *Virginia Journal of International Law* 46, no. 3 (Spring 2006): 501–62.

16. Paul Kennedy, *The Parliament of Man: The Past, Present, and Future of the United Nations* (New York: Random House 2006), 179. Among the Nigerians examined by Ibhawoh, "the introduction of the UDHR did not stimulate the kind of impassioned debates about the right to self-determination that followed the Atlantic Charter" (160). This is not surprising, given that the UDHR did not mention self-determination.

17. Mohandas Gandhi, "A Letter Addressed to the Secretary-General of UNESCO," in *Human Rights: Comments and Interpretations*, ed. Jacques Maritain (New York: Columbia University Press 1948).

18. Jawaharlal Nehru, "To the United Nations" (November 1948), in *Independence and After* (Delhi: Day, 1949). Cf. G. S. Pathak, "India's Contribution to the Human Rights Declaration and Covenants," in *Horizons of Freedom*, ed. L. M. Singhvi (Delhi: National Publishing House,1969). For a different account (whose main contribution, in spite of the title, is about Nehru's aspirational globalism), Manu Bhagavan, "A New Hope: India, the United Nations and the Making of the Universal Declaration of Human Rights," *Modern Asian Studies* 44, no. 2 (March 2010): 311–47.

19. For a panoramic view, see Christopher Bayly and Tim Harper, *Forgotten Wars: Freedom and Revolution in Southeast Asia* (Cambridge, MA: Harvard University Press, 2007), esp. 127, 141 for the impact of the Atlantic and UN Charters.

20. "Declaration to the Colonial Peoples of the World," in Kwame Nkrumah, *Revolutionary Path* (New York: International Publishers, 1973).

21. C. L. R. James, *The Black Jacobins: Toussaint L'Ouverture and the San Domingo Revolution* (New York: Vintage, 1963), 24, 116, 139. James thought that what mattered for Toussaint was that the "cascade" of citizenship did not happen by itself; it had to be forced through violence, and what these radicals insisted on was mainly their right to be masters of their fate; the same was to be true in twentieth-century history.

22. Aimé Césaire, *Discourse on Colonialism*, trans. Joan Pinkham (New York: Monthly Review Press, 1972), 15.

23. Gary Wilder, *The French Imperial Nation-State: Negritude and Colonial Humanism between the World Wars* (Chicago: University of Chicago Press, 2005); see also Wilder, "Untimely Vision: Aimé Césaire, Decolonization, Utopia," *Public Culture* 21, no. 1 (Winter 2009): 101–40.

24. Frantz Fanon, *The Wretched of the Earth*, preface Jean-Paul Sartre, trans. Constance Farrington (New York: Grove Press, 1963), 317.

25. W. E. B. Du Bois, "750,000,000 Clamoring for Human Rights," *New York Post*, May 9, 1945, rpt. in *Writings by W.E.B. Du Bois in Periodicals Edited by Others*, 4 vols., ed. Herbert Aptheker (Millwood, NY: Kraus-Thompson, 1982), vol. 4, 2–3. See also Du Bois, "The Colonies at San Francisco," *Trek* [Johannesburg], April 5, 1946, rpt. in *Writings by W.E.B. Du Bois,* Aptheker, ed., vol. 4, 6–8.

26. For the figure, Harold Karan Jacobson, "The United Nations and Colonialism: A Tentative Appraisal," *International Organization* 16, no. 1 (Winter 1962): 45.

27. For an excellent rendition, see Mark Mazower, *No Enchanted Palace: Empire, War, and the Ideological Origins of the United Nations* (Princeton, NJ: Princeton University Press, 2009), ch. 1.

28. The transition is well captured by the subtitles of Evan Luard's two-volume early UN history, *A History of the United Nations*, 2 vols. (New York: St. Martin's Press, 1982, 1989), covering 1945–55 as "the years of Western domination" and then 1955–65 as "the age of decolonization." Compare Jacobson, "The United Nations and Colonialism," and David W. Wainhouse, *Remnants of Empire: The United Nations and the End of Colonialism* (New York: Harper & Row, 1964).

29. For some specific analyses of the percolation of self-determination in UN politics on which I have drawn, see Benjamin Rivlin, "Self-Determination and Colonial Areas," *International Conciliation* 501 (January 1955): 193–71; Muhammad Aziz Shukri, *The Concept of Self-Determination at the United Nations* (Damascus: Al Jadidah Press, 1965); and Rupert Emerson, "Self-Determination," *American Journal of International Law* 65, no. 3 (July 1971): 459–75. For larger effects on the organization, see D. N. Sharma, *The Afro-Asian Group in the United Nations* (Allahabad: Chaitanya Publishing, 1969); David A. Kay, "The Politics of Decolonization: The New Nations and the United Nations Political Process," *International Organization* 21, no. 4 (Autumn 1967): 786–11; and Kay, *The New Nations in the United Nations, 1960–1967* (New York: Columbia University Press, 1970).

30. Cited in Kweku Ampiah, *The Political and Moral Imperatives of the Bandung Conference: The Reactions of the US, UK, and Japan* (Folkestone: Global Oriental, 2007), 147.

31. UN General Assembly, A/C.3/SR.292 (1950), 133.

32. UN General Assembly, UN GA Res. 421(V), December 4, 1950.

33. UN General Assembly A/C.3/SR.361 (1951), 84.

34. UN General Assembly, A/C.3/SR.362 (1951), 90.

35. UN General Assembly, A/C.3/SR.366 (1951), 115.

36. UN General Assembly, A/PV.375 (1952), 517–18.

37. UN GA Res. 545(VI), February 5, 1952. The resolution also called for the covenant to "stipulate that all States, including those having responsibility for the administration of Non-Self-Governing Territories, should promote the realization of that right," which in effect, if unofficially, revised the Charter Chapter XI. Down into the 1970s, leading international lawyers could attack this retroactive change as an illegitimate revision of the Charter outside its own amendment procedures. See Leo Gross, "The Right of Self-Determination in International Law," in *New States in the Modern World*, ed. Martin Kilson (Cambridge, MA: Harvard University Press, 1975). For the continuing debate on self-determination and rights at the UN, see Roger Normand and Sarah Zaidi, *Human Rights at the UN: The Political History of Universal Justice* (Bloomington: Indiana University Press, 2008), 212–24.

38. Clyde Eagleton, "Excesses of Self-Determination," *Foreign Affairs* 31, no. 4 (July 1953): 604.

39. Louis Henkin, "The United Nations and Human Rights," *International Organization* 19, no. 3 (Summer 1965): 513.

40. Vernon Van Dyke, *Human Rights, the United States, and the World Community* (New York: Oxford University Press, 1970), 77.

41. Kay, *New Nations*, 87; cf. Kay, "The Politics of Decolonization," 802. See also many of the analyses in Hedley Bull and Adam Watson, eds., *The Expansion of International Society* (New York: Oxford University Press, 1984), esp. Bull's "The Revolt against the West" and R. J. Vincent's "Racial Equality."

42. Amilcar Cabral, "Anonymous Soldiers for the United Nations" (December 1962), in *Revolution in Guinea: Selected Texts*, trans. Richard Handyside (New York: Monthly Review Press, 1969), 50–51.

43. See UN GA Res. 1598(XV), April 15, 1961, passed with only Portugal voting no; and later 1663(XVI), November 28, 1961; 1881(XVIII), October 11, 1963; and 1978(XVIII), December 17, 1963. And, for comment, Ballinger, Moses E. Akpan, *African Goals and Diplomatic Strategies in the United Nations* (North Quincy, MA: Christopher Publishing House, 1976); and Audie Klotz, *Norms in International Relations: The Struggle against Apartheid* (Ithaca, NY: Cornell University Press, 1995), esp. 44–55. In the same years, there were also resolutions on the long-simmering South West Africa dispute, and the shocking decision by the International Court of Justice that other African countries had no standing in the forum to bring an action. See, e.g., John Dugard, *The South West Africa-Namibia Dispute* (Berkeley: University of California Press, 1973), 220–31 and ch. 8.

44. UN GA Res. 1775(XVII), December 7, 1962.

45. UN GA Res. 1904(XVIII), November 20, 1963, 2106A(XX), December 21, 1965, and 2131(XX), December 21, 1965.

46. For some of this, esp. the Human Rights Commission's Sub-commission on Prevention of Discrimination, see Jean-Bernard Marie, *La Commission des droits de l'homme de l'ONU* (Paris: A. Pedone, 1975); Moses Moskowitz, *The Roots and*

Reaches of United Nations Actions and Decisions (Alphen aan den Rijn: Sijthoff & Nordhoff, 1980); and Howard Tolley, *The United Nations Commission of Human Rights* (Boulder, CO: Westview Press, 1987).

47. On the first topic, see Roland J. Burke, "'The Compelling Dialogue of Freedom': Human Rights and the Bandung Conference," *Human Rights Quarterly* 28 (2006): 947–65. On the second topic, see Fabian Klose, *Menschenrechte im Schatten kolonialer Gewalt: Die Dekolonisierungskriege in Kenia und Algerien 1945–1962* (Munich: Oldenbourg Verlag, 2009), written in the shadow of Matthew Connelly's *A Diplomatic Revolution: Algeria's Fight for Independence and the Origins of the Post-Cold War Order* (New York: Oxford University Press, 2002). If my approach in this chapter is correct, neither topic should be pursued in isolation from the larger anticolonialist picture.

48. See, e.g., Faisal Devji's fascinating attempt to read contemporary terrorism as Gandhian in *The Terrorist in Search of Humanity* (New York: Columbia University Press, 2009).

49. David H. Bayley, *Public Liberties in the New States* (Chicago: Rand McNally, 1964), 142.

50. Rupert Emerson, "The Fate of Human Rights in the Third World," *World Politics* 27, no. 2 (January 1975): 223.

51. Daniel Patrick Moynihan, "The Politics of Human Rights," *Commentary* 64, no. 2 (August 1977): 22.

8

"THE FIRST RIGHT"

The Carter Administration, Indonesia, and the
Transnational Human Rights Politics of the 1970s

BRAD SIMPSON

In June 1977, U.S. National Security Council staffer Michael Armacost wrote National Security Advisor Zbigniew Brzezinski of the "perplexity" in Jakarta regarding the new U.S. emphasis on human rights. Despite the Indonesian government's intention to release tens of thousands of political prisoners arrested when General Suharto rose to power in 1965–1966, the U.S. Congress continued to condemn Indonesia's December 1975 invasion and occupation of the former Portuguese territory of East Timor. "The Indonesian decision is irreversible," he argued. "The U.S. government has accepted it. Continued Congressional hearings are regarded as unwarranted and mischievous interference in their internal affairs."[1]

While Armacost wrote to Brzezinski, Indonesian Foreign Minister Adam Malik admitted to journalists that at least fifty thousand Timorese had died since Indonesia invaded. During this period, Indonesian forces employed mass killings, forced resettlement, mass arrests, forced sterilization, and torture to crush East Timorese military and civilian resistance.[2] Yet the Carter administration continued to pursue closer relations with Indonesia, partly in the name of human rights, pressing it to release political prisoners and investing substantial resources to this end. In doing so, it joined numerous nongovernmental and multilateral organizations, as well as the Western media in framing the fate of *tapols* (*tahanan politik*, or political prisoners) as Indonesia's chief human rights challenge. Through nonstate channels at the United Nations and among the nations of the Non-Aligned Movement, meanwhile, East Timor's resistance fought for recognition of its claim to self-determination as the fulcrum on which transnational debates about human rights should pivot.

This contrast between the international human rights community's priorities and those of many East Timorese and their supporters raises the question how and why some conceptions of human rights ascended over others during the 1970s. Despite a wealth of scholarship exploring the explosion of transnational human rights organizations and the institutionalization of norms in state bureaucracies and multilateral forums, historians have largely told a story of diffusion of civil and political rights, generally radiating from the West outward. But a reexamination of the Carter administration's human rights policies toward Indonesia and East Timor, and Indonesia's own emerging human rights movement demonstrate that in the 1970s there was no single "human rights movement" with clear goals or agreement on what constituted core human rights. Moreover, this history challenges the teleological, self-referential, and self-congratulatory story that scholars have told about campaigns against torture and political imprisonment during the 1970s. Instead, it treats the human rights politics and discourses of the decade as an ongoing contest in which alternative conceptions of rights, especially the right of self-determination, were subordinated as a result of often bitter political conflict within and among state bureaucracies, international forums, and NGO boardrooms. These disputes often transcended not only Cold War limits but North–South divides as well.

Indonesia invaded the former Portuguese colony of East Timor on December 7, 1975, following a brief but bloody civil war won by the radical pro-independence party Fretilin. Indonesia was determined to prevent the emergence of a potentially destabilizing neighbor on its eastern border, while allies in London, Canberra, Washington, and elsewhere agreed that absorption by Indonesia, rather than independence, was the preferred outcome of the decolonization process.[3] Facing imminent attack, Fretilin declared East Timor's independence on November 28, 1975. The announcement prompted Indonesia's invasion a week later, just after U.S. President Gerald Ford and Secretary of State Henry Kissinger visited Suharto in Jakarta, offering explicit approval for Indonesia's actions. East Timorese guerrillas mounted a fierce resistance for six years before Indonesia consolidated its control, during which time between 108,000 and 180,000 Timorese were massacred or died of starvation and disease, out of a population of perhaps 600,000.[4]

The invasion of East Timor provoked divergent international responses. The UN Security Council condemned the invasion and affirmed East Timor's right to self-determination, but the United States prevented it from enforcing this and subsequent resolutions. The State Department wrote

President Ford that the United States "has no interests in Portuguese Timor" and should "follow Indonesia's lead on the issue." Most Western governments concurred, though many of their citizens did not.[5] Australia's support for Indonesia prompted the emergence of a vocal and well-organized movement to support Timorese self-determination.[6] Several European nations, including Portugal, the Netherlands, and Great Britain, also witnessed the rise of East Timor solidarity groups. NGOs such as Amnesty International, the Catholic Institute for International Relations, and Tapol, a human rights group started in 1973 by former political prisoner Carmel Budiardjo, eventually took up East Timor's cause.[7] Following the invasion, however, Indonesia effectively closed East Timor to the outside world, barring journalists and aid workers from the territory and making it extremely difficult to gather and disseminate information about the situation in the territory. In the United States, East Timor remained the concern of a tiny coterie of journalists, Catholic Church activists, Portuguese Americans, human rights activists, and academics, who founded Tapol US in 1974 and the East Timor Defense Committee in 1975.[8] But the fate of East Timor barely resonated with the American public, whose concern for Soviet dissidents and Latin American torture victims contributed to the "phenomenal burst of human rights activism in the United States" in the mid 1970s.[9]

The 1976 election of Jimmy Carter as U.S. president raised expectations worldwide of a change in U.S. policy toward repressive regimes. Suharto's supporters recognized that Indonesia, which held more political prisoners than any nation on earth, was vulnerable to condemnation. After Suharto rose to power in the wake of the failed September 30th movement in 1965, his regime killed an estimated five hundred thousand alleged communists and imprisoned an estimated one million more, overwhelmingly without trial. Some were eventually executed, while the rest were held in local prisons, released with onerous restrictions or "forcibly resettled to penal colonies in remote areas of the archipelago."[10]

A wide range of national, multilateral, and nongovernmental organizations condemned Indonesia's detention practices. In 1966, Amnesty International (AI) began to focus on the plight of Indonesia's long-term detainees, as did many local and country chapters. In 1973, as Carmel Budiardjo founded Tapol in London, AI released a series of reports on Indonesian political detainees and called for the UNCHR to demand their unconditional release. The next year, the World Council of Churches, International Labor Organization, and International Commission of Jurists issued similar calls. Such demands had little effect on the Suharto regime—insulated from criticism by skyrocketing oil revenues—or its international donors.[11]

Two years later, however, Indonesia was more vulnerable to international pressure because of a major debt scandal in 1974 involving the national oil company Pertamina; investigations into bribes paid to the Suharto
regime by Ford Motor Company and Hughes Aerospace; mounting student
protests against corruption; and preparations for the invasion of East
Timor.[12] In April 1975, the Suharto regime began lobbying donors for
increased foreign aid and for the first time faced sharp questioning from the
Inter-Governmental Group on Indonesia, a forum of donor governments
which AI had targeted the previous two years. When Suharto visited
Washington in July, officials warned him that Congress would likely cut aid
to Jakarta unless it released political prisoners.[13] Three months later, a delegation led by General Ali Murtopo and Lim Bian Kie of the Center for
International Studies—two architects of the East Timor invasion—also
traveled to Washington to lobby U.S. officials, initiating quiet negotiations
over the mechanisms of a prisoner-release program and issuing public statements "designed to appeal to Congress as a sign of the regime's progress in
human rights." But few detainees saw the light of day, and criticism from
human rights groups continued.[14]

In December 1976, following months of negotiations with U.S., Japanese,
and other policymakers, Jakarta announced that it would begin a three-year,
phased release of thirty thousand political prisoners.[15] In Washington,
Indonesia's prisoner-release program muted congressional opposition to
increased economic and military assistance, despite continued reports of
mass killings in East Timor and at a time of declining aid to the rest of
Southeast Asia.[16] The State Department's annual human rights report for
1976, issued shortly before Carter's inauguration, reflected this contradiction. It characterized the Suharto government as "a moderate authoritarian
regime" with "no consistent pattern of violation of human rights," identifying
political detainees as *"the single major human rights problem in the country"*
(emphasis added). The report did not mention Timor.[17] The State Department's assessment coincided with AI's publication of a more damning report,
which estimated that one hundred thousand political prisoners crowded Indonesian jails and that torture was employed "systematically" during interrogation.[18] Amazingly, the Amnesty report did not mention East Timor either, nor
did AI Secretary General Martin Ennals raise the abuses in Timor in meetings
in 1976 and 1977 with top World Bank leaders and Indonesian military and
diplomatic officials.[19]

By the end of 1976, however, abundant evidence was emerging that
Indonesia was engaged in ferocious military operations and committing
massive atrocities in the territory. At the end of April, Chief of Staff of the

U.S. Pacific Command Lt. General Joseph Moore met with Indonesia's Assistant Minister for Defense Planning Major General Yoga Supardi, who warned that Indonesia was encountering a "serious drain on resources" because of its operations in East Timor, "with shortages of ammunition for small arms, artillery, tank and naval guns." Other Indonesian officials admitted that Fretilin forces controlled perhaps three-quarters of the territory.[20] In November, a group of pro-integration Indonesian church officials publicly charged that Indonesian troops had killed sixty thousand Timorese.[21]

As the new administration settled in, Secretary of State Cyrus Vance and Zbigniew Brzezinski ordered a review of U.S. policy toward Southeast Asia. Ominously, Brzezinski ranked human rights dead last on his list of planning priorities, reprimanding staffers who proposed to cut assistance to Indonesia, the Philippines, and South Korea on these grounds.[22] Before the policy review even commenced, Indonesian officials told the U.S. embassy that President Suharto would refuse aid "if it's tied to human rights pressures," a bluff to be sure, given Jakarta's dependence on Washington for military assistance, but indicative of the Suharto regime's concern.[23] He should not have worried. Carter administration officials saw no need to reevaluate the foundations of U.S.-Indonesian relations, long premised on forging closer relations with Jakarta through increased foreign investment, military assistance, and enmeshment with the IMF, World Bank, and regional organizations such as ASEAN.[24]

Further reports of continued Indonesian atrocities in East Timor quickly tested the Carter administration's professed commitment to human rights. In March 1977, former Australian consul to East Timor James Dunn alleged that Indonesian forces had killed up to one hundred thousand civilians in East Timor.[25] Testifying before Congress, Dunn concluded that East Timor might be "the most serious case of contravention of human rights facing the world at this time."[26] Indonesian and Western officials quickly sought to discredit Dunn, whose claims contradicted their position that the fighting in Timor was effectively over and atrocities exaggerated. The Carter administration's response to his charges might have been scripted in Jakarta. The State Department wrote to Congressman Donald Fraser that Dunn's figures were "greatly exaggerated" and argued, citing no evidence, that "a more accurate estimate" of deaths would be "a few thousand, most of whom would have been fighting men on both sides."[27] Whatever the facts, State Department officials concluded, the basic question before Congress was "whether the situation in ET should be allowed to affect our overall policy goals in Indonesia." Clearly, they thought, it should not.[28]

Indonesian officials recognized the implications of the Carter administration's approach to Congress and responded accordingly. Shortly after the
Fraser hearings, a Congressional delegation led by Lester Wolff (D-NY)
and William Goodling (R-PA), accompanied by Assistant Secretary of State
Richard Holbrooke, visited Indonesia and East Timor, meeting with President Suharto and collaborating Timorese officials.[29] Upon their return,
Wolff and Goodling hailed Indonesia's actions in East Timor and mused
that "the Indonesians should have entered the fray much earlier and perhaps
more lives could have been spared."[30] Holbrooke's visit to Jakarta, the first
by a high-ranking Carter administration official, took place shortly before
tightly controlled general elections in which hundreds of Suharto opponents
were arrested and critical newspapers shuttered. The assistant secretary's
trip was, the U.S. embassy reported, an "unusual opportunity" to advance
concerns about human rights and democracy. In meetings with Suharto,
Foreign Minister Adam Malik, and Defense Minister General Maraden
Panggabean, however, Holbrooke offered no criticism of Indonesia's human
rights record.[31] President Suharto and other officials were "pleased" and
"reassured" with the results of these stage-managed visits, which Carter
administration officials appeared to view primarily as a means for deflecting
international criticism of Jakarta. Officials in Canberra agreed, viewing the
visit as a de facto U.S. recognition of East Timor's integration into
Indonesia.[32]

Shortly after Holbrooke's return, the NSC completed its review of U.S.
regional policy and recommended deeper military and economic ties with
ASEAN countries.[33] "All are eager to preserve close links with the United
States," Zbigniew Brzezinski wrote the president. "All provide a hospitable
climate for our investments; all take a moderate and pragmatic stance in
North–South gatherings"; and "all share apprehensions about our current
interests and future role in that part of the world."[34] All were also authoritarian states. To build on the Ford administration's initiatives, the NSC recommended a vice presidential visit to the region, expanded economic
assistance, and more generous terms for Foreign Military Sales (FMS) that
the Indonesian Armed Forces hoped to use to pursue its long-delayed program of military modernization.[35] Brzezinski urged a continued "focus on
the human rights pressures directed at Indonesia" and praise regarding the
release of political prisoners, but deleted any mention of East Timor.[36]

Suharto got the message. Over the summer, Indonesian officials paraded
to Washington to pledge progress on human rights in exchange for more
military and economic aid. Indonesian officials were particularly worried
about the prospective phasing out of the Military Assistance Program for

Jakarta at the end of 1977 and were determined to extract as much aid as possible to make up for it. Between 1978 and 1980, the Suharto regime requested $167 million worth of A-4 and F-5 ground attack fighters, surveillance radar, armored car and personnel carriers, and a co-production facility for M-16 rifles—a near doubling of U.S. military assistance compared to the Ford administration.[37] Two years prior, the Suharto regime had been able to exploit the Ford administration's anticommunism and concern with regional credibility in the aftermath of the end of Vietnam War to help secure U.S. support for the invasion of East Timor. While such concerns lurked in the background they did not animate the Carter administration's high-level deliberations on Indonesia or the region more generally, where, as Zbigniew Brzezinski told the president, "our prospect for nurturing effective relationships with the countries of East Asia" were "more favorable than at any time since World War II."[38]

During this period, the State Department Bureau of Human Rights and Humanitarian Affairs, working with congressional supporters and prodded by grassroots activists, sought to block the expansion of military assistance to Indonesia and link economic assistance to an improvement in human rights. However, Secretary of State Vance, Assistant Secretary of State Holbrooke, and especially Brzezinski formed a formidable wall of opposition, as they did for human rights supporters seeking to cut or condition U.S. assistance to other authoritarian states. When Assistant Secretary of State for Human Rights Patricia Derian's office sought to identify Indonesia as a "consistent and gross violator of human rights," rendering it ineligible for military assistance, the NSC intervened, arguing that Indonesia had human rights "problems" but did not engage in systematic abuses.[39] Attempts to delay plans for an M-16 co-production facility and the sale of F-5 fighter planes to Jakarta met a similar fate, when Secretary of State Vance personally intervened after Indonesian officials threatened to seek European weapons suppliers.[40]

The U.S. silence on East Timor contrasts sharply with the dramatic expansion of human rights activism and media attention directed at Latin America. There congressional activists mounted significant efforts to halt U.S. military assistance and restrict multilateral development aid to rights-abusing regimes, while country and regionally based campaigns sought to raise awareness of torture and shift public debate over U.S. interests in the western hemisphere. These groups benefited from geographic proximity, relatively high public awareness, refugees and immigrants living in the United States, a long history of travel by U.S. citizens, and extensive religious and missionary ties.[41] None of these conditions prevailed in East

Timor, where Indonesia enforced a near total news blackout and blocked journalists and other visitors access. However, activists still managed to covertly gather and distribute information about atrocities in the territory.[42]

Indonesia's nascent human rights movement fared no better. The two main human rights organizations in Indonesia—the Institute for Defense of Human Rights (LPHHM), founded in 1966 by Dutch activist H. J. C. Princen, and the Indonesian Legal Aid Foundation (LBH), founded in 1970 by lawyer Adnan Buyung Nasution—initially focused their work on the "extension of legal, civil and political rights" as well as "social justice and popular participation in development projects." Both organizations cultivated transnational ties to make political prisoners an international concern and lobbied Attorney General Ali Said for their release. But their fear of repression, nationalist identification, and lack of access to information concerning abuses in East Timor prevented Indonesian human rights groups from taking on the far more dangerous task of challenging Indonesia's invasion and occupation of Timor.[43]

The Suharto regime adroitly exploited nationalist sentiment to delegitimize the work of Amnesty International and other human rights groups, charging that it "still suffers from a 'moral arrogance' of the West." It also periodically targeted the first generation of human rights activists for harassment and arrest. Restrictions on discourse, funding, activism, and travel severely restricted local NGOs' ability to develop transnational links, forcing LBH and LPHHM to couch their work within the rhetorical confines of the regime's nationalist project, presenting it as a contribution to the legal reform and modernization of the state rather than as a challenge to its legitimacy.[44]

The legal aid approach of LBH and LPHHM also appealed to international donors who were considering funding human rights work.[45] Ford Foundation officials often framed these questions in functional terms, asking of Indonesia in 1976: "Is the present level of repression necessary to maintain an orderly society and carry on the variety of development efforts?" Initially, the Ford Foundation supported the International Commission of Jurists and ICRC, both of which worked directly with LBH and LPHHM to gather and disseminate information about political prisoners. Ford also began funding the Jakarta Public Defenders office, the Institute for Legal Aid, and other programs to give higher prominence to " legal aid and the rule of law" as a framework for human rights advocacy and development.[46]

Foreign donors soon came to dominate human rights funding in Indonesia, a development with dramatic and sometimes contradictory long-term consequences. External funding helped make NGO work an "alternative middle class career path for those with critical ideas," while serving as "transmitters into Indonesia of new paradigms for thinking about social, economic, and political change."[47] By the late 1970s, LBH began to engage in recognizably "Western" human rights work, establishing a human rights division and issuing its own annual reports on Indonesia. But foreign funding also imposed subtle constraints, giving a higher profile to NGOs that could frame goals, analyze problems, report abuses, and compile information in ways useful to the transnational human rights community. One former Amnesty researcher described an accretive process by which Amnesty's institutional needs indirectly worked to shape the language, style, and structure of human rights reporting from Indonesian and Timorese activists, imposing over time a discursive discipline that stripped their accounts of politics and ideology to appear neutral for international consumption.[48]

But the sidelining of East Timor as a human rights concern stemmed from more than mere great power hypocrisy, limited information, or geopolitics. The individualistic, liberal human rights discourse in the West, which ranked civil and political over collective economic and social rights and, in particular, the right to self-determination, compounded the difficulties faced by East Timor advocates working to reverse U.S. and Western support of Indonesia. As political scientist Kathryn Sikkink observed regarding Latin America, "The focus on the rights of the person found an echo in the liberal ideological tradition of the Western countries, where the human rights movement had the bulk of its members. But [it] was also consonant with the human rights problems in the main target countries of the early movement"—all long independent states in which rights-talk grew out of legal and political traditions of individual rights rather than recent anticolonial struggles. This narrow vision also reflected the original mandate of Amnesty International, which for the first twenty years of its existence focused almost exclusively on prisoners of conscience, torture victims, and the death penalty.[49]

If Western human rights advocates during the 1970s focused on crimes against the individual and the body, many postcolonial states and more politically radical solidarity campaigns continued to frame human rights demands in an anticolonial context. The leaders of Fretilin organized themselves along lines similar to FRELIMO, Mozambique's political party which ousted the Portuguese colonial regime in 1975. Many East Timorese sought refuge in Mozambique after 1975 and found in FRELIMO's colonial past Marxist analysis and organizational principles that paralleled their struggle. In their view, East Timor was fighting not for human rights in a Western context but for self-determination from colonialism, both Portuguese and Indonesian, which it exercised when it declared independence on November 28, 1975.[50]

Though historians of human rights have produced a small torrent of scholarship in the last decade, we still lack broad historical treatments of self-determination's descent through the twentieth century and its intersection with contemporary debates about minority protection, human rights, and related concepts.[51] Yet the limited studies we do have suggest that, from the moment of the December 1948 signing of the Universal Declaration of Human Rights, significant fissures opened within the postcolonial world, and between the colonial powers and the scommunist bloc as to the scope and meaning of self-determination as a human right. These debates, every bit as fierce as those over the UDHR itself, were inseparable from the dynamics of the Cold War and broader contests over postcolonial social, political, and economic organization.

Underlying these conflicts was a series of unanswerable questions: "Was self-determination a human right or a general principle? Did it implicate economic as well as political independence? Did it encompass the right to internal democratic participation? Did it apply only to colonial or non self-governing territories, or did it apply to national groups seeking to secede from recognized states?"[52] Inclusion of an explicit "right to self-determination" in the first two UN human rights charters and in the 1960 Declaration on the Granting of Independence to Colonial Countries and Peoples did little to clarify matters. Few national liberation movements or postcolonial states claiming the right to self-determination practiced internal democracy, and new multiethnic states rejected the application of self-determination to internal minorities. Indonesia's first President Sukarno, for example, threatened war with the Netherlands in 1962 in order to "recover" the territory of West New Guinea, which he argued could only exercise its right to self-determination as part of the unitary republic of Indonesia. These fissures sometimes burst into the open when ethnic, religious, and political minorities claiming the right of secession or internal rule, as in Biafra and Bangladesh, challenged the sanctity of colonial borders that served as the basis for independence claims—and for the nation-state system itself—in the postwar era.[53]

It is no coincidence that the last gasp of European colonialism in the early 1970s paralleled the explosion of human rights activism in Europe and the United States, or that postcolonial states continued to insist that self-determination broadly construed was the "first right" from which all other human rights derived.[54] Western nations in the 1970s, however, "did not agree that this was a fundamental human right," often viewing movements for self-determination as the untidy leftovers of decolonization. U.S. officials were particularly opposed to claims by members of the Non-Aligned Movement that effective self-determination required economic sovereignty and control over natural resources, a challenge to the prerogatives of multinational corporations also reflected in calls for a New International Economic Order.[55]

The U.S. stance on East Timor at the United Nations illustrates the difficulty U.S. and other Western officials had in reconciling self-determination with other framings of human rights. Immediately following Indonesia's December 1975 invasion, the United States voted in favor of UN Security Council resolutions affirming East Timor's right to self-determination and calling on Indonesia to withdraw from East Timor "without delay," while working mightily behind the scenes to make sure the resolution would never be enforced. A few months later, convinced that Indonesia's takeover of East Timor was a fait accompli, the Ford administration ordered U.S. Ambassador to the UN Daniel Patrick Moynihan to simply abstain from voting on a similar resolution.[56] On November 19, 1976, the United States voted against a General Assembly resolution rejecting Indonesia's July 1976 annexation of the territory (which Jakarta argued constituted an act of self-determination), thereafter maintaining the position that "while we have never recognized that a valid act of self-determination by the Timorese people has occurred, we accept the incorporation of East Timor into Indonesia."[57]

The Carter administration between 1977 and 1980 reiterated its predecessor's position at the UN recognizing Indonesia's incorporation of East Timor. At the 32nd UN General Assembly meeting in the fall of 1977, Mozambique and Guinea Bissau introduced a resolution calling for a ceasefire and the admission of a UN fact-finding mission to East Timor, significantly diluting the previous year's submission in the hopes of gaining U.S. support.[58] Not even Assistant Secretary of State Patricia Derian—a former civil rights activist—supported the resolution, though doing so would "dramatically underscore our human rights concerns" and "conform to our position that the UN has a responsibility to deal with problems relating to human rights, *including self-determination*"(emphasis added).[59] The United States, Australia, New Zealand, and other regional supporters of Indonesia in succeeding years continued to vote against UN resolutions rejecting Indonesia's invasion of East Timor and worked to remove the territory from the agenda of the UN Decolonization committee.[60] These efforts reflected a desire on the part of the United States and other countries both to support the Suharto regime's position on East Timor and to close off international forums where the territory's status could be contested.

The United States and Australian position was strikingly at odds with the Non-Aligned Movement, Lusophone nations, the communist bloc, and older human rights groups such as the International League for Human Rights.[61] The Fifth Conference of the Non-Aligned Countries in Colombo, Sri Lanka, for example, in August 1976 rejected Indonesia's claim that its annexation of Timor constituted an act of self-determination and affirmed support for East Timor's independence in accordance with recent UN resolutions.[62] The United States and other Western governments, however, were not alone in seeking to wall-off self-determination from other framings of human rights. Amnesty International's International Secretariat in a worldwide directive reminded members that "while governments may regard the human rights situation in East Timor as having a bearing on their stand on the issue of self-determination, AI does not urge governments to take any particular position on the issue." Most solidarity groups focusing on East Timor rejected Amnesty's analysis and sought explicitly to link human rights abuses to the denial of self-determination—exposing a gulf between differing visions of NGO human rights politics that historians have accorded little consideration.[63]

Western diplomats, while affirming East Timor's rights in principle, effectively ruled out independence and framed self-determination squarely in the context of integration with Indonesia. Developmental discourses, moreover, provided shorthand for dismissing Timor as too small and primitive to merit self-government; New Zealand's ambassador mused that "considered as human stock they are not at all impressive." Britain's Foreign and Commonwealth Office, which worried about the precedent set for decolonization in Belize, in March 1976 frankly argued that "morals and the law do not always go hand in hand. Self-determination is a laudable principle, but it may not always be morally right to grant it."[64]

Carter administration officials, like their regional allies, continued to formulate policy on the assumption that Indonesia's incorporation of East Timor was irreversible, and that any abuses, while regrettable, had occurred in the past and that the international community's priority should be gaining access for humanitarian organizations such as Catholic Relief Services and the Red Cross.[65] Not until contending claims over self-determination were resolved, in other words, would human rights in East Timor emerge as an acceptable subject of discussion for Western governments. But reports smuggled out of the territory by Catholic Church activists and journalists suggested that the Indonesian armed forces were not only still carrying out mass killings, but that they struggled to assert control over rural areas where most of Timor's population had fled.[66] In September 1977, Australian Labor Party leaders, citing reports smuggled out of East Timor, warned that Indonesia was planning a major offensive to wipe out Fretilin resistance, following an offer of "amnesty" to tens of thousands of Timorese living outside of army-controlled areas. Rather than allowing the refugees to return to their homes, however, Indonesian officials forced them into resettlement camps where starvation and disease killed thousands.[67]

Indonesian officials continued to admit privately that they controlled less than half and perhaps only 20 percent of East Timor's population. Meeting with U.S. embassy officials, General Benny Murdani complained that the armed forces lacked "manpower, supplies and expertise" to defeat Fretilin guerrillas. In July, the CIA observed that Indonesian military forces were engaged in their largest military operations since independence but "have had difficulties extending their control to the countryside and in some cases, even pacifying areas near the large population centers."[68] Moreover, despite a near doubling of U.S. military aid since 1976 the Armed Forces were "running out of military inventory," their operations in Timor having "pushed them to the wall."[69]

The continued reports of Indonesian atrocities and the military stalemate in East Timor at the end of 1977 provide the crucial backdrop for evaluating the Carter administration's framing of human rights in Indonesia, as well as its continued commitment to expanding military assistance to the Suharto regime. After two years of accumulating evidence of a possible genocide in East Timor, the State Department's annual human rights report for Indonesia, released in January 1978, acknowledged reports of atrocities by Indonesian troops in East Timor in 1975 and 1976 but claimed that "the Indonesian government withdrew and disciplined offending units guilty of individual excesses, [and] most of the human losses appear to have occurred prior to Indonesia's intervention."[70]

As the U.S. embassy was preparing its human rights report, Congressman Fraser wrote Secretary of State Vance concerning reports of indiscriminate killings in East Timor and the use of defoliants by U.S.-supplied OV-10 Bronco counterinsurgency aircraft. The State Department acknowledged the use of OV-10 aircraft to attack East Timor but noted that Indonesia had limited the weapons employed to "machine guns, rockets, and perhaps bombs" used in the "aerial bombing" of Fretilin-controlled areas—at the time sheltering tens of thousands of refugees fleeing Indonesian attacks.[71]

In the face of continued criticism, Carter administration officials sought to recast Indonesia's assault as a counterinsurgency effort. In February

1978, Assistant Secretary of State Robert Oakley appearing before Congress defended continued Indonesian military operations in East Timor as a legitimate response to "armed groups such as Fretilin who are employing armed force against the government."[72] The day after Oakley's testimony, the State Department notified Congress of its intent to sell to Indonesia sixteen F-5 fighter planes and spare parts worth $125 million, just as Australian ham-radio operators received broadcasts from East Timor reporting that Indonesian forces had massacred the entire population of the town of Atabai for supporting Fretilin, killing an estimated five hundred people.[73]

Three months later, in the culmination of the Carter administration's efforts to forge closer relations with Indonesia, Vice President Walter Mondale visited Jakarta, meeting with President Suharto and other Indonesian officials.[74] "This will be an especially important moment for U.S.-Indonesian relations," the NSC argued, an opportunity to "erase doubts as to U.S. policy toward Indonesia and Southeast Asia."[75] Both U.S. and Indonesian officials recognized the importance of such a visit. Mondale's briefing papers for the visit accordingly stated that one of his chief objectives was to "affirm our commitment to promote progress on human rights." Yet the NSC urged the vice president to discuss human rights in both countries "with a very light touch," emphasizing "our determination not to impose our values, our understanding of local cultural and historical factors, [and] our recognition of recent progress."[76]

The Suharto regime viewed Mondale's visit as an opportunity to plead for expedited approval and shipment of military assistance, including twenty-eight A-4 ground attack aircraft.[77] Mondale agreed, requesting that Carter accelerate approval of the A-4 sale, since "the underlying purpose of my visit is to affirm that we want to work with Indonesia." As the vice president arrived in Indonesia, Carter issued a special Presidential Guidance approving the sale, seeking clarification "on the circumstances in which . . . the planes will be used, *in particular in East Timor*," an acknowledgement that the new U.S. weapons would be used there (emphasis in original).[78] Following Washington's lead, Great Britain and Australia immediately announced the sale of Hawk ground attack aircraft, transports, and helicopters to Jakarta.[79]

In his meeting with Suharto, the vice president treated human rights as a matter of perception and politics whose effective management would enable still closer relations with Jakarta.[80] Mondale noted that the recent release of detainees had "helped create a favorable climate of opinion in the Congress" for expanded arms sales. He suggested that releasing smaller numbers of prisoners more regularly would further improve public opinion and deflect criticism—a suggestion the regime later implemented. The vice president likewise noted the two nations' "mutual concerns regarding East Timor," in particular "how to handle public relations aspects of the problem." He suggested that allowing humanitarian groups such as Catholic Relief Services access to East Timor would not only help refugees in the area (overwhelmingly generated by Indonesian military operations) but "have a beneficial impact on U.S. public opinion."[81] Suharto was "exuberant" over the visit, finding Mondale "completely friendly and open and to have an excellent understanding of the Indonesian situation," a sign that the regime expected no more real pressure on either human rights or East Timor, at least none that could not be effectively managed.[82]

As the White House worked to "consolidate the Administration's position" with the regime, Indonesian army and navy units launched a campaign of "encirclement and annihilation" against Fretilin guerrillas lasting through the end of 1978. In one of many such incidents reported during the campaign, Indonesian troops using U.S.-supplied Bronco aircraft massacred upwards of five hundred people assembled at the foot of Vadaboro Mountain in the Matebian range on the eastern end of the island.[83]

When Western ambassadors and journalists finally gained access to the territory in September they were shocked by the extent of starvation and misery among the tens of thousands of refugees in forced resettlement camps.[84] Horrific pictures of emaciated Timorese refugees finally forced Indonesia to permit the reentry of the ICRC, but not before many thousands had died of starvation and preventable disease. In July 1979—ten months after his visit to East Timor—U.S. Ambassador to Indonesia Ed Masters finally requested U.S. emergency assistance, a move which the administration trumpeted as a symbol of the U.S. and Indonesian commitment to the welfare and human rights of the Timorese.[85]

Between 1977 and 1979, the Carter administration did succeed in its goal of deepening relations with the authoritarian Suharto regime and advancing U.S. regional interests. Indonesia continued to play a politically moderate role in ASEAN and the Non-Aligned Movement on issues of North–South conflict. It welcomed U.S. investment and served as a reliable anticommunist counterweight to China and Vietnam. Indonesia also continued to release political prisoners detained after 1965, enabling Washington to claim progress on human rights and keep the pipeline of economic and military assistance flowing. Improved relations with Jakarta, however, enabled a near-genocidal assault on the people of East Timor and negated Indonesia's human rights "progress." There is no indication, however, that the Carter administration ever reconsidered U.S. support for Indonesia's occupation of East Timor or viewed mounting Indonesian atrocities there as a human rights violation. Rather, U.S. officials, almost without exception, treated East Timor as a public relations or humanitarian problem, significant not for the abuses occurring there but for the problems it might pose for U.S. plans to expand economic and military assistance to Indonesia. The United States, together with its British, Australian, and Japanese allies, denied East Timor's right to self-determination, a right accorded little weight even by the emerging human rights establishment.

If human rights were "preeminently a politics of the information age," then the handful of Westerners knowledgeable about East Timor faced a formidable challenge.[86] Into the 1980s, East Timorese refugees and church activists periodically smuggled out letters and messages describing the appalling human rights situation, and journalists penned occasional stories about Southeast Asia's "forgotten war."[87] However, the U.S. government, Indonesia's primary military patron, could and did ignore this trickle of information, aided by a pliant media which generally refused to cover East Timor and often accepted Indonesian government propaganda at face value when it did. Without consistent and reliable sources of information, mobilized constituencies, or organized pressure on Congress, and other institutions the small and scattered community of East Timor supporters—relying largely on information provided by activists elsewhere—was unable to effectively challenge U.S. support for the Indonesian occupation. In addition, the focus of the organized human rights movement on civil and political rights at the expense of postcolonial self-determination enabled the Carter administration to argue that discussions of East Timor should focus on improving the conditions of the Timorese under Indonesian rule rather than pressing for an Indonesian withdrawal.

As he began hearings on East Timor in June 1977, Congressman Donald Fraser stated that "to write off the rights of 600,000 people because we are friends with the country that forcibly annexed them does real violence to any profession of adherence to principle or to human rights." De facto foreign minister in exile José Ramos-Horta framed the same issue in anticolonial terms: "What in the final act of analysis, is an act of self-determination? When one-tenth of our nation has been massacred by the Nazi army of Java, but in spite of this the whole nation continues the struggle for liberation, is this not the supreme act of self-determination?"[88] To recall Fraser's and Horta's words is not to elevate self-determination to a privileged position in the history of human rights but to place a certain vision of self-determination *as* human rights in its proper perspective, and to suggest that historians have yet to sufficiently and critically unpack the complicated international and organizational politics of human rights in the 1970s.

The diplomatic and discursive fight over East Timor exposed a major fissure in transnational conceptions and hierarchies of human rights at the end of the colonial era that the Indonesian armed forces and its sponsors were able to manipulate to their advantage for twenty-four years. Human rights, in this reading, was not a trajectory or a gradually expanding set of norms and institutions but an arena of contestation over expertise and representation and therefore power, waged on highly unequal terms. The final report of East Timor's Commission for Reception, Truth and Reconciliation rightly situates both the human rights politics and denial of self-determination to East Timor in both a Cold War and a postcolonial context.[89] The persistent and countervailing demands of East Timorese and their outnumbered and outgunned supporters for a different ordering of rights would await the collapse of the Cold War, the reemergence of a transnational movement for East Timor, and a reconsideration of the meaning of self-determination and human rights in an age of accelerating globalization.

NOTES

1. Memo, Armacost to Brzezinski, June 14, 1977, NSA Staff Materials, Far East, Box 6, James Carter Presidential Library (hereafter NSA SMFE JCPL).

2. Taylor, "'Encirclement and Annihilation': The Indonesian Occupation of East Timor," in *The Specter of Genocide: Mass Murder in Historical Perspective*, ed. Robert Gellately and Ben Kiernan (Cambridge: Cambridge University Press, 2003), 166–68.

3. Note on Meeting With [excised], Note New Zealand Embassy in Jakarta to Wellington, July 5, 1975, declassified document in authors possession; Memo, C. W. Squire, South East Asian Department, "The Future of Portuguese Timor," March 5, 1975, FCO 15/1703, UK National Archives; Cablegram O.JA1201 Australian Embassy in Jakarta to Canberra, August 14, 1975, quoted in *Australia and the Indonesian Incorporation of Portuguese Timor, 1974–1976* (Melbourne: Department of Foreign Affairs and Trade, 2000), 306–9.

4. Brad Simpson, "'Illegally and Beautifully': The United States, the Indonesian Invasion of East Timor and the International Community," *Cold War History* 5, no. 3 (August 2005): 281–315.

5. Telegram 286596, the State Department to US Delegation Secretary's Aircraft, December 7, 1975, NSA Country Files, East Asia and the Pacific, Indonesia, Box 6, Gerald Ford Library (hereafter GFL).

6. Cable Canberra to Jakarta, October 7, 1975, cited in *Australia and the Indonesian Incorporation of Portuguese Timor,* 447; Nancy Viviani, "Australians and the Timor issue," *Australian Outlook* 30, no. 2 (August 1976): 197–226.

7. James Dunn, *Timor: A People Betrayed* (Sydney: ABC Books for the Australian Broadcasting Corporation, 1996), 311, 333; Pedro Pinto Leite, ed., *The East Timor Problem and the Role of Europe* (Leiden: International Platform of Jurists, 1998), passim.

8. Arnold Kohen, "Human Rights in Indonesia," *The Nation,* November 26, 1977, 553–57; Richard Franke, *East Timor: The Hidden War,* (New York: East Timor Defense Committee, 1976).

9. Kenneth Cmiel, "The Emergence of Human Rights Politics in the United States," *Journal of American History* 86, no. 3 (December 1999): 1231–50.

10. Greg Fealy, "The Release of Indonesia's Political Prisoners: Domestic Versus Foreign Policy, 1975–1979" (working paper 94, Centre for Southeast Asian Studies, Monash University, 1995, 7); Memo, Executive Committee Meeting of August 26, 1976, "Proposal for an Indonesia Campaign," RG IV, Box 10, Amnesty International USA Papers, Columbia University (hereafter AI Papers).

11. Fealy, "The Release of Indonesia's Political Prisoners," 13–14; David Hinkley, "The Work of Amnesty International for Indonesian Prisoners of Conscience," TAPOL US, US Campaign for the Release of Indonesian Political Prisoners, Bulletin no. 1, October 1, 1975; "ILO Given Indonesia Pledge on Prisoners," *The Guardian,* June 17, 1976, 4.

12. *Indonesia: Economic Prospects and the Status of Human Rights*, Center for International Policy, Vol. II, no. 3 (Washington, DC, 1976).

13. Memo, sec. gen., "The Forthcoming meeting of the Intergovernmental Group on Indonesia," November 20, 1973, RG II, Box 7, AI Papers; Memo, Ingersoll for Ford, July 1, 1975, Indonesia, Box 6, GFL.

14. Fealy, "The Release of Indonesia's Political Prisoners," 28; Telegram 252899, State to Jakarta, October 23, 1975, declassified as a result of author's Freedom of Information Act request (hereafter FOIA).

15. Telegram 15467 Jakarta to State, November 30, 1976, FOIA; Jusuf Wanandi, *Kebijakan Luar Negri President Carter Dan Peranan Kongress AS*, (Jakarta, Centre for Strategic and International Studies, Monograf No. 5, February 1978), 9–13.

16. Jan Pluvier to Cong. Donald Fraser, October 25, 1976, Subject Committee Files 1976, Box 149.G.9.8F, Fraser Papers, Minnesota State Historical Society, Minneapolis, MN (hereafter MSHS); TAPOL, US Bulletin no. 4, New York, April 15, 1976.

17. Telegram 13695, Jakarta to State, October 20, 1976, FOIA.

18. *Indonesia* (London: Amnesty International, 1977), 21; Telegram 12787, Jakarta to State, September 30, 1976, FOIA.

19. "Note of a Conversation with Indonesian Delegation led by Lt. General Ali Moertopo," November 18, 1976, RG II, Box 7, AI Papers; Memo for the Files, Meeting With Representatives of AI, October 26, 1977, Accession A1994–021, Box 53, Indonesia General Vol. I, Fol. 1388105, World Bank Archives, Washington, DC.

20. Telegram 5605, Jakarta to State, April 29, 1976, FOIA; *Indonesian Times,* February 1, 1976; Telegram 0021, Jakarta to State, January 3, 1978, FOIA.

21. "Indons Killed 60,000: Report," *Melbourne Age*, November 19, 1976, 2.

22. Memo, for Zbigniew Brzezinksi from Armacost, January 28, 1977, NSA SMFE, Box 4, JCPL; Memo, for Brzezinksi from Jessica Tuchman and Robert M. Kimmitt, February 7, 1977, NSA SMFE, Box 4, JCPL.

23. Memo, for Zbigniew Brzezinksi, East Asia Evening Report, January 18, 1977, NSA SMFE, Box 4, JCPL.

24. Telegram 059033, State to Jakarta, March 17, 1977, FOIA.

25. Telegram 1472, Canberra to State, March 3, 1977, FOIA.

26. Subcommittee on International Organizations and Asian and Pacific Affairs, "Human Rights in East Timor and the Question on the Use of U.S. Equipment by the Indonesian Armed Forces," March 23, 1977, 95th Congress, First Session (Washington, DC, 1977), 26; Memo, to Asst. Secretary Maynes from USUN, October 10, 1977, FOIA.

27. Submission to Peacock by A. R. Parsons, Canberra, March 17, 1977, cited in *Australia and the Indonesian Incorporation of Portuguese Timor,* 829–34; Ali Murtopo to Donald Fraser, March 16, 1977, Subject Committee Files 1977 Box 151.H.3.7B, Fraser Papers, MSHS; Telegram 3166, Jakarta to State, March 12, 1977, FOIA.

28. Telegram 066813, State to Jakarta, March 25, 1977, FOIA.

29. "Congressmen [*sic*] Back Takeover of Timor," *Melbourne Age,* April 17, 1977, cited in Taylor, *Indonesia's Forgotten,* 83–84.

30. Telegram 4724, Jakarta to State, April 14, 1977, FOIA; Telegram 100498, State to Jakarta, May 4, 1977, FOIA.

31. Telegram 4980, Jakarta to State, April 18, 1977, FOIA; Telegram 4893, Jakarta to State, April 18, 1977, FOIA.

32. Cablegram O.JA13174, Jakarta to Canberra, Lisbon, New York, May 26, 1977, quoted in *Australia and the Indonesian Incorporation of Portuguese Timor,* 836–38; Telegram 5572, Jakarta to State, May 2, 1977, FOIA.

33. W. W. Rostow, *The United States and the Regional Organization of Asia and the Pacific* (Austin: University of Texas Press, 1986). In 1977 ASEAN's member states were Indonesia, the Philippines, Thailand, Singapore, and Malaysia.

34. Memo, for the President from Brzezinski, May 16, 1977, NSA SMFE, Box 4, JCPL.

35. Memo, for Brzezinski from Armacost, June 14, 1977, NSA SMFE, Box 4, JCPL.

36. Memo, for the President from Brzezinski, July 8, 1977, NSA SMFE, Box 4, JCPL.

37. Memo, for Brzezinski from Armacost, October 21, 1977, FOIA.

38. Memo, from Brzezinski to the President, May 16, 1977, NSA SMFE, Box 4, JCPL.

39. Memo, from Armacost to Jessica Tuchman, August 24, 1977, NSA SMFE, Box 6, JCPL.

40. Rep. Helen S. Meyner to Secretary of State Cyrus Vance, June 22, 1978, Box 14, Box 14, East Timor and Indonesia Action Network Papers, Tamiment Library, New York University (hereafter ETAN Papers); Fraser to Vance, February 23, 1977, Subject Files 1977, Box 151.H.3.7B, Fraser Papers, MSHS.

41. Kathryn Sikkink, *Mixed Signals: U.S. Human Rights Policy and Latin America* (Ithaca, NY: Cornell University Press, 2004), chs. 2–4; James Green, *"We Cannot Remain Silent": Opposition to the Brazilian Military Dictatorship in the United States, 1964–85* (Durham, 2009).

42. "East Timor Information Bulletin," no. 3, March 1976, British Campaign for an Independent East Timor, Box 16, ETAN Papers.

43. Edward Aspinall, *Opposing Suharto: Compromise, Resistance and Regime Change in Indonesia* (Stanford, CA: Stanford University Press, 2005), 103–5; Anja Jetschke, "Linking the Unlinkable? International Norms and Nationalism in Indonesia and the Philippines," in *The Power of Human Rights: International Norms and Domestic Change*, ed. Thomas Risse, Stephen C. Ropp, and Kathryn Sikkink (Cambridge: Cambridge University Press, 1999), 134–72.

44. Jetschke, "Linking the Unlinkable?" 140.

45. William Korey, *Taking on the World's Most Repressive Regimes: The Ford Foundation's International Human Rights Policies and Practices* (New York: Palgrave Macmillan, 2007), 28–37; Rosalyn Higgins, "Human Rights: Needs and Practices," September 1973, Ford Foundation Archives New York (hereafter FFA).

46. Ford Foundation, "Notes on Human Rights and Indonesian Development," Paper for Southeast Asia Development Advisory Group Seminar, May 14–15, 1976, Box 14, ETAN Papers; "Human Rights and Intellectual Freedom," Ford Foundation Information Paper 005527, March 1978, FFA.

47. Aspinall, *Opposing Suharto*, 93–95.

48. "East Timor: Indonesian Armed Aggression," Speech by José Ramos-Horta, Representative of Fretilin (n.d.), Box 14, ETAN Papers; Author correspondence with Geoffrey Robinson, November 2008.

49. Sikkink, *Mixed Signals*, 57.

50. David Webster, "Non-State Diplomacy: East Timor, 1975–1999," *Portuguese Studies Review* 11, no. 1 (2003): 10; excerpt from *People's Daily* of the People's Republic of China, December 10, 1975, published in F. X. do Amaral, *East Timor: A People's War* (New York: Ministry of External Relations, Democratic Republic of East Timor, April 12, 1976), 5.

51. Eric Weitz, "From the Vienna to the Paris System: International Politics and the Entangled Histories of Human Rights, Forced Deportations, and Civilizing Missions," *The American Historical Review* 113 (December 2008):1313–1343; Erez Manela, *The Wilsonian Moment: Self-Determination and the International Origins of Anticolonial Nationalism* (New York: Oxford University Press, 2007).

52. Roger Normand and Sarah Zaidi, *Human Rights at the UN: The Political History of Universal Justice* (Bloomington: Indiana University Press, 2008), 212–20.

53. M. Rafiquil Islam, "Secessionist Self-Determination: Some Lessons From Katanga, Biafra and Bangladesh," *Journal of Peace Research* 22, no. 4 (1985): 217–27; Daniel Sargent, "From Internationalism to Globalism: The United States and the Transformation of International Politics in the 1970s" (PhD diss., Harvard University, 2008), 278–344.

54. Rupert Emerson, "The Fate of Human Rights in the Third World," *World Politics* 27, no. 2 (January 1975): 204; Press release No. 288/1006, June 28,1977, Indonesian Mission to the United Nations, New York.

55. Cmiel, "The Recent History of Human Rights"; Telegram 1290, Geneva to State, "Human Rights Commission—Self-Determination," March 23, 1973, FOIA.

56. Geoffrey Gunn, *East Timor and the United Nations: The Case for Intervention* (Lawrenceville, NJ: Red Sea Press, 1997), 107–11.

57. State Department Press Advisory, "East Timor—Self Determination," August 4, 1982, FOIA.

58. Memo, for Richard Holbrooke from Andrew Young, USUN, August 4, 1977, FOIA; Telegram 2776, State to Jakarta, August 30, 1977, FOIA.

59. Memo, for Philip Habib from Maynes, Holbrooke, Hansen and Derian, November 1, 1977, FOIA.

60. Telegram 5688, USUN to State, December 6, 1978, FOIA; Telegram 04413, USUN to State, October 21, 1980, FOIA; Memo, New Zealand Embassy in Jakarta to Wellington, June 16, 1976, declassified document in author's possession.

61. Petition from International League for Human Rights to Fourth Committee of the UN General Assembly, October 14, 1980, Box 14, ETAN Papers.

62. Ton Duc Thang, President of the Democratic Republic of Vietnam to Francisco Xavier do Almaral, President of Fretilin, January 27, 1976, Box 14, ETAN Papers; Memo, Grozney to Rundell, July 21, 1976, FCO 020/1(333), UKNA.

63. Memo, Asia Research Department to All Sections, "AI's concerns in East Timor," August 1983, RG IV, Box 25, AI Papers.

64. Memo, Roger Peren to New Zealand Secretary of Foreign Affairs, January 13, 1978, released under Official Information Act request; Foreign and Commonwealth Office Diplomatic Report no. 182/76, March 15, 1976, FCO 15/1709, UKNA.

65. Submission, Roger Holdich to Fraser, August 6, 1976, quoted in *Australia and the Indonesian Incorporation of Portuguese Timor,* 825–26.

66. Telegram 5366, Jakarta to State, April 25, 1978, FOIA; Telegram 6209, Jakarta to State, May 12, 1978, FOIA.

67. Telegram 6150, Canberra to State, September 1, 1977, FOIA.

68. Telegram 000345, Jakarta to State, January 3, 1978, FOIA; CIA National Foreign Assessment Center Weekly Military Review, July 26, 1978, FOIA.

69. "Indonesia Quietly Starting to Modernize Its Hopelessly Outmoded Military Force," *Los Angeles Times,* December 4, 1977, B18.

70. U.S. Department of State Country *Reports on Human Rights Practices 1978,* February 3, 1978 (Washington, DC: GPO, 1978), 235.

71. Assistant Secretary for Congressional Relations Douglas Bennett to Fraser, January 7, 1978, FOIA; Telegram 0333, Jakarta to State, January 8, 1978, FOIA.

72. Subcommittee on International Relations of the Committee on International Relations, *U.S. Policy on Human Rights and Military Assistance: Overview and Indonesia,* February 15, 1978, 96th Congress, 1st Sess. (Washington, DC: GPO, 1978).

73. Telegram 040604, State to Jakarta, February 16, 1978, FOIA; John Taylor, *Indonesia's Forgotten War,* 85.

74. Scope paper for Vice President's Visit to Southeast Asia, March 17, 1978, NSA SMFE, Box 7, JCPL; Raymond Bonner, *Waltzing with a Dictator*, Expanded and Updated Ed. (New York: Vintage, 1988), 231–49.

75. Inventory of Vice Presidential Trip to Indonesia, February 28, 1978, NSA SMFE, Box 7, JCPL.

76. Scope paper for Vice President's Visit to Southeast Asia, March 17, 1978, NSA SMFE, Box 7, JCPL.

77. Telegram 1874, Jakarta to State, February 10, 1978, FOIA.

78. Memo, for the President from the Vice President, April 26, 1978, NSA SMFE, Box 7, JCPL; Memo, for Deputy Executive Secretary of State Frank Wisner, "Presidential Guidance on A-4s," May 9, 1978, FOIA.

79. Carmel Budiardjo and Liem Soei Liong, *The War in East Timor* (London: Zed, 1984), 30.

80. Telegram 5613, Jakarta to Manila, May 1, 1978, FOIA.

81. Telegram 6004, Jakarta to State, May 9, 1978, FOIA; Telegram 8864, Jakarta to State, July 5, 1978, FOIA; Telegram 6076 Jakarta to State, FOIA.

82. Telegram 8736, Jakarta to State, May 15, 1978, FOIA; Memo, for Brzezinski from Armacost, May 16, 1978, NSA SMFE, Box 7, JCPL.

83. Taylor, *Indonesia's Forgotten War*, 86–87.

84. Telegram 12189, Jakarta to State, September 8, 1978, FOIA.

85. Telegram 313771, State to Jakarta, December 6, 1979, FOIA.

86. Cmiel, "The Emergence of Human Rights Politics in the United States," 1235.

87. Sharon Scharfe, "Human Rights and the Internet in Asia: Promoting the Case of East Timor," in *Human Rights and the Internet,* ed. Stephen Hick, Edward F. Halpin, and Eric Hoskins (New York: Palgrave Macmillan, 2000), 129–37.

88. *Human Rights in East Timor*, June 28 and July 19, 1977, hearings before the Subcommittee on International Relations of the Committee on International Relations (Washington, DC: GPO 1977); Horta quoted in Francisco Xavier do Amaral, *East Timor: A People's War,* April 12, 1976, p. 44, Box 14, ETAN Papers.

89. *Chega! Final Report of the Commission for Reception, Truth and Reconciliation in East Timor (CAVR)* (Dili, 2006), Executive Summary, 47–55.

9

ANTI-TORTURE POLITICS

Amnesty International, the Greek Junta, and the
Origins of the Human Rights "Boom" in the United
States

BARBARA KEYS

In 1970, Tower Books, publisher of such mass-market titles as *The Amazing Hypno-Diet, Games Women Play,* and *ESP and Psychic Power*, released a pocket-sized paperback edition of *Barbarism in Greece*. Authored by James Becket, a Harvard Law School graduate who had worked for Amnesty International (AI), the book was a grim compilation of firsthand accounts by political prisoners of torture by the military dictatorship in Greece, supplemented with the texts of investigative reports. The cover reminded readers that torture was a crime with tangible victims and victimizers: on the front, the face of an attractive young woman was captured in an agonized scream, the Acropolis visible in the background; the back featured a photograph of a man identified as "a practicing torturer" in Athens. Among the enthusiastic endorsements of the book were five by members of Congress.[1]

The book was part of a concerted liberal campaign in the United States against the Greek junta that seized power in April 1967. Although the repercussions of repression in Greece for the development of post-1970 human rights movements have been given scant attention, anti-junta activism helped lay the groundwork for the worldwide "human rights boom" of the 1970s.[2] Junta opponents cultivated public interest, provided tactics, and shaped priorities that would influence later, more powerful campaigns. The overthrow of constitutional democracy in the "cradle of democracy," combined with tales of brutal tortures inflicted on well-educated, middle-class Greeks who opposed the regime, energized left-leaning groups in Europe and the United States into activism that began to draw on the language of human rights. Overshadowed by the national obsession with the Vietnam War, repression in Greece never attained in the United States the prominence it did in Europe, where proximity and the power of socialist parties gave Greece a higher profile. But as Becket's book suggests, Greece generated enough attention in the United States to offer a testing ground for new strategies of political mobilization and a new liberal foreign-policy agenda.[3]

Surveying the U.S. response to repression in Greece through 1970, this chapter argues that tales of Greek torture—or physical and psychological maltreatment loosely labeled torture—became a nascent liberal human rights coalition's most effective tool in mobilizing public opposition to the Greek junta and, more broadly, in U.S. strategies for fighting the Cold War. Amnesty International's reporting on Greece raised torture to the top of the human rights agenda.[4] American liberals then made torture a central part of the indictment against the junta, successfully using allegations of torture to transform the nature of the debate about U.S. support for right-wing dictatorships. Their concern and outrage at abuses were genuine, but they also consciously designed strategies to engage the public at an emotional level. At a time when the Cold War consensus was crumbling, leftist outrage about torture helped develop a new political language, one that abandoned Cold War dichotomies in favor of purported universalisms.[5] By the mid-1970s, condemnations of torture, tested in the context of opposition to the colonels' regime in Greece, had become a critical catalyst for surging interest in human rights. In the public mind, torture attained the status of the most recognized and most reviled of all human rights abuses.

The Greek campaign taught Amnesty International officials valuable lessons about credibility and documentation.[6] As historian Kenneth Cmiel noted, the human rights movement of the 1970s was a product of the information age, and AI officials created a "politics of the global flow of key bits of fact" by devising ways "to collect accurate accounts" of abuses.[7] By the late 1970s, Amnesty's reports would be lauded for their reliability and regarded as required reading for the world's diplomats, and the organization's success was driven by what one historian calls the "meticulous and verifiable accuracy" of its reports.[8] But achieving this status was neither simple nor easy. The allegations in AI's two Greek reports were weakly documented and vulnerable to counterattack. They generated media attention, but they also sparked two years of charges and countercharges in a battle for public trust and credibility.[9] For every charge lobbed by Amnesty and its supporters, the Greek regime, its supporters, and nonaligned skeptics denied that there was credible evidence of mistreatment. It was not until the

December 1969 leak of a European Commission of Human Rights report that substantiated charges of torture, in hundreds of pages of detailed legal analysis, that public doubts were quelled and the mainstream media began to treat claims of official torture as established fact.[10] In building public trust, Amnesty officials learned that reports were perceived as credible when they provided names, dates, and firsthand testimony.[11] Meticulous detail and a clinically detached style became a form of prophylaxis against the charges of propagandizing that inevitably greeted criticisms of right-wing regimes.

The dividing line between those who accepted the early allegations of torture in Greece and those who disputed them was not determined by evidence but by political ideology: liberals believed, conservatives denied. Liberal receptivity to torture charges was heightened by a loss of faith in American benevolence that was a legacy of the Vietnam War. A new sense of moral responsibility for crimes committed by U.S. allies coincided with rising public consciousness of the Holocaust, the central lesson of which equated silence with complicity.[12] These developments shaped the liberal political response to the Greek regime. Anti-junta groups united around a single goal: cutting off U.S. aid to Greece, choosing the limited objective of moral dissociation over positive incentives to mitigate abuses.[13]

The focus on torture as the preeminent symbol of repression and on reductions in aid as the solution, hallmarks of the anti-junta campaign, would also become central to the more broad-based U.S. human rights campaigns of the mid-1970s. As the Greek case shows, the roots of those campaigns lie in shifts that began in the late 1960s. Liberal human rights initiatives prioritizing the promotion of civil and political rights abroad gained momentum after the Vietnam War ended, but they originated earlier, in tandem with growing opposition to that war after 1967.

Opposition to the Greek Junta

In April 1967, following two years of parliamentary instability in Greece, a group of right-wing military officers headed by Colonel George Papadopoulos seized power in a bloodless coup. Fearing that new elections called by King Constantine would bring a swing to the left, the colonels seized power in the name of anticommunism and promptly imprisoned or forced into exile thousands of leftist, centrist, and monarchist Greeks, including union leaders, journalists, and intellectuals. Replacing democracy with dictatorship, they instituted martial law, prohibited strikes and political demonstrations, and severely curtailed civil liberties, empowering the police to arrest people for making statements "likely to arouse anxiety among citizens or lessen their sense of security and order."[14] Many of the regime's edicts, including bans on modern music, long hair on men, Russian caviar, and books by Sophocles, invited ridicule at home and abroad.[15] Until it was brought down in 1974 by an ill-advised attempt to "reunite" Cyprus with Greece, the junta faced ineffectual resistance, including small-scale bombings.[16]

Intelligence services and civil and military police routinely used brutal methods in the interrogation of political prisoners; estimates of the number of torture victims run into the thousands.[17] State-sanctioned maltreatment of prisoners on this scale was not new. Earlier Greek governments had held thousands of political prisoners, and physical mistreatment of prisoners, criminal and political, was a common practice. The Metaxas dictatorship of the late 1930s engaged in widespread torture of political prisoners, and during and after the Greek civil war of the late 1940s, torture was widely practiced in concentration camps holding tens of thousands of communists.[18] Whether mistreatment was significantly more widespread and brutal under the colonels is difficult to determine given the lack of hard numbers and questions of what constitutes torture. The post-1967 junta was the first to use electric shock, but it also favored a method with a long history in Greece: *falanga*, or beating the soles of the feet.[19]

Governments on both sides of the Atlantic responded temperately to events in Greece. West European governments saw the suppression of democracy as regrettable but outweighed by Greece's value as a NATO ally and trading partner. Britain and France continued to sell weapons to Greece; West Germany imposed a ban only in 1971. Public opinion in Europe, particularly in Scandinavia, was responsible for moving some governments—in Denmark, Norway, Sweden, and sometimes Italy, West Germany, and the Netherlands—to oppose Greece in European forums such as the Council of Europe. In a significant move, the Scandinavian countries brought a case against Greece before the European Commission on Human Rights in late 1967. The list of charges, initially based on the suppression of democracy, was amended in 1968 to include torture after AI's reports received significant media attention. After a year-long series of hearings in Strasbourg and elsewhere, the commission ruled that democracy had been suppressed without justification and that torture was officially sanctioned. Under threat of expulsion from the Council of Europe, Greece withdrew in December 1969.[20]

The Johnson and Nixon administrations adopted a position one official characterized as "do business with the Junta but do it with some show of reluctance."[21] Viewing Greece as an important NATO ally and eager to maintain valued Mediterranean bases and overflight rights, neither Johnson nor Nixon exerted genuine pressure on the Greek junta to moderate repression or to return to democracy.[22] Under pressure from liberals, the Johnson administration cut off the supply of heavy weapons to Greece immediately after the coup, but the suspension was first evaded and then ended.[23] U.S. support for the colonels offered legitimacy to the regime and identified the United States with the dictatorship in the minds of many Greeks, contributing to the rise of anti-Americanism in Greece after its return to democracy in 1974.[24]

Making Torture Credible

The junta's suppression of democracy and civil liberties was the initial trigger for foreign public opposition, but the issue soon became intertwined with, and in many ways overshadowed by, allegations of torture.[25] To many opponents of the regime, nothing symbolized what was wrong with the colonels' regime more than its embrace of torture. Yet torture in Greece might have remained a historical footnote if not for Amnesty International's efforts. Still a young, small organization with a weak financial base, it was weathering an internal crisis over the clandestine acceptance of British government funding and the resignation of its founder, Peter Benenson, when the Greek colonels seized power.[26] Amnesty's handling of the Greek case proved critical for its future development, spurring its growth (and its tiny, new U.S. section), by at first testing—but ultimately enhancing—its credibility, garnering a bonanza of media attention, and providing a blueprint for future campaigns.

A few scattered reports of torture in Greece appeared in the European press in the last months of 1967, but it was AI's work that made torture a prominent issue.[27] At the end of 1967, AI's International Secretariat in London sent two attorneys to Greece to investigate the Greek government's announced amnesty for political prisoners. British barrister Anthony Marreco and American lawyer James Becket published their report in January 1968 after four weeks in Athens.[28] Its findings on the amnesty were unremarkable, and the few paragraphs they wrote on the status of political prisoners might have languished unnoticed in AI's files if not for the inclusion of an incendiary final point that caught the attention of the European media. At the end of the brief and inconclusive report, the authors noted that they had come across charges that the Greek government was "practising the infliction of pain as an aid to interrogation." They concluded that "torture is deliberately and officially used" against political opponents as "a widespread practice." The report listed eighteen techniques that allegedly constituted torture, including falanga, electric shock, pulling out fingernails, and sexual torture.[29]

In retrospect, the report appears to have been accurate in its essentials, but it offered such weak substantiation that doubters had solid grounds for skepticism.[30] The lack of firsthand testimony from victims willing to be named in public left AI open to charges of propagandizing. Becket and Marreco found sixteen people who testified to having been physically or psychologically brutalized, as well as others who offered secondhand reports regarding the alleged torture of thirty-two victims who remained in prison. The two lawyers "verified" the claims of victims though "oral testimony" and the testimony of (unspecified) "professional people" and relatives. They found secondhand claims of torture "convincing" when offered by more than one person.[31] Although neither lawyer had medical training, they verified torture claims by seeing "scars," despite that even medical professionals find linking scarring to torture notoriously difficult.[32] Becket later recalled being persuaded by signs of psychological trauma: shaking hands, chain smoking, and emotional distress. They had hoped that victims would sign an affidavit to be stored abroad with a "reliable person" who would attest that the affidavit was signed without revealing the name of the signatory, but even this weak measure was abandoned when they met the first victim. "One look into this woman's eyes," Becket said, "and any legalistic demands on her suffering were out of the question."[33]

The Greek junta's efforts to defend itself were often clumsy and inept, but its vociferous denials of Amnesty's charges were taken seriously in the press. Public relations firm Thomas J. Deegan Co., hired by the government to burnish its image in the United States, assailed the charges in AI's first report as "totally undocumented . . . political propaganda" and noted that opponents of the junta had close ties to communists.[34] Greek officials dismissed torture allegations as communist propaganda and suggested the alleged victims claimed torture to justify divulging names of co-conspirators during interrogation.[35] Occasionally the regime engaged in factual rebuttals, pointing out, for example, that one prisoner who claimed to have had teeth broken had a full set of healthy teeth.[36] When the foreign press reported that Alexander Panagoulis, who had attempted to assassinate Papadopoulos, had been brutally tortured, Greek officials allowed foreign correspondents to observe him looking healthy and fit as he played soccer in the prison yard.[37] When the wife of arrested law professor George A. Mangakis told foreign news agencies in July 1969 that her husband was wounded from "inhuman tortures," reporters allowed to visit him found him in apparent good health. He denied he had been tortured, and a pathologist who examined him found no signs of torture.[38] Both cases demonstrated the unreliability of cursory examination: when the post-junta government put torturers on trial, it was revealed both Panagoulis and Mangakis had been subjected to brutal mal-treatment.[39] On several occasions government officials admitted that iso-lated cases of violence may have occurred, but the regime never initiated its own investigations or punished offenders.

A second AI report in April 1968 failed to settle the controversy. Marreco was allowed back into Greece at the request of Francis Noel-Baker, a British Labour MP who was a large landowner in Greece and a staunch defender of the regime. Marreco gathered testimony from nine current pris-oners who claimed to have been tortured and a tenth prisoner who refused to confirm or deny in the presence of prison officials.[40] What Marreco called "prima facie evidence" that ten men had been tortured did not sway the junta's allies abroad. Noel-Baker told the press that the allegations of bru-tality were grossly exaggerated.[41] Two other MPs toured Greece and pub-licly discounted claims of torture.[42]

Of most significance to the debate was what Becket characterized as the "skeptical and unresponsive" stance of the International Committee of the Red Cross (ICRC).[43] Concerned more with detention standards than with interrogation techniques and wedded to private diplomacy rather than public shaming, the ICRC had a different agenda than AI. In early 1968, the ICRC wrote a favorable report on detention conditions on the island of Yáros. A separate report on police headquarters at Bouboulinas Street in Athens, no-torious as an alleged torture center, maintained strict neutrality: the ICRC representative interviewed prisoners who claimed to have been tortured, but noting some inconsistencies, as well as denials by authorities, the represen-tative confined himself to relaying "these contradictory declarations" with-out drawing "conclusions about the reality of the alleged tortures."[44] In keeping with its practice of maintaining confidentiality in its dealings with governments, the Red Cross did not publish its report. Taking advantage of ICRC's policy of silence, in 1968 the junta used selective quotations from ICRC reports to refute torture charges.[45]

Not until May 1969 did a major media outlet in the United States give significant play to torture allegations, in the form of *Look* magazine's breathless exposé by Christopher Wren, who had been given "abundant in-formation and documentation" by Becket.[46] Wren's article adopted a trope common in media reports on torture: disbelief followed by conversion. The article opened with the statement, "I didn't believe [the stories]"; they were "so grotesque as to seem unreal." Torture victim Pericles Korovessis, a young actor from Athens who became the most well-known Greek torture survivor in the West, was the central character of Wren's article. Wren emphasized that Korovessis had not believed the stories either—until he was arrested and tortured. "Smuggled reports," mostly anonymous, of "nearly 200 cases" of "torture" helped convince Wren; but, above all, it was his visit to Greece where "a succession" of former prisoners let Wren "see, and touch, the scars," that persuaded him "thousands" had been tortured.[47]

The Greek leadership was apoplectic about the *Look* article, but its rebuttals, as the Australian ambassador aptly characterized them, were "abusive, undignified and irrelevant."[48] Government officials labeled the article "a cheap collection of stories by mentally unbalanced persons, anonymous informers," or communists. Papadopoulos called a press conference to condemn the article, denouncing Korovessis as "a mentally deranged person, who has been an inmate in an asylum for disturbed persons."[49] Korovessis' father, apparently under pressure from the Greek police, wrote to *Look* that Pericles had complained of "hardships" during the first days of his interrogation but had never "mentioned to me the miseries . . . in your article," and suggested that the claims of torture were "the exaggeration of an imaginative editor's pen."[50] Government officials did not stop at questioning the sanity of the alleged victims; in their view the article also raised questions about Wren's "mental equilibrium."[51] In a similar vein, Catherine "Kitty" Arseni—another torture victim who became well-known through AI reports, testimony to the European Subcommission, a memoir in Italian, and television interviews—was publicly described by a police officer as "mentally retarded."[52]

Conservative Skeptics

Prolific conservative columnist William F. Buckley Jr. was among the most ardent supporters of the colonels. Although he would later join the board of Amnesty's U.S. section and was an early critic of the Brazilian dictatorship's use of torture, Buckley questioned charges of torture in Greece.[53] In a July 1968 column on Greece with the skeptical subheading "Who Put the Scar on Mr. Ambatielos' Foot?" Buckley drew on the Greek government's selective release of ICRC reports to argue that the Red Cross had found the charges of torture "circumstantially implausible." He concluded, "the case against the Junta is not sustained, as of this moment, by documented charges of torture as state policy."[54] In other columns, Buckley railed against charges of torture "used for the sake of advancing a political movement." Casting doubt in 1974 on a torture account from Chile publicized by the muckraking journalist Jack Anderson, Buckley concluded, "it is callousing to read about torture while never quite knowing whether the accounts of it are (a) accurate; or (b) fictitious, and politically inspired. Those who give currency to account of torture of this kind are friends not of the tortured, but of the torturers."[55] As late as 1976 Buckley called for a definitive investigation to "discover who was right" about torture in Greece—an issue that by then was settled both in Greece and abroad.[56] When corrected, he issued an apology, conceding that the evidence showed the junta had engaged in systematic torture. Although he maintained that the colonels may not have used torture more than some earlier Greek governments, it was, he wrote, "embarrassing to conscientious inquirers who, in 1968, having done their best to investigate the situation," had concluded that the charges "were for the most part politically inspired." Amnesty's reports "were, on the whole, justified; sad to say."[57]

Unlike liberals, who took umbrage at human rights violations in proportion to the degree of U.S. support for offending states, conservatives claimed to use an absolute measuring stick, according to which the worst violations were committed by communist regimes. This attitude sometimes blinded them to abuses committed by anticommunist regimes. In early 1968, Buckley's National Review colleague William Rickenbacker visited Greece at the invitation of the junta to "have a look for [himself]." He found not "even the basic symptoms of mass repression," baldly declaring detention of political prisoners to be "humane" and arguing there is "no satisfactory documentation" of torture. In a footnote, he dismissed Amnesty's second report as dealing merely with the "mistreatment of ten prisoners," and found more persuasive the reports of the ICRC that allegedly uncovered no evidence of torture. Above all, in Rickenbacker's view, "Greece isn't Cuba."[58]

Until 1970, U.S. conservatives sympathetic to the Greek regime remained skeptical of allegations of official torture. They argued that Greek police had a long-standing reputation for brutality, and they saw accusations that the junta was unusually brutal as politically motivated. New York Times correspondent C. L. Sulzberger, a friend of the regime, wrote in October 1969 that "systematic use of torture is certainly not government policy, although it is occasionally practiced. Greek police under all regimes have been given to brutality."[59] An American expatriate in Greece wrote the State Department that reports of torture had been proven to be "vicious . . . lies" and that the "sex-angled" Look article was designed to "sell many copies" of the magazine.[60]

Behind closed doors, Western diplomats admitted that some prisoners had been brutally treated, but were slow to conclude that such treatment was officially sanctioned or to define it as torture. In early 1968, Amnesty's reporting pushed the British and U.S. embassies into investigations of their own. As British Ambassador Michael Stewart put it, the findings were "not agreeable" but "not as bad" as the AI report.[61] The Australian, American, British, and Dutch ambassadors echoed the same world-weary refrain: sorting fact from fiction in allegations of torture was "exceedingly difficult"— the U.S. embassy repeatedly claimed it was beyond its capabilities—but brutal treatment of prisoners in Greece was neither new nor unexpected.[62] What *was* new was "the interest taken by journalists and parliamentarians outside Greece" due to the fact that those arrested and tortured were no longer villagers or "lower order elements" but middle-class citizens, often with Western educations and Western connections.[63]

The *Look* article alone prompted at least ten congressmen to express concern to the State Department, but officials steadfastly denied that torture was officially sanctioned or widespread.[64] Before 1970, the department's standard response was that there had been cases of prisoner mistreatment— most often of communist prisoners and primarily in connection with the investigation of terrorist bombings—but these were mostly in the past.[65] In the department's view, many of the charges in the international press were "false or gross distortions by political enemies of the regime."[66] In private discussions, the U.S. embassy seems to have uncritically taken up the Greek government's line, parroting, for example, the claim that Korovessis was mentally unbalanced and that charges of torture were often "aimed at the gallery and to *Pravda* and *Izvestia* reporters."[67] The U.S. ambassador to Greece told the press that ICRC had not found evidence of systematic torture.[68] The State Department also tried to take advantage of a lack of coordination between AI's International Secretariat and its U.S. branch, which at the time did not have official relations. The department noted that the U.S. branch had "not adopted" the first AI report on Greece "as an official report," but instead issued its own in March 1968. The department also claimed that Paul Lyons, executive director of the U.S. section of Amnesty International (AIUSA), had "informed us that with the exception of the case of Patriotic Front prisoners, the American Chapter of Amnesty International does not have evidence of systematic mistreatment of Greek prisoners."[69]

The battle for credibility devolved into farce at a session of the European Human Rights Commission in Strasbourg in November 1968. Two former Greek prisoners, scheduled to testify on behalf of the Greek government that they had not been maltreated, reversed their testimony and then sought asylum in Norway. One of the men then reversed his testimony again, apparently after the Greek embassy threatened his family in Greece with reprisals. He explained his first reversal with the implausible story that he had been kidnapped by the Norwegian counsel and a Greek opposition group.[70] U.S. Ambassador Phillips Talbot reported that the "publicity debacle" made the Greek government look both "guilty" *and* "stupid."[71] But defenders found ways to explain away the incongruities. David Holden, a prominent critic of torture allegations, saw in the "black comedy" of the Strasbourg affair more reason to believe that some of the "atrocity stories" were "exaggerated, if not fabricated." Even if "this sort of thing" (beatings) had increased under the colonels, he wrote, it would have been "remarkably un-Greek" for the regime to have entirely avoided physical maltreatment.[72]

It was not until the commission's investigation gathered more witnesses over the course of 1969 that the debate died down. Late that year, when its detailed and legalistic report chronicling 213 cases of torture in hundreds of pages of analysis was leaked to the press, the mainstream media was reporting torture as a proven fact. An eight-minute-long primetime NBC news segment on August 5, 1969, reported that the commission had heard "sworn testimony" from "several Greeks," which was "verified by Amnesty International," to the effect that "the ugly rumors were all true": torture was "a tool of government." The segment included interviews with three victims who described falanga, psychological torture, and pressure clamping the head.[73] When Greece withdrew from the Council of Europe in December 1969, NBC ran a three-minute-long interview with Korovessis, then living in London, who recounted in halting English his experience with falanga and electric shock.[74] These were the first in what would become a steady stream of young, sympathetic, and well-educated victims of brutality who would tell their stories to the world in the 1970s.

Liberals and the Torture Issue

Public opposition to the Greek junta in the United States came from a committed group of liberal Democrats. The vast majority of the Greek-American community was either supportive of the junta or indifferent, and the handful of Greek-American congressmen, unwilling to antagonize pro-junta donors, adopted supportive positions.[75] A few Greek-American academics spoke out against the junta, along with the indefatigable exiled journalist Elias Demetracopoulos, who acted as a one-man lobby in Washington.[76] In Congress the leading anti-junta voices were those of non-Greek liberal internationalists searching for a new moral basis for U.S. foreign policy.[77]

In building a case against the junta, liberal internationalists made torture one of the key indictments against Greece. In a July 1968 interview on NBC, Paul O'Dwyer, an antiwar liberal who had recently won the Democratic nomination for New York's U.S. Senate seat, cited widespread reports of torture "à la [the] Middle Ages" as the prime example of how the Greek junta has "suppressed every symbol and expression of democracy."[78] Minnesota Congressman Donald Fraser, an early opponent of the Vietnam War who became a leader of congressional human rights efforts in the mid-1970s, later saw Greece as a turning point in shaping his views. After visiting Greece in May 1968, he concluded that it was "a full-blown police state," in part because of torture.[79] For a time, Greece was the primary concern of the fledgling AIUSA, headquartered just outside Washington in Chevy Chase, Maryland. In March 1968, its newsletter ran a special issue on torture in Greece titled "The People vs. Papadopoulos."[80]

The liberal Democrats who came together in the U.S. Committee for Democracy in Greece played an important role in laying the groundwork for the human rights movement of the 1970s in the United States—and in centering the human rights agenda on issues such as torture.[81] Formed in October 1967 and headquartered in Washington, DC, the committee was intended as "a fact-finding service" aimed at lobbying Congress, policymakers, and other opinion makers.[82] It was the brainchild of social activist Jack T. Conway, an AFL-CIO official and executive director of the liberal organization Americans for Democratic Action. Jack's wife LuVerne Conway, a former attorney working on the staff of liberal California congressman and civil rights proponent Don Edwards, had a long-established interest in Greece, and it was the Conways who spurred both Edwards and Fraser into anti-junta activism in 1967.[83] Edwards and Fraser would each later serve as chairman of the committee. Other prominent members included liberal establishment names, most with backgrounds in civil rights, antiwar, and labor issues, including John Kenneth Galbraith, Michael Straight, A. Philip Randolph, United Auto Workers International Director Victor Reuther, old New Dealers such as Francis Biddle, journalist and former socialist Maurice Goldbloom, and Senators Joseph Clark and Claiborne Pell.[84]

The committee raised the issue of torture early, writing in the opening paragraph of a May 1968 fundraising letter that many opponents of the Greek junta "have been subjected to sadistic torture," and its publications often gave prominent attention to torture.[85] A draft of one early appeal,

later toned down, described the junta's torture as "unspeakable in its besti-
ality, unprintable in its detail, [and] unshakeably documented."[86] Many
members of Congress who eventually came to support efforts to cut off aid
to Greece cited torture in their reasoning. Senator Birch Bayh said "the
regime's policy of torture and denial of constitutional rights had been a
matter of deep concern to me." Pell wrote in 1970, "What most distresses
me is their past practices of permitting torture."[87] Spurred also by contacts
with European parliamentarians who were equally outraged about torture,
bills to cut off aid to Greece were introduced in 1969 and 1970, failing on
close votes until the Hays Amendment, after a long fight in 1971, cut off
aid to Greece at the beginning of 1972. Nixon promptly took advantage of
the loophole for a waiver on national security grounds, but the legislative
effort was an important precedent for later congressional human rights
efforts.[88]

   In the postscript to his 1969 memoir of torture, Korovessis wrote, "This
book would never have been written but for peace-loving and fair-minded
people all over the world, who by their silence and indifference have contributed to the continuation and spread of the tortures."[89] This view resonated with a rising liberal sense of responsibility for abuses perpetrated by
U.S. allies. Christopher Wren's *Look* article suggested that the Nixon
administration's support for the junta linked Americans to torture: U.S.
equipment—M1 rifles and hospital blankets—were used in Greek prisons;
the torturers even smoked American cigarettes. In large font over a picture
of Korovessis' haunted face, the article asked, "Why should we hand over
American taxpayers' money to a government that rules by torture?"[90]
Korovessis, Wren, and the liberal internationalists in Congress saw a clear
solution: cut off aid to the regime. As Becket wrote, "If American support is
obvious to the Greeks, it is vital to the torturers. The torturers themselves
not only use American equipment in their military and police work, but they
rely on the fact that the U.S. supports them."[91] As Edwards put it, the Greek
junta, and hence Greek torture, "could not survive" without the United
States.[92]

   By 1970, the debate over whether the Greek junta sanctioned torture had
largely been settled. In a 1971 radio interview Republican Congressman
Guy Vander Jagt, when asked why hearings before the House Foreign Affairs Subcommittee on Europe had persuaded him to support the Hays
Amendment banning aid to Greece, answered: "I think probably one of the
reasons was [that during the hearings] we've had all kinds of witnesses, eye-
witnesses, former members of government, journalists, who have brought

back a unanimous report of the torture that is taking place in Greece."[93] In 1968, the presidential campaigns had ignored Greece; by 1972, all prospective candidates for the Democratic presidential nomination went on record opposing aid to the Greek junta.[94]

Many of the well-meaning liberals who campaigned against the Greek junta went on to lead or to participate in similar campaigns in the 1970s against Brazil, Chile, Argentina, South Korea, the Philippines, and other right-wing dictatorships allied with the United States. All of these campaigns featured charges of state-sponsored torture. Beginning in 1972, AI's International Secretariat led a global "Campaign against Torture" that depicted torture as a growing "epidemic," and much of the energy of the human rights boom in the 1970s was directed toward ending state-sponsored torture. In the United States, torture in Greece proved an important stimulus to the rise of a liberal coalition that would push to integrate human rights into U.S. foreign policy in the 1970s.[95] Among a vast spectrum of human rights abuses in the world, it was "gross abuses," defined, above all, as torture and prolonged detention without charges that congressional activism on human rights targeted. This activism began with Greece in the late 1960s, rather than, as most accounts have it, with the 1973 hearings on human rights held by Fraser's Subcommittee on International Organizations. The agenda for those hearings, which in turn laid the groundwork for the human rights legislation of the mid-1970s and for the Carter human rights policies, was in many ways formed in the crucible of opposition to Greece.

Although Buckley and other skeptics were proven wrong about abuses in Greece, their critique of the anti-torture campaign was not entirely without merit. The embrace of torture allegations combined genuine outrage with political calculation. Tales of torture did "sell": accounts of "barbarism" generated headlines and helped mobilize opposition. However well intentioned, the preponderance of attention devoted to torture necessarily obscured other human rights abuses, many of which affected vastly greater numbers of people in even more prolonged and debilitating ways—often with attendant physical pain.[96] Tales of torture simplified the story of injustice in the world, reducing it to stereotypes of good and evil, and suggested that eradicating abuse was a matter of changing U.S. aid policy. Cutting off U.S. aid to the Greek junta may well have been good policy—it might have weakened the junta, hastened its end, and prevented the rise of Greek anti-Americanism. But the craving for moral dissociation also amounted, in part, to an evasion of hard choices and a preference for easy solutions that assigned "bad people" to other countries while affirming U.S. goodness.[97]

NOTES

I would like to thank Katerina Lagos for sparking my interest in Greece, and Roland Burke, Jan Eckel, and Sarah Snyder for useful comments on a draft of this essay. Research for this article was supported by an Early Career Researcher Award from the University of Melbourne, a United States Studies Centre research award, and a Visiting Scholarship at the Center for the Study of Law and Society at UC Berkeley.

1. James Becket, *Barbarism in Greece* (New York: Tower Books, 1970). Congressional blurbers were Don Edwards, Edward Koch, Abner Mikva, and Stephen Young; Claiborne Pell wrote the foreword. Becket's book was also translated into several European languages and excerpted in "Inquisition Greek Style," *Ramparts*, April 1970, 45–8; and "Torture in Democracy's Homeland," *Christianity in Crisis*, May 27, 1968, 115–20. See also Becket, "Greece: The Rack and the Bomb," *The Nation*, July 7, 1969, 6–7.

2. There is no detailed study of anti-junta efforts. Studies that mention the European public's response to events in Greece typically laud it as an admirable moralism that helped transform the international status of human rights from mere principles into genuine guides to action. See, e.g., Effie G. H. Pedaliu, "Human Rights and Foreign Policy: Wilson and the Greek Dictators, 1967–1970," *Diplomacy and Statecraft* 18 (2007): 185, and A. H. Robertson and J. G. Merrills, *Human Rights in the World*, 4th ed. (Manchester: Manchester University Press, 1996), 136–8. Ann-Marie Clark's study of Amnesty International presents the organization's efforts to publicize torture in Greece as an effort to get "the right information" to governments, to combine "facts" with "pressure," and thereby to strengthen "underdeveloped" norms against torture: *Diplomacy of Conscience: Amnesty International and Changing Human Rights Norms* (Princeton, NJ: Princeton University Press, 2001), 42–43. In studies of official U.S.-Greek relations, the role of U.S. public opinion is typically mentioned only in passing. See James Edward Miller, *The United States and the Making of Modern Greece: History and Power, 1950–1974* (Chapel Hill: University of North Carolina Press, 2009). Uta Devries passes over Greece in a sentence: *Amnesty International gegen Folter: Eine kritische Bilanz* (Frankfurt: Peter Lang, 1997), 81. There has been very little Greek scholarship on the junta; Neni Panourgiá, *Dangerous Citizens: The Greek Left and the Terror of the State* (New York: Fordham University Press, 2009), 126–7.

3. James Green has argued that a similar campaign against the Brazilian regime, which began in 1969 (slightly after the one against Greece), "initiated a gradual shift in official and public opinion" that laid the basis for more extensive campaigns against human rights abuses in Latin America beginning in the mid-1970s. James N. Green, *"We Cannot Remain Silent": Opposition to the Brazilian Military Dictatorship in the United States, 1964–85* (Durham, NC: Duke University Press, 2010).

4. Just a few years earlier, the systematic torture of hundreds of thousands of Algerians by the French army had elicited no audible global outcry.

5. On this point, see Tom Buchanan, "'The Truth Will Set You Free': The Making of Amnesty International," *Journal of Contemporary History* 37 (2002): 579.

6. For AI's own analysis of the Greek case, see Amnesty International, *Report on Torture* (London: Duckworth, 1973), 23, 75–95.

7. Kenneth Cmiel, "The Emergence of Human Rights Politics in the United States," *Journal of American History* 86, no. 3 (1999): 1232–35.

8. Paul Gordon Lauren, *The Evolution of International Human Rights: Visions Seen* (Philadelphia: University of Pennsylvania Press, 1998), 77.

9. American opponents of the Brazilian dictatorship similarly highlighted torture and worked to gain mainstream media attention in 1970; see Green, *"We Cannot Remain Silent,"* ch. 5.

10. The credence given to allegations of torture in Greece is, in part, a story of diminishing media deference to government.

11. AI, *Report on Torture*, 83–4.

12. Peter Novick, *The Holocaust in American Life* (Boston: Houghton Mifflin, 1999), 255. Rising fascination with the Holocaust also made "evil" fashionable outside a Cold War context.

13. Barbara Keys, "Congress, Kissinger, and the Origins of Human Rights Diplomacy," *Diplomatic History* 34, no. 4 (November 2010): 823–51.

14. Quoted in Keith R. Legg, *Politics in Modern Greece* (Stanford, CA: Stanford University Press, 1969), 238.

15. C. M. Woodhouse, *The Rise and Fall of the Greek Colonels* (London: Granada, 1985), 35.

16. The opposition published leaflets and underground newspapers; there were also two assassination attempts. Ibid., 36–8.

17. Becket, *Barbarism*, 1. On the training of Greek torturers, see Mika Haritos-Fatouros, *The Psychological Origins of Institutionalized Torture* (London: Routledge, 2003).

18. Haritos-Fatouros, *Psychological Origins*, 23–25; Polymeris Voglis, *Becoming a Subject: Political Prisoners during the Greek Civil War* (New York: Berghahn Books, 2002), 131–4.

19. On the centuries-long history of falanga, see Panourgiá, *Dangerous Citizens*, 260–2. On electric shock, see Darius Rejali, *Torture and Democracy* (Princeton, NJ: Princeton University Press, 2008), 181, 202.

20. Woodhouse, *Rise and Fall*, 39–40, 51–2, 67–72.

21. Quoted in David Schmitz, *The United States and Right-Wing Dictatorships, 1965–1989* (New York: Cambridge University Press, 2006), 77.

22. See Miller, *United States*, 157–75.

23. Woodhouse, *Rise and Fall*, 40.

24. That U.S. support of the junta undercut U.S. interests when Greece returned to democracy was acknowledged almost immediately; see "U.S. Policies on Human Rights and Authoritarian Regimes," n.d. [1974], Policy Planning Staff, Director's Files (Winston Lord), Box 348, RG 59, National Archives, College Park, Maryland.

25. Many reports attest to the centrality of torture in shaping public opinion; see, e.g., Becket, *Barbarism*, 19.

26. Jonathan Power, *Against Oblivion: Amnesty International's Fight for Human Rights* (Glasgow: Fontana, 1981), 29–31.

27. The first significant report was Cedric Thornberry's "Letters Tell of Plight in Greek Political Prisons," *The Guardian*, October 21, 1967.

28. Becket, *Barbarism*, 11–13. Amnesty's focus was on political prisoners, and it did not formally include torture in its mandate until 1968. Becket recalled that torture had not been part of the team's mandate, and that it was only as he heard secondhand reports about torture that he grew interested in the issue, but other reports suggest the delegation was sent in order to gather reliable documentation on torture. Clark, *Diplomacy of Conscience*, 39–40; *Torture in Greece: The First Torturers' Trial 1975* (London: Amnesty International, 1977), 11.

29. *Situation in Greece: Report by Amnesty International*, January 27, 1968 (London: Amnesty International, 1968). Thanks to a lengthy appendix listing torture techniques, three of the report's four pages dealt with torture. Its findings on numbers of prisoners and their backgrounds took up less than half a page. The report is reprinted in full in several books, including Becket, *Barbarism*.

30. According to torture expert Darius Rejali, false claims of torture are not uncommon. Rejali, personal communication, October 28, 2009. In Greece the hurdles to gathering credible evidence were significant. Whether released or still in detention, victims of maltreatment feared that public accusations would invite retaliation against themselves or their families.

31. AI, *Situation in Greece*.

32. See, e.g., Council of Europe, *Yearbook of the European Convention on Human Rights*, vol. 12a (1972), 288.

33. Becket, *Barbarism*, 11–12.

34. "Greece Using N.Y. Firm to Aid Image," *Washington Post*, March 4, 1968, 8.

35. Council of Europe, *Yearbook*, 222–3.

36. Enclosure to Airgram A-538, April 6, 1968; and Telegram, Athens to Washington, "Torture of Greek Political Prisoners," April 9, 1968, Box 2154, National Archives and Records Administration, College Park, Maryland, Record Group 59, Central Foreign Policy Files 1967–1969, Subject-Numeric (hereafter NARA).

37. Airgram, Macomber to Washington, May 27, 1969, Box 2155, NARA.

38. Athens to Canberra, "Arrest of Professor Mangakis," August 20, 1969, Barcode 56242, National Archives of Australia, Canberra (hereafter NAA).

39. *Torture in Greece,* 48–9; Haritos-Fatouros, *Psychological Origins*, 5.

40. "Torture of Political Prisoners in Greece," reprinted in Becket, *Barbarism*, 155–61.

41. Becket, *Barbarism*, 196–7.

42. Ibid., 24; Telegram, Athens to Washington, April 27, 1968, Box 2154, Pol 23–9 Greece, NARA. It was later revealed that one of them, Labour MP Gordon Bagier, had been paid by the Greek government's British public relations firm.

43. Becket, *Barbarism*, 13. Some detainees on Yáros reported that the Red Cross covered up evidence of torture and at times even participated. Panourgiá, *Dangerous Citizens*, 146.

44. ICRC, "Political Detainees in the Hands of the Police Authorities," reproduced in Becket, *Barbarism*, 165; Roland Siegrist, *The Protection of Political Detainees: The International Committee of the Red Cross in Greece, 1967–1971* (Montreuz: Éditions Corbaz, 1985), 114. Note that Yáros is alternately rendered Yioura.

45. Becket, *Barbarism*, 164–73; "Political Prisoners in Greece," *The Guardian*, April 9, 1968. The quotations appeared in a brochure entitled "The Truth About Greece." Pressure from international public opinion and NATO allies led the Papadopoulos regime to sign an agreement with the ICRC giving it access to all police stations, places of detention where political prisoners were held, and the families of detainees, from late 1969 to late 1970. ICRC access resulted in some improvements in conditions of detention and some releases on medical grounds, and may have diminished the use of torture—one likely reason the agreement was not renewed in 1970. Siegrist, *Protection*, 120–2; David P. Forsythe, *Humanitarian Politics: The International Committee of the Red Cross* (Baltimore, MD: Johns Hopkins University Press, 1977), 76–84.

46. James Becket, letter to the editor, *International Herald Tribune*, June 11, 1969.

47. Christopher S. Wren, "Government by Torture," *Look*, May 27, 1969, 19–20. U.S. embassy officials in Athens speculated that Wren's editors, fearing a libel suit, had left the article deliberately vague and imprecise. Athens to Canberra, "Greece: Allegations of Torture," June 27, 1969, Barcode 562242, NAA.

48. Gilchrist to Canberra, June 1969, Barcode 562242, NAA.

49. John Corry, "Greece: The Death of Liberty," *Harper's*, October 1969, 72. Papadopoulos famously promised to execute anyone found guilty of torture in Constitution Square. See also Airgram, Athens to Washington, "Greek Government Answers (in a way) Look Article on Torture," June 4, 1969, Box 2155, Pol 29 Greece, NARA.

50. Quoted in Council of Europe, *Yearbook*, 282.

51. Report on Greek Government comments, May 31, 1969, p. 36, Barcode 562242, NAA.

52. Testimony of police officer Evangelos Mallios, March 1969, in Council of Europe, *Yearbook*, 230.

53. Charles Lam Markmann, *The Buckleys: A Family Examined* (New York: W. Morrow, 1973), 214. AIUSA director Paul Lyons, responding to the *National Review* article, noted that "Amnesty is getting ready [for] a delightful fight" with Buckley. Lyons to Fraser, July 3, 1968, Box 41, F. 4, Don Edwards Papers, Special Collections, San Jose State University Library, San Jose, California (hereafter Edwards Papers).

54. Buckley, "Understanding Greece," *National Review*, July 16, 1968, 711–2. Anthony Ambatielos was a Greek Communist and torture victim who testified to the European Commission.

55. William F. Buckley, "Assessing Torture Claims," *Washington Star News*, December 24, 1974. Anderson's response offered no further evidence or rebuttals, but accused Buckley of taking the word of the U.S. Embassy and the Chilean government without consulting the victim. Jack Anderson, "A Rebuttal to William F. Buckley," *Washington Post*, January 3, 1975, D15.

56. William F. Buckley, Jr., "What's Going On in Chile?" *National Review*, April 30, 1976, 467.

57. William F. Buckley, Jr., "On the Right," *National Review*, July 23, 1976, 803.

58. William F. Rickenbacker, "Greece under the Junta," *National Review*, June 18, 1968, 607–8.

59. C. L. Sulzberger, "Foreign Affairs: Greece: I—Frozen Custard," *New York Times*, October 5, 1969, E12.

60. Nicholas C. Cummins to William Rogers, November 8, 1969, Box 2146, NARA. Mangakis's wife served a year in prison for "falsely" alleging torture. "Greece: Escape by Red Carpet," *Time*, May 1, 1972, 27.

61. Michael Stewart to London, March 11, 1968, FCO 9/141, United Kingdom National Archives.

62. Telegram 8115 (2), Talbot to Washington, December 4, 1968, Box 2155, NARA; Airgram A-558, Athens to Washington, April 29, 1968, "An Assessment of the Situation in Greece a Year after the April 21, 1967 Coup," Box 2146, NARA; Telegram 2047, Athens to Washington, May 20, 1969, "Look Article," Box 2155, NARA; C. D. Barkman, *Ambassador in Athens* (London: Merlin, 1989), 4–5. "Exceedingly difficult" is from Airgram A-558; "interest" quotation from Gilchrist to Canberra, "Greece: Torture Allegations," December 3, 1969, Barcode 562242, NAA.

63. Gilchrist to Canberra, "Greece: Torture Allegations," December 3, 1969, Barcode 562242, NAA.

64. Letters from Thomas Foley, William Dickinson, Claiborne Pell, J. W. Fulbright, Jennings Randolph, William Saxbe, Herman Talmadge, Charles Teague, Lloyd Meeds, and Robert Michel, in Box 2154, NARA.

65. Lucius Battle to Claiborne Pell, April 9, 1968, Box 2154, Pol 29 Greece, NARA.

66. Lucius Battle to Clairborne Pell, July 10, 1968, Box 2155, NARA. In March 1969 Secretary of State William Rogers acknowledged the existence of torture, telling the Senate Foreign Relations Committee: "Yes, Senator [Pell]! We share your concern not only for the torture but for other civil liberties." Quoted in Maurice Goldbloom, "United States Policy in Post-War Greece," in *Greece Under Military Rule*, ed. Richard Clogg and George Yannopoulos (London: Secker & Warburg, 1972), 246.

67. Athens to Canberra, 27 June 1969, Barcode 562242, NAA; Telegram 114, Thessaloniki to Washington, May 23, 1969, Box 2155, NARA. The consulate in Thessaloniki reported in July 1968, however, that many Greeks believed torture was widespread and that the consulate had come across enough reports to believe torture was "regularly employed" there. Telegram 291, Thessaloniki to Washington, July 16, 1968, Box 2155, NARA.

68. "Two Groups Accuse Greece on Torture," *New York Times*, October 18, 1972, 12.

69. William Macomber, Jr. to Frank Thompson, Jr., May 10, 1968, Box 2154, NARA.

70. Woodhouse, *Rise and Fall*, 57; Becket, *Barbarism*, 13–6. In another problem of evidence, a film of a torture session on the infamous terrace on Bouboulinas Street that came to the commission's attention was discounted because its provenance remained obscure. John Barry, "Watching Torture," *Newsweek*, December 10, 2007.

71. Telegram 8115, Talbot to Washington, December 4, 1968, Box 2155, NARA.

72. David Holden, *Greece without Columns* (London: Faber and Faber, 1972), 241–2.

73. "First Tuesday: Greek Victims," Media ID M690805, n.d. [August 5, 1969], NBC News Achives, at www.nbcnewsarchives.com (accessed September 28, 2009); NBC News press release, Box 74, F. 35, Edwards Papers; and George Mougious to Senator Sam Ervin, October 20, 1971, Box 41, F. 2, Edwards Papers.

74. NBC News, December 12, 1969, 443693, Vanderbilt Television News Archives, Nashville, Tennessee.

75. Jim Pyrros, "Memories of the Anti-Junta Years," 1991, Box 2, Greek Junta Papers, Special Collections Library, University of Michigan.

76. Russell Warren Howe and Sarah Hays Trott, *The Power Peddlers: How Lobbyists Mold America's Foreign Policy* (Garden City, NY: Doubleday, 1977), 410–34.

77. On liberal internationalists, see Robert David Johnson, *Congress and the Cold War* (Cambridge: Cambridge University Press, 2006), 190–241.

78. Film abstract, Paul O'Dwyer interview, July 15, 1969, NBC Archives, www.nbcarchives.com. O'Dwyer's campaign officially came out in favor of a cut-off in aid to Greece. O'Dwyer press release, July 15, 1968, Box 74, F. 24, Edwards Papers.

79. Donald Fraser in *Congressional Record* vol. 114, May 27, 1968, E4666. Fraser's views on Greece are discussed in Sarah B. Snyder, "The Rise of Human Rights During the Johnson Years," in *The United States and the Dawn of the Post-Cold War Era*, ed. Francis J. Gavin and Mark Atwood Lawrence (New York: Oxford University Press, forthcoming).

80. Memorandum, Paul Lyons to Board Members and Key List, July 10, 1967, Box 29, AI 1967 folder, International League for Human Rights Records, Manuscripts and Archives Division, New York Public Library, New York City, New York (hereafter ILHR); *Amnesty Action*, March 1968.

81. I have found only two discussions of the committee, both brief: James G. Pyrros, "PASOK and the Greek Americans: Origins and Development," in *Greece under Socialism: A NATO Ally Adrift*, ed. Nikolaos A. Stavrou (New Rochelle, NY: Aristide Caratzas, 1988), 228–33; Howe and Trott, *Power Peddlers*, 435.

82. Paul Lyons to Michael Carsiotis, January 29, 1968, Box 41, F. 1, Edwards Papers.

83. Pyrros, "Memories."

84. U.S. Committee for Democracy in Greece, Newsletter, n.d. [1968], Box 41, F. 4, Edwards Papers; Pyrros, "PASOK," 228.

85. "Dear Friend" fundraising letter, May 17, 1968, Box 34, Greece 1968, ILHR.

86. Draft, Committee Newsletter, n.d. [April 1968], p. 2, Box 41, F. 5, Edwards Papers.

87. Quoted in *Common Heritage*, April 1970, 18.

88. Clifford Hackett, "The Role of Congress and Greek-American Relations," in *Greek-American Relations: A Critical Review*, ed. Theodore Couloumbis and John O. Iatrides (New York: Pella, 1980), 132–3; Woodhouse, *Rise and Fall*, 94.

89. Pericles Korovessis, *The Method: A Personal Account of the Tortures in Greece*, trans. Les Nightingale and Catherine Patrakis (London: Allison & Busby, 1970 [Greek ed. 1969]), 87.

90. Wren, "Government by Torture," 20.

91. Becket, *Barbarism*, 42.

92. Don Edwards in *Congressional Record* vol. 114, April 27, 1970, 12634.

93. U.S. Committee for Democracy in Greece, *News of Greece*, 4 no. 4 (July–August 1971), 1, Box 41, Edwards Papers. New York Democrat Ben Rosenthal, a good friend of Edwards and Fraser, chaired the committee.

94. The candidates were Muskie, McGovern, Humphrey, Jackson, and Wilbur Mills. Goldbloom, "United States Policy," 245, 253.

95. As Van Gosse suggests, the antiwar movement did not dissipate after the war ended but consolidated in the 1970s; "Unpacking the Vietnam Syndrome: The Coup in Chile and the Rise of Popular Anti-Interventionism," in *The World the Sixties Made: Politics and Culture in Recent America*, ed. Van Gosse and Richard Moser (Philadelphia: Temple University Press, 2003), 111.

96. For an incisive view of how claims to care about suffering abroad have been co-opted for "false ends," see Samuel Moyn, "Spectacular Wrongs: Gary Bass's *Freedom's Battle*," *The Nation*, September 24, 2008; on how a focus on acts such as torture can obscure less visible wrongs that cause pain, see Moyn, "On the Genealogy of Morals," *The Nation*, March 29, 2007.

97. See also Novick, *Holocaust*, 13–15.

10

FROM THE CENTER-RIGHT

Freedom House and Human Rights in the 1970s
and 1980s

CARL J. BON TEMPO

On the morning of October 6, 1977, the National Conference on Human Rights (NCHR) brought together an extraordinary collection of human rights activists and policymakers in New York City. B'nai Brith, Amnesty International, the International League for Human Rights, the AFL-CIO, and the International Rescue Committee—to name just a few—and a scattering of U.S. government officials met with the goal of creating a more effective institutional framework for human rights activism. One of the more prominent organizations at the NCHR was Freedom House, a bipartisan, foreign-policy think tank and advocacy organization that was at the center of debates about international affairs in the United States for the preceding three decades. Freedom House's president John Richardson was a co-convener of the NCHR, its personnel was well represented on the day's panels, and the event's main organizer—civil rights activist Bayard Rustin—was a longtime Freedom House member.[1]

Rustin's opening remarks about human rights were capacious and welcoming. "We must oppose the suppression of human rights anywhere, whatever the ideology of the oppressor," Rustin began. He then took a stab at defining human rights, highlighting the "importance of social and economic well-being for all peoples . . . I point out that this means stretching the definition of human rights beyond civil and political to include all matters which affect human welfare."[2] Yet, about one month after the conference, Rustin received a letter from Ronald Young of the American Friends Service Committee (AFSC), an NGO led by Quakers. Long active in liberal-left politics in the United States and a supporter of the welfare state and civil rights, the AFSC's foreign policy agenda (nuclear and conventional disarmament, aid to refugees and immigrants, and world peace) reflected those leanings. Young agreed to work further with Rustin to meet the NCHR's goals, but he also sounded some sour notes. Most pointedly, he stressed, "We were disturbed by a number of speeches . . . in which the speakers seem to place more emphasis on reasserting a cold war framework than on advancing the cause of human rights." Instead of the Cold War, Young asserted human rights should be part of a "movement toward social justice, disarmament, and transferring resources from the military budget to programs to meet real human needs at home and abroad."[3] The Rustin-Young exchange highlighted the ideological, political, and geopolitical divides inherent in the human rights movement of the 1970s and 1980s. Were human rights principles mainly political and civil in nature, or did they encompass social and economic rights as well? Was the Cold War the main front in the battle for human rights—or should authoritarianism of all kinds be subjected to the light of human rights?

The Rustin-Young correspondence raised issues that, as the essays in this volume demonstrate, defined the post-1945 history of human rights: the emergence of multiple and evolving definitions of human rights; the changing place and importance of human rights on the crowded agenda of international politics; and the challenge for nation-states, international organizations, and advocacy groups of translating human rights principles into concrete policy initiatives. During the 1970s, however, with the modern human rights regime almost three decades old, these issues only grew in salience. Disaffection with the Cold War—the governing paradigm of international affairs since the late 1940s—peaked not only in the United States but also in Europe and the so-called Third World. As a result, more political and cultural space opened up in the 1970s for the consideration of human rights ideals and their actualization into policy.[4] At the same time, human rights, with the stunning growth of NGOs and interconnected transnational activist networks—as well as greater institutionalization within governments and international organizations—had become mass politics, preached and practiced by an ever-wider circle. This expansion gave human rights concerns more prominence but also led to a more raucous and contentious debate about what human rights were, when they ought to be cited, and how they ought to be enforced.[5]

As part of this ferment—symbolized by both the Rustin-Young exchange, as well as the larger NCHR—human rights principles emerged in the 1970s and 1980s as a vital part of debates in the United States about politics, culture, and foreign policy. The American Friends Service Committee was emblematic of how liberals and the left answered these questions, offering a vision of human rights that grew in power and prestige during the human rights revolution of the 1970s. On the right and in the center, though, a different vision emerged. Beginning in the late 1960s and early 1970s, conservatives trumpeted human rights principles and politics, largely as weapons in the war against communism and the Soviet Union. By the late 1970s and 1980s, Freedom House had emerged as an important proponent of this view. The organization's broader foreign policy agenda during these years identified the Soviet Union as the chief threat to the United States and the Cold War as the principal framework of international politics. Freedom House's human rights position tracked along these lines, stressing the Cold War, anticommunism, and political and civil rights to the neglect of economic and social rights. While Freedom House reflected a variety of positions—for instance, Rustin's capacious definition of human rights—on signature issues of the day, the group found itself more often contesting the liberal-left vision of human rights. As Freedom House dealt with the larger human rights frameworks offered by the Carter and Reagan administrations and as it addressed controversial issues like the Helsinki Accords and the role of UNESCO, it helped consolidate and further elaborate a conservative vision of human rights, grounded in anticommunism and opposition to the Soviet Union, that emerged in the 1970s.[6]

Freedom House formed in the fall of 1941 in response to the threat of fascism. Its original leadership was bipartisan—featuring 1940 Republican presidential candidate Wendell Willkie and former First Lady Eleanor Roosevelt—and included intellectuals (Reinhold Niebuhr), labor leaders (A. Philip Randolph), journalists (Dorothy Thompson), and civil rights activists (Walter White), an eclectic mix the group maintained over the decades. By the 1960s and 1970s, Freedom House claimed several thousand members, most of whom resided in the northeast United States. The majority of Freedom House's budget came from its investments, its endowment, and the grants it received from charitable foundations. Raising funds became more of an issue in the 1980s. Freedom House's leadership complained that foundations like Smith Richardson and Olin, who had been supporters in the late 1970s, financed more partisan think tanks in the 1980s, leaving the group in more difficult financial straits.[7]

Freedom House sought to educate the public about the issues of the day and influence policymakers in Washington.[8] The group tirelessly publicized the efforts of prodemocracy groups in other countries and participated in election monitoring. Like other think tanks, such as the Washington, DC-based Center for Strategic and International Studies, it opened research centers dedicated to particular issues (the Center for Caribbean and Central American Studies and the Afghanistan Information Center) and it hosted foreign leaders. Freedom House periodically released policy statements, crafted by its Executive Committee and Board of Directors, which addressed current events and international trends. All of these activities were publicized via radio, television, newspapers, press conferences, and the organization's own monthly magazine, *Freedom at Issue (FATI)*. Freedom House's most well-known effort was its annual survey of freedom across the globe, which judged nations on the scale of "Free," "Partly Free," and "Not Free." Freedom House stressed that these judgments were based on rigorous and impartial research and analysis, but the "Comparative Survey of Freedom," as it came to be known in 1972, often came under critical fire. Nonetheless, the survey was the way most Americans encountered the organization's work.[9]

It is difficult to measure how much influence Freedom House had either among the public or in Washington. Many of the Reagan administration's records remain closed, making it difficult to assess the group's impact on the White House in the 1980s. Yet evidence suggests that the organization did effectively reach politicians and policymakers. Politicians approvingly cited Freedom House statements and the group's members routinely testified on Capitol Hill.[10] The Comparative Survey's rankings were regular fodder for reporters, columnists, and politicians—and the State Department often consulted the Survey's authors as it assessed human rights records.[11] This influence in policymaking circles arose because key figures at Freedom House had long experience in government, because the group assiduously maintained its bipartisanship, and because the group's statements seemed calculated to avoid partisan controversy and embrace consensus rather than advocate bold new approaches.[12]

Freedom House often described its goal as protecting and promoting freedom at home and abroad—yet this depiction obscured more than clarified.[13] Instead, it is more useful to see Freedom House as an exemplar of Cold War liberalism. On domestic issues, the organization strongly favored African American civil rights and ethnic pluralism, castigated McCarthy's red scare, and generally supported labor rights.[14] The group concentrated more, though, on the central foreign policy issues of the postwar era. Like other Cold War liberal organizations, it saw the Soviet Union as the main menace to global stability, liberal democracy, and capitalism, and as the chief threat to American national security. It urged that only "clear-eyed realism" and attendant military, moral, and political strength on the part of the United States and its allies could face down Soviet totalitarianism.[15] As such, the organization supported the anticommunist and anti-Soviet foreign policies of the Truman and Eisenhower White Houses. While Freedom House's leadership divided over Johnson's 1965 escalation in Vietnam, it rather quickly got behind the war effort, lauding the "nation's firm commitment" to South Vietnam.[16]

As Cold War liberalism buckled in the late 1960s, Freedom House urged a reestablishment of consensus politics and decried the rising anger of the new left and the far right, particularly George Wallace.[17] Anti-Vietnam War protestors were a frequent target, and Freedom House even engaged in some red-baiting attacks on Martin Luther King as he publicly turned against the war.[18] Freedom House's Board of Directors and the Executive Committee generally supported what it saw as the Nixon administration's "orderly withdrawal from Vietnam," but it could not agree on how to publicly announce this position.[19] The group divided over the Nixon administration's détente policy as well, with some in the organization describing it as "embarrassing" while others saw potential benefits. Freedom House leaders grew more disenchanted with détente as the 1970s wore on, criticizing the policy for according the Soviets too much political legitimacy, for naively downplaying Soviet military advances, and for tolerating Soviet repression at home and in Eastern Europe.[20]

Détente, of course, was but one response to the foreign policy challenges created by the Vietnam quagmire and attendant political and cultural discord at home. Another—orienting U.S. foreign policy around human rights principles—found advocates across the political spectrum. On the liberal left, a comprehensive articulation of human rights emerged from liberal Democrats like Senator Ted Kennedy and Representative Donald Fraser and a whole host of liberal activists and organizations. These human rights advocates refused to see international affairs solely through a Cold War lens and were deeply suspicious of the efficacy of an anticommunist U.S. foreign policy. They reached these conclusions because they believed global politics rotated on a North–South axis and that the world's problems—the arms race, poverty, the maldistribution of wealth, ethnic and national rivalries, and the deprivation of individual rights and democracy by rightist and leftist repressive governments—could not be addressed by those mired in Cold War thinking. Instead, they urged participation in international organizations and multilateral efforts. They saw the 1948 Universal Declaration of Human Rights not as some distant star to shoot for, but rather as a tangible guide for American foreign policy.[21]

Human rights principles and rhetoric also found supporters among two sets of conservatives. A group of disaffected liberals—known as the neoconservatives—worried in the late 1960s and 1970s that the Democratic Party and the larger liberal-left alliance had lost its grounding in Cold War liberalism and given way to dangerous radicalism. Neoconservatives like Norman Podhoretz, Irving Kristol, and Daniel Patrick Moynihan urged Democrats to maintain a strongly anticommunist and anti-Soviet foreign policy that used human rights as a cudgel to pound the Soviet Union. Such thinking led to criticism of Nixon's détente policies as well. Senator Henry Jackson deftly used the Soviet Union's restriction of the right of Jews to emigrate to bash the Kremlin and the Nixon administration, the latter for tolerating these practices within the détente framework. Jackson argued that Soviet emigration policies and Nixon's pursuit of détente were an affront to human rights.[22]

The right wing of the Republican Party—including Ronald Reagan, William F. Buckley, and Phyllis Schlafly—joined the neoconservatives in blasting Nixon for accommodating rather than confronting the Soviets (and China) and for failing to rebuild the U.S. military. The Republican right initially eschewed human rights principles in this critique of détente, but that stance began to change in the late 1970s. The 1976 Republican campaign platform's foreign policy planks—large parts of which were drafted by conservative Jesse Helms—praised the Soviet dissident and human rights leader Alexander Solzhenitsyn and called for the Soviets to implement the Universal Declaration of Human Rights and honor the Helsinki Accords' human rights agreements. The latter was particularly striking, as conservatives earlier had attacked the Ford administration for signing the accords and derided the human rights benchmarks as toothless.[23] Although real differences existed between the neoconservatives and the Republican right, the two groups both wanted an aggressive anticommunist foreign policy that aimed to defeat the Soviets through military strength and moral certitude. For these conservatives, human rights principles were most useful in winning the Cold War.

In this period of fluidity in American foreign policy, Freedom House held fast to its faith in the basic precepts of the Cold War consensus even while acknowledging both an erosion of American power and a drastically reconfigured geopolitical map. As Freedom House declared in late 1970, the first "imperative" of U.S. foreign policy was "To maintain the stability of the present balance of power, and especially the continuing need for an adequate and credible American offset to rapidly expanding Soviet strategic power."[24] Unsurprisingly, Freedom House was slow to engage in the human rights moment of the mid-1970s. Part of this reluctance surely arose from the cracks within the organization's leadership in this tumultuous period. Yet, Freedom House also was unsure about human rights as a political agenda. Instead, echoing its early Cold War stance, it believed in privileging "freedom" over human rights concerns.[25] By late 1976, however, Freedom House began thinking more rigorously and more seriously about the place of human rights in American foreign policy. In part, this new attention grew from an understanding of the newfound prominence of human rights. Self-interest was also in play; some at Freedom House believed the high tide of human rights was the perfect wave to carry the group's publications and programs to a larger audience.[26]

Leonard Sussman, the group's executive director, urged Freedom House members in 1976 to consider how the United States might "more effectively advance human rights abroad." While a policy statement was never publicly released, the drafts reveal a number of themes that would characterize the organization's position in the years to come. Freedom House asserted that "a traditional and fundamental American concern for advancing human rights around the world" existed and that "inherent humanitarian reasons" and "pragmatic national interests" were served by the promotion of human rights. Several caveats followed this general endorsement. Freedom House warned against strict laws that might force policymakers to punish human rights violators, noting that the United States had to recognize that "over-riding reasons for maintaining relationships with a repressive nation abroad" might exist—though the government should make clear the public's "abhor-rence of repression." Moreover, any human rights policy had to differentiate between "basic human decencies (the abrogation of human rights) and the actual level of political or civil rights permitted individual citizens in a country." On this score, Freedom House seemed more concerned with the latter than the former, a privilege that would solidify in the coming years.[27] With the Carter administration taking office in the new year, Freedom House would have the opportunity to think about—and critique—policymakers' efforts to put human rights at the center of American foreign policy.

Soon after entering office, the Carter administration began articulating its vision of a human-rights-based foreign policy. In a speech at Notre Dame in the spring of 1977, Carter questioned the centrality of the Cold War and containment doctrine to American foreign policy. Instead, he described global politics as encompassing the Cold War and "the new global questions of justice, equity, and human rights." While making clear he wanted to continue détente and to work with the Soviets toward arms control, he embedded this aim within broader objectives, including the promotion of human rights and democracy, the establishment of peace in the Middle East, and the reduction of the global arms trade. At Notre Dame, Carter did not precisely define human rights—other than make plain the assumption that American values and ideals were identical to human rights principles—but Secretary of State Cyrus Vance did later that spring. Vance asserted that human rights encompassed three sets of rights: the "right to be free from governmental violation of the integrity of the body," the "right to the fulfillment of such vital needs as food, shelter, health care, and education," and "civil and political liberties."[28] While historians engage in brisk debate about whether Carter's foreign policy actually accomplished some (or any) of these goals, most agree that he laid out an ambitious agenda and that his administration was a high point in U.S government human rights activism.[29]

Vance's definition of human rights was not quite consonant with Freedom House's, but relations between Freedom House and the administration were not fated to fail. If, as was well reported, the administration was divided between those (in the State Department) sympathetic to human rights and those (in the National Security Council) more partial to a Cold War–based approach, Freedom House actually maintained solid contact with members of both groups. John Richardson, Freedom House's president, had just finished a tour at the State Department and was on good terms with Patricia Derian, who headed the department's human rights operation. Most striking, National Security Adviser Zbigniew Brzezinski (who had neoconservative leanings) had been an active participant on Freedom House's Board for a number of years. Upon leaving for Washington, Brzezinski's membership in Freedom House was deactivated, but he remained in contact with executive director Leonard Sussman.[30]

Initially, Freedom House was equally energized by and uncomfortable with the Carter administration's foreign policy initiatives and emphasis on human rights.[31] The organization's emerging critique centered on the fear that the administration was not up to the task of implementing its agenda. At the end of 1977, John Richardson warned Carter's White House Counsel Robert Lipschutz that the human rights agenda was endangered "due in part to the necessary refinement of early formulations, and in part to a failure, so far, to persuade even the most favorably disposed that there is a considered long-term strategy."[32] (This charge was not unfamiliar; Stanley Hoffman's scathingly titled "The Hell of Good Intentions," which appeared in *Foreign Policy* in the winter of 1977/1978, attacked the administration for failing to understand the relationship between strategy and goals.)[33] Richardson's solution was for Freedom House and the Center for Strategic and International Studies to organize a conference bringing together academics and administration officials to work through these structural issues.[34]

But Freedom House's criticisms were more than just structural or mechanical. In the late 1970s, the group revealed its own definition of human rights, one that was not always in tune with Carter or Vance, much less liberal-left activists and organizations. In 1978, Richardson and Raymond Gastil argued that any effective human rights strategy must avoid "stretching the term 'human rights' to cover all sorts of human wants from sound nutrition to formal schooling." This "stretching" was problematic for two reasons. First, it was impossible for the United States to hold another government to human rights standards if those standards involved state promotion of "human welfare." Gastil and Richardson suggested a more low-key lobbying approach—an effort not tied to human rights promotion—to encouraging development. Second, the inclusion of social and economic rights under the rubric of human rights would only "confuse American human rights policy which in practice (and of necessity) focuses on political rights and civil liberties."[35] Gastil continued this line of thinking in 1980, arguing that while conventional definitions of human rights had three components—political and civil rights, economic and social rights, and rights to bodily integrity—it was vital for the United States to base its policies on the promotion and protection of political and civil rights. Gastil reckoned that such a focus would encompass the protection of bodily integrity—the prevention of torture, for instance—as this right was subsumed under political and civil rights. At the same time, Gastil reasoned that political and civil liberties formed the basis, and, in fact, were a precondition, of economic development and social rights like education.[36]

The human rights issue that most concerned Freedom House during the Carter years was the Soviet Union's and the Eastern bloc's compliance with the 1975 Helsinki Accords. Arduous negotiations among thirty-five nations—hampered by the lack of enthusiasm from the Soviet and American representatives taking their cues from Brezhnev and Kissinger, respectively—produced a wide-ranging agreement in Helsinki. The accords, much to the Soviets' liking, ratified the postwar political divisions in Europe and guaranteed each signatory's "sovereignty" and "territorial integrity." (These conditions fueled the right's disenchantment with Helsinki and the Ford administration.) The signatories of the accords also promised—at the urging of European governments—to "respect human rights and fundamental freedoms, including the freedom of thought, conscience, religion or belief, for all" and to "encourage the effective exercise

of civil, political, economic, social, cultural and other rights and freedoms."
In the long term, the human rights benchmarks would prove the most vital
of the agreement, in large part because of the encouragement that dissidents
behind the Iron Curtain took from them.[37]

In the short term, though, how was the United States to judge Soviet
compliance and to press the Soviets to meet the accords' human rights stipulations? Shortly after the accords' conclusion, Freedom House publicly
called for rigorous monitoring of the Soviets on all aspects of the Helsinki
agreement and soon mounted its own "Helsinki Watch."[38] In fact, Freedom
House insisted that only strict oversight could redeem the accords. According to Leonard Sussman, "America and its allies paid a heavy price . . .
immediate recognition of the USSR's 'right' to dominate Eastern Europe"
in return for a "promised opening to the East" that "if implemented . . .
could significantly ventilate the closed communist societies."[39] On this
score, Sussman echoed conservatives in the Republican Party, except that
they were more fixated on the price rather than the potential payoff.

While the accords contained a review process that led to meetings in
Belgrade in 1978 and Madrid in 1980, Freedom House insisted that private
groups—like the Helsinki Watch—monitor Soviet actions and that the
United States and its allies aggressively use the official review process to
hold the Soviets accountable. As a result, the pages of *Freedom at Issue*
were filled in the late 1970s with articles about the state of the Helsinki
agreement. In advance of the 1978 Belgrade meeting, Freedom House exco-
riated those in the administration—leaving them unnamed—who wished to
abandon the review process because any vigorous discussion of the accords'
implementation might stand in the way of progress on issues like arms control. Freedom House instead urged an "energetic" American posture at Belgrade, as well as the continuation of the summit reviews, "so that human
freedom, as reflected in the issues of expanded human rights and information exchange, remains high on the conscience and the agenda of the
world."[40] The group continued this stance, for the most part, in advance of
the Madrid meeting two years later.[41] In looking at the accords, Freedom
House focused intently on the codicils insuring a free flow of information
between the East and West, unsurprising given the group's general interest
in freedom of the press issues.[42] By 1980, Freedom House cited the Soviet
invasion of Afghanistan and crackdowns by Eastern European governments
on dissidents as evidence of Soviet noncompliance with Helsinki.[43]

The overall thrust of these efforts—both to define human rights and to
monitor the Helsinki Accords—was remarkably clear. Richardson and Gastil defined human rights as political and civil rights, while all other rights

were secondary or logical outgrowths. The definition emerged starkly as the group confronted Helsinki and chose to focus on the particular issues of freedom of the press and freedom of dissent, which did not deviate from its traditional concerns with political and civil rights. More important, Freedom House's focus on Helsinki's human rights codicils—and the group's use of them to criticize the Soviet Union—makes clear it believed that the most striking and pressing human rights issues of the day were intertwined with the Cold War and the rejection of communism. This approach was not limited to Helsinki—for instance, Freedom House in 1979 trumpeted Jonas Savimbi as a human rights leader for his campaign against the Soviet- and Cuban-aligned communist government of Angola[44]—but it achieved its most convincing articulation there.

Ronald Reagan came to office promising a bold reassertion of American power, a more confrontational approach with the Soviet Union, and a renewed emphasis on military strength. Underlying this agenda was a promise to break with what Reagan saw as the impotent foreign policies of the Carter administration. Reagan did believe in human rights, but of a particular kind. For Reagan, communism and Soviet power were the chief affronts to human rights in the modern world. As he declared in 1982: "The record is clear. Nowhere in its whole sordid history have the promises of communism been redeemed. Everywhere it has exploited and aggravated temporary economic suffering to seize power and then to institutionalize economic deprivation and suppress human rights."[45] On this score, Reagan borrowed heavily from the neoconservatives and Republican right of the 1970s. Indeed, several neoconservatives joined his foreign policy team.[46]

Freedom House's leadership understood that Reagan's election heralded a new era and the organization thought about where it might fit. Sussman described the group's ideology as "hard-line liberalism," a clear reference to 1940s and 1950s Cold War liberalism, and he aimed to position Freedom House as an alternative to what he believed were weak-kneed Democrats ("the McGoverns") and to the Reagan administration, which he viewed with uncertainty. "Certainly we shall have many friends in the new government," he wrote, "but will we accept all of the objectives the new administration may set for itself and for the country?"[47] Furthermore, Sussman asked in January 1981, "How do we stand *now* on human rights in international affairs?" He and other key members answered over the coming months.[48] Sussman reiterated that human rights were subordinate to a broader agenda of "freedom" and hinted strongly that the Soviets and their allies were the chief threats to freedom. Freedom House leaders recognized that human rights ought to be "one of several factors in the formulation of foreign policy"[49] but that the U.S. ought not to be "rigid" in pursuing human rights objectives.[50] Rather, "We may have to support a partly free regime today to prevent a more totalitarian take-over tomorrow. It may be necessary to abide short-term violations of human rights in order to avoid long-term irreversible denials of human rights."[51] Likewise, Sussman continued to deride the concept of economic rights, insisting that "Rights and liberties are the key to all of society. Given these freedoms, the citizens can choose priorities: more food now, better housing later, or even circuses first."[52]

Sussman hoped that this approach might find favor in the Reagan administration, and the first human rights controversy, involving the staffing of key human rights positions at the State Department, indicated that it might.[53] Reagan nominated Ernest Lefever as assistant secretary of state for Human Rights and Humanitarian Affairs, a position previously held by the strong human rights advocate Patricia Derian. Critics in the Democratic Party and the human rights community were alarmed by the choice, for Lefever had criticized the Carter administration's human rights policies, questioned the efficacy of linking foreign military and economic aid to respect for human rights, and seemed to condone torture by rightist Latin American governments.[54] With the Senate poised to reject Lefever's nomination, the White House withdrew his name from consideration in the summer of 1981. Rumors flew that the post would remain vacant and the human rights office downgraded.[55] Freedom House, along with other human rights activists, lobbied the administration against such moves. In early November, the Reagan White House resolved the problem, nominating the neoconservative Elliot Abrams as assistant secretary.

More important, Abrams, Deputy Secretary of State William Clark, and Undersecretary of State for Management Richard Kennedy began outlining the administration's human rights approach in a memo that soon leaked to the *New York Times*. The administration saw human rights as "central to what America is and stands for," but it offered a very specific and limited definition of human rights, one oriented toward the Cold War and the Soviet Union: "'Human rights'—meaning political rights and civil liberties—conveys what is ultimately at issue in our contest with the Soviet bloc. The fundamental distinction is our respective attitudes towards freedom." The memo's authors noted that the United States should call attention to human rights violations among American adversaries and allies. They also declared that "the human rights element in making decisions affecting bilateral relations must be balanced against U.S. economic, security, and other interests." Thus, a human rights policy under the Reagan administration would always take larger strategic—Cold War-based—realities into account, which seemed to promise cover for rightist authoritarian regimes allied with the United States. Much of this thinking was neoconservative orthodoxy on human rights policy, reflecting, most obviously, the influence of Abrams.[56]

Freedom House was pleased with the statement, and with good reason. On the most important issues—the definition of human rights, the focus on the Cold War, and the place of human rights within a larger strategic framework—the Reagan administration had followed the Freedom House line. It is not clear whether this was deliberate, but the emerging neoconservative-influenced policies of the administration were closely aligned with what Freedom House had been arguing for years. Moreover, Sussman—along with leaders of other human-rights-based NGOs—had met with William Clark in late September in an effort to keep the human rights portfolio active at State. Sussman's notes of that meeting indicate that "Clark, I thought, acknowledged formally my reference to 'political rights and civil liberties' rather than human rights or human needs."[57] Sussman followed up by sending a congratulatory note to Abrams that acknowledged the administration's and Freedom House's similar thinking.[58]

This close thinking and cooperation continued on another key issue: monitoring the Helsinki Accords. Max Kampelman, chairman of Freedom House's Board in the early and mid-1980s, was a longtime conservative Democrat with neoconservative ties—he helped found the Committee on the Present Danger—who served as the American representative to the Helsinki Final Act review process at Madrid in 1980. Reagan kept Kampelman in this position, until assigning him in 1985 to head up arms control negotiations with the Soviets. Kampelman fit in well with the Reagan administration's hard-line approach toward the Soviet Union. He hammered away at Soviet human rights abuses through the early 1980s, decrying the Soviet leadership's failure to live up to the Helsinki human rights codicils. As an example of his aggressive approach, Kampelman's opening statement at the 1984 CSCE review conference in Stockholm raised the cases of famed Soviet dissidents Andrei Sakharov and Elena Bonner, "only one example of the many thousands of other human tragedies that have resulted from the increased repression that we sadly note in the Soviet Union."[59] Freedom House, unsurprisingly, supported Kampelman's efforts at using the Helsinki review process to blast Soviet human rights violations.[60]

Freedom House's narrow definition of human rights, as well as the trickiness of its relations with the Reagan administration, came to the fore during a controversy over the United Nations Education, Scientific, and Cultural Organization (UNESCO). The problem originated in the mid-1970s. A group of Third World nations, led by UNESCO's head, Amadou Mahtar M'Bow of Senegal, put forward a plan for a "new world information order" that provided guidelines for the relationship between the press and governments around the world. The U.S. delegation at UNESCO, on which Freedom House's Sussman served, strenuously objected to the proposal, arguing that it attacked freedom of the press, the right to communicate freely and openly, and civil rights more generally. Third World nations responded that the press was Western-dominated and that governments—facing crushing social and economic problems—needed some of the tools the press provided. Such claims, backed by the Soviet Union, only heightened fears in the United States about the goals of the new world information order.[61] A succession of American administrations opposed the proposal from its introduction, but Third World nations and the Soviet Union just as doggedly stood behind it.

Freedom House contended that the proposal, if enacted, would trample on the freedom of the press, a vital and central human right. Moreover, Sussman argued that "Third World regimes" enacted such restrictions "to minimize challenges to the regime's power," in turn dealing a death blow to democracy and basic political rights.[62] Conservatives in the Reagan administration shared these concerns and saw UNESCO and M'Bow as implacable opponents of American interests. In late 1983, the administration announced that it was considering withdrawing the United States from UNESCO altogether by the end of 1984. Sussman and Freedom House responded angrily when they learned of these plans, opening up a significant rift. While Freedom House acknowledged that UNESCO was deeply flawed and antagonistic toward the United States, it also believed that the country needed to remain in UNESCO to reform it. Moreover, withdrawal would only leave the field to the Soviets and their allies. Here, Freedom House's internationalism ran headlong into those in the administration who were deeply skeptical of the efficacy of American participation in international organizations. The administration paid little heed to these warnings and withdrew from UNESCO at the beginning of 1985. The United States did not rejoin until 2003.[63]

The UNESCO new world information order controversy revealed that Freedom House did not move in lockstep with the Reagan administration. Yet the disagreement revolved around how the United States should deal with UNESCO rather than a difference in the assessment of UNESCO's program. Both the administration and Freedom House worried that UNESCO's new world information order assaulted a particular set of political and civil rights. More important, both believed that UNESCO served as a forum in which Third World nations and the Soviet Union campaigned to recast human rights into "people's rights."[64] People's rights, according to Sussman, were nothing less than an effort by the Soviets and their Third World allies to overturn the traditional definition of human rights. Two definitions of people's rights had emerged, one that "would have governments guarantee fulfillment of human needs (employment, food, housing, health care, etc.)" and the other "would emphasize the self-determination of peoples in opposition to neocolonialism and imperialism." Sussman concluded that "[t]hese two expansions of human rights emphasize the role of the group, not the individual . . . In the Western approach the individual receives guarantees of rights against the government. In a collectivist system the individual is given duties to perform in the interest of the state, and the state holds 'rights' that insure the performance of the individual."[65]

The price of the ascendancy of "people's rights" principles and rhetoric was high according to Freedom House's Raymond Gastil: "The trivialization of human rights into empty rhetoric or the use of human rights rhetoric to clothe or obscure tyranny." Gastil proposed that Freedom House work to "develop a hierarchy of human rights that would emphasize the dignity of the individual as the core of the concept."[66] To this end, Freedom House held a one-day conference in August, 1983—before the UNESCO new world information order controversy emerged fully—that brought together academics, members of the Reagan administration (Charles Fairbanks of the State Department's Bureau of Human Rights and Alan Keyes of the National Security Council), along with Sussman and Gastil—to discuss "People's Rights and the Redefinition of Human Rights." A long, searching conversation ensued, proceeding from the assumptions that the Third World was more interested in "people's rights" than Euro-American human rights and that the Third World's embrace of people's rights damaged the United States in the international arena. Among Freedom House organizers and Reagan administration officials, the rejection of people's rights—and the reification of a certain brand of human rights that stressed political and civil rights—was never in doubt. People's rights were merely a difficulty to be analyzed and either transformed or vanquished.[67]

Throughout the 1970s and 1980s, Freedom House held fast to its beliefs that the Cold War was the defining aspect of international affairs, that the Soviet Union was the chief threat to the United States, and that communism was a dangerous ideology that could not be allowed to spread. The group's stance on human rights flowed from this larger understanding of global politics: human rights were political and civil rights and human rights principles should be another weapon in the West's Cold War arsenal. This thinking

238 The Globalization of Human Rights History

found few allies in the Carter White House, but such views were common-place among neoconservatives and the Republican right, and Freedom House proved welcoming of the former and found common cause with the latter. The larger intellectual project of constructing a centrist-conservative alternative vision of human rights principles and policies was well under-way by 1980 and achieved a degree of influence under Reagan theretofore unknown.

Freedom House was central to this process: articulating and defining a distinct vision of human rights, demonstrating how it applied to particular policy challenges, and bringing it to the attention of the general public and the Washington policymaking and political communities. Through these ac-tivities, Freedom House, as much as other NGOs and activists discussed in this volume, contributed to the human rights revolution of the postwar years. But Freedom House's larger political and foreign policy outlook, so rooted in the consensus of the early Cold War and resonant with the conservative right of post-Vietnam America, set it apart from those NGOs and activists of the liberal-left. Indeed, Freedom House serves as a reminder that human rights principles and politics were not solely the province of the liberal-left and that the political center and right also launched important efforts to participate in, shape, and utilize the human rights revolution. Too often, human rights scholars have overlooked this history.[68]

In no way, however, did Freedom House vanquish the liberal-left's vi-sion of human rights, which in some respects grew stronger during the 1980s as its advocates protested the Reagan White House's foreign policies, not to mention the administration's "rights" policies in the domestic sphere. Instead, Freedom House offered an alternative to the liberal-left's—both in the United States and abroad—more capacious vision of human rights that encompassed economic and social, as well as political and civil, rights. Freedom House's advocacy of its definition of human rights, then, was not a case of a vision lost or an ideological victory, but rather a battle joined. That battle continues to this day in American politics and culture, as well as among human rights advocates of all stripes, in debates con-cerning terrorism, genocide, religious freedom, and economic and social development.

NOTES

I would like to thank Kristin Celello, Mark Bradley, Ara Keys, and Temple University's International History Workshop for their helpful comments. Thank you to Dan Linke at Princeton University's Mudd Library for guiding me through the Freedom House archival collection.

1. Bayard Rustin, "Dear Friend," June 3, 1977, Box 45, Folder 3, Freedom House Archives (hereafter FHA), Princeton University (hereafter PU); Memorandum, John Richardson to Members, Board of Trustees, September 14, 1977, Box 6, Folder 7, FHA, PU; "Conference Participants," National Conference on Human Rights," n.d., Reel 4, Bayard Rustin Papers, Library of Congress.

2. "Summary of Discussion, Meeting of the Steering Committee, National Conference on Human Rights," August 8, 1977, Box 45, Folder 3, FHA, PU; Rustin to Sussman, September 9, 1977, Box 45, Folder 3, FHA, PU; "Program: Toward an American Coalition for Human Rights," n.d., Box 45, Folder 3, FHA, PU. For Rustin quotes, see "Bayard Rustin Address at National Conference on Human Rights," October 6, 1977, Box 45, Folder 3, FHA, PU.

3. Young to Rustin, November 9, 1977, Box 45, Folder 3, FHA, PU.

4. John Lewis Gaddis, *The Cold War: A New History* (New York: Penguin, 2005), especially chapters 4, 5, and 6; Tony Judt, *Postwar: A History of Europe Since 1945* (New York: Penguin, 2005), 484–503.

5. Tom Buchanan, "The Truth Will Set You Free: The Making of Amnesty International," *Journal of Contemporary History* 37, no. 4 (October 2002): 575–97; Ken Cmiel, "The Emergence of Human Rights Politics in the United States," *Journal of American History* 86, no. 3 (December 1999): 1231–50; Margaret Keck and Kathryn Sikkink, *Activists Beyond Borders: Advocacy Networks in International Politics* (Ithaca, NY: Cornell University Press, 1998).

6. The historiography on Freedom House is very limited and written largely by the group's members and journalists. See Leonard Sussman, *Democracy's Advocate: The Story of Freedom House* (New York: Freedom House, 2002); Diana Barahona, "The Freedom House Files," *Monthly Review Zine*, March 3, 2007, http://monthlyreview.org/mrzine/barahona030107.html#_edn1 (accessed July 28, 2009).

7. William E. Farrell, "Freedom House Honors Truman," *New York Times*, April 14, 1965, 20; Sussman, *Democracy's Advocate*, 7–26; "Instructions for Membership List," Box 6, Folder 6, "Meeting Materials, 1977 January—June," FHA, PU; "Freedom House Program Audit Committee Report," November 4, 1974, Box 2, Folder 5, FHA, PU. On Freedom House's relationship with the Heritage Foundation, see Sussman to John Riehm, April 1, 1983, Box 18, Folder 5, FHA, PU; Memorandum, Sussman to Executive Committee, September 14, 1982, Box 8, Folder 6, FHA, PU; Memorandum, Sussman to Kampelman and Riehm, January 18, 1985, Box 15, Folder 10, FHA, PU; R. Bruce McColm to Sussman, "Restructuring Freedom House," c. 1986, Box 10, Folder 1, FHA, PU.

8. See Sussman to Kampelman and Riehm, January 18, 1985, Box 15, Folder 10, FHA, PU.

9. Sussman, *Democracy's Advocate*, 61–63. For an internal critique of the Survey, see "Minutes: Executive Committees Willkie Memorial Freedom House," December 1, 1983, Box 3, Folder 15, FHA, PU.

10. See, for instance, "Johnson is Backed by Freedom House on Vietnam Policy," *New York Times,* July 21, 1965, 3; Memorandum, Sussman to Board of Trustees, December 5, 1975, Box 6, Folder 3, FHA, PU.

11. For newspaper editorials, see, Editorial, "The Fading Ring of Freedom," *Chicago Tribune*, January 5, 1973, 12; Editorial, "Perspective on Freedom," *Wall Street Journal*, January 9, 1974, 16; Editorial, "The New Colonialism," *Christian Science Monitor*, January 30, 1975, 6. For politicians and policymakers, see Ernest LeFever, "Rhodesia: From Irony to Tragedy," *Wall Street Journal,* June 2, 1976, 18; Edward Luttwak, "United States Policy: Between the Two Chinas," *New York Times*, August 1, 1977, 14; Patrick Buchanan, "A Selective Policy on South Africa," *Chicago Tribune*, April 25, 1978, B4.

12. Members of Freedom House's leadership included Margaret Chase Smith (former Republican Senator from Maine), Paul Douglas (former Democratic Senator from Illinois), and Leo Cherne (former chairman of the President's Foreign Intelligence Board).

13. Sussman, *Democracy's Advocate*, 4.

14. Ibid., 43–44, 33–35.

15. Ibid., 37.

16. "Regular Meeting of the Board of Directors of Freedom House," February 25, 1965, Box 1, Folder 23, FHA, PU; Ralph Blumenthal, "Vietnam Backers Urged to Shout," *New York Times*, November 29, 1965, 1; "Johnson is Backed by Freedom House on Vietnam Policy," *New York Times*, July 21, 1965, 3; "Johnson is Picked for Annual Award by Freedom House," *New York Times*, January 28, 1966, 3; John Pomfret, "Johnson Denies 'Blind Escalation' in Vietnam War," *New York Times*, February 24, 1966, 1; Lyndon Johnson, "Remarks in New York City Upon Receiving the National Freedom Award," February 23, 1966, American Presidency Project website, http://www.presidency.ucsb.edu/ws/index.php?pid=28101 (accessed October 11, 2008).

17. "Both Parties Urged to Shun Radicalism of Left and Right," *Washington Post*, September 22, 1968, A5; "Extremes on Foreign Policy Deplored," *New York Times*, December 13, 1970, 24.

18. "Freedom House Rips Dr. King Viet Efforts," *Chicago Tribune*, May 21, 1967, 13; "McCarthyites, Rev. King Says of His Critics," *Chicago Tribune*, May 23, 1967, B10.

19. Memorandum, Sussman to Board of Trustees, November 6, 1969, Box 1, Folder 27, FHA, PU; "Minutes, Freedom House Board of Trustees," November 10, 1969, Box 1, Folder 27, FHA, PU.

20. "Minutes, Willkie Memorial Building and Freedom House," May 22, 1972, Box 2, Folder 3, FHA, PU; Memorandum, Sussman to Board of Trustees, September 14, 1973, Box 2, Folder 4, FHA, PU; quote from Gerald L. Steibel, "Détente Item for Board Meeting, September 24" n.d., Box 2, Folder 4, FHA, PU; "Minutes, Freedom House Board," October 30, 1973, Box 2, Folder 4, FHA, PU; "Minutes, Freedom House Board of Trustees, Special Meeting," November 14, 1974, Box 2, Folder 5, FHA, PU.

21. Cmiel, "The Emergence of Human Rights Politics in the United States"; David Schmitz and Vanessa Walker, "Jimmy Carter and the Foreign Policy of

Human Rights," *Diplomatic History*, January 2004, 117–18; Buchanan, "The Truth Will Set You Free."

22. John Ehrman, *The Rise of Neoconservatism: Intellectuals and Foreign Affairs, 1945–1994* (New Haven, CT: Yale University Press, 1995); John Judis, "Trotskyism to Anarchism: The Neoconservative Revolution," *Foreign Affairs*, July/ August 1995, 123–29; George Nash, *The Conservative Intellectual Movement in America since 1945* (Wilmington, DE: Intercollegiate Studies Institute, 1998), 304–6; Julian Zelizer, "Conservatives, Carter, and the Politics of National Security," in *Rightward Bound*, ed. Bruce Schulman and Julian Zelizer (Cambridge: Harvard University Press, 2008), 265–87.

23. Jeremi Suri, "Détente and its Discontents," in *Rightward Bound*, ed. Schulman and Zelizer, 243; William Link, *Righteous Warrior: Jesse Helms and the Rise of Modern Conservatism* (New York: St. Martin's Press, 2008), 163–64; Zelizer, "Conservatives, Carter, and the Politics of National Security," 269–71; Donald Critchlow, *The Conservative Ascendancy* (Cambridge, MA: Harvard University Press, 2008), 93–96, 142–49; The Republican Party Platform, August 18, 1976, American Presidency Project website, http://www.presidency.ucsb.edu/ws/index. php?pid=25843 (accessed on August 6, 2009).

24. Quote from "Extremes on Foreign Policy Deplored," *New York Times*, December 13, 1970, 24; Robert Scalapino and Paul Seabury, "Urgent: Foreign Policy Debate," *Freedom at Issue*, May–June 1972, 1–10; "Minutes, Willkie Memorial Building and Freedom House," May 22, 1972, Box 2, Folder 3, FHA, PU; "Minutes, Freedom House Board," October 30, 1973, Box 2, Folder 4, FHA, PU.

25. "Freedom House Program Audit Committee Report," November 4, 1974, Box 2, Folder 5, FHA, PU; "Minutes, Freedom House, Board of Trustees, Special Meeting," November 14, 1974, Box 2, Folder 5, FHA, PU.

26. Memorandum, Sussman to Executive Committee, October 6, 1976, Box 3, Folder 8, FHA, PU.

27. Sussman to Smith, September 21, 1976, Box 2, Folder 7, FHA, PU; "Outline of a Draft Statement on Human Rights and Foreign Policies," September 16, 1976, Box 6, Folder 5, FHA, PU; "Minutes, Boards of the Willkie Memorial Building and Freedom House," September 27, 1976, Box 2, Folder 7, FHA, PU.

28. President Jimmy Carter, "University of Notre Dame—Address at Commencement Exercises at the University," May 22, 1977, American Presidency Project website, www.presidency.ucsb.edu/ws/index.php?pid=7552 (accessed November 15, 2008). Cyrus Vance, "Human Rights and Foreign Policy," U.S. Department of State, *Bulletin* (May 23, 1977): 505–8. See also Schmitz and Walker, "Jimmy Carter and the Foreign Policy of Human Rights," 119–21.

29. The key works in this evolving literature are Gaddis Smith, *Morality, Reason, and Power: American Diplomacy in the Carter Years* (New York: Hill and Wang, 2006); Schmitz and Walker, "Jimmy Carter and the Foreign Policy of Human Rights,"; John Soares, "Strategy, Ideology, and Human Rights," *Journal of Cold War Studies* (Fall 2006): 57–91; Kenton Clymer, "Jimmy Carter, Human Rights, and

Cambodia," *Diplomatic History* (April 2003): 245–78; Robert Strong, *Working in the World* (Baton Rouge: Louisiana State Press, 2000); Itai Sneh, *The Future Almost Arrived: How Jimmy Carter Failed to Change U.S. Foreign Policy* (New York: Peter Lang Publishing, 2008); Scott Kaufman, *Plans Unraveled: The Foreign Policy of the Carter Administration* (Dekalb: Northern Illinois Press, 2008).

30. Memorandum, John Richardson to Members, Board of Trustees, September 14, 1977, Box 6, Folder 7, FHA, PU; Richardson to Derian, September, 19, 1977, Box 18, Folder 2, FHA, PU.

31. Sussman to Richardson, March 10, 1977, Box 18, Folder 2, FHA, PU; Memorandum, Sussman to Gruson, Hauser, and Sargeant, February 10, 1977, Box 23, Folder 20, FHA, PU.

32. Richardson to Lipschutz, November 7, 1977, Box 45, Folder 3, FHA, PU.

33. Stanley Hoffman, "The Hell of Good Intentions," *Foreign Policy* (Winter 1977–1978): 3–26.

34. "Draft for Washington Conference in January," December 2, 1977, Box 45, Folder 3, FHA, PU.

35. "Draft for Wash Post, file John Richardson," n.d., Box 18, Folder 1, FHA, PU. See also, Richardson, "Human Rights in a Global Context," April 22, 1977, Box 18, Folder 2, FHA, PU; John Richardson, "Human Rights Strategy," *Freedom at Issue*, May–June 1977, 3.

36. Raymond Gastil, "Human Rights: A Policy Guide for the U.S.," *Freedom at Issue,* March–April 1980, 12–15.

37. Text of the "Conference on Security and Co-Operation in Europe Final Act, Helsinki, 1975," http://www.csce.gov/ (accessed on November 23, 2008). Also see, Daniel Thomas, *The Helsinki Effect: International Norms, Human Rights, and the Demise of Communism* (Princeton, NJ: Princeton University Press, 2001); Judt, *Postwar*, 501–3.

38. Sussman, "Mount the Helsinki Watch, draft," September 9, 1975, Box 2, Folder 6, FHA, PU; "Mount the Helsinki Watch!" *Freedom at Issue*, November–December 1975, 4.

39. "Mount the Helsinki Watch!" *Freedom at Issue*, November–December, 1975, 4.

40. "Public Diplomacy versus Quiet Diplomacy," *Freedom at Issue*, May–June 1977, 4–6.

41. "Should the United States Abrogate the Helsinki Accords?" *Freedom at Issue*, November–December 1980, 7–9.

42. "A Freedom House Advisory: An Analysis of Compliance with the Information Section of Basket Three of the Helsinki Accords of 1975," *Freedom at Issue*, September–October 1977, 16–22.

43. "Should the United States Abrogate the Helsinki Accords?" *Freedom at Issue*, November–December 1980, 7–9.

44. Memorandum, Sussman to Board of Trustees, Advisory Council, November 9, 1979, Box 7, Folder 1, FHA, PU.

45. Ronald Reagan, "Remarks on the Caribbean Basin Initiative," February 24, 1982, American Presidency Project website, http://www.presidency.ucsb.edu/ws/index.php?pid=42202 (accessed November 27, 2008).

46. Ehrman, *Rise of Neoconservatism*, 154–157.

47. Freedom House did have good connections with the administration. Jeane Kirkpatrick, the U.S. ambassador to the United Nation's during Reagan's first term, was a Freedom House board member and also a leading neoconservative. Memorandum, Sussman to Executive Committee, December 29, 1980, Box 7, Folder 6, FHA, PU; "The Opportunties for Freedom House to Sustain the New National Spirit," c. 1981, Box 7, Folder 7, FHA, PU; Sussman to Richardson, January 16, 1981, Box 7, Folder 7, FHA, PU.

48. Sussman to Richardson, January 16, 1981, Box 7, Folder 7, FHA, PU.

49. John Richardson "Regarding the draft statement for the Board of Trustees, Master—4th Draft, 3/10/81–LRS," March 10, 1981, Box 7, Folder 7, FHA, PU.

50. Leonard Sussman, "The Opportunities for Freedom House to Create a New National Spirit, 4th Draft" March 10, 1981, Box 7, Folder 7, FHA, PU; "Minutes, Executive Committee," February 25, 1981, Box 3, Folder 13, FHA, PU.

51. Richardson "Regarding the draft statement for the Board of Trustees, Master—4th Draft, 3/10/81–LRS," March 10, 1981, Box 7, Folder 7, FHA, PU.

52. Sussman, "The Opportunities for Freedom House to Help Sustain the New National Spirit, Draft," February 23, 1981, Box 7, Folder 7, FHA, PU.

53. Sussman to Brzezinksi, March 4, 1981, Box 7, Folder 8, FHA, PU; "Minutes, Boards of the Willkie Memorial Building and Freedom House," January 26, 1981, Box 2, Folder 12, FHA, PU.

54. Charles Mohr, "Human Rights Choice Abhors Scolding as U.S. Tool," *New York Times*, February 13, 1981, 2; Ernest Lefever, "The Tyranny of Chaos—a Footnote on Chile," *Freedom at Issue*, January–February, 1975, 23.

55. Judith Miller, "Rebuffed in Senate, Lefever Pulls out as Rights Nominee," *New York Times*, June 6, 1981, 1; David Carliner to William Clark, July 2, 1981, Box 7, Folder 9, FHA, PU; Memorandum, Sussman to Case, Cherne, Richardson, van Slyck, July 7, 1981, Box 7, Folder 9, PHA, PU.

56. "Excerpts from State Department Memo on Human Rights," *New York Times*, November 5, 1981, A10; Barbara Crossette, "Strong U.S. Human Rights Policy Urged in Memo Approved by Haig," *New York Times*, November 5, 1981, A1; "Reagan Rights Policy Confirmed," *New York Times*, November 9, 1981, A4; Editorial, "Human Rights Revisited," *The New Republic*, November 25, 1981, 5–6.

57. Memorandum, Sussman to Board of Trustees, November 5, 1981, Box 7, Folder 10, FHA, PU; "Meeting with Deputy Secretary of State Wiliam P. Clark—September 24, 1981," Box 7, Folder 10, FHA, PU.

58. Sussman to Abrams, November 5, 1981, Box 37, Folder 9, FHA, PU.

59. Max Kampelman, "East-West Relations," May 24, 1984, Box 15, Folder 12, FHA, PU; Francis X. Cline, "Skeptical Optimist for Talks: Max M. Kampelman," *New York Times*, January 20, 1985, 12; "Conservatives Have Some Doubts About

Kampelman," *Human Events*, February 2, 1985, 2–3, Box 10, Folder 15, FHA, PU; "Ambassador Max Kampelman Links Human Rights and the Conference on Disarmament in Europe, Opening Press Statement in Stockholm," September 18, 1984, Box 15, Folder 11, FHA, PU.

60. Leonard Sussman, "In Support of the Helsinki Process," *Freedom at Issue*, September–October 1985, 14–17.

61. "American Warns UNESCO on Proposed Press Code," *New York Times*, October 9, 1980, A7; Jonathan Friendly, "U.S. Press Curbs in Grenada May Affect International Debate," *New York Times*, November 8, 1983, A10; E.J. Dionne, "U.S. Weighs UNESCO Pullout Over Budget and Policy Fight," *New York Times*, December 15, 1983, A1.

62. Leonard Sussman, "Opposing Assaults on the World's Free Press," *Wall Street Journal*, June 16, 1981, 30.

63. Richardson to Reagan, December 6, 1983, Box 9, Folder 1, FHA, PU; Memorandum, Sussman to Executive Committee, December 14, 1983, Box 9, Folder 1, FHA, PU; Memorandum, Sussman to Executive Committee, December 30, 1983, Box 9, Folder 1, FHA, PU; Memorandum, Sussman to Executive Committee, February 1, 1984, Box 9, Folder 2, FHA, PU; Sussman to Robert Bartley, September 6, 1984, Box 9, Folder 5, FHA, PU; Abrams to Sussman, August 15, 1984, Box 15, Folder 11, FHA, PU; Sussman to Armacost, November 20, 1984, Box 41, Folder 10, FHA, PU; E.J. Dionne, "U.S. Weighs UNESCO Pullout Over Budget and Policy Fight," *New York Times*, December 15, 1983, A1; Richard Bernstein, "Distortion Laid to U.S. on UNESCO," *New York Times*, August 9, 1984, A9; Editorial, "The UNESCO Lobby," *Wall Street Journal*, August 28, 1984, 26; Alex Jones, "UNESCO Reported to Move Away From Issue of Licensing Reporters," *New York Times*, November 6, 1984, A16; Frank Prial, "U.S. Move Praised by Conservatives," *New York Times*, December 20, 1984, A10.

64. E,J. Dionne, "U.S. Weighs UNESCO Pullout Over Budget and Policy Fight," *New York Times*, December 15, 1983, A1; Transcript, "People's Rights and the Redefinition of Human Rights," August 24, 1983, Box 52, Folder 9, FHA, PU.

65. Leonard Sussman, "Peoples' Rights and the Redefinition of Human Rights," n.d., 1983, Box 52, Folder 9, FHA, PU.

66. Raymond Gastil, "On the Expansion of the Concept of Human Rights," n.d., 1983, Box 52, Folder 9, FHA, PU.

67. Transcript, "People's Rights and the Redefinition of Human Rights," August 24, 1983, Box 52, Folder 9, FHA, PU.

68. See Ken Cmiel, "The Recent History of Human Rights," *American Historical Review* 109, no. 4 (February 2004): 117–35.

11

"FOR OUR SOVIET COLLEAGUES"

Scientific Internationalism, Human Rights, and the Cold War

PAUL RUBINSON

In late November 1980, during yet another day of "backbreaking forced labor behind a lathe," Yuri Orlov closed his eyes and rested his head on his arms. Although it was a designated break period, Officer Salakhov told Orlov that rest was forbidden. For his transgression, Orlov was placed in the labor camp's prison for a month. By June 1981, Orlov had been in the labor camp for three years, much of that time spent in the camp's prison and "punishment cell." Inside the prison, boots and warm clothes were prohibited. Not surprisingly Orlov fell ill, suffering at various times from low blood pressure, rheumatic pains, cystitis, insomnia, and vitamin deficiency. Desperate for nourishment, he took to eating the grasses that grew on the grounds of the labor camp.[1]

Hunger and abuse wrecked Orlov's body; another form of torture battered his mind. Before his arrest for establishing a human rights group in Moscow, Orlov had been a physicist. And while the Soviet state tried to impose an identity of prisoner upon him, Orlov defied this fate by remaining, as best he could, a scientist. According to his wife, "He secretly, by snatches, continued his scientific work in the unbearable conditions of the camp." Despite the frequent seizure of his books and notes, Orlov somehow managed to draft an article on wave logic. But his attempt to send the article to a journal was rewarded with another six months in the camp prison. In a letter to his wife, Orlov wrote, "I cannot carry out my ideas on logic; this is almost obvious, due to lack of time and including a lack of health." At one point in his draconian prison, a member of the KGB scoffed, "Orlov, forget that you're a scientist. You'll never get out of this camp."[2]

The plight of Orlov and his attempts to resist his fate show how the objective realities of science can be brought to bear on human rights activism. The connection between human rights, social movements, and the Cold War is well established. During the second half of the twentieth century, as Cold War bipolarity attempted to divide the globe along political and economic lines, a simultaneous movement attempted to reunite the globe on the basis of respect for human rights.[3] Less well-known, however, is how science and human rights became intertwined. Science itself is often envisioned, promoted, and celebrated as valid truth, regardless of nation, era, or political system, much like the concept of human rights. But in reality, science and human rights have not always gone hand in hand. In fact, the alignment of these two belief systems during the late 1970s only occurred because of the direct action of scientists and activists who sought to redefine science as a human rights endeavor.

Human Rights and Scientific Internationalism

Modern conceptions of science and human rights emerged from the intellectual ferment of the Enlightenment. The enthusiasm for the Age of Reason and the drafting of the Declaration of the Rights of Man and Citizen during the early days of the French Revolution suggested a mutually beneficial relationship between rational scientific thought and human rights. Inspired to an extent by the U.S. Revolution against Britain, French revolutionaries occasionally (and overzealously) credited Benjamin Franklin, the scientist and former U.S. ambassador to France, with sparking the revolutionary ideals of reason and democracy in Paris. At one point, vendors even sold statuettes of Franklin carved out of stones allegedly pulled from the rubble of the Bastille. But science and the new human rights regime in Paris got off to a rough start, demonstrated most clearly when the great chemist Lavoisier was put on trial, where a judge told him, "The Republic has no need of scientists." He was subsequently marched to the scaffold and beheaded by guillotine.[4]

In the early twentieth century, science fell more in line with the political and military demands of the nation-state, contradicting the values of scientific internationalism. During the Great War, chemists of all nations rushed to serve their homelands by eagerly concocting poison gases. The head of the wartime German chemical weapons program, Fritz Haber, ominously declared scientific internationalism secondary to nationalism when he said "science belongs to humanity in peacetime and to the fatherland in war." The efforts of U.S. chemists matched their German peers; at the war's height, roughly 1,700 U.S. chemists worked for the military, and the rate of mustard-gas production alone reached thirty tons per day by November 1918.[5]

The Second World War both reinforced and challenged the alliance of science and scientists with the nation. When Hitler rose to power and renowned physicists began to leave Germany, Hungarian physicist Leo Szilard worked frantically to locate jobs overseas for these exiled scientists. By finding homes for many of the scientific diaspora, Szilard demonstrated the scientist's status as a true citizen of the world. But many of these same scientists, including Szilard himself, willingly took part in the distinctly anti-internationalist move of censoring and keeping secret the results of experiments with uranium in a futile attempt to keep German scientists from learning about the feasibility of an atomic bomb. Szilard and his peers would eventually participate in the U.S. effort to construct an atomic bomb, a weapon used unilaterally against two Japanese cities and symbolically (according to some interpretations) against the Soviet Union in the first salvo of the Cold War.[6]

After the Second World War, scientists in many Western nations attempted to reestablish a scientific internationalism that, as they understood it, had been only suspended during two world wars. Bringing the scientific ethos to bear on geopolitics, they mobilized for world government and international control of nuclear weapons. Eventually, however, Cold War tensions demanded that Western scientists view science from within a Cold War paradigm. In one scholar's words, the Cold War produced a "bipolar scientific internationalism" that united the scientific community under an anticommunist and pro-Western ideology. With Western governments dispensing larger and larger amounts of funding and influence, scientists had professional reasons to oppose the Soviets.[7]

Scientific Exchanges and Scientific Boycotts

During the mid 1970s, before Orlov's exile to labor camp, the issue of human rights transformed U.S.-Soviet relations, as well as the scientific discipline. Although scientists had played a large role in debates over nuclear weapons and arms control in the 1950s and 1960s, antinuclear scientists had not met much success in trying to push U.S. nuclear policy toward disarmament. But during the 1970s, the growing détente between the United States and Soviet Union led scientists to question the bipolar internationalism that had divided U.S. scientists from their Soviet peers. Rather than fight the

Cold War on a scientific level, scientists began to try and transcend the Cold War by embracing a transnational rather than bipolar vision of scientific internationalism—one based on the ideals of the scientific discipline itself, rather than geopolitics.

Meanwhile, the concurrent surge of interest in human rights around the world created another opportunity for science to play a role in geopolitics and transnational relations. The connection between science and human rights got a boost from the Helsinki Final Act, signed on August 1, 1975. This landmark agreement between East and West, relatively dismissed by Western leaders at the time, focused mainly on social, political, and economic rights, but the agreement also included a section that described science and technology as activities that "contribute to the reinforcement of peace and security in Europe and in the world as a whole." Scientific cooperation between nations in particular "assists the effective solution of problems of common interest and the improvement of the conditions of human life." The Helsinki Final Act specifically recommended joint projects, research, contact, communication, and exchange programs in many fields, including agriculture, energy, physics, chemistry, meteorology, hydrology, and oceanography.[8] In the spirit of Helsinki, U.S. scientists undertook cooperative, scientific exchange programs with their Soviet counterparts aimed at increasing scientific knowledge, as well as diffusing Cold War tensions. The U.S. National Academy of Sciences (NAS) coordinated exchanges with the Soviet Academy of Sciences at the rate of roughly thirty scientists from each of the two countries for a total of one hundred working months per year. The two academies also discussed working groups on arms control and joint planetary explorations.[9]

Just as Helsinki enabled the formation of human rights networks to monitor adherence to the political and social aspects of the agreement, Western scientists were energized by the Helsinki Final Act and their role as transnational actors. The increased contact with Soviet scientists, however, quickly revealed the deplorable Soviet record on human rights. Most upsetting to the scientific community was the fate of Andrei Sakharov, the esteemed Soviet physicist and dissident who came under increasing oppression as he became more outspoken. Orlov's sham trial and hard labor sentence also disgraced the Soviet Union in Western eyes. The scientists empowered by Helsinki quickly took to using science as a means of enforcing human rights—the NAS, for example, established a Human Rights Committee as did the New York Academy of Sciences. In 1976, the American Association for the Advancement of Science established a Clearinghouse on Science and Human Rights, described as "a conduit for information about and advocacy on behalf of members of the scientific community in foreign countries whose human rights and/or scientific freedoms have been violated."[10] The American Mathematical Society created a Committee on Human Rights of Mathematicians, while the Society for Industrial and Applied Mathematics Council established its own Committee on Human Rights in the late 1970s.[11] In some cases, ordinary academic rituals took on added significance, such as the International Congress of Mathematicians in August 1978 in Helsinki, where the nonappearance of Soviet scientists took on the stigma of a violation of an international agreement.[12]

As oppression of Soviet scientists—most notably Sakharov, Orlov, and Anatoly Shcharansky[13]—worsened, U.S. scientists were further drawn into debates over human rights.[14] Orlov, scientist and chairman of the Moscow Helsinki Watch Group that monitored Eastern bloc adherence to the Helsinki Final Act, had been arrested in 1977. Jeri Laber, head of the U.S. Helsinki Watch Group, wrote to President Jimmy Carter that "No prisoner of conscience is of more concern to the American scientific community." The imprisonment of Orlov, she asserted, "casts a cloud over the development of relations between the scientific communities of the United States and the Soviet Union." According to Laber, the president of the NAS had expressed to Brezhnev "the deep sorrow of US scientists" over Orlov's arrest, and Laber then informed Carter that many scientists refused to participate in scientific exchange with the Soviets.[15] Thus began the boycott of U.S.-Soviet scientific exchanges, the preferred method of protest of many U.S. scientists. It was hoped the boycott would shame the Soviet government into improving its treatment of its scientists and citizens.

In early 1978, announcing a six-month suspension of Soviet-American scientific exchanges, NAS president Philip Handler termed the sentencing of Sakharov to exile in Gorky "shocking." A statement from the NAS further elaborated on the boycott decision and the Soviet actions that inspired it: "These actions represent, from our perspective, an intrusion upon the human rights and scientific activities of an eminent scientist." The NAS expressed "a deep conviction that both [the U.S. and Soviet science] academies work toward peace, détente and disarmament . . . But we are keenly aware of the reaction of American scientists and the American public to the actions of the Soviet Government."[16]

In the process of standing up for their fellow scientists, U.S. scientists formulated a defense of human rights based on the advocacy of science. When four U.S. scientists withdrew from a macromolecular chemistry symposium slated for Tashkent in October 1978, they wrote directly to their Soviet colleagues to personally explain the boycott. They had made, they wrote, a "painful decision" informed by the recent show trials of scientists in the Soviet Union that had "gravely hampered" the objectives of international scientific cooperation and communication. The trials were indicative of "repression in the Soviet Union and its stifling effect on scientific communication and cooperation." In the symbiotic relationship between science and human rights, repression of scientists made the conduct of science all but impossible, even for scientists on opposite sides of the globe.[17]

John T. Edsall of Harvard similarly expressed a "sense of outrage" over the fate of Orlov and Shcharansky when he wrote to W. A. Engelhardt of the Institute of Molecular Biology in Moscow: "These profoundly disturbing events seem to belong to an alien world that repels us." Spelling out a commitment to human rights, he continued: "We are concerned with the maintenance of human rights throughout the world, and as a scientific community we are particularly concerned with the defence of the rights of our fellow scientists."[18] The Soviets had offended the values and mores of the scientific community, and in the late 1970s and early 1980s, human rights trumped internationalism.

In mid-July 1978, Stanford scientist Paul J. Flory wrote to Anatoly Aleksandrov, president of the Soviet Academy of Sciences, to express the "widespread revulsion" over the accusations of treason brought against Soviet scientists including Orlov and Shcharansky. Referring to the Helsinki Final Act, Flory affirmed the importance of scientific cooperation to friendly relations between East and West, mentioning "international scientific cooperation as one of the avenues for achieving peace and for advancing human welfare." Flory described science as the free exchange of ideas, an ideal hampered by the repression of scientists. "Science itself cannot flourish in such an atmosphere," he wrote. Flory personally promised that at an October scientific conference in the Soviet Union he fully intended to publicly excoriate the Soviet government for its violations of human rights. In closing, he wrote, "I fully agree that scientific meetings should not be politicized, but the issues involved transcend politics."[19]

Despite Flory's claim, politics and science had often mingled in the past, and as the year went on, they became increasingly entangled. A September 1978 article in the prestigious scientific journal *Nature* claimed that the Soviets saw "that the threat of a severance of scientific relations was a real one." But the same article highlighted the diverse views scientists held on the issue, mentioning that "not all scientists" thought a boycott was the best method of aiding imprisoned and repressed Soviet colleagues. In place of a boycott, some scientists thought "the stricter insistence on the norms of scientific life—including proper representation at conferences, a more fitting form of protest." The NAS pointed to these opposing views—glossed over as the "individualistic" nature of U.S. scientists—in explaining its refusal to formally endorse an indefinite boycott. "Each American scientist . . . must determine his or her own course of action," an NAS statement concluded. In contrast, French physicists facing the same quandary had recommended the cessation of every form of "official scientific relations."[20]

The boycott did not mean a break of informal contacts between U.S. human rights activists and Soviet scientists. Instead, official exchanges were halted, but U.S. scientists continued to reach out to their oppressed colleagues. President Carter's science advisor Frank Press even served as a conduit between U.S. Helsinki Watch and Soviet scientists. After a meeting in February 1979, Helsinki Watch managed to get Press to take with him on a trip to Europe letters for Orlov and Sakharov; one letter detailed for Sakharov the formation of U.S. Helsinki Watch and asked him for advice.[21]

Further threats to Sakharov led to increasing efforts by U.S. scientists to help him. The Committee of Concerned Scientists (CCS) counted four thousand members in late February 1979 and dedicated itself to "constructive action to protect and advance the scientific and human rights of colleagues the world over." In a telegram the CCS implored Aleksandrov not to expel Sakharov from the Soviet Academy of Sciences, an action foreshadowed by the failure of the academy to invite Sakharov to its general meeting in March. Such an ouster, the telegram stated, "would be an act of hostile disrespect." Blaming the Soviet Union's repression of Sakharov for straining scientific relations, the telegram made a veiled threat to end scientific exchange permanently if Sakharov suffered any more: "By resisting efforts to further isolate him from his Soviet colleagues, the academy, under your leadership, can begin to restore the confidence of American scientists in the value of our bilateral efforts and strengthen their desire to participate in exchanges with Soviet colleagues." The telegram closed by placing responsibility for relations squarely on the Soviet Academy: "We look to your academy to set the tone for improved scientific relations between our nations."[22]

With no change in official Soviet attitudes, the group Scientists for Orlov and Shcharansky (SOS) announced in March 1979 that "they would severely restrict their cooperation with the Soviet Union in response to the jailing of Orlov, Shcharansky, and other dissidents." SOS counted more than 2,400 members at this point, most of them scientists, engineers, and computer scientists. From the ranks of the NAS, 113 members joined the SOS protest, including thirteen Nobel Prize winners.[23]

This social movement of scientists found a sympathetic audience in Congress. In late May 1979, Aleksandrov was once again the target of a letter of protest, this time from the congressional Subcommittee on Science, Research and Technology. The letter began by expressing "concern for the deterioration of Soviet-American scientific relations during this past year." The subcommittee members refused "acquiescence in the violation of scientists' human rights . . . as a price of scientific exchange." The letter further noted that U.S. scientists had complained that Soviet authorities often only let scientists of "low calibre" travel abroad for conferences—last-minute substitutes for more prestigious and controversial scientists. Making it clear that the protests were of a grassroots nature, the subcommittee emphasized that "none of these actions have been stimulated or suggested by the American Government." Still, "the Congress is slowly becoming aware of the need to include human rights as an essential component of national and international science and technology policy."[24] Scientists continued to push the government on this issue. A lawyer for the State Department writing to Helsinki Watch about the official stance on exchange policy admitted that the Soviet invasion of Afghanistan and the exile of Sakharov had brought this policy into question. But the lawyer also credited scientists and scientific organizations with driving postponements. In addition to the NAS refusal to participate in seminars for six months, the lawyer credited Lawrence Livermore National Laboratory physicists' refusal to receive Soviet scientists in an atomic energy exchange and unnamed U.S. scientists' postponement of an electrometallurgy seminar.[25] The paradigm, to use a scientific term, had shifted.

With momentum building, the CCS continued to agitate on behalf of Soviet scientists. In June 1980, the organization sent a letter to scientists attending the Eleventh International Quantum Electronics Conference in Boston, once again infusing an ordinary academic event with geopolitical significance. The CCS letter to participants characterized the meeting as "a unique opportunity to help several of our fellow scientists who are currently persecuted in the Soviet Union" and suggested discussing the plight of the dissidents with Soviet scientists at the conference. Scientists were transformed into amateur diplomats by conducting, as the CCS recommended, "informal discussion with a view toward persuading them to intervene in these cases." The letter concluded, "In this way, you will underscore for our Soviet colleagues the widespread concern among American scientists about the status of scientific freedom in the USSR." A simultaneous CCS letter to Aleksandrov, Brezhnev, and the Soviet Ambassador to the United States Anatoly Dobrynin (also publicized in a press release) protested the treatment of Sakharov, Orlov, and others: "The status of scientific freedom in the USSR is linked to scientific progress worldwide. Only when cases such as those above have been justly and humanely resolved will productive scientific exchange be made possible." In essence, the CCS told the Soviets that by failing to free Sakharov and the others, they not only violated the Helsinki human rights guidelines but also the act's science and technology guidelines.[26]

The mobilization of the U.S. scientific community came as the direct result of Soviet scientists reaching out to their peers and appealing to the international scientific community's respect for human rights. Sakharov had not initially looked for help overseas, but when his fellow Soviet scientists abandoned him, he turned to the West. In 1979, Sakharov praised the group Scientists in Defense of Orlov and Scharansky: "Active participation by scientists and specialists in the fight for human rights the world over is a burning need of our time."[27] But after two years, Sakharov remained in exile, and he continued to need contact with his U.S. peers. In a 1981 letter to Stanford physicist Sidney Drell, Sakharov detailed his exile in Gorky. A policeman guarded his front door. This was not quite house arrest, Sakharov observed, "for I am not in my own house." The totalitarian state imposed its will on him. Authorities confiscated his mail, and only his wife was allowed to visit him. KGB agents, Sakharov was certain, frequently broke into his apartment, which he saw as "a direct threat to my life." He found comfort in alerting scientists to his fate, writing simply: "I want my Western colleagues to know about it." This constant abuse not surprisingly hampered his professional endeavors. His son's fiancée was being "held hostage" in an insane asylum, he told Drell. "There is no way that I can do any scientific work so long as we have to spend every hour of every day worrying about her fate." Nor was he allowed to attend scientific conferences, which violated his "purely academic rights." In closing he implored Western scientists to "go directly to high officials of their own governments and beseech them to appeal to the Soviet leaders."[28]

Elsewhere, Sakharov repeated how his exile kept him from working. In announcing a hunger strike, he declared: "There can be no question . . . of any scientific work while this tragedy of my loved ones continues." The failure of Soviet scientists to make any attempt to intervene on his behalf he described as a "bitter disappointment to me, not only on the personal level but as a manifestation of a pernicious abandoning of responsibility and of the possibility of influencing events."[29] Sakharov thus averred that scientists have a greater role to play in society, a responsibility to risk their elite status for the sake of human rights.

Sakharov so clearly embodied this commitment to human rights and this willingness to sacrifice that U.S. scientists could hardly refuse to boycott the exchanges. At one point Sakharov's wife, Elena Bonner, wrote to a friend that her husband was frequently drugged, his papers then stolen. His exile deprived him of "the right to free scientific and human intercourse." Sakharov, Bonner wrote, was "miserable" without the ability to discuss science with his friends and without the right to pick up the phone and discuss a scientific problem or insight. Over three years, he was visited by only six colleagues; occasions that were more "humiliation" than "normal scientific discourse" because of his imposed deprivation. In fact, Bonner admitted, Sakharov was so desperate for scientific discussion that he even discussed physics with her, though "it would be hard to find a more unprepared listener."[30]

Debating the Boycott

Strong support for the boycott came from those who had direct experience with the plight of scientists in the Soviet Union. Irene Gildengorn Lainer, a PhD in metallurgical science, credited contacts in the West with securing her release from the Soviet Union in 1979. At an American Physical Society meeting she delivered a paper calling on scientists to take action. "Any support that the Western scientific community can give to its Soviet colleagues is of utmost importance," she stated.[31]

Valentin F. Turchin, born in Russia and a friend of Sakharov's, had been forced to leave Russia in the late 1970s, ending up in New York by 1979. In a letter to the CCS he gave the boycott a heavy endorsement: "I am sure it made impression on the Soviets and saved from arrest some unknown number of potential prisoners." But, he added, if more scientists boycotted, "the effect would be more spectacular. I do not understand how people can collaborate with the Soviet regime, thereby supporting it, notwithstanding its crimes and the threat it presents to humanity."[32]

Despite enthusiasm for the cause, the boycott continued with little discernable effect. Most significantly, Sakharov, Orlov, and Shcharansky remained in prison and in exile, causing some scientists to question this tactic and wonder if cooperation held more promise than exclusion. In a letter to Helsinki Watch, the physicist Victor Weisskopf, for decades a respected U.S. government arms control advisor, stated that he opposed the six-month NAS boycott of exchanges. He feared that such actions might only cause the Soviet government to take even harsher measures against Sakharov.[33]

The congressional Subcommittee on Science, Research and Technology celebrated the diverse views of scientists. Noting a "budding professional ethic," the subcommittee praised SOS's boycott of exchanges, as well as the opposite tactic of transforming conferences and exchanges into vehicles "for maintaining contact with and public awareness of oppressed colleagues. Both approaches share the recognition by scientists that individual and collective action is required in the face of human rights violations."[34]

But many scientists realized that the desires for different tactics threatened to break the movement apart. At its heart, the debate came down to the very meaning of scientific internationalism. What, after all, *was* scientific internationalism? Was it the simple, neutral-value act of crossing borders and working with scientists regardless of the political context? Or was it defending the rights of humans and principles of scientific freedom? Was scientific internationalism a worthwhile endeavor if it tacitly endorsed the actions of a repressive nation? On the other hand, was it worth sacrificing scientific internationalism for what was ultimately a political dispute over ideals?

At the center of the boycott debate stood Philip Handler and the NAS. For decades the NAS had coordinated U.S. science policy, including the exchanges, and advised the government on scientific research priorities. Naturally the NAS was expected to formulate a position on the Soviet scientist controversy. Handler addressed the dilemma in a long statement to the U.S. Commission on Security and Cooperation in Europe (a liaison to Helsinki activists overseas) and the congressional subcommittees on International Security and Scientific Affairs and on Science, Research and Technology. First, Handler discussed Sakharov's plight, largely brought on by the physicist's heavy criticism of the Soviet invasion of Afghanistan. He then turned to what to do about scientific cooperation in a "post-Afghanistan, post-Sakharov period." "I find it difficult to imagine scientific exchange continuing in the spirit we had created heretofore," Handler admitted. For every new Soviet scientist deprived of his or her rights, the NAS received, he said, "a shower of letters . . . urging that we terminate our exchange program." Yet the NAS "considered that unwise because . . . there also remain strong voices within the community insisting that we sustain the lines of communication." Handler actually endorsed both approaches, claiming that the NAS, in fact, had little power over the exchanges since the programs were voluntary. "Neither the Congress nor the Academy can *make* exchange programs happen," he stated.[35]

Handler ultimately decided that the exchanges should continue, befitting the international spirit of science. But he confessed that he was also "sorely pressed to find any justification for merely proceeding as usual." Handler thus announced that the NAS would defer "all bilateral seminars and the like, while permitting the activities of individual scientists to proceed on our usual basis, leaving the decision to the individual consciences of American scientists." The NAS president made a distinction, however, between his official role and his personal principles, adding that if he had the opportunity to participate in an exchange as an ordinary scientist, "I would not go." Handler essentially implemented a scaling back of the exchange program: "It should be slowed down markedly, there should be no new starts, no high-level, visible interactions," with the framework left intact for the future if relations improved.[36]

This compromise lacked the vigor of a comprehensive boycott, causing many boycott advocates to defend their chosen tactic. The boycott, they argued, sent a valuable message of solidarity to their oppressed Soviet peers. The chairman of SOS, Morris Pripstein, complained about boycott naysayers. Claiming that SOS had made a "somewhat dramatic impact," he stated he was "amazed and appalled" by a *Nature* editorial that opposed the boycott. "Despite these reactions," he told Jeri Laber, "our point of view is gaining ground in the scientific community."[37] In defense of his tactics, he pointed directly to the words of Sakharov himself, who had endorsed the boycott in an open letter: "I believe that in order to protect innocent persons it is permissible and, in many cases, necessary to adopt extraordinary measures such as an interruption of scientific contacts or other types of boycott."[38]

The American University physicist Earl Callen disagreed and led a move to resume the exchanges. In a letter to SOS, CCS, and others, he wrote: "I think that the time has come to take the initiative in encouraging a deal with the Russians, and to end endorsement of the boycott." He argued that with the Cold War intensifying, "scientists will now feel more and more that we need a scientific bridge to the Russians," and that "the boycott will erode away . . . and with no price extracted." If this happened, the boycott could not be used as a threat in the future nor would U.S. scientists be inclined to try one again. On the other hand, he did not want to end the boycott "without a quid pro quo" to "maintain credibility." He suggested floating a deal to the Soviets: that for the release of Sakharov, Orlov, or Shcharansky, U.S. scientists might be "encouraged to maintain contacts with their Soviet counterparts."[39] From a social movement perspective, he hoped to preserve the threat of the boycott as a tactic for future bargaining.

Callen's move to resume the exchanges touched off a heated debate as scientists endeavored to assess the political impact of their activism. Paul Flory took exception to Callen in strong terms in a memo of July 15, 1981. He saw himself as up against "a growing body of opinion that scientists in the West should relax their policies of restriction on scientific exchange and cooperation with their counterparts in the U.S.S.R." Flory first rejected the idea that boycotting had no effect. Though Orlov and Shcharansky remained imprisoned and Sakharov in exile, Flory boasted that "many scientists who could have been imprisoned have not been, and others have received lighter sentences than would have been their fate if American scientists had been indifferent. My informants are positive of this." As evidence he mentioned a computer scientist named Irina Grivina who received a five-year exile sentence, far less harsh than what had been expected.[40]

Flory then suggested that, out of solidarity with their Soviet colleagues, U.S. scientists should "follow their examples in upholding principles." Instead of cutting a deal for the release of scientists, he advocated renewed commitment to the principles of human rights. "Sakharov, Orlov and Shcharansky do not ask for ransom at a price. They suffer for the principles to which they are irrevocably committed," he wrote. "None of these three (among others) would agree to barter principles for release from prison or exile . . . It is the least that we can do." Flory described the situation as a "war of nerves" in which "our resolve is under test. Clearly, we must stand firm. To do otherwise would jeopardize many courageous people, deprive them of hope, and discourage others from trying." He closed by stating, "We should redouble our efforts, not relax them." To support his arguments, Flory explained that he drew upon the views of Yuri Yarim-Agaev, a recently emigrated scientist expelled from the Soviet Union in 1980. Flory claimed, "I am sure other Russian exiles would support him strongly."[41]

The views of Anthony Ralston, a professor in SUNY Buffalo's Department of Computer Science, steered a middle course between Callen and Flory. Ralston did not oppose a "deal" with the Soviets over the fate of Sakharov, Orlov, and Shcharansky, but he felt strongly that "we must be as steadfast as the Soviets." The boycott "should be continued until Sakharov is released from exile *and* the other two (at least) from jail."[42]

In further correspondence, Callen responded with a respectful but crystal clear rejection of continuing the boycott. Confronting the idea that the boycott had been effective, Callen wrote, the "religious" view was that without a boycott, Sakharov, Orlov, and Shcharansky would have been treated even more harshly than they had been. "Maybe," Callen continued, though such a view was "certainly a non-falsifiable assertion, more a statement of faith than a proof," the fact remained that none of the three had been released. Instead, Callen thought it would "be better to gain some *major* concessions now, resume lots of exchange, re-establish good ties, visit dissidents, demonstrate to the Soviets and to ourselves the success of our tactics, and use all that as a brake against the next atrocity." Scientists could always "ratchet back to withdrawal at the next major affront." Callen's sense of urgency that something had to be done soon came from his belief that the apolitical nature of scientists would eventually cause their enthusiasm for political action to "fade away." The focus should be on "finite, limited goals—like the release of particular persons—and respond favorably when we achieve these goals."[43]

A Fading Enthusiasm

Over time, the oppression of many Soviet scientists improved. In 1986, scientists worldwide celebrated the granting of Sakharov's freedom; one year later Orlov was able to leave the Soviet Union to accept a position at Cornell University. It was not the boycott, however, that freed Sakharov or his peers. Despite the intense debate over deals and boycotts, there was never any indication the Soviets were interested in negotiating over the fate of Sakharov or Orlov. Though the efforts of U.S. scientists cannot be dismissed, it was Mikhail Gorbachev, general secretary of the Communist Party and leader of the Soviet Union, who released Sakharov as part of his *perestroika* campaign. While sympathy for Soviet dissidents remained high, the boycott itself essentially petered out in the early 1980s. Coordinated political action by scientists could only last so long—as early as 1982, Helsinki Watch chose Orlov as its "Forgotten Man of the Year," a title granted to those "who would have been in the news if he or she had not been silenced by imprisonment" and "governmental terrorism."[44]

Three years after earning that dubious distinction, Orlov's plight was no better. Stuck in Kobyai, Yakutia, in northeastern Siberia, Orlov was assaulted by two drunken thugs, his glasses smashed. According to a Helsinki Watch memo, Orlov was "shunned and hated by many of the townspeople." Unable to procure housing, he lived in a workers' dorm, where his scientific papers were stolen. Lack of food and medical supplies put his health at risk to the extent that life might have been better for him in the labor camp, where he could at least sleep safely at night. "Scientific work is the only way for Orlov to keep his sanity under these conditions," one of his correspondents noted. "But even that possibility is being taken away from him." Scientific journals provided a comfort for the physicist and allowed him to keep up with scientific developments. But Orlov had not received any journals *"since November of last year,"* leaving him all but scientifically lost. Though Orlov's mail was clearly being confiscated by authorities, Helsinki Watch implored scientists "to keep sending journals and greetings to Orlov, in order to let Soviet leaders know that he is not forgotten." Working as a scientist was simply "impossible" for Orlov, but science could still provide a way out. Helsinki Watch encouraged U.S. scientists to ask their universities to offer Orlov lecture invitations, which it hoped might lead to an exit visa.[45]

While some considered Orlov's plight a call for increased activism, others saw only evidence that the boycott had failed. In 1985, the NAS came to that conclusion and decided to resume exchanges. With Cold War tensions rising and nuclear fears increasing, the NAS believed that exchanges would help soothe tense U.S.-Soviet relations. The *New York Times* quoted the new president of the NAS, Frank Press: "These are times of change in the Soviet Union. We feel that we can best help Sakharov and the dissident scientists by having channels of communication open rather than not." Edsall concurred, citing the renewed threat of nuclear war. The head of the American Association for the Advancement of Science echoed support for the academy's move, as did the Federation of American Scientists and its leader Jeremy Stone.[46]

As organizations moved to resume exchanges, some scientists tried to keep the boycott alive. In 1985, Joseph Birman of the City College of New York physics department vehemently objected to the NAS decision to resume cooperation and exchange with the Soviet Union. While in 1980 the NAS had demonstrated "moral leadership," according the Birman, the NAS of 1985 was "abandon[ing] its interest in its member, Prof. Sakharov" (Sakharov had been made a Foreign Associate of the NAS). Birman accused the NAS of "a regretful and disappointing lack of sensitivity to Human Rights of scientists" and a lack of respect for the Helsinki Final Act.[47] Meanwhile, Joel L. Lebowitz of Rutgers defended the resumption of exchanges to Morris Pripstein of SOS. He described the difference between a boycott and a resumption of exchanges as one of "tactics rather than principle as far as human rights are concerned." He argued that "having an agreement" might be a useful way to help Sakharov and other dissidents, though he recognized that not everyone would concur.[48]

But the resumption of exchange and the boycotting of exchange were decidedly not two sides of the same coin. Without a boycott, it became all too easy to set human rights aside in pursuit of scientific internationalism. Scientific internationalism, after all, had been a core scientific value longer than human rights. By the late 1990s, with the Cold War over and the Soviet Union disintegrated, the journal *Science* detected a sense of apathy among scientists, declaring in a headline, "Human Rights Fades as a Cause for Scientists."[49]

Such had not always been the case. For a time, it appeared that science would be impossible without human rights. Arthur L. Shawlow, president of the American Physical Society, expressed as much in a 1981 letter to Sakharov. "The American Physical Society is actively working for the civil rights of individual scientists in many countries around the world." He stated, "In this regard, we continue to look for inspiration and leadership from your words and actions." Linking science to human rights, he declared: "The progress of science depends on the creative ideas of scientists, tested and refined by lively discussions with their peers. We all hope that we will soon again be able to greet you in person, and to discuss with you the frontier areas of our science."[50]

The scientists' boycott and embrace of human rights in the late 1970s and early 1980s reflects the growing salience of human rights to an extensive array of human activities. Having transcended bipolar internationalism, human rights gave scientists a way to criticize the Soviet government while sympathizing with those who lived under its brutal regime. Human rights also gave U.S. scientists a way to avoid the partisan domestic bickering over nuclear weapons yet still claim relevance to geopolitics. The human rights of the West—including freedom of speech, intellectual freedom, and the right to dissent—would also be the values of the international scientific community, and both would flourish. Human rights served not just as a platitude but as a force that shaped the mores of a discipline that, on the surface, appeared to have little to do with human rights.

At the same time, the transformation of human rights from noble idea to political reality is not irreversible—human rights could regress to being simply a noble idea. Scientists, as the exchange boycott demonstrates, embraced and then lost interest in human rights. During the boycott debate, Earl Callen argued for a discrete movement with limited goals. He demanded of Paul Flory: "We better ask what our goals are, and at what point we are willing to resume exchange. The SOS pledge (and the very name of that organization) focuses on the maltreatment of particular individuals." If the boycott and human rights campaign was to be a broad, indefinite campaign, where should it end? What about reform of the whole Soviet system? Callen wondered. South Africa? Argentina? What about a boycott of the United States for not having signed the SALT agreements? Should the human rights campaign ever end or become a dominant feature of scientific life? He needn't have worried about this slippery slope. The same American Physical Society that Shawlow had declared "actively working" for human rights in 1981 changed noticeably: at the annual APS meeting in 1998, despite attempts to raise concerns over the human rights of scientists in China, only two participants out of several thousand registered for a workshop on human rights.[51] Science would be international, but noncontroversial.

NOTES

1. Irina Valitova (Mrs. Yuriy Orlov) to Max M. Kampelman, June 23, 1981, Box 34, Folder: Files of Cathy Fitzpatrick: USSR: Orlov, Yuri: 1981, Series III: Files of Cathy Fitzpatrick, Country Files, Human Rights Watch Records, Columbia University (hereafter HRWR).

2. Ibid.

3. See Akira Iriye, *Global Community: The Role of International Organizations in the Making of the Contemporary World* (Berkeley: University of California Press, 2004); Elizabeth Borgwardt, *A New Deal for the World: America's Vision for Human Rights* (Cambridge, MA: Harvard University Press, 2007).

4. On the French Revolution as the origin of modern human rights, see Lynn Hunt, *Inventing Human Rights: A History* (New York: Norton, 2008). Officially Franklin was appointed minister plenipotentiary rather than ambassador. On Franklin, Lavoisier, and the French Revolution, see Stacy Schiff, *A Great Improvisation: Franklin, France, and the Birth of America* (New York: Henry Holt, 2005), xv, 254, 404, 409; John Marks, *Science and the Making of the Modern World* (London: Heinemann, 1983), 125; and John Gribbin, *The Scientists: A History of Science Told Through the Lives of Its Greatest Inventors* (New York: Random House, 2002). Lavoisier had controlled the government gunpowder monopoly during Louis XVI's war with Britain, and his participation in the unpopular tax farming system led to his beheading.

5. James G. Hershberg, *James B. Conant: Harvard to Hiroshima and the Making of the Nuclear Age* (New York: Knopf, 1993), 42, 45–46.

6. On Szilard, see William Lanouette, *Genius in the Shadows: A Biography of Leo Szilard, the Man Behind the Bomb* (New York: C. Scribner's Sons, 1992); and Michael Bess, *Realism, Utopia, and the Mushroom Cloud: Four Activist Intellectuals and Their Strategies for Peace, 1945–1989* (Chicago: University of Chicago Press, 1993). On the use of the atomic bomb as a means to intimidate the Soviets, see Gar Alperovitz, *Atomic Diplomacy: Hiroshima and Potsdam: The Use of the Atomic Bomb and the American Confrontation with Soviet Power* (New York: Penguin, 1985).

7. Joseph Manzione, "'Amusing and Amazing and Practical and Military': The Legacy of Scientific Internationalism in American Foreign Policy, 1945–63," *Diplomatic History* 24, no. 1 (Winter 2000): 49–55.

8. Helsinki Final Act, 14–26, Organization for Security and Co-operation in Europe website, www.osce.org/. On the creation and consequences of the act, see Sarah B. Snyder, "The Helsinki Process, American Foreign Policy, and the End of the Cold War" (PhD diss., Georgetown University, 2006).

9. "Statement of Philip Handler," January 31, 1980, Box 63, Folder: Files of Jeri Laber: USSR: Scientists: General, 1979–1980, HRWR.

10. Joel L. Lebowitz, form letter to unknown recipients, March 30, 1981, Box 62, Folder: Files of Jeri Laber: USSR: Sakharov, Andrei, General, 1981–1984; Andy Sommer to Bob Berstein, October 4, 1979, Box 63, Folder: Files of Jeri Laber: USSR: Scientists: AAAS, 1975–1979, Series I: Jeri Laber Files, HRWR.

11. John A. Nohel to Amadou Mahtar M'Bow, August 4, 1980; Richard C. DiPrima to Leonid Brezhnev, July 29, 1980, Box 62, Folder: Files of Jeri Laber: USSR: Sakharov: General, 1969–1980, Series I: Jeri Laber Files, HRWR.

12. Vera Rich, "Boycott of Soviet Contacts Is for Individuals, Says NAS," *Nature*, September 7, 1978, 3.

13. Contemporary Americanized spellings of most of the Russian names mentioned in this chapter varied greatly: Sakharov versus Sacharov, Scharansky versus Shcharansky, Orlov versus Orlove, Aleksandrov versus Alexandrov, etc. I have attempted to employ the spellings most frequently used in my sources, except in direct quotations where I have retained the original spelling.

14. Rich, "Boycott of Soviet Contacts Is for Individuals, Says NAS."

15. Jeri Laber to Carter, January 5, 1979, Box 59, Folder: Files of Jeri Laber: USSR: Orlov, Yuri: Defense, 1978–1980, Series I: Jeri Laber Files, HRWR.

16. United Press International, "Academy Halts Soviet Exchanges," February 25, 1978, Box 58, Folder 14, National Academy of Sciences, Series I: Jeri Laber Files, HRWR.

17. H. F. Mark, W. H. Stockmayer, N.W. Tschegl, P.J. Flory to V. V. Korshak, September 18, 1978, Box 63, Folder: Files of Jeri Laber: USSR: Scientists: AAAS: 1975–1979, Series I: Jeri Laber Files, HRWR.

18. John T. Edsall to W. A. Engelhardt, August 18, 1978, Box 63: Folder: Files of Jeri Laber: USSR: Scientists: AAAS: 1975–1979, Series I: Jeri Laber Files, HRWR.

19. Paul J. Flory, Stanford University, to Anatoly Aleksandrov, Soviet Academy of Sciences, July 13, 1978, Box 63, Folder: Files of Jeri Laber: USSR: Scientists: AAAS, 1975–1979, Series I: Jeri Laber Files, HRWR.

20. "Boycott of Soviet Contacts Is for Individuals, Says NAS."

21. Bob Bernstein to Sakharov, February 1, 1979, and David Fishlow, Executive Director Helsinki Watch, to Dr. Herbert Fusfeld, Director of Center for Science and Technology Policy, February 1, 1979, Box 67, Folder: Files of Jeri Laber: USSR: U.S. Scientific Exchange, 1978–1979, Series I: Jeri Laber Files, HRWR. See also: Memo from Mark Mellman, February 9, 1979, Box 45, Folder 8: Committee of Concerned Scientists, Series I: Jeri Laber Files, HRWR. The fate of these letters is unclear. At the same time, Richard Sennett, director of the New York Institute for the Humanities, asked Press to deliver a speaking invitation to Orlov. In April, Sennett wrote to Press expressing his dissatisfaction that the State Department had told him the letter had been delivered to Malcolm Toon, the U.S. ambassador in Moscow, who had passed it on to "personal friends." According to Sennett, no one could confirm that these unspecified people ever delivered the invitation to Orlov. Sennett to Press, April 16, 1979, Box 59, Folder: Files of Jeri Laber: USSR: Orlov, Yuri: Defense: Reception for J. MacDonald, 1978–79, HRWR.

22. News Release, Committee of Concerned Scientists, February 28, 1979; Cable to Academician A. P. Aleksandrov, President of Soviet Academy of Sciences, Box 45, Folder 8: Committee of Concerned Scientists, Series I: Jeri Laber Files, HRWR.

23. Program for MacDonald Reception, April 16, 1979, p. 2, Box 59, Folder: Files of Jeri Laber: USSR: Orlov: Defense: Reception for J. MacDonald, 1978–1979, Series I: Jeri Laber Files, HRWR.

24. Brown, Scheuer, Hollenbeck, Ritter, Harkin, Pease, Hance, and Ertel to Alexandrov, May 24, 1979, Box 63, Folder: Files of Jeri Laber: USSR: Scientists: General, 1979–1980, HRWR.

25. Memo, by Rozanne L. Ridgway, April 8, 1980, Box 63, Folder: Files of Jeri Laber: USSR: Sakharov: Questionnaire: 1977–1980, HRWR.

26. CCS News Release, June 27, 1980; CCS letter to Aleksandrov, Brezhnev, Marchuk, and Dobrynin; CCS letter to EIQE Conference, June 23, 1980, Box 63, Folder: Files of Jeri Laber: USSR: Scientists: General, 1979–1980, HRWR.

27. Sakharov and Naum Meiman to Scientists in Defense of Orlove and Scharansky, March 10, 1979, Box 63, Folder: Files of Jeri Laber: USSR: Scientists for Orlov and Scharansky: 1979–1981, HRWR.

28. Sakharov to Drell, January 30, 1981, Box 62, Folder: Files of Jeri Laber: USSR: Sakharov: General: 1981, HRWR.

29. Sakharov, "A Letter to My Foreign Colleagues," October 9, 1981, Box 62, Folder: Files of Jeri Laber: USSR: Sakharov, Andrei: Hunger Strike: 1980–1982, HRWR.

30. Elena Bonner to Professor Michelle, November 16, 1982, Box 62, Folder: Files of Jeri Laber: USSR: Sakharov, Andrei: Hunger Strike: 1980–1982, HRWR.

31. Irene Gildengorn Lainer, "Human Rights of Scientists in the Soviet Union," Box 63, Folder: Files of Jeri Laber: USSR: Scientists: General: 1979–1980, HRWR.

32. Valentin F. Turchin letter, July 15, 1979, Box 34: Folder: Files of Cathy Fitzpatrick: USSR: Orlov, Yuri: 1979, Series III: Cathy Fitzpatrick Files, HRWR.

33. Victor Weisskopf to Edward Kline, Helsinki Watch, March 11, 1980, Box 63, Folder: Files of Jeri Laber: USSR: Sakharov: Questionnaire, 1977–1980, Series I: Jeri Laber Files, HRWR.

34. Brown, Scheuer, Hollenbeck, Ritter, Harkin, Pease, Hance, and Ertel to Alexandrov, May 24, 1979, Box 63, Folder: Files of Jeri Laber: USSR: Scientists: General, 1979–1980, HRWR.

35. "Statement of Philip Handler," January 31, 1980, Box 63, Folder: Files of Jeri Laber: USSR: Scientists: General, 1979–1980, HRWR. Emphasis in original.

36. "Statement of Philip Handler," January 31, 1980, Box 63, Folder: Files of Jeri Laber: USSR: Scientists: General, 1979–1980, HRWR.

37. Morris Pripstein, Chairman of SOS, to Jeri Laber, December 9, 1980, Box 63, Folder: Files of Jeri Laber: USSR: Scientists for Orlov and Scharansky, 1979–1981, Series I: Jeri Laber Files, HRWR.

38. Andrei Sakharov, "The Responsibility of Scientists," *Nature*, May 21, 1981, 84–85.

39. Memo to CCS, SOS, Others, by Earl Callen, June 16th, 1981, Box 63, Folder: Files of Jeri Laber: USSR: Scientists: Exchange, 1980–1981, Series I: Jeri Laber Files, HRWR.

40. Paul Flory, "U.S. Soviet Scientific Relations," July 15, 1981, Box 63, Folder: Files of Jeri Laber: USSR: Scientists: Exchange, 1980–1981, Series I: Jeri Laber Files, HRWR.

41. Ibid.

42. Anthony Ralston, Prof. in SUNY Buffalo Dept. of Computer Science, to Earl Callen, July 22, 1981, Box 63, Folder: Files of Jeri Laber: USSR: Scientists: Exchange, 1980–1981, Series I: Jeri Laber Files, HRWR. Emphasis in original.

43. Earl Callen, Department of Physics, American University, "U.S.-Soviet Scientific Relations—A Response to Paul Flory," July 23, 1981, Box 63, Folder: Files of Jeri Laber: USSR: Scientists: Exchange, 1980–1981, Series I: Jeri Laber Files, HRWR. Emphasis in original.

44. Press Release, "Forgotten Man of the Year," December 1982, Box 59, Folder: Files of Jeri Laber: USSR: Orlov, Yuri: Poster [Campaign] 1982–1983, Series I: Files of Jeri Laber, HRWR.

45. Memorandum, Helsinki Watch, "Yuri Orlov: Current Status," May 1985, Box 35, Folder: Files of Cathy Fitzpatrick: USSR: Orlov, Yuri: 1985, HRWR. Emphasis in original.

46. Philip M. Boffey, "Science, Sakharov, and Soviet," May 9, 1985, *New York Times*, 16.

47. Joseph Birman to Frank Press, April 10, 1985, Box 7, Folder: Files of Cathy Fitzpatrick: USSR: Committee of Concerned Scientists: 1984–May 1985, Series III: Files of Cathy Fitzpatrick, HRWR. Press, the president of the NAS at that point, disputed Birman's charges. Press to Birman, May 2, 1985, Box 7, Folder: Files of Cathy Fitzpatrick: USSR: Committee of Concerned Scientists: 1984–May 1985, HRWR.

48. Joel L. Lebowitz to Morris Pripstein, May 28, 1985, Box 51, Folder: Files of Cathy Fitzpatrick: USSR: Scientists [General], 1985–1988, HRWR.

49. James Glanz, "Human Rights Fades as a Cause for Scientists," *Science* 282 (October 9, 1998): 216.

50. Arthur L. Schawlow, President of American Physical Society, to Andrei Sakharov, April 16, 1981, Box 62, Folder: Files of Jeri Laber: USSR: Sakharov: General, 1981, Series I: Jeri Laber Files, HRWR.

51. Earl Callen, Department of Physics, American University, "U.S.-Soviet Scientific Relations—A Response to Paul Flory," July 23, 1981, Box 63, Folder: Files of Jeri Laber: USSR: Scientists: Exchange, 1980–1981, Series I: Jeri Laber Files, HRWR. Glanz, "Human Rights Fades as a Cause for Scientists."

12

PRINCIPLES OVERWHELMING TANKS

Human Rights and the End of the Cold War

SARAH B. SNYDER

Upon becoming Soviet General Secretary, Mikhail Gorbachev faced a myriad of domestic problems including a stagnating economy, decaying infrastructure, and environmental degradation. Abroad, he was locked in an expensive arms race with the United States, was bogged down in an exhausting war in Afghanistan, suffered strained relations with Europe and China, and was overextended in Eastern Europe and the Third World. Gorbachev also presided over a system with a long record of repression and human rights abuses, which had invited considerable international criticism and domestic activism. At the time, Soviet human rights violations seemed of secondary importance, but the Soviet record proved to be a stubborn obstacle to successfully addressing the country's other problems. Gorbachev's approach to human rights evolved; the transformation was most evident during the 1986–1989 Conference on Security and Cooperation in Europe (CSCE) Review Meeting in Vienna, thus making a focus on the meeting's negotiations essential to gauging the role of human rights in the end of the Cold War.

Influenced by exposure to Western ideas, advice from like-minded aides, and the circumstances of his generation, Gorbachev believed the appropriate response to his many challenges was fundamental reform of the Soviet system. He chose to pursue *glasnost'*, or openness, *perestroika*, or restructuring, and new political thinking, which together significantly altered Soviet diplomacy and the domestic system. Above all, Gorbachev undertook reform to address the USSR's economic problems, which had become particularly glaring, because increased contacts with the West, among other factors, highlighted the disparity between Soviet and Western standards of living. In order to ease the strain on the Soviet economy, Gorbachev sought to curb the arms race with the United States, withdraw troops from Afghanistan, limit aid to socialist allies, and improve relations with Western Europe. As time went on, he also recognized the need for some liberalization of the Soviet political system to facilitate his economic reforms. To encourage international cooperation with his economic agenda, Gorbachev worked to improve the Soviet human rights record.

That Gorbachev saw improving Soviet human rights practices as a step to developing deeper relations with the West points to the reach of human rights activism. Numerous studies have examined how different external and internal pressures shaped Gorbachev's course of reform, although there is limited historical research demonstrating the role of human rights activism and ideals on Soviet policies.[1] In 1975, the Soviet Union was one of thirty-five signatories of the Helsinki Final Act, which outlined a commitment to respect human rights and facilitate East-West contacts.[2] In the years that followed, a network of governmental and nongovernmental actors arose that was dedicated to monitoring compliance with the agreement. Given the Soviet Union's record of human rights abuses, the USSR was often subject to international criticism, in part at the international CSCE meetings held to review implementation of the agreement. Evidence suggests that over time Soviet leaders shifted from solely resenting such scrutiny as interference in their internal affairs to identifying ways to use it for Soviet purposes. Under Gorbachev, Soviet leaders saw improving human rights practices as a way to advance relations with the West, which was an essential part of Gorbachev's reform policies.

Recognition of the need to improve the Soviet human rights record evolved slowly, eventually influencing Gorbachev and his aides to move away from long-standing policies of heavy-handed repression in order to gain cooperation from Western policymakers, whose approach was shaped, in large part, by a transnational network of activists that had lobbied for years for greater Helsinki compliance. Soviet leaders experienced Western concerns about human rights violations in many ways. For example, while posted to Ottawa as the Soviet ambassador to Canada, Gorbachev adviser Alexander Yakovlev frequently faced questions from Canadian politicians about the plight of human rights activist Andrei Sakharov and the treatment of other dissidents in the Soviet Union.[3] Conversations with Western leaders such as British Prime Minister Margaret Thatcher, United States President Ronald Reagan, and United States Secretary of State George Shultz led Gorbachev and his close advisers to see human rights as a necessary element of Soviet foreign policy—an interlocking component of their larger agenda.[4] Describing his reform efforts, Gorbachev wrote:

For many long years the Soviet Union considered human rights as some sort of false issue that had been manufactured artificially (even the phrase human rights was published in our country only in quotation marks preceded by the word so-called). For a totalitarian system, the very posing of the question of human rights is a challenge, a vicious assault on the very essence of its policies. And only perestroika brought this to an end.[5]

Although Western and neutral governments, their CSCE delegates, and a broader coalition of Helsinki activists and groups had pressed the Soviets to improve their human rights record, for years their efforts had produced few results, but that changed under Gorbachev's leadership.[6] The CSCE review meetings, and in particular the 1980–1983 Madrid meeting, had put the Soviets "in [the] dock before public opinion." Gorbachev recognized in particular the damage Soviet human rights violations were causing to relations with Western Europe and determined the situation needed to change.[7]

Soviet leaders' attitudes toward human rights evolved slowly after the signing of the Helsinki Final Act. Initially, in the late 1970s, Soviet officials repressed private citizens who sought to monitor implementation of the agreement and criticized international inquiries into human rights abuses as interference in internal affairs. Their intransigence continued for so many years that when the Soviet Union began criticizing Western countries' records in propaganda counterattacks, it was a welcome shift because it acknowledged human rights were a matter of international concern. The eventual willingness of Soviet Foreign Minister Eduard Shevardnadze and Gorbachev to discuss domestic human rights violations in diplomatic negotiations was seen as important progress.

Their readiness to engage on human rights manifested itself most strikingly in the years of the CSCE Vienna Review Meeting (1986–1989), during which the Soviet attitude toward compliance with the Helsinki Final Act seemingly transformed. Gorbachev and his aides sought to comply with their commitments on human rights and human contacts to prevent their isolation and estrangement from Western Europe and the United States. The Soviet proposal at the Vienna CSCE Review Meeting to host a conference on human rights in Moscow demonstrates the influence of transnational Helsinki activism, as well as subsequent efforts to secure consensus for the proposed meeting, such as inviting the International Helsinki Federation for Human Rights (IHF), an umbrella group of Helsinki monitoring groups, and the Commission on Security and Cooperation in Europe to Moscow.[8]

The Soviet proposal became the defining issue of the Vienna negotiations; for many observers, progress on the proposed Moscow conference served as a barometer of Eastern advancement on human rights, as the acceptance of the conference proposal and thus agreement on a concluding document was conditioned on Soviet progress on human rights.[9] Some delegates were adamant that they would not consider the proposal given the USSR's abysmal rate of Helsinki compliance, whereas others thought its merits should be explored. As the Soviets were slow to expand fully on their proposal, Western delegations, in consultation with nongovernmental organizations (NGOs), began amassing a list of conditions that might be necessary for its acceptance.[10]

The Soviet proposal for a human rights conference in Moscow was a preemptive strike to limit international criticism of the Soviet record at Vienna and was the centerpiece of a calculated strategy to respond to Western scrutiny by projecting an improved Soviet image to the West. With the Moscow conference proposal, Gorbachev and Shevardnadze were pressuring others in the Soviet government to make rapid, far-reaching progress. Shevardnadze explained the rationale for the conference proposal: "I was convinced that the conference was essential in order to show the country and world how far we intended to go and, beyond that, to provide an impetus for democratization and the perestroika of legislation in everything relating to human affairs."[11] It is unclear if the conference's proponents realized the degree of concessions that would be necessary for its achievement, but they nonetheless remained committed to the proposal and to demonstrating a changed stance on human rights.[12]

To this end, the Soviet delegation went to extensive lengths to interact with journalists in the early stages of the Vienna meeting, holding six press conferences in one week alone. According to Shevardnadze, the Soviet Union's policy of increased contact with the press there was due to the influence of glasnost'.[13] In the analysis of Helsinki Watch, a United States-based Helsinki monitoring group:

> The Gorbachev government, in an unexpected series of acts and declarations, has apparently put human rights concerns at the top of its public agenda and is taking the initiative in related matters. Whatever the motivation behind the gestures that have been made, certain implications are clear. International concern about human rights abuses in the Soviet Union has not gone unnoticed by Soviet leaders.[14]

In contrast with previous meetings, Soviet delegates were willing to accept lists of *refuseniks* and political prisoners, as well as to meet with a range of interested NGOs and individuals. In the words of one observer, the Soviets tried to draw a contrast between their new openness and "the bad old days."[15]

Nonetheless Western observers were frustrated by the incongruity between Gorbachev's talk about *perestroika* and *glasnost'* and the Soviet negotiating positions at Vienna. As at past conferences, the Soviet Union and its allies employed varied strategies to deflect Western human rights criticisms, including introducing new proposals and accusing the West of violations. The strategy of the Soviet Union and its allies at Vienna was to insist on compliance with economic, social, and cultural rights to counteract the Western emphasis on civil and political rights, causing the first year of debate in Vienna to be unproductive because diplomats there avoided working together to reach mutual compromises.[16]

An additional tactic the Soviets pursued to deflect attention from their human rights record was creating governmental bodies that supposedly addressed domestic human rights problems. First, they established a bureau on humanitarian affairs in the foreign ministry whose leader, Yuri Kashlev, also led the Soviet delegation in Vienna.[17] Second, the Soviet Union formed the Public Commission for International Cooperation in Humanitarian Problems and Human Rights in late 1987. Headed by Fedor Burlatsky, a Gorbachev adviser, it was charged with monitoring Soviet and other CSCE states' Helsinki compliance as well as reforming Soviet legislation.[18] The development of new Soviet institutions tasked with monitoring human rights demonstrated recognition that a new stance was advantageous to Soviet interests. Nevertheless a meaningful commitment to reducing human rights violations did not come until later in the Vienna negotiations.

Many observers viewed the Soviet Union as making only cosmetic changes, and Western delegates largely perceived the Soviets to be unwilling to engage in productive negotiations at Vienna. By March 1987, the Soviet Union had sponsored 32 proposals, none of which addressed human rights issues. In the words of one Western diplomat: "We have heard a lot from Moscow and various Soviet officials about new thinking in regard to such problems as exit visas for those who want to go abroad to meet their families. One would expect the USSR to show it is serious by presenting some of these ideas in Vienna. But the table is bare."[19]

Moscow's push to hold a human rights conference prompted considerable dialogue among dissidents, human rights activists, and CSCE diplomats, who over the years had developed a well-coordinated transnational network. Interested groups and individuals shared their views with CSCE delegates as to what conditions should be imposed on Moscow in exchange for agreeing to the conference.[20] By and large, conditions for the meeting focused on two categories: improvements in Soviet human rights practices before agreeing to the meeting; and commitments on the circumstances of the meeting in Moscow, such as open sessions, guaranteed entry for activists to the Soviet Union for the meeting's duration, and opportunities for parallel meetings, demonstrations, etc. Months after Shevardnadze made his proposal, the IHF urged the Western delegations to support it as long as the Soviet Union met certain requirements, including the release of all Helsinki monitors and other political prisoners from jails, labor camps, internal exile, and psychiatric institutions.[21] Separately, former Soviet dissident Yuri Orlov advocated considerable stipulations, including freeing all political prisoners and admission to the meeting for journalists, human rights groups, activists, and Soviet citizens. If such steps were taken, Orlov said that he would travel to Moscow himself for the meeting.[22] Sakharov, whom Secretary of State George Shultz queried as he sought to formulate the American position, said that the United States should have two key conditions: Soviet withdrawal from Afghanistan and the release of political prisoners.[23] United States Ambassador to the Vienna meeting. Warren Zimmermann also enumerated an ambitious list of changes he felt the Soviet Union needed to undertake to demonstrate compliance with the Helsinki Final Act; in addition to steps such as amnestying all political prisoners, he called for an institutionalization of such changes by abolishing the articles in the Soviet criminal code that facilitated politically motivated arrests and sentences.[24]

The litany of conditions considered by Western governments would have seemed entirely implausible a few years earlier, but by 1987 there was meaningful movement by the Soviets. The Soviet Union made important strides that year, including releasing 140 political prisoners in February, ceasing to jam Voice of America in May, and allowing German and Jewish emigration to rise significantly. As the deliberations wore on, the USSR continued to offer concessions.[25] For example, Kashlev proactively asked Zimmermann for a list of prisoners about whom the United States was concerned.[26] In addition, Soviet diplomats engaged in bilateral negotiations with Shultz and Assistant Secretary of State for Human Rights and Humanitarian Affairs Richard Schifter to secure American support for the conference.[27] Over time, the Soviets demonstrated a willingness to resolve outstanding cases in order to gain acceptance of their conference proposal; American and Soviet negotiators would later outline a timetable for Soviet changes, and the United States granted formal approval of the conference in the last days of the Reagan administration.[28]

In the intervening months, pressure on the Soviet Union and its allies to resolve human rights cases continued unabated. The Soviet government responded for the first time to Commission on Security and Cooperation in Europe entreaties by resolving 137 of the 442 cases the commission had raised previously.[29] Shultz began to see genuine change in the Soviet position when Shevardnadze told him in September 1987, "Give me your lists and we will be glad to look at them."[30] By October 1987, the Soviets had granted exit visas to six thousand people, more than six times the number in 1986. Nevertheless, 7,500 cases remained, which raised questions about the depth of the Soviet commitment to change.

Soviet leaders also pursued other steps to win support for their proposed conference, including inviting some of their most ardent critics to Moscow: the IHF and the Commission on Security and Cooperation in Europe. The IHF was established in 1982 to coordinate the monitoring activities of Western, neutral, and Eastern national Helsinki committees, and the umbrella organization vocally criticized human rights abuses in the Soviet Union. Since its establishment in 1976, the commission had successfully influenced the United States' approach to the CSCE and served as a key forum for reports of violations of the Helsinki Final Act. Describing Soviet motivations for the invitations, Kashlev said, "We are engaged in a dialogue on human rights in the Soviet Union not only with those who like us but those who criticize us as well."[31]

Despite the changed image Soviet officials tried to project during these visits, old practices remained. Soviet authorities moderated their repressive tactics somewhat during the IHF's stay, but nevertheless recorded its meetings with Soviet activists.[32] In Helsinki Watch Executive Director Jeri Laber's view, the meeting between the IHF and Soviet officials in Moscow was "strictly window dressing" and demonstrated the USSR was run by the "same old bureaucrats" doing only a "slightly different number."[33] Laber regarded her Soviet hosts as disingenuous and argues they had no intention of examining the prisoner lists presented by IHF.[34]

Swedish delegate Frantisek Janouch's firsthand account of his time in Moscow with the IHF delegation, however, illustrates the extent to which Soviet officials wanted to cultivate the support of human rights activists from Western and neutral countries. Janouch wrote, "Almost anything was permitted during that one week: Jewish demonstrations as well as demonstrations of Hare Krishna devotees, and many more things, unknown or at least unusual in Moscow."[35] According to Janouch, Shevardnadze's deputy, Anatoly Adamishin, tried hard to persuade the IHF to support the conference proposal, going so far as "promising everything under the sun."[36] Although the IHF representatives encountered a wide spectrum of views on the proposed conference among those they met in Moscow, Janouch personally saw value in using agreement on a conference to induce the Soviets to develop a favorable human rights record:

> I am convinced that the organization of a conference on humanitarian issues in Moscow could have a positive influence on future developments in the USSR. The earliest date the conference could meet in Moscow is 1990, probably one or two years later. During the period of preparation the Soviet authorities will logically make sure that fundamental human rights are respected. This means that the present relatively liberal attitude of the Soviet authorities will go on for several more years—and will clearly progress even further during the actual conference.[37]

In Janouch's view and many others', agreeing to the conference would ensure an initial period of respect for human rights and by the time the conference closed, it would be too late for the Soviets to reverse course and return to repressive human rights practices.

Janouch's thinking was in line with the approach the IHF adopted, and after returning from Moscow, the organization began a public campaign in support of a Moscow conference. Leading the effort, Laber wrote an opinion piece for the *International Herald Tribune* outlining the argument in favor of the meeting:

> A Moscow human rights conference would . . . give the Soviet people a forum for discussing their government's past, present and future human rights practices. It would allow an infusion of Western ideas and values, including the concept that respect for human rights cannot merely be legislated from above but requires the active participation and vigilance of private citizens.[38]

Soviet authorities saw value in winning over Helsinki activists, and that tactic likely aided their efforts to garner supporters for their conference proposal.

During the commission's visit to Moscow, the Soviets similarly worked to convey an impression of progress and openness, while also conceding more needed to be done and articulating a commitment to undertake further improvements.[39] One member of the delegation reported a changed attitude among Soviet officials: "There was a willingness not only to discuss the issues, but a forthcoming [*sic*] that I've never seen from Soviet officials, one of [whom said]: 'We have made a lot of mistakes, and we are going to change and concern ourselves more with individual liberties. And we're going to do it because it's in the best interest of our people and it's going to help our economy do better.'"[40] At the conclusion of the congressional visit, the Soviets resolved 147 exit visa cases, though none of the two hundred political prisoners about whom members of Congress had inquired were released.[41]

By the end of 1988, there were more improvements in the Soviet human rights situation: Six hundred political prisoners had been released and emigration had swelled to eighty thousand. In addition, Gorbachev announced he was ending Soviet involvement in Afghanistan, withdrawing all troops by February 15, 1989, and reducing Soviet force levels in Eastern Europe by five hundred thousand soldiers and ten thousand tanks.[42] Soviet actions and commitment to continued reform enabled Western agreement on the Moscow conference and paved the way to a concluding document and closing ceremony in January 1989.

The close of the Vienna meeting represented the end to the traditional East-West divide that characterized the CSCE and Europe.[43] The Soviet proposal to host a human rights conference, Western conditions for their agreement, and Soviet efforts to meet those terms denoted a remarkable shift for the CSCE and a significant moment of change in the Cold War.[44] Shevardnadze later described the Vienna meeting as a "watershed." According to him, "Europe had never known such a dialog-intense, at times dramatic, but purposeful and democratic in a way that was without precedent."[45] Kashlev wrote that "without the achievements reached in Vienna, communist regimes in Eastern European countries would have fallen much later."[46] Zimmermann characterized the concluding document as "the most comprehensive statement of human rights commitments that has ever existed in the East-West framework."[47]

The pace of progress accelerated in the months following the Vienna meeting, ushering in significant developments in the Helsinki process. Within the CSCE framework, almost all contentious issues were resolved, enabling agreements on such significant topics as adherence to the principles of pluralistic democracy, market capitalism, and the rule of law. Furthermore, between 1989 and 1991, stunning changes transformed Eastern and Central Europe, and Helsinki monitors, long persecuted by Eastern regimes, were active in the movements that toppled communist leaderships in Czechoslovakia and Poland. The broader Helsinki network was one element in a constellation that shaped changes across Eastern Europe and the Soviet Union throughout this period.

Following the Vienna meeting, the Soviet Union continued its new role as a cooperative participant in CSCE meetings. The Soviet approach to the Conferences on the Human Dimension (CHD) that followed Vienna demonstrate that Soviet steps during Vienna were not purely tactical moves designed to insure the acceptance of their conference proposal but also signified a new approach to human rights practices. The changes in Eastern Europe fostered improvements in East-West relations and facilitated some

positive steps at the 1989 Paris CHD. In advance of the Paris conference, a
Soviet Foreign Ministry memorandum outlined the negative ramifications
of Soviet restrictions on emigration:

> In contrast to the majority of countries of the world community, substantial
> restrictions continue to be maintained in the socialist community in the area
> of contacts between people [and] private trips of citizens. In the political area
> this does not serve our interests [and] has an adverse effect on the develop-
> ment of trade and economic, scientific, cultural, athletic, and other ties. At the
> present time, the question of the maximum removal of restrictions on trips of
> citizens of socialist countries to the USSR and of Soviet citizens to these
> countries and the creation of corresponding facilities for this has become
> unavoidable.[48]

During the meeting, the Soviet Union took additional steps to resolve human
contact cases such as those awaiting exit visas and releasing political
prisoners.

The dramatic changes in Eastern Europe in the year between the CHD
meetings in Paris and Copenhagen meant that many traditional Helsinki
points of controversy between East and West were no longer contentious.
Instead, the 1990 CHD meeting in Copenhagen charted the way for Eastern
Europe to adopt democratic pluralism.[49] One of the most far-reaching and
widely supported proposals at Copenhagen advocated the significance of
the rule of law and such rights as freedom of expression; freedom to as-
semble and demonstrate; freedom of association, including membership in
a trade union; freedom of thought; freedom of movement; and freedom to
own private property.[50] That such a proposal could gain support from both
Eastern and Western states was evidence of the striking shifts that had taken
place in Europe. United States ambassador to the Copenhagen meeting Max
Kampelman described the new dynamic: "The Soviets have been extremely
cooperative with me and ready to accept most anything within reason. The
newly initiated democracies began to feel their oats."[51]

At the November 1990 Paris CSCE summit, which many CSCE observers regarded as marking the end of the Cold War, the sweeping shifts in
the East-West relationship were formalized and, as Gorbachev noted, it
"heralded a new, post-confrontational era in European history."[52] Representatives from all CSCE states signed two documents there: the Charter of
Paris for a New Europe and the Vienna Document on Confidence and Security Building Measures, which expanded and strengthened the confidence
and security-building measures agreed to at the Stockholm conference in

1986.[53] The Charter of Paris for a New Europe declared, "The era of confrontation and division of Europe has ended" and further emphasized the CSCE commitments to human rights, democracy, rule of law, and market economics.[54] Also at Paris, NATO and Warsaw Pact states signed the Treaty on Conventional Armed Forces in Europe and the Joint Declaration of Twenty-Two States, which declared an end to the East-West conflict between the two alliances.[55] The important agreements on democracy and market economics signed at Copenhagen and Bonn, as well as the declaration of an end to East-West military animosity, suggested an end to the Cold War.[56]

Although the Paris summit was hailed as an achievement for Gorbachev and evidence of the transformation of the communist bloc, the period after the summit was at times difficult for the Soviet leadership. Gorbachev, Shevardnadze, and their aides faced many who believed Gorbachev's reforms undermined the role of the party, the communist system, and Soviet power. Shevardnadze wrote about his struggle to change human rights in the Soviet Union:

> It cost immense effort to bring back from exile and banishment several outstanding scientists, writers, and theater directors—honest, conscientious people whose only offense had been refusing to accept the canon of violence and falsehood. But it was even harder to restore the good name of the country where the best people had been treated that way.
>
> It was difficult to persuade even my colleagues on the simplest point: Since we had signed the Helsinki Final Act and had assumed obligations under international conventions and agreements, we had thereby acknowledged the right of other participants in these agreements to inquire into all issues and to insist that we observe the obligations we had undertaken. By that time it had become perfectly obvious to me that the human dimension in international security was crucial. But many of our partners had yet to believe in the sincerity of my statements on that score.[57]

The long-awaited Moscow Conference on the Human Dimension opened in September 1991, three weeks after the failed coup that would overshadow much of the meeting. In his opening speech, Gorbachev characterized the defeat of the coup against him as a triumph for human rights.[58] Secretary of State James Baker echoed Gorbachev in his opening statement: "[The] CSCE has no divisions of tanks. It has instead the moral authority that flows from [the Paris Charter] principles. But as we saw on the streets of this city three weeks ago, at critical moments people armed with principles have overwhelmed tanks."[59] Most of the issues originally slated for discussion at Moscow, such as the release of political prisoners and freedom to leave one's country, had been addressed in the earlier Conference on the Human Dimension meetings in Paris and Copenhagen and implemented in the intervening months. Instead, the Moscow conference closely examined the outbreak of nationalist tensions, among other issues.[60] One of the most significant concerns about a human rights meeting in Moscow had been access for NGOs, which had become increasingly part of the fabric of the CSCE, to the conference and delegations; given subsequent developments, openness was not a problem, and abundant Soviet NGOs were active in connection with the meeting.[61]

The Moscow Concluding Document, like the text agreed to at Copenhagen, demonstrated how far acceptance of human rights had progressed in the previous years. The CSCE states noted continuing progress on Helsinki compliance and the challenges of rising ethnic, national, and religious discrimination and violence. They expressed concern about human rights, democracy, and the rule of law, as well as capital punishment, migrant workers, the protection of journalists, and artistic freedom.[62]

Many observers and policymakers on both sides of the East-West divide have attributed significance to the influence of the Helsinki process on Soviet reforms. According to Soviet diplomat Yuri Kashlev, "It is difficult to imagine what our society would have become without all of those democratic changes that were to a very large extent related to our participation in the Helsinki process."[63] In former Jewish refusenik and Soviet human rights activist Natan Sharansky's view, reform in the Soviet Union was possible because Soviet dissidents were "ready to risk their freedom to speak the truth" and "leaders of the free world who [were] ready to support [them] directly and consistently."[64]

Understanding how and why the multilateral CSCE structure positively shaped Soviet human rights reforms offers important lessons on the possibilities for achieving peaceful change and improving human rights observance internationally. Official support from political leaders and diplomats committed to Helsinki compliance heightened the effectiveness of transnational activism by tying progress on trade, arms control, and political support to improvements in human rights practices. The diverse network united by a common commitment to improving the lives of those living behind the Iron Curtain positively influenced the course of East-West relations and the liberalization of Eastern European society and politics at the end of the Cold War. Furthermore, Helsinki monitoring groups learned from and contributed to a broader human rights movement at the end of the twentieth century, ensuring the issue became a permanent fixture of international diplomacy.

NOTES

1. See for example, Archie Brown, *The Gorbachev Factor* (New York: Oxford University Press, 1996); Jeffrey T. Checkel, *Ideas and International Political Change: Soviet/Russian Behavior and the End of the Cold War* (New Haven, CT: Yale University Press, 1997); Robert D. English, *Russia and the Idea of the West: Gorbachev, Intellectuals and the End of the Cold War* (New York: Columbia University Press, 2000); Matthew Evangelista, *Unarmed Forces: The Transnational Movement to End the Cold War* (Ithaca, NY: Cornell University Press, 1999); Jack Matlock, *Reagan and Gorbachev: How the Cold War Ended* (New York: Random House, 2004); and Vladislav Zubok, *A Failed Empire: The Soviet Union and the Cold War from Stalin to Gorbachev* (Chapel Hill: University of North Carolina Press, 2007).

2. The 1975 Helsinki Final Act was the culmination of three years of negotiations at the Conference on Security and Cooperation in Europe (CSCE) and contained principles to govern East-West interactions in Europe. In addition to reaching an agreement on the inviolability of frontiers, which was the original impetus for the Soviet desire to hold the conference, the Helsinki Final Act committed the CSCE states to respect human rights and facilitate human contacts across East-West borders. The agreement also contained a follow-up mechanism, setting a meeting to be held in two years time to review implementation of the act. The most important scholarly work on the Helsinki Final Act thus far is Daniel Thomas, *The Helsinki Effect: International Norms, Human Rights, and the Demise of Communism* (Princeton, NJ: Princeton University Press, 2001), which analyzes the influence and acceptance of human rights norms, using reaction to the Helsinki Final Act in the Soviet Union, Czechoslovakia, and Poland as his case studies. Thomas argues that the establishment of human rights as a "formal norm" in the Helsinki Final Act transformed Soviet bloc states and East-West relations. My research on the Helsinki process has led me to emphasize human rights advocacy as opposed to the power of human rights norms. Helsinki activism grew increasingly effective as the movement gained supporters who would incorporate Helsinki compliance into high-level diplomacy.

3. Yakovlev also faced protesters at the Soviet embassy who pressed for family reunification. Christopher Shulgan, *The Soviet Ambassador: The Making of the Radical Behind Perestroika* (Toronto: McClelland and Stewart, 2008), 146, 165, 191. Thomas argues that some who were close to Gorbachev had considerable exposure to human rights literature. Daniel C. Thomas, "Human Rights Ideas, the Demise of Communism, and the End of the Cold War," *Journal of Cold War Studies* 7, no. 2 (Spring 2005): 119–21; Christopher Andrew and Vasili Mitrokhin, *The Sword and the Shield: The Mitrokhin Archive and the Secret History of the KGB* (New York: Basic Books, 1999), 333; Daniel C. Thomas, "The Helsinki Accords and Political Change in Eastern Europe," in *The Power of Human Rights: International Norms and Domestic Change*, ed. Thomas Risse et al. (New York: Cambridge University

Press, 1999), 229; Mikhail Gorbachev and Zdeněk Mlynář, *Conversations with Gorbachev: On Perestroika, the Prague Spring, and the Crossroads of Socialism* (New York: Columbia University Press, 2002); and Xinyuan Dai, "Compliance Without Carrots or Sticks: How International Institutions Influence National Policies" (PhD diss., University of Chicago, 2000), 196.

4. Oral History Interview, Fedor Burlatsky, Folder 9, Box 1, The Hoover Institution and the Gorbachev Foundation (Moscow) Collection, Hoover Institution Archives, Stanford, California. Copyright Stanford University.

5. Mikhail Gorbachev, *Gorbachev: On My Country and the World*, trans. George Shriver (New York: Columbia University Press, 2000), 267.

6. Thomas, "Human Rights Ideas, the Demise of Communism, and the End of the Cold War," 118.

7. Handwritten Notes, Warren Zimmermann, Zimmermann Papers, Special Collections Research Center, Georgetown University, Washington, DC.

8. Some observers dispute the suggestion that pressure from Helsinki activists influenced Soviet behavior. See for example, Sandra Louise Gubin, "International Regimes, Agenda Setting and Linkage Groups in U.S.-Soviet Relations: The Helsinki Process and Divided Spouses" (PhD diss., University of Michigan, 1990), 168; N. Edwina Moreton, "Security, Change, and Instability in Eastern Europe," in *European Security: Prospects for the 1980s*, ed. Derek Leebaert (Lexington, MA: Heath, 1979); and Jonathan Luxmoore, "And So to Vienna . . . The CSCE Eleven Years On," *Contemporary Review* 249, no. 1451 (1986): 307. The Commission on Security and Cooperation in Europe was made up of members of the executive and legislative branches of the United States government that was devoted to monitoring compliance with the Helsinki Final Act; it came to serve as a clearinghouse for reports of Helsinki violations and was an effective advocate for Helsinki monitors repressed and imprisoned in Eastern Europe. Formed in 1976, it was an essential element of the transnational Helsinki network. For further discussion of the commission's role, see Sarah B. Snyder, *Human Rights Activism and the End of the Cold War: A Transnational History of the Helsinki Network.* (New York: Cambridge University Press, 2011), 38–52.

9. CSCE/WT.2, December 10, 1986, Organization for Security and Cooperation in Europe Archives, Prague, Czech Republic (hereafter OSCE Archives); Eduard Shevardnadze (USSR), November 5, 1986, CSCE/WT/VR.3, OSCE Archives; and Bohdan Nahaylo, "Shevardnadze Proposes International Conference on Humanitarian Issues in Moscow," November 5, 1986, Human Rights, 1986–1987, Box 692, Old Code Subject Files, Soviet Red Archives, Records of Radio Free Europe/Radio Liberty Research Institute, Open Society Archives, Budapest, Hungary (hereafter OSA).

10. Roland Eggleston, "West Considers Soviet Proposal for Humanitarian Meeting in Moscow," Radio Liberty Research, December 4, 1986, Helsinki: Vienna, 1986–1989, Box 1118, Old Code Subject Files, Soviet Red Archives, Records of Radio Free Europe/Radio Liberty Research Institute, OSA; and Howe to Avebury,

May 7, 1987, Correspondence: National Committees: United Kingdom, 1986–1992, Box 19, Correspondence and Memoranda, Records of the International Helsinki Federation for Human Rights, OSA.

11. Eduard Shevardnadze, *The Future Belongs to Freedom*, trans. Catherine Fitzpatrick (New York: Free Press, 1991), 86.

12. The degree to which Soviet actions embodied a new approach rather than merely a recognition of the value of conveying a new approach would evolve over the course of the meeting.

13. Shevardnadze, *The Future Belongs to Freedom,* 44.

14. A Report from Helsinki Watch: Annual Report, 1986, Box 1, General Files, Helsinki Watch: New York Office Files, Human Rights Watch Records, Center for Human Rights Documentation and Research, Rare Book and Manuscript Library, Columbia University, New York (hereafter HRWR).

15. William Korey, "Helsinki, Human Rights, and the Gorbachev Style," *Ethics and International Affairs* 1 (1987): 113–33; Roland Eggleston, "The New Soviet 'Openness' in Vienna: Many Words, Little Substance," Radio Liberty Background Report, November 10, 1986, Helsinki: Vienna, 1986–1989, Box 1118, Old Code Subject Files, Soviet Red Archives, Records of Radio Free Europe/Radio Liberty Research Institute, OSA; Memorandum, Nagler and Minnema to National Committees, November 20, 1986, Memos, 1986, Box 20, Correspondence and Memoranda, Records of the International Helsinki Federation for Human Rights, OSA; William Korey, *The Promises We Keep: Human Rights, the Helsinki Process and American Foreign Policy* (New York: Institute for East West Studies, 1993), 227, 271; and Orest Deychakiwsky, "Helsinki Review Process: Making Progress Slowly, but Surely," *Ukrainian Weekly* January 18, 1987, CSCE General 1987, Box 17 Unprocessed, Joint Baltic American National Committee Records, Immigration History Research Center, University of Minnesota, Minneapolis, (hereafter JBANC).

16. Stefan Lehne, *The Vienna Meeting of the Conference on Security and Cooperation in Europe, 1986–1989* (Boulder, CO: Westview Press, 1991), 74.

17. Transcript, Press Conference with Ambassador Zimmermann, December 3, 1986, CSCE Vienna—November 1986, Box 6 Unprocessed, JBANC; and Korey, *The Promises We Keep*, 220.

18. Julia Wishnevsky, "Burlatsky on Goals of Soviet Human-Rights Commission," Radio Liberty Research February 17, 1988, Human Rights, 1988–1988, Box 692, Old Code Subject Files, Soviet Red Archives, Records of Radio Free Europe/Radio Liberty Research Institute, OSA; Rahr, "USSR-Fedor Burlatsky to Head New Human Rights Commission," December 1, 1987, Politics: Human Rights: General, 1987–1988, Box 20, New Code Subject Files, OSA; and Korey, *The Promises We Keep*, 220.

19. Roland Eggleston, "Gorbachev's 'New Thinking' and the Vienna Conference," Radio Liberty Research, March 18, 1987, Helsinki: Vienna, 1986–1989, Box 1118, Old Code Subject Files, Soviet Red Archives, Records of Radio Free Europe/Radio Liberty Research Institute, OSA; and Lehne, *The Vienna Meeting of the*

Conference on Security and Cooperation in Europe, 75. Helsinki Watch was concerned about the makeup of Burlatsky's commission given indications that some members were not committed to human rights, including one person a staff member described as a "real bad egg in psychiatry." Memorandum, n.d., USSR: Burlatsky, Fyodor: Meetings, 1988, Box 44, Country Files, Jeri Laber Files, Record Group 7, HRWR.

20. Memorandum, IHF to Delegations to the Vienna CSCE Meeting, February 4, 1987, Memos 1987, Box 20, Correspondence and Memoranda, Records of the International Helsinki Federation for Human Rights, OSA; Howe to Avebury, May 7, 1987, Correspondence: National Committees: United Kingdom, 1986–1992, Box 19, Correspondence and Memoranda, Records of the International Helsinki Federation for Human Rights, OSA; "Appeal by Doctor Yuri Orlov to the Vienna CSCE Meeting," January 27, 1987, 1987, Box 20, Correspondence and Memoranda, Records of the International Helsinki Federation for Human Rights, OSA; and Official Response of U.S. Helsinki Watch Committee, January 21, 1987, USSR: CSCE: Vienna, 1986–February 1987, Box 10, Country Files, Cathy Fitzpatrick Files, Record Group 7, HRWR.

21. Memorandum, IHF to Delegations to the Vienna CSCE Meeting, February 4, 1987, Memos 1987, Box 20, Correspondence and Memoranda, Records of the International Helsinki Federation for Human Rights, OSA.

22. Yuri Orlov, *Dangerous Thoughts: Memoirs of a Russian Life,* trans. Thomas P. Whitney (New York: William Morrow and Company, 1991), 304–5; and Eggleston, "Yuri Orlov Sets Conditions for Moscow Human Rights Conference," November 22, 1988, Human Rights, Declarations, 1988–1990, Box 693, Old Code Subject Files, Soviet Red Archives, Records of Radio Free Europe/Radio Liberty Research Institute, OSA.

23. Matlock, *Reagan and Gorbachev,* 291. The Vladimir Bukovsky Foundation, located in Amsterdam, also undertook an assessment of what conditions would make a conference in Moscow acceptable. Robert van Voren, "Is a Human Rights Conference in Moscow Acceptable?" August 1987, Folder 2, Box 37, Human Rights Collection, Andrei Sakharov Archives, Houghton Library, Harvard University.

24. Whitehead Statement, June 23, 1987; and Zimmermann Statement, May 5, 1987, both in Zimmermann Papers.

25. Lehne, *The Vienna Meeting of the Conference on Security and Cooperation in Europe,* 106.

26. Cable, AmEmbassy Vienna to SecState, June 20, 1988, Eastern Europe (General) 1987–1988 Memos, Cables, Reports, Articles (1 of 2), Box 92440, Nelson Ledsky Files, Ronald Reagan Library, Simi Valley, California.

27. As high-level discussions ensued about agreement to the conference, the State Department carefully followed political prisoners' releases in the Soviet Union. John Finerty, written communication with the author, June 24, 2008.

28. Alexis Heraclides, *Security and Co-operation in Europe: The Human Dimension, 1972–1992* (Portland: Frank Cass, 1993), 99; and Lehne, *The Vienna Meeting of the Conference on Security and Cooperation in Europe,* 128–29.

29. "Soviets Announce Resolution of Commission Cases," *CSCE Digest* April 1987, CSCE Digest, Box 6, JBANC.

30. George P. Shultz, *Turmoil and Triumph: Diplomacy, Power, and the Victory of the American Ideal* (New York: Simon and Schuster, 1993), 986.

31. Judy Dempsey, "Moscow Go-ahead for Rights Group," Annual Report 1988, Box 1, Publications, Records of the International Helsinki Federation for Human Rights, OSA.

32. International Helsinki Federation for Human Rights, *On Speaking Terms: An Unprecedented Human Rights Mission to the Soviet Union, January 25–31, 1988* (Vienna: International Helsinki Federation for Human Rights, 1988), 5, 7; Mickey Edwards, "Is Moscow Due That Rights Session?" *Washington Times,* January 10, 1989, F1–4; Memorandum, Susan to Edwards, January 10, 1989, Folder 11, Box 56, Mickey Edwards Collection, Carl Albert Center Congressional Archives, University of Oklahoma, Norman.

33. Jeri Laber, interview, April 29, 2008. Helsinki Watch was a member of the IHF.

34. Jeri Laber, *The Courage of Strangers: Coming of Age with the Human Rights Movement* (New York: Public Affairs, 2002), 288; "Political Prisoners," *News from Helsinki Watch* II:1 (February 22, 1988) in Delegation to Moscow: General, 1987, Box 3, Project Files, Records of the International Helsinki Federation for Human Rights, OSA; and Schwarzenberg to Adamishin, March 15, 1988, Delegation to Moscow, Correspondence 1987–1988, Box 3, Project Files, Records of the International Helsinki Federation for Human Rights, OSA.

35. Diary, Frantisek Janouch, January 24–31, 1988, Box 3, Project Files, Records of the International Helsinki Federation for Human Rights, OSA.

36. The IHF's report, however, characterized Adamishin's comments on the conditions for such a conference to be "evasive." International Helsinki Federation for Human Rights, *On Speaking Terms*, 45–7; and Diary, Frantisek Janouch, January 24–31, 1988, Box 3, Project Files, Records of the International Helsinki Federation for Human Rights, OSA.

37. Diary, Frantisek Janouch, January 24–31, 1988, Box 3, Project Files, Records of the International Helsinki Federation for Human Rights, OSA; International Helsinki Federation for Human Rights, *On Speaking Terms*, 46–47.

38. Laber, *The Courage of Strangers,* 304–5.

39. "Commission Delegation Holds Human Rights Discussions in Moscow," *CSCE Digest* January–February 1989, CSCE 1989: London Conference, Box 2 Unprocessed, JBANC; and Steno Notebook, November 1988, Folder 18, Box 175, Dennis DeConcini Papers, University of Arizona, Tucson.

40. Sean Griffin, "De Concini Observes New Soviet Attitude," *Phoenix Gazette,* November 24, 1988, Folder 18, Box 175, DeConcini Papers. See also Mickey Edwards, "Is Moscow Due That Rights Session?" *Washington Times,* January 10, 1989, F1, F4; and Memorandum, Susan to Edwards, January 10, 1989, Folder 11, Box 56, Edwards Collection.

41. Press Conference: Soviet Union Trip, November 23, 1988, Folder 18, Box 175, DeConcini Papers.

42. Laber, *The Courage of Strangers,* 304; and Milan Hauner, "A Softening of the Soviet Stance on Human Rights?" Radio Liberty Research, December 7, 1988, Human Rights, 1988–1989, Box 693, Old Code Subject Files, Soviet Red Archives, Records of Radio Free Europe/Radio Liberty Research Institute, OSA.

43. The Vienna Concluding Document included a mandate to begin Conventional Forces in Europe talks, leading many to point to the close of the Vienna meeting as marking the beginning of a new era for Europe. Schifter and Adamishin see the Vienna Concluding Document as marking the end of the Cold War. Richard Schifter, "Concluding Thoughts," in Anatoly Adamishin and Richard Schifter, *Human Rights, Perestroika, and the End of the Cold War* (Washington, DC: United States Institute of Peace Press, 2009), 243.

44. Activists such as Orlov also saw Vienna as a significant breakthrough in Soviet thinking about political prisoners and human rights. Yuri Orlov, interview, March 27 and 28, 2008.

45. Shevardnadze, *The Future Belongs to Freedom,* 128–29.

46. Yuri Kashlev, "The CSCE in the Soviet Union's Politics," *International Affairs* (USSR) 7 (1992): 71.

47. Heraclides, *Security and Co-operation in Europe,* 102.

48. Soviet Foreign Ministry, "The Political Processes in the European Socialist Countries and the Proposals for Our Practical Steps Considering the Situation Which Has Arisen in Them," February 24, 1989, *Cold War International History Project Bulletin* 12/13 (Fall/Winter 2001): 70–1.

49. The Copenhagen meeting was held in the context of the international showdown with Saddam Hussein over Kuwait and a recent show of force by Soviet troops in Lithuania.

50. CSCE/CHDC.16, June 8, 1990, OSCE Archives.

51. Telegram, AmEmbassy Copenhagen to SECSTATE, June 27, 1990, Box 35, Max M. Kampelman Papers, Minnesota Historical Society, St. Paul, Minnesota.

52. Mikhail Gorbachev, *Memoirs* (New York: Doubleday, 1996), 548.

53. The negotiations that produced the Vienna Document on Confidence and Security Building Measures had been in session since March 9, 1989, and were the second phase of the Stockholm conference held from 1984–1986.

54. "Charter of Paris for A New Europe," November 1990, at Organization for Security and Co-operation in Europe website www.osce.org/ (accessed May 22, 2006); and Rob Zaagman, "The Second Basket of the CSCE: History, Helsinki-II and Afterwards," in *The Challenges of Change: The Helsinki Summit of the CSCE and its Aftermath,* ed. Arie Bloed (Boston: Martinus Nijhoff Publishers, 1994), 181.

55. Joint Declaration of Twenty-Two States, Conference on Security and Cooperation in Europe, Box 1, Subject Files, Press Office, George Bush Presidential Library, College Station, Texas; and Heraclides, *Security and Co-operation in Europe,* 144–45.

56. The Negotiation on Conventional Armed Forces in Europe (CFE) produced an agreement that limited conventional forces in Europe and was described by a Bush administration official as "probably the most ambitious arms control treaty ever concluded." Press Briefing, November 15, 1990, Conference on Security and Cooperation in Europe, Box 1, Subject Files, Press Office, George Bush Presidential Library.

57. His memoirs offer important evidence of the adoption of Helsinki ideals by Gorbachev's aides and other Soviets leaders at the time. Shevardnadze, *The Future Belongs to Freedom,* 86, 204.

58. The Soviets questioned going forward with the Moscow meeting given the turmoil in the Soviet Union but polled CSCE ambassadors in Moscow who argued that it would offer support to the reforms undertaken by the Gorbachev government. Anatoly Chernyaev, *My Six Years with Gorbachev* (University Park: Pennsylvania State University Press, 2000), 390.

59. Korey, *The Promises We Keep,* 393.

60. CSCE/CHDM.33, September 25, 1991, OSCE Archives; CSCE/CHDM.36, September 25, 1991, OSCE Archives; CSCE/CHDM.37, September 26, 1991, OSCE Archives; CSCE/CDHM.46, September 26, OSCE Archives; CSCE/CHDM.47, September 26, 1991, OSCE Archives; and Laber, *The Courage of Strangers,* 365.

61. DeConcini and Hoyer to Petrovskiy, June 14, 1991, Box 36, Kampelman Papers; and Laber, *The Courage of Strangers,* 366–69.

62. CSCE/CHDM.49/Rev.1, October 3, 1991, OSCE Archives.

63. Yuri Fokine, et al., "Helsinki 30 Years Later," *International Affairs* (May 2005): 188.

64. Natan Sharansky, interview, November 19, 2009.

13

THE RIGHT TO BODILY INTEGRITY

Women's Rights as Human Rights and the
International Movement to End Female Genital
Mutilation, 1970s–1990s

KELLY J. SHANNON

In September 1994, CNN ignited an international firestorm over the practice of female genital mutilation (FGM).[1] While covering the United Nations International Conference on Population and Development (ICPD) in Cairo, CNN correspondent Christiane Amanpour decided to report on the practice of FGM in Egypt. Working through a freelance producer, CNN convinced an Egyptian family to allow Amanpour and her crew to film their daughter's clitoridectomy. Amanpour then showed the footage at the UN conference, and it aired on television worldwide.[2] The graphic video depicted ten-year-old Nagla Hamza having her clitoris removed without anesthesia or sanitary instruments. *Time* magazine described the footage, which depicted

a crowded living room, where relatives smiled and ululated in celebration. As a voice-over explained that no sanitary precautions would be taken, no anesthetic applied, Nagla was tilted onto her back by two men—a plumber and a florist—and her legs prodded into the air in a wide V. While the florist cradled her from behind, the plumber wrapped Nagla's hands around her ankles. Then the plumber quickly leaned in between Nagla's legs and cut off her clitoris with a pair of barber's scissors. The girl barely had time to emit her first gasp of pain before her legs were lowered and her mutilated genitalia were bound with rags.[3]

Nagla, who was dressed in a party dress and smiling before the procedure began, clearly experienced agony as she cried, "Father! Father! A sin upon you! A sin upon you all!"[4]

The video did not show Nagla's genitals during or after the procedure, but her screams were enough to cause "an immediate worldwide public outcry."[5] Official delegates to the UN conference, policymakers, and the mainstream global public were outraged when the footage aired. The UN issued its harshest condemnation of FGM to date, and people worldwide called for the eradication of the practice. Despite the fact that Egyptian law did not ban clitoridectomy, Egyptian authorities arrested Nagla's father, the two men who performed the procedure, and the freelance producer who arranged for CNN to film it. Egyptian President Muhammad Hosni Mubarak denied that FGM was practiced in Egypt, but the film was evidence to the contrary.[6] Despite Mubarak's attempts to quell the uproar, international condemnation of FGM continued to intensify.

The Cairo conference brought global public attention to the international movement to eradicate FGM, which had been gaining momentum since the late 1970s. For decades, anti-FGM activists from around the globe had been working tirelessly without significant mainstream recognition. Not only did the CNN video create intense public scrutiny and broad support for anti-FGM campaigns, but a simultaneous shift in international human rights law allowed activists to recast FGM as a human rights issue. As a result, several countries took steps over the next few years to outlaw the practice within their borders, grant political asylum to women fleeing mutilation, and participate in international efforts to end the tradition.

In the early 1990s, the stage was set for a revitalization of international human rights law. The United Nations, freed from the confines of the Cold War era superpower struggle, could pursue the protection of human rights with renewed purpose. Over the course of the 1990s, it convened six international conferences that were critical to the reconceptualization of human rights, including the 1993 World Conference on Human Rights in Vienna and the International Conference on Population and Development in Cairo in 1994.[7] The amount and scale of activity focused on human rights undertaken by the United Nations during the last decade of the twentieth century was revolutionary, comparable only to the period immediately following World War II when the UN was formed.[8] Of the many momentous developments in human rights during this period, the most important were the UN's formal recognition that women's rights *are* human rights and the drafting of several international documents which enshrined that principle in the international human rights regime.[9]

This shift in the conception of human rights to include women's rights and abuses in the "private" sphere represents an important turning point in the history of human rights, one that must fundamentally alter the way scholars assess the human rights movement. Put another way, the 1990s represent the moment when individual rights trumped government sovereignty in the long-standing tension between the two. The history of human rights in the twentieth century is mainly the story of the development of protections for civil and political rights and of international human rights agencies' concern with state abuses against individuals. Social, economic, and cultural rights, which scholars often refer to as "second generation" human rights, were downplayed or ignored at the international level, and violations of women's rights in particular did not receive attention because they usually involved abuses committed by private citizens, not states.[10] Although the 1945 UN Charter and the 1948 Universal Declaration of Human Rights endorsed the principle of gender equality, women continued to face discrimination worldwide. The UN did little to advance women's rights before it convened the Decade for Women from 1975 to 1985.[11] Even then, it took until the 1990s for the principle of gender equality to find its way into international human rights instruments. It was then that the international community declared it could intervene when states failed to protect their citizens from human rights abuses committed in the "private" realm. This important shift subordinated state sovereignty to international human rights law, bridging the public-private divide that prevented the universal application of human rights protections. The campaign against female genital mutilation epitomized this moment of transformation.

Without this shift in human rights discourse, anti-FGM activists faced an uphill battle in securing international support for their efforts, even from the UN and its affiliates. For example, a group of African women urged the World Health Organization (WHO) to study female circumcision in 1961. The WHO refused on the grounds that it was a cultural practice, not a medical problem, so FGM was none of its concern. In any case, WHO policy precluded the organization's intervention in the domestic matters of sovereign states, and no government had invited it to take up the issue of female circumcision.[12] Consequently, there was no discussion of FGM at the UN's first World Conference on Women in 1975.[13]

The reason for this refusal by international organizations like the WHO to discuss FGM in the 1960s and 1970s was the construction of certain categories as being beyond the purview of international law. Culture, religion, and the family supposedly belonged to a "private" sphere, not subject to "public" debates or action. This sphere, of course, was where societies constructed and defined women's roles and rights. Declaring the private sphere off-limits to international human rights intervention effectively ensured the perpetuation of women's subordination worldwide. Accordingly, international organizations like the UN and WHO concerned themselves only with state violations of human rights; they pointed to the "private" nature of FGM, as well as other abuses committed against women, when explaining their reluctance to insert themselves into the matter.[14] They felt it better to allow individual states or ethnic groups to work out solutions for themselves. So common was this premise that the private sphere was beyond the purview of public intervention at the time that women's rights activists in the United States had to struggle to get the public and government involved in protecting women from such abuses as domestic violence and rape.[15] Anti-FGM activists faced the same battle at the international level.

Despite the resistance of the UN and other intergovernmental organizations to take up the issue of FGM, Arab and African grassroots activists worked steadily to combat the custom in their home countries and to build international support networks. By the late 1970s, their efforts began to pay off, as Western feminists threw their support behind the anti-FGM campaign, and women built an international movement that eventually succeeded in getting the UN, its affiliate organizations, and national governments to take up the issue.

The first step in the campaign was the collection of data to prove that the practice was widespread and harmful to women and girls. While some physicians had published national studies in medical journals, no comprehensive international study of FGM existed in the 1970s.[16] American feminist Fran Hosken helped remedy the problem. The Austrian-born Hosken, who immigrated with her family to the United States in 1938, was a Harvard-educated journalist and urban planner. She was horrified when she learned about female circumcision when traveling in Africa in 1973 and was equally shocked to learn that the international community was largely silent on the issue.[17] Hosken made it her goal to push for the eradication of the practice. After UNICEF and the WHO rebuffed her requests to examine FGM in the mid-1970s, she set out to conduct her own study. To acquire the necessary expertise, she took three trips across Africa to interview midwives and doctors, sent hundreds of questionnaires to women and institutions in Africa and the Middle East, and wrote to the authors of existing medical publications on FGM.[18] The result of these efforts was the 370-page *Hosken Report*, which appeared in 1979.[19]

The *Hosken Report* documented the geographic scope and history of the practice, described the various types of FGM, enumerated its health effects, explained its purpose, and provided statistics for how many women and girls were mutilated worldwide. Most subsequent studies relied heavily on Hosken's figures.[20] Because Hosken was the first person to study genital mutilation comprehensively, her work framed subsequent debates on the subject in the international arena.

In fact, it was Hosken who coined the term "female genital mutilation." She argued, "Female circumcision is the popular, but medically incorrect, name for a variety of mutilating genital operations to which female children and young women are subjected in Africa and the Middle East" and that "genital mutilation is the correct definition."[21] Hosken hoped the new name would combat the perception that female genital operations were akin to male circumcision.[22] So great was her influence on debates about female circumcision that "female genital mutilation" soon became the official term used by the United Nations and much of the NGO community for female genital cutting practices.

Notwithstanding its substantial research base, *The Hosken Report* was a manifesto against FGM that combined research with moral outrage. For Hosken, medical concerns, feminist theory, and human rights were inextricably intertwined with genital mutilation. She declared, "I am concerned first of all with health," a right to which all human beings were guaranteed in the 1948 Universal Declaration of Human Rights.[23] She defined health broadly, as "physical integrity and psychological well-being, freedom of [sic] fear and a quality of life that assures the fullest development of the human personality."[24] This holistic definition allowed her to frame her arguments in terms of the larger position of women in the societies where FGM was practiced, alongside concerns about the custom's health effects. She thus connected her arguments with the strand of feminist theory popular at the time that critiqued global patriarchy.[25] According to Hosken, FGM remained pervasive in so many countries because of "contempt for the female of the species." The practice became "a means to prove male sexual superiority."[26] Genital mutilation was the most horrific form of male oppression because it struck at the heart of what defines a woman as female according to most societies: her genitalia. Therefore, according to Hosken, the international community should become involved in efforts to eradicate FGM because it violated the basic human right to health and because it hindered the physical and psychological well-being of women.

While Hosken attempted to raise American women's consciousness about FGM and build a broad-based international coalition to eradicate the practice, her report had the potential to alienate the very people with whom she was trying to build an alliance. Although she argued that Westerners who opposed FGM must first and foremost support the efforts of African and Arab women to combat the practice, she claimed in her report, "The victims of the practices described here are, for the most part, illiterate and too young to speak for themselves, unaware of the rest of the world and of their own bodies' biological functions. They are quite unable to communicate their needs."[27] Hosken's characterization of the "victims" of FGM as wholly ignorant of biology and as unconscious of their own oppression offended adult African and Arab women. Her approach proved problematic when it came to dealing with women from FGM-practicing countries who should have been ready allies.

Hosken's report alienated men who opposed the practice by stating that she was "deeply ashamed for all men because ultimately they are all responsible."[28] Persuading global leaders to make FGM their concern was difficult under any circumstances; Hosken's rhetoric thwarted her ability to do so. Indeed, while Hosken stated repeatedly that international organizations were crucial to bringing about the eradication of FGM, she heaped criticism upon the UN, WHO, and UNICEF for their characterizations of the practice as a cultural issue outside of their purview. She accused these international agencies of upholding the patriarchal status quo and creating a global "conspiracy of silence" about FGM.[29]

Recognizing that her criticism of the organizations was backfiring, Hosken's contemporaries urged her to tone down her rhetoric for the good of the cause. In her 1981 review of the second edition of Hosken's report, Africanist Margaret Jean Hay praised Hosken's research but called her a "crusader" who weakened the overall impact of her own report with her "general tone of outrage and sarcasm."[30] Similarly, after Hosken criticized *Ms.* magazine's March 1980 feature article on FGM and its inclusion of the respected Egyptian activist and author Dr. Nawal El Saadawi's account of her own clitoridectomy, *Ms.* editors Robin Morgan and Gloria Steinem cautioned Hosken about her "troubling . . . cultural bias" which "could overshadow the enormous value of the work you actually have done" and "confirm the understandable suspicions of Third World women that outside criticism of their countries may have a racist base and agenda."[31]

Despite Hosken's approach, her efforts and those of other activists to draw international attention to FGM began to yield results. In particular, *The Hosken Report* had exposed the pervasive nature of FGM; it reported that female genital cutting rituals occurred in over two dozen countries, cutting a swath across Africa and into the Middle Eastern countries of Oman and Yemen. According to Hosken's initial estimates, at least 60 million women and girls worldwide had undergone some form of genital mutilation, a figure she later revised to 120 million.[32] The report's hard facts demonstrated that FGM occurred on a scale greater than anyone had imagined and gave the anti-FGM movement ammunition to galvanize the international community. Shortly after its publication in 1979, the WHO hosted an international seminar in Khartoum on Traditional Practices Affecting the Health of Women and Children. There, official delegations from nine African and Middle Eastern countries, as well as Hosken, discussed FGM openly for the first time and drew up specific recommendations for eradicating the practice.[33] Following the seminar, the UN and its affiliates paid increasing attention to FGM. Newspaper, magazine, and journal articles, as well as scholarly studies, appeared with increasing frequency throughout the 1980s.[34]

As genital mutilation gained greater international attention, anti-FGM activists expanded their organizational reach. The NGO Forums which paralleled the two UN conferences on women during the decade—in Copenhagen in 1980 and Nairobi in 1985—brought women together from across the globe to discuss FGM face-to-face. At first, the women who met in Copenhagen disagreed fiercely over how best to approach the issue. During several sessions devoted to genital mutilation at the NGO Forum, women from African and Arab countries took offense at how American and European women discussed the practice. For example, when Hosken encountered Dr. Nawal El Saadawi, the two clashed, despite their common opposition to FGM. El Saadawi, an influential international spokesperson against FGM, complained that Hosken seemed intent on blaming Islam and Africans for female genital mutilation, whereas El Saadawi argued, "It has to do with patriarchy and monogamy . . . But she doesn't want to hear any of this."[35]

African and Arab women at the sessions felt that Hosken and other Western women were either amplifying female circumcision for their own benefit or were neoimperialists bent on "saving" FGM's victims from a barbaric, exotic practice. El Saadawi argued that "the West is exploiting this issue," while Marie Angelique Savane of African Women for Research and Development (AAWORD), one of the NGOs that sponsored the sessions on FGM, protested that Westerners "have fallen back on sensationalism, and have become insensitive to the dignity of the very women they want to 'save.'"[36] For their part, many Western women at Copenhagen encountered the issue for the first time. The *New York Times* reported that Western women at the sessions "seemed visibly shocked to learn that girls in African and Arab villages are circumcised . . . Waving a pamphlet entitled, 'Genital and Sexual Mutilation of Females,' a Swedish student asked an American, 'Have you read this? This is barbarism, what they are doing.'"[37] Such statements incensed African and Arab women, prompting Savane to characterize the Westerners' comments as "latent racism."[38] African and Arab women wanted support for their efforts to eradicate FGM, but they did not want American and European women to see them as ignorant victims of barbaric cultures that needed Western enlightenment.

This controversy prompted AAWORD to issue a statement condemning "this new crusade of the West" and asking Western women to allow African and Arab women to speak for themselves.[39] In response, some Western women expressed resentment that they were being told to leave FGM for African and Arab women to deal with. A Swedish woman, for example, wrote in protest to the NGO forum newspaper, "We cannot accept the idea that because we have no experience of genital mutilation we should therefore not express our views on the subject . . . we feel so strongly that no human being has the right to decide over another person's body."[40] It was difficult to set goals and strategies for the eradication of FGM when women who opposed the practice could not even agree on whom had the right to speak. There was little consensus by the end of the forum about how best to proceed in the fight against FGM.

Sessions on the topic at the next UN women's conference in Nairobi in 1985 were not marked by such fierce acrimony, largely because in the intervening years Western women had deferred to the leadership of African and Arab women. The forum newspaper commented that "a big shift has occurred in the fight to stop circumcision," as the sessions were "run like an annual report meeting to donor agencies . . . This is a far cry from the confusion and rumour surrounding the issue at the mid-Decade meeting in Copenhagen."[41] Finally, women were able to coalesce around FGM and develop clear strategies to end it.[42]

That the practice was a problem related to the global lack of women's rights was clear to the women who met in Nairobi and elsewhere to organize the international anti-FGM campaign.[43] Yet those involved in the movement recognized that international agencies were unlikely to draw upon feminist arguments against the custom due to the potential to offend the governments and citizens of countries where FGM was practiced. NGOs and members of the UN were sensitive to the legacy of colonialism in the African and Arab countries where, in the nineteenth and early twentieth centuries, European imperial powers had often used arguments about the oppression of women by indigenous men to justify their domination.[44] To avoid charges of neoimperialist interference, those who worked to end FGM chose to adopt a more neutral discourse that focused on the practice as an issue of public health. Hosken, of course, had been arguing for several

years that FGM was a health issue, but other leaders of the international movement against FGM made a calculated decision to avoid linking it to patriarchy
or culture and to focus exclusively on the physical effects of FGM.[45] This
paved the way for the UN to get involved in anti-FGM campaigns without
threatening countries' sovereignty.

Health arguments against genital mutilation were more palatable to governments and practitioners, for whom the custom was deeply tied to issues
of culture and religion. Especially in the 1980s, opponents of non-Western
traditional practices, which oppressed women, faced the obstacle of cultural relativists, who claimed that universal human rights were simply a
form of Western cultural imperialism and that all cultural practices are
equally valid.[46] Practitioners of traditions that subordinated women claimed
that those customs were legitimate and that the imposition of women's
equal rights undermined their right to cultural identity. According to these
groups, writes Iranian feminist Mahnaz Afkhami, women "have rights
because they belong to certain cultures or religions, not because they are
individual human beings."[47] Maintaining women's subordinate status
became an integral part of maintaining cultural identity for these communities, and any woman from the community who expressed a desire for
change could be labeled a culturally inauthentic tool of Western imperialism. Arguments against FGM based on notions of universal women's
rights were unlikely to be successful, whereas arguments based on the medical consequences of FGM could theoretically avoid charges of cultural
insensitivity because they did not criticize the cultures that practiced FGM
or challenge the overall status of women in these societies.

A medically focused campaign was not only politically acceptable to
international leaders, but the practice did have serious health consequences
for women. Health professionals, activists, and scholars agreed that various
genital cutting rituals could be placed into three categories based on the
amount of tissue removed: clitoridectomy, excision, and infibulation. Clitoridectomy, the mildest form, involves the removal of the clitoris. Excision
is a clitoridectomy with the additional removal of some or all of the inner
labia. The most severe form of FGM is infibulation, in which all of a woman's or a girl's genital tissue is removed, and the wound is sutured, leaving
only a tiny opening about the size of a matchstick through which menstrual
blood and urine can pass.[48] Research on FGM demonstrated that, most
often, these surgeries took place in nonsterile environments and were performed by women (and sometimes men) with no formal medical training.
Those performing the procedure outside hospital settings used no anesthetic and crude instruments, such as broken glass, knives, and razor blades;

along with ash, herbs, and other substances to stop the bleeding; and, in the case of infibulation, thorns or catgut to suture wounds. These operations led to a host of short- and long-term physical complications, such as severe blood loss, shock, pain, chronic infection, urine retention, infertility, incontinence, painful menstruation, difficult childbirth, and even death.[49] Infibulated women faced the most difficulty; if they survived the initial surgery and its complications, they faced a lifetime of cutting and suturing to facilitate marital intercourse and childbirth.[50]

Because of Hosken's report and the work of other researchers, anti-FGM activists knew that roughly two million women and girls worldwide underwent FGM each year, leading to the deaths and the physical impairment, infection, and pain of many African and Arab women.[51] For this reason, the Voltaic Women's Federation, Somali Women's Democratic Organization, and Cairo Family Planning Association—all organized and run by women from FGM-practicing countries—worked for change by educating their countrymen and countrywomen about the negative effects of female circumcision on women's health.[52] International NGOs, such as the New York-based Research Action Information Network for Bodily Integrity of Women (RAINBO), did the same and also attempted to educate the West. Dr. Nahid Toubia, the director of RAINBO, the first female surgeon in the Sudan, and an official advisor to UNICEF, the WHO, and the United Nations Development Program (UNDP), published a booklet targeted at an American audience that took the medical approach to FGM.[53] Organizations like RAINBO scrupulously avoided criticizing FGM as a "barbaric" and exotic practice and instead utilized a neutral medical discourse.

At first, the public health campaign seemed to be effective. The combined efforts of NGOs succeeded in getting FGM on the agenda of the UN, WHO, and UNICEF. In 1984 the UN formed the Inter-African Committee on Traditional Practices Affecting the Health of Women and Children (or IAC), which appointed a special rapporteur to deal with "Traditional Practices Affecting the Health of Women and Children," including FGM. The IAC, composed of representatives from twenty African nations, conducted studies of FGM and adopted the medical approach to educate people across Africa.

Yet despite the hard work of grassroots activists and their success in getting UN organizations to address FGM, they struggled to get mainstream public attention and to change local practices. By the start of the 1990s, millions of women still underwent some form of FGM each year. Without significant funding and public attention, it was difficult for grassroots activists to reach each community that practiced FGM, and many Westerners still had no idea it existed. In places where anti-FGM activists were able to reach out to the community, they often faced resistance. Tribal and religious leaders—invariably men—often castigated local women who worked to end FGM as tools of imperialists bent on eradicating indigenous cultures in favor of "Westernization."[54] In addition, the women who performed the surgeries often depended on the income they received from the families of the girls and women they cut, so they had no economic incentive to cease the practice. Even many mothers who believed circumcision was wrong still chose to practice it because they feared their daughters would be unmarriageable without undergoing the procedure. In societies where marriage was a woman's only option for survival, parents would be irresponsible to jeopardize their daughters' marriage prospects. Many communities saw FGM as an important initiation into womanhood, while many people in African Muslim societies believed that circumcising their daughters was a religious requirement, although it is not in the Koran.[55] For those reasons, convincing practitioners to give up their custom was difficult.

Even worse, it appeared that the medical approach to FGM had backfired. Once they launched education initiatives, activists realized that many FGM-practicing peoples already knew about the consequences of cutting rituals, but they perceived the health risks as less dangerous than the social ostracism they or their children would experience if they chose not to follow tradition. In addition, the medical discourse focused largely on infibulation. However, clitoridectomy was more widespread; therefore, those who practiced clitoridectomy or excision deemed the health warnings inapplicable to them. Others started paying medical professionals to cut their daughters, resulting in the medicalization—and further entrenchment—of FGM, while some Muslim groups who practiced infibulation shifted toward clitoridectomy, which they assumed was a "safer" form of female circumcision that allowed them to uphold their religious requirements.[56] Activists now had to rethink their arguments.

The conceptual shift in human rights theory that occurred in the early 1990s allowed anti-FGM activists to change their tactics and amass more broad-based international support. This conceptual transformation was due to the lobbying efforts of women's rights groups, particularly the Center for Women's Global Leadership (CWGL), headed by American feminist Charlotte Bunch. Women's rights NGOs had learned during the Decade for Women how to lobby the UN effectively, and they used that expertise to create a well-organized campaign to put women's rights on the international agenda in the 1990s. During the preparatory period for the 1993 World Conference on Human Rights in Vienna, Bunch and the CWGL joined forces with other NGOs to create clear goals for putting women's rights at the center of the conference and any human rights policy that resulted from it.[57] Their goals included breaking down the public-private dichotomy that prevented the international community from addressing human rights abuses that occurred in the private realm and exposing the specious nature of claims to cultural or religious rights that perpetuated practices that violated women's human rights.[58] To that end, they organized a series of seminars in several countries starting in 1991 that brought women together to develop strategies. They also organized an annual 16 Days of Activism Against Gender Violence, which included, among other activities, an international petition drive to get women's human rights included on the agenda for the Vienna conference.[59] They submitted reports and recommendations to the UN preparatory meetings and eventually succeeded in getting on the official agenda.

Their most effective tactic was the Global Tribunal on Violations of Women's Human Rights, held on June 15, 1993, the second day of the conference, at the NGO Forum which paralleled the official conference activities. There, thirty-three women from twenty-five countries testified about human rights abuses they had suffered because of their sex, as four prominent human rights advocates presided as judges over the event.[60] The witnesses spoke out about issues as diverse as bride burning in Pakistan and the abuse of migrant women in the United States. FGM was included because Charlotte Bunch believed, "Traditional practices which are intrinsically injurious to women and girls can find no justification or immunity in a human rights framework that claims to be universal."[61] Recounting the stories of several women who had undergone FGM, Dr. Toubia of RAINBO testified that FGM is "a cruel and unnecessary tradition" that "is not a private issue nor the concern of one nation" and called for the international community to take immediate action to end it.[62] Citing the right to bodily integrity, Toubia made a strong argument for the categorization of FGM as a human rights abuse.

The tribunal provided clear evidence that women across the globe lacked human rights protections. One thousand people attended, including "community leaders, human rights activists, UN delegates and other high-ranking government officials."[63] The tribunal organizers issued a report to the official conference arguing that women's rights must be included in human rights law if "the promise of universal human rights will be realized" in the twenty-first century.[64] Their arguments proved persuasive. In the Vienna Declaration and Programme of Action, the UN stated unequivocally, "The human rights of women and of the girl-child are an inalienable, integral and indivisible part of universal human rights," and "the equal status of women and the human rights of women should be integrated into the mainstream of United Nations system-wide activity."[65] The Vienna declaration also called for "the eradication of any conflicts which may arise between the rights of women and the harmful effects of certain traditional or customary practices," clearly negating claims that rights to cultural or religious identity trumped women's rights.[66]

Before Vienna, the UN had treated women's rights and human rights as separate categories, even though the UN Charter and the Universal Declaration on Human Rights had declared the equality of men and women in the 1940s, and the UN had adopted the Convention on the Elimination of All Forms of Discrimination against Women (CEDAW) in 1979. In practice, member states of the UN had ignored women's rights for decades, and many of the countries that ratified CEDAW did so with so many reservations as to make the convention effectively useless. The Vienna conference represented a concrete step toward the protection and promotion of women's human rights by the international community.

This expansion of human rights allowed feminists to pressure states at the international level to take action to protect individuals from human rights abuses that occurred in the "private" sphere, condemning an array of private cultural practices as "violence against women."[67] This move paralleled the efforts of women's activists in the United States and elsewhere to subject private abuses, such as rape, sexual abuse, and domestic violence, to public scrutiny and government action. Thus, the inclusion of women's rights into the human rights agenda was part of a larger move within states and the international community to cast the private categories of culture, religion, and the family as areas for legitimate public and governmental involvement.

With this shift in the conception of human rights, the door opened for anti-FGM activists to pursue their opposition to the practice within the framework of the existing international human rights agenda, such as CEDAW and the Convention on the Rights of the Child, adopted in 1989. Notwithstanding FGM's negative health consequences, activists now argued that an even more basic problem with the practice was that it violated women and girls' rights to bodily integrity and freedom from abuse and violence. Situating FGM under the umbrella of human rights allowed activists to argue that no solution was acceptable other than complete eradication, which rendered insufficient efforts to medicalize cutting procedures and empowered activists to shame states into taking positive steps toward ending FGM.[68] The UN and other international agencies only moved away from the medical discourse because of the efforts of anti-FGM activists to recast the problem as a human rights abuse. By 1995, the transition from the medical approach to a human rights discourse was so complete that the UNFPA, UNICEF, WHO, and UNDP issued a joint statement calling the medically based opposition to FGM a "mistake" and insisting on a human rights basis for anti-FGM policies thereafter.[69]

Women's rights NGOs built on the Vienna experience to prepare for the UN International Conference on Population and Development in Cairo: they lobbied the UN and member states to include FGM as one of the major items of discussion. Meanwhile, FGM began to receive increasing visibility in public venues. In the United States, popular authors Alice Walker and Gloria Naylor published novels in 1992 that featured infibulated main characters, bringing the issue of FGM into American fiction for the first time.[70] Abe Rosenthal condemned FGM in his regular *New York Times* column throughout the 1990s, while ABC's *Day One*, hosted by the respected news anchor Forrest Sawyer, ran a segment on FGM in September 1993 that won a prestigious Peabody Award.[71] The momentum built by international anti-FGM activists and the media created sufficient pressure for the UN to include FGM on the official conference agenda in Cairo in 1994.

While organizations including the Cairo Family Planning Association, Equality Now, Sisterhood Is Global Institute, and RAINBO lobbied the UN and member states successfully to make FGM a topic of discussion, proponents of "traditional" practices and gender roles combined forces to contest the official conference program. In particular, Muslim groups decried the conference as a Western imperialist plot to reduce the number of Muslims worldwide, and they put aside theological differences to join forces with the Vatican to create a conservative, patriarchal bloc opposed to the inclusion of women's issues in the Cairo conference. News of this unusual alliance grabbed headlines before the conference began.[72]

Christiane Amanpour's CNN video, however, upstaged the opponents of the conference and spurred the conference delegates to denounce all forms of FGM. In its "Report of the International Conference on Population and Development," the UN declared, "In a number of countries, harmful practices meant to control women's sexuality have led to great suffering. Among them is the practice of female genital mutilation, which is a violation of basic rights and a major lifelong risk to women's health."[73] The report continued, "Governments and communities should urgently take steps to stop the practice of female genital mutilation and protect women and girls from all such similar unnecessary and dangerous practices," and it listed recommendations for how governments and communities might do so.[74] This final statement from the ICPD was the "strongest language opposing FGC in the history of the U.N. system."[75]

Amanpour did not single-handedly thrust FGM into the international spotlight—anti-FGM activists were the ones who got female genital mutilation on the agenda for Cairo and forced states to grapple with the issue—but her video did what women's rights activists, the UN, and the few journalists who wrote about FGM had been unable to do during the previous two decades: bring FGM to the international public. Her position as a major media figure with the power to bring issues to millions of television viewers worldwide gave her a unique ability to publicize the campaign. Thus, the combination of the UN's condemnation of FGM at Cairo and the significant reaction to the CNN video put FGM on the map in a way that allowed for real progress in the international campaign to end the practice.

The CNN piece spurred a heated debate in the United States, as Americans watched the footage on television and journalists reported on its aftermath. For many American viewers, it was their first encounter with the existence of FGM. Paige Prill, spokeswoman for CNN, commented that one caller to the station said that she had not believed written reports on FGM until she saw the video footage from Cairo. The images on screen proved far more powerful than any written testimony. Judy Mann of the *Washington Post* concluded, "That's probably the best argument for showing shocking and horrifying footage of any atrocity. The world has far too long pretended that female genital mutilation isn't happening . . . It's a ritual born of ignorance and superstition that can no longer be excused in a modern world."[76] Meanwhile, a flood of articles began to appear in newspapers across the country, and U.S. scholars began taking a greater interest in the subject.[77]

American lawmakers proved equally susceptible to the persuasive power of the CNN video. Representative Constance Morella (R-MD) viewed the film at the Cairo conference. When she met later that week with President Mubarak, Morella pressed him: "I asked him about female genital mutilation, and he said that it does not happen, that it's not legal in Egypt. I said that [the law] must not be enforced . . . that I'd seen the CNN film."[78] Reports later surfaced that at least 80 percent of Egyptian women had undergone FGM in some form. The international pressure brought to bear as a result of Amanpour's video eventually forced the Egyptian government to ban FGM and implement programs to eradicate it.[79]

Senator Harry Reid (D-NV) first learned about FGM when a longtime friend called him to describe the CNN footage. As he told his fellow Senators, "I became almost sick to my stomach by listening to her describe what she watched on television."[80] Reid was so horrified by his friend's description that he watched the video, commissioned his staff to undertake a thorough study of FGM, and co-sponsored legislation in late 1994 with Representative Patricia Schroeder (D-CO) to ban the practice in the United States and to tie U.S. foreign aid to eradication efforts. A staunch advocate for women's rights in the House, Rep. Schroeder first introduced anti-FGM legislation to Congress in 1993 as part of the Women's Health Equity Act, but the bill did not pass.[81] She kept pushing the issue in the House, but it took Amanpour's video for other legislators to support her efforts.[82] Taking up Schroeder's earlier arguments that FGM violated women and girls' rights to bodily integrity, Senator Carol Moseley-Braun (D-IL) declared during the introduction of the legislation in the Senate, "This is not just a matter of difference in cultural points of view. This really goes to . . . a concern for human rights that I think as Americans we all share."[83]

With bipartisan support, Schroeder and Reid's proposals resulted in the passage of anti-FGM legislation in September 1996. The act criminalized FGM, bound the United States to oppose nonhumanitarian loans or other funding from international financial institutions for countries that had not taken steps to eradicate it, and mandated that immigrants from FGM-practicing countries receive information about the negative effects of the custom and of the criminal penalties they would face if they practiced it in the United States.[84] Along the way, in June 1995, the House also passed Rep. Schroeder's resolution "urging the President to help end the practice of female [circumcision] worldwide," which pressured President Clinton to take up the issue at the executive level.[85] On September 30, 1996, Clinton signed the ban on FGM into law, and fifteen states followed suit with anti-FGM legislation of their own.[86] The U.S. legal system underscored these developments by making the United States a safe haven for women fleeing genital mutilation when the courts ruled that fear of FGM for oneself or one's children was sufficient grounds for a woman to seek and receive political asylum.[87]

The anti-FGM legislation and asylum cases in the United States were part of a larger trend that saw the criminalization of genital mutilation across the globe. By 2000, twenty nations had passed laws specifically targeting female genital mutilation, and seven others recognized that their existing civil, criminal, and child protection laws applied to the practice. These ranged from Western countries like Australia, the United Kingdom, and France to countries with the highest prevalence of FGM, such as Ethiopia, Burkina Faso, Djibouti, and Egypt.[88] In addition, Canada and some other Western nations also recognized FGM as a basis for asylum during the 1990s.[89]

These developments, while encouraging, did not eradicate the practice of female genital mutilation. Today, the struggle to end FGM is far from over. Indeed, scholars and activists have questioned whether national legislation is enough to combat the practice, or if it is even an effective way to approach the issue.[90] For those who support the legislative efforts, the struggle to get governments to commit the resources and political will to uphold their laws is ongoing. For example, no person was prosecuted for violating the U.S. ban on genital mutilation until 2006.[91] Most governments that passed anti-FGM legislation have yet to dedicate enough funding and attention to enforcement. After passing the laws, many turned their attention to other pressing problems, and FGM faded from their agendas. Enforcing the legislation must be accompanied by culturally sensitive, on the ground efforts to change the views of practitioners. NGOs and grassroots activists have led the way, but they often lack adequate resources. They still struggle to counter the arguments of cultural relativists who argue the practice should continue. Scholars even continue to argue about what to call the customs that constitute FGM.[92] Thus, at the end of the first decade of the twenty-first century, the debate about FGM and how best to bring about its eradication continued unabated.

Yet the developments of the 1990s opened up space for progress in the campaign to end FGM. The story of human rights in the twentieth century is that of the continuous expansion of rights, increasingly due to the efforts of grassroots activists and NGOs rather than governments or the United Nations. It was the rise of NGOs and grassroots activism in the last quarter of the twentieth century that both created the campaign against FGM and helped expand the international human rights regime so that FGM could be considered a human rights abuse. Without the efforts of nonstate actors and the media, FGM would have remained on the margins of the human rights agenda. Activists caused the crucial shift in human rights discourse and practice that led to the categorization of abuses in the "private" realm as human rights violations. Women's human rights could no longer be ignored in the name of cultural autonomy or state sovereignty. This development paved the way for activists and the international community to use human rights instruments in new ways to broaden and strengthen human rights protections, as they did in the campaign against FGM. The revolutionary breakdown of the public-private dichotomy, which had dominated human rights law for most of the twentieth century, created the potential for a truly universal application of human rights.

NOTES

I would like to thank Richard Immerman, Petra Goedde, Will Hitchcock, Beth Bailey, and Harvey Neptune, as well as the participants in Temple University's International History Workshop on the history of human rights, for their critical feedback and support in the writing of this chapter.

1. The various rituals that involve cutting the female genitalia are also referred to as "female genital cutting" (FGC), "female circumcision," "female genital modification," and "female genital surgeries" (FGS). "Female circumcision" was the earliest term, while FGM came into use by the late 1970s. FGC, FGS, and female genital modification are more recent terms created due to the debate about finding terminology that is accurate but not offensive to practitioners. This chapter is not concerned with these debates; I have utilized "female genital mutilation" because it was the most commonly used term during the period under examination.

2. Gail Young reporting from Cairo, *The World Today*, CNN, September 7, 1994, DVD, Television News Archive, Vanderbilt University Libraries.

3. Jill Smolowe, "A Rite of Passage—or Mutilation?" *Time*, September 26, 1994, 65 and at http://www.time.com/time/magazine/article/0,9171,981483,00.html (accessed September 13, 2008).

4. Young, *World Today*, CNN.

5. Nada Khader, "Hope for Our Sisters: Ending Female Genital Mutilation," Proutworld, 2001, http://www.proutworld.org/ (accessed October 22, 2008).

6. "Egypt: UN Conference on Population and Development and FGM," *Women's International Network News* 20, no. 4 (September 1994): 29; Judy Mann, "When Journalists Witness Atrocities," *The Washington Post*, September 23, 1994, E3; and Elizabeth Heger Boyle, *Female Genital Cutting: Cultural Conflict in the Global Community* (Baltimore, MD: The Johns Hopkins University Press, 2002), 3.

7. Berta Esperanza Hernandez-Truyol, "Human Rights Through a Gendered Lens: Emergence, Evolution, Revolution" in *Women and International Human Rights Law*, vol. 1, *Introduction to Women's Human Rights Issues*, ed. Kelly D. Askin and Dorean M. Koenig (Ardsley, NY: Transnational Publishers, Inc., 1999), 31–32. The six conferences were the 1992 "Earth Summit" in Rio, the 1993 World Conference on Human Rights in Vienna, the ICPD in Cairo in 1994, the 1995 World Summit for Social Development in Copenhagen, the Fourth World Conference on Women in Beijing in 1995, and the 1996 Conference on Human Settlements.

8. For scholarship on the formative years of the UN, see Elizabeth Borgwardt, *A New Deal for the World: America's Vision for Human Rights* (Cambridge, MA: The Belknap Press of Harvard University Press, 2005); Micheline R. Ishay, *The History of Human Rights: From Ancient Times to the Globalization Era* (Berkeley: University of California Press, 2004), 174–243; Jack Mahoney, *The Challenge of Human Rights: Origin, Development, and Significance* (Malden, MA: Blackwell Publishing, 2007), 42–53; Marilyn Lake, "From Self-Determination via Protection to Equality via Non-Discrimination: Defining Women's Rights at the League of

Nations and the United Nations," in *Women's Rights and Human Rights: International Historical Perspectives*, ed. Patricia Grimshaw, Katie Holmes, and Marilyn Lake (Houndmills: Palgrave, 2001), 254–71; Stephen C. Schlesinger, *Act of Creation: The Founding of the United Nations* (Boulder, CO: Westview, 2003); M. Glen Johnson, *The Universal Declaration of Human Rights: A History of Its Creation and Implementation, 1948–1998* (Paris: UNESCO Publishers, 1998); Mary Ann Glendon, *A World Made New: Eleanor Roosevelt and the Universal Declaration of Human Rights* (New York: Random House, 2001); A. W. Brian Simpson, "The Road to San Francisco: The Revival of the Human Rights Idea in the Twentieth Century," *Human Rights Quarterly* 14 (1992): 447–77; and Hernandez-Truyol, "Human Rights Through a Gendered Lens," in *Women and International Human Rights Law*, Askin and Koenig, 3–39.

9. These include the Vienna Declaration and Programme of Action, the 1994 Cairo Programme of Action, the Beijing Declaration and Platform for Action, and the Declaration on the Elimination of Violence against Women.

10. Hernandez-Truyol, "Human Rights Through a Gendered Lens" in *Women and International Human Rights Law*, Askin and Koenig, 25–26; Kenneth Cmiel, "The Recent History of Human Rights," *American Historical Review* 109, no. 1 (February 2004): 123.

11. Charter of the United Nations, preamble and Article I, at the UN website, http://www.un.org/en/documents/charter/index.shtml (accessed August 12, 2009); Universal Declaration of Human Rights, http://www.un.org/en/documents/udhr/ (accessed August 12, 2009). The UN Charter declares "the equal rights of men and women" (preamble) and upholds "promoting and encouraging respect for human rights and for fundamental freedoms for all without distinction as to race, sex, language, or religion" (Art. 1). The UDHR declares the equality of all human beings and specifically addresses sex: "Everyone is entitled to all the rights and freedoms set forth in this Declaration, without distinction of any kind, such as race, colour, sex, language, religion, political or other opinion, national or social origin, property, birth or other status" (Art. 2).

12. Boyle, *Female Genital Cutting*, 41.

13. Ibid., 45.

14. Hernandez-Truyol, "Human Rights Through a Gendered Lens," in *Women and International Human Rights Law*, Askin and Koenig, 3.

15. Karen Lindsey, Holly Newman, and Fran Taylor, "Rape: The All American Crime" (1973), in *Dear Sisters: Dispatches from the Women's Liberation Movement*, eds. Rosalyn Baxandall and Linda Gordon (New York: Basic Books, 2000), 195–96; Susan Brownmiller, *Against Our Will: Men, Women, and Rape* (New York: Simon & Schuster, 1975); and Estelle B. Freedman, *No Turning Back: The History of Feminism and the Future of Women* (New York: Ballantine Books, 2002), 276–302.

16. For a good list of the publications available before 1979, see the bibliography in Fran P. Hosken, *The Hosken Report: Genital and Sexual Mutilation of Females*,

4th rev. ed. (Lexington, MA: Women's International Network News, 1993), 429–39. Hereafter Hosken, *Report* (1993).

17. Fran P. Hosken, "A Personal View," in *The Hosken Report: Genital and Sexual Mutilation of Females* (Lexington, MA: Women's International Network News, 1979), 1. Hereafter Hosken, *Report* (1979). Hosken numbers each chapter separately in her report, so I must refer to the chapter title as well as the page number for the purposes of citation.

18. Hosken, "A Personal View," in *Report* (1979), 1–20.

19. Hosken, *Report* (1979); Fran P. Hosken, *Female Sexual Mutilations: The Facts and Proposals for Action* (Lexington, MA: Women's International Network News, 1980); Fran P. Hosken, *The Hosken Report: Genital and Sexual Mutilation of Females*, 3rd rev. ed. (Lexington, MA: Women's International Network News, 1982); Hosken, *Report* (1993).

20. For example, Dr. Nahid Toubia states that she relied upon Hosken's figures when no national studies were available. Nahid Toubia, *Female Genital Mutilation: A Call for Global Action* (New York: RAINBO, 1995), 22.

21. Hosken, "Medical Facts and Summary," in *Report* (1979), 1; and Hosken, "A Personal View," in *Report* (1979), 2.

22. Hosken, "Medical Facts and Summary," in *Report* (1979), 1. As Hosken and many subsequent anti-FGM activists have pointed out, the male equivalent of female "circumcision," even the mildest form, would involve partial or total amputation of the penis.

23. Hosken, foreword to her *Report* (1979), 2, 4.

24. Hosken, "Medical Facts and Summary," in *Report* (1979), 1.

25. For example, see Mary Daly, *Gyn/Ecology: The Metaethics of Radical Feminism* (Boston: Beacon Press, 1978); and Gerda Lerner, *The Creation of Patriarchy* (New York: Oxford University Press, 1986).

26. Hosken, foreword to her *Report* (1979), 1–2.

27. Ibid., 6.

28. Hosken, "A Personal View," in *Report* (1979), 1.

29. Hosken, "The Politics of Genital Mutilation," in *Report* (1979), 12.

30. Margaret Jean Hay, review of *The Hosken Report: Genital and Sexual Mutilation of Females* in *International Journal of African Historical Studies* 14, no. 3 (1981): 523–26.

31. Robin Morgan and Gloria Steinem, "The International Crime of Genital Mutilation," *Ms.*, March 1980, 65–67, 98, 100; Nawal El Saadawi, "The Question No One Would Answer," *Ms.*, March 1980, 68–69; Gloria Steinem and Robin Morgan to Fran Hosken, March 26, 1980, letters to *Ms.*, 1972–1980, Schlesinger Library, Radcliffe Institute, Harvard University. The dispute between Hosken and *Ms.* arose because, when Hosken heard the magazine was considering running a piece on FGM, she proposed that she be the author. She was insulted when Morgan and Steinem decided to write the articles themselves, and she objected when they included El Saadawi's article rather than focus on Hosken's campaign. Hosken

objected to El Saadawi's socialist politics and accused her of being a "tool of the PLO." Steinem and Morgan to Hosken, March 26, 1980, letters to *Ms.*, 1972–1980, Schlesinger Library, Radcliffe Institute, Harvard University; Fran Hosken to Gloria Steinem, May 28, 1979, Gloria Steinem Papers, 1940–2000, Sophia Smith Collection, Smith College.

32. Hosken, "Personal View," in *Report* (1979), 5. Hosken, "Health Facts and Overview," in *Report* (1993), 1.

33. World Health Organization, "Seminar on Traditional Practices Affecting the Health of Women and Children," February 10–15, 1979, A/CONF.94/BP/9, microfiche, Women's Rights Collection, 1789–2000, Sophia Smith Collection, Smith College.

34. For example, see Nawal El Saadawi, *The Hidden Face of Eve: Women in the Arab World* (London: Zed Press, 1980); Olayinka Koso-Thomas, *The Circumcision of Women: A Strategy for Eradication* (London: Zed Books, 1987); Hanny Lightfoot-Klein, *Prisoners of Ritual: An Odyssey into Female Genital Circumcision in Africa* (New York: Haworth Press, 1989); Raqiya Haji Dualeh Abdalla, *Sisters in Affliction: Circumcision and Infibulation of Women in Africa* (New York: Zed Books, 1982); Blaine Harden, "Africans Keep Rite of Girls' Circumcision," *Washington Post*, July 13, 1985, A12, A13; and Margaret Strobel, "African Women," *Signs* 8, no. 1 (Autumn 1982): 109–31.

35. Nawal El Saadawi, quoted in Tiffany Patterson and Angela Gillam, "Out of Egypt: A Talk with Nawal El Saadawi," *Freedomways* 23, no. 3 (1983): 190–91.

36. Maggie Jones, "African Women Must Speak Out on Circumcision," *Forum80*, July 21, 1980, 2, International Women's Tribune Centre Records, Sophia Smith Collection, Smith College (hereafter IWTC, Smith).

37. Gorgia Dullea, "Female Circumcision a Topic at U.N. Parley," *New York Times*, July 18, 1980, B4.

38. Jones, "African Women Must Speak Out on Circumcision," 2.

39. AAWORD, "A Statement on Genital Mutilation," in *Third World, Second Sex: Women's Struggles and National Liberation*, vol. 1, ed. Miranda Davies (London: Zed Press, 1983), 217–20; and Dullea, "Female Circumcision a Topic at U.N. Parley," B4.

40. Gertrud Anljung, letter to the editor, *Forum80*, July 22, 1980, 7, IWTC, Smith.

41. Nadia Atif, "Workshops: Circumcision," *Forum '85*, July 15, 1985, 6, microfiche, IWTC, Smith.

42. Nadia Hijab, "Attempting to Tackle a Sensitive Issue," *Forum '85*, July 25, 1985: 2, microfiche. IWTC, Smith.

43. For example, one hundred participants from twenty countries met in Dakar, Senegal, for the 1984 Seminar on Traditional Practices Affecting the Health of Women and Children in Africa, sponsored by WHO, UNICEF, and the UNFPA. It was there that the Inter-African Committee was formed. International Women's Studies Institute, "A Report and Recommendation Based on Selected Sessions of

the 1985 NGO Forum Held in Conjunction with the U.N. Conference on Women," 95–97. IWTC, Smith.

44. For example, French colonialists justified their domination of Algeria by pointing to the oppression of Algerian women. Franz Fanon, *A Dying Colonialism* (New York: Grove Press, 1965), 23–68; Todd Shepard, *Inventing Decolonization: The Algerian War and the Remaking of France* (Ithaca, NY: Cornell University Press, 2006), 186–89; and Hal Lehrman, "Battle of the Veil in Algeria," *New York Times Sunday Magazine*, June 13, 1958, SM14–SM16.

45. Boyle, *Female Genital Cutting*, 48.

46. Christina M. Cerna and Jennifer C. Wallace, "Women and Culture" in *Women and International Human Rights Law*, vol. 1, Askin and Koeing, 626; Mahnaz Afkhami, "Cultural Relativism and Women's Human Rights," in *Women and International Human Rights Law*, vol. 2: *International Courts, Instruments, and Organizations and Select Regional Issues Affecting Women*, ed. Kelly D. Askin and Dorean M. Koenig (Ardsley, NY: Transnational Publishers, Inc., 2000), 481; and Mahanz Afkhami, introduction to *Faith and Freedom: Women's Human Rights in the Muslim World* (Syracuse, NY: Syracuse University Press, 1995), 3.

47. Afkhami, "Cultural Relativism," 481.

48. Toubia, *Female Genital Mutilation*, 9–10.

49. Ibid., 14.

50. Ibid., 14–15. For firsthand accounts of infibulation, see Ayaan Hirsi Ali, *Infidel* (New York: Free Press, 2007); Fadumo Korn, *Born in the Big Rains: A Memoir of Somalia and Survival,* with Sabine Eichhorst (New York: The Feminist Press, 2006); and Waris Dirie, *Desert Flower: The Extraordinary Journey of a Desert Nomad,* with Cathleen Miller (New York: William Morrow and Company, Inc., 1998).

51. Toubia, *Female Genital Mutilation,* 5; and Nahid Toubia, "Female Circumcision as a Public Health Issue," *The New England Journal of Medicine* 331, no. 11 (September 15, 1994): 712–16. There are no exact figures available for the number of deaths caused by FGM each year, although most believe a considerable number of women and girls have died as a result of complications of various genital cutting procedures. The author of "Razor's Edge—The Controversy of Female Genital Mutilation" writes, "It is difficult to determine the actual numbers of women who die from FGM-related complications, given the highly guarded nature of the practice. Medical record-keeping systems are also rarely configured to record FGM and FGM-related complications as causes of death." IRIN (Integrated Regional Information Networks), a project of the UN Office for the Coordination of Humanitarian Affairs, "Razor's Edge—The Controversy of Female Genital Mutilation," http://www.irinnews.org/ (accessed August 24, 2009).

52. The Voltaic Women's Federation was created by women from Upper Volta, now known as the country of Burkina Faso.

53. Toubia, *Global Action.*

54. Cerna and Wallace, "Women and Culture," in *Women and International Human Rights Law*, Askin and Koeing, 646.

55. Boyle, *Female Genital Cutting*, 136–51. While many Muslim practitioners believe that FGM is required by their religion, there is no reference to FGM in the Koran.

56. Ibid., 51.

57. Charlotte Bunch and Niamh Reilly, *Demanding Accountability: The Global Campaign and Vienna Tribunal for Women's Human Rights* (New Brunswick, NJ: Center for Women's Global Leadership, 1994), 10–13. The Global Campaign was co-sponsored by the CWGL, Asian Women's Human Rights Council, Austrian Women's Human Rights Working Group, Feminist International Radio Endeavor (FIRE), Human Rights Watch Women's Project, International Women's Tribune Centre (IWTC), ISIS International, the United Nations Development Fund for Women (UNIFEM), Women in Law and Development in Africa (WiLDAF), and Women Living Under Muslim Laws (WLUML).

58. Ibid., 10–11.

59. Ibid., 4–5, 103. The 16 Days of Activism begin on November 25, the International Day Against Violence Against Women and end December 10, International Human Rights Day. Their petition drive succeeded in collecting a half-million signatures by June 1993.

60. Ibid., 14–16. The judges included Gertrude Mongella, secretary-general of the UN Fourth World Conference on Women, Justice P.N. Bhagawati, former chief justice of the Supreme Court of India, Ed Broadbent, former Canadian MP and president of the International Centre for Human Rights and Democratic Development, and Elizabeth Odio, the minister of justice in Costa Rica and member of the UN Committee Against Torture.

61. Ibid., 11.

62. Nahid Toubia, statement during "Violations of Bodily Integrity" session of the Global Tribunal on Violations of Women's Human Rights, Vienna, June 15, 1993, in *Testimonies of the Global Tribunal on Violations of Women's Human Rights at the United Nations World Conference on Human Rights*, ed. Niamh Reilly (New Brunswick, NJ: Center for Women's Global Leadership, 1994), 45–47.

63. International Women's Tribune Centre, *Rights of Women: A Guide to the Most Important United Nations Treaties on Women's Human Rights* (New York: Women, Ink., 1998), 92.

64. "Report of the Global Tribunal on Violations of Women's Human Rights," in *Demanding Accountability*, Bunch and Reilly, 132.

65. UN General Assembly, "Vienna Declaration and Programme of Action," July 12, 1993, A/CONF.157/23, Section I, para. 18; Section II, para. 36–37, United Nations High Commissioner for Human Rights, http://www.unhchr.ch/huridocda/huridoca.nsf/(Symbol)/A.CONF.157.23.En (accessed October 8, 2008).

66. Ibid., Section II, para. 38.

67. Boyle, *Female Genital Cutting*, 53.

68. Ibid., 56.

69. Ibid., 55.

70. Alice Walker, *Possessing the Secret of Joy* (New York: Washington Square Press, 1992); Gloria Naylor, *Bailey's Café* (New York: Vintage Books, 1992).

71. See for example, A. M. Rosenthal, "Female Genital Torture," *New York Times*, December 29, 1992, A15; Rosenthal, "The Torture Continues," *New York Times*, July 27, 1993, A13; Rosenthal, "The Possible Dream," *New York Times*, June 13, 1995, A25; and transcript of "Scarred for Life," *Day One*, ABC News, September 20, 1993.

72. Samia Nakhoul, "U.N. Conference Draws Cairo Criticism," *Philadelphia Inquirer,* August 17, 1994, A9; Conor Cruise O'Brien, "A Holy and Explosive Alliance," *The Independent* (London), August 26, 1994, 16; Eugene Linden, "Showdown in Cairo: A Feminist Agenda at Next Week's Population Conference Stirs Protests," *Time*, September 5, 1994, 52; and Christine Gorman, "Clash of Wills in Cairo," *Time*, September 12, 1994, 56.

73. UN, "Report of the International Conference on Population and Development," October 14, 1994, A/CONF.171/13, para. 7.35.

74. Ibid., para. 7.40.

75. Boyle, *Female Genital Cutting*, 3.

76. Mann, "When Journalists Witness Atrocities."

77. See, for example, Barbara Crossette, "Female Genital Mutilation by Immigrants Is Becoming Cause for Concern in US," *New York Times*, December 10, 1995, http://www.nytimes.com/ (accessed November 28, 2008); Linda Burstyn, "Female Circumcision Comes to America," *The Atlantic*, October 1995, http://www.theatlantic.com/unbound/flashbks/fgm/fgm.htm (accessed November 28, 2008); Bettina Shell-Duncan and Ylva Hernlund, eds., *Female "Circumcision" in Africa: Culture, Controversy, and Change* (Boulder, CO: Lynne Rienner Publishers, 2000); Rosemarie Skaine, *Female Genital Mutilation: Legal Cultural, and Medical Issues* (Jefferson, NC: MacFarland & Co., 2005); Obioma Nnaemeka, ed., *Female Circumcision and the Politics of Knowledge: African Women in Imperialist Discourses* (Westport, CT: Praeger, 2005); and Stanlie M. James and Claire C. Robertson, *Genital Cutting and Transnational Sisterhood: Disputing U.S. Polemics* (Urbana: University of Illinois Press, 2002).

78. Mann, "When Journalists Witness Atrocities."

79. Smolowe, "A Rite of Passage—or Mutilation?" 65; and Boyle, *Female Genital Cutting*, 5.

80. Senator Harry Reid, speaking on September 21, 1994, to express the sense of the Senate condemning the cruel and tortuous practice of female genital mutilation, S. Res 263, 103rd Cong. 2nd sess., *Congressional Record*, 140, pt. 133: 140 Cong. Rec. S. 13100, page 2 of 5 (from LexisNexis Congressional, accessed October 2, 2008).

81. Anika Rahman and Nahid Toubia, eds., *Female Genital Mutilation: A Guide to Laws and Policies Worldwide* (London: Zed Books, 2000), 237. However, the U.S. Agency for International Development (USAID) began to provide assistance to prevent FGM in Africa in 1993, and, after the public outcry over FGM that

followed the Cairo conference, USAID formed a Working Group in 1994 to integrate efforts to eradicate FGM into existing reproductive health programs (Rahman and Toubia, 240).

82. Reid's bill was co-sponsored by Senator Carol Moseley-Braun (D-IL) and Senator Paul Wellstone (D-MN), while Rep. Constance Morella (R-MD) co-sponsored Schroeder's bill in the House.

83. Senator Carol Moseley-Braun, speaking on introduced bills and joint resolutions, 103rd Cong. 2nd sess., *Congressional Record*, 140 Cong. Rec. S. 14244, page 6 of 9 (from LexisNexis Congressional, accessed October 2, 2008).

84. U.S. Congress *Omnibus Consolidated Appropriations Act of 1997*, HR 3610, September 30, 1996, Pub. L. 104–208, 110 Stat. 3009, 104th Cong., 2nd sess.: sec. 579, 645. The law identifies "international financial institutions" as the International Bank for Reconstruction and Development, the Inter-American Development Bank, the Asian Development Bank, the Asian Development Fund, the African Development Bank, the African Development Fund, the International Monetary Fund, the North American Development Bank, and the European Bank for Reconstruction and Development (sec. 352(b)).

85. "House Passes Schroeder Resolution on Female Genital Mutilation," *Congressional Press Releases*, June 7, 1995.

86. Rahman and Toubia, *Female Genital Mutilation*, 237.

87. "In re: Fauziya Kasinga, Applicant," Interim Decision #3278, File A73 476 695—Elizabeth, Decided June 13, 1996, U.S. Department of Justice, Executive Office for Immigration Review, Board of Immigration Appeals: 1–22; Corinne A. Kratz, "Seeking Asylum, Debating Values, and Setting Precedents in the 1990s: The Cases of Kassindja and Abankwah in the United States," in *Transcultural Bodies: Female Genital Cutting in Global Context*, ed. Ylva Hernlund and Bettina Shell-Duncan (New Brunswick, NJ: Rutgers University Press, 2007), 167–201; Charles Piot, "Representing Africa in the Kasinga Asylum Case," in *Transcultural Bodies*, Hernlund and Shell-Duncan, 157–66; Equality Now, "Women's Action 9.3," June 1996, http://www.equalitynow.org/english/actions/action_0903_en.html (accessed June 18, 2008); Celia W. Dugger, "Woman's Plea for Asylum Puts Tribal Ritual on Trial," *New York Times*, April 15, 1996, A1, B4; Pamela Constable, "INS Says Mutilation Claim May Be Basis for Asylum," *Washington Post*, April 24, 1996, A3; and Patricia D. Rudloff, "In Re Oluloro: Risk of Female Genital Mutilation as 'Extreme Hardship' in Immigration Proceedings," *St. Mary's Law Journal* 26 (1995): 877.

88. Rahman and Toubia, *Female Genital Mutilation,* 101–41.

89. A Malian woman was allowed to stay in France under a humanitarian exception to French asylum law, see Bronwyn Winter, "Women, the Law, and Cultural Relativism in France: The Case of Excision" *Signs* 19 (1994): 939. A Somali woman was given refugee status in Canada after she fled there to prevent her daughter's infibulation, see Clyde Farnsworth, "Canada Gives a Somali Mother Refugee Status," *New York Times*, July 21, 1994, A14. Fauziya Kasindja was granted political asylum in a precedent-setting case in the United States in 1996 because she feared

she would be subjected to FGM if sent home to Togo, and Lydia Oluloro of Nigeria received asylum so that she could protect her two daughters from undergoing FGM if sent back home. For these two cases, see note 87.

90. IWTC, *Rights of Women,* 64; and Isabelle R. Gunning, "Female Genital Surgeries: Eradication Measures at the Western Local Level—A Cautionary Tale," in *Genital Cutting and Transnational Sisterhood,* James and Robertson, 114–25.

91. "Man Sentenced for Mutilating Daughter," *Washington Post,* November 2, 2006, A2.

92. Nahid Toubia, for example, uses the term "female genital mutilation." See Toubia, *Call for Global Action.* See also Skaine, *Female Genital Mutilation.* Others, however, still use the term "female circumcision." See Nnaemeka, *Female Circumcision and the Politics of Knowledge:* and Shell-Duncan and Hernlund, *Female "Circumcision" in Africa.* Still others prefer the terms "female genital surgeries" and "female genital cutting." See James and Robertson, *Genital Cutting and Transnational Sisterhood*; Gunning, "Female Genital Surgeries" in *Genital Cutting and Transnational Sisterhood,* James and Robertson; and Boyle, *Female Genital Cutting.*

14

IS HISTORY A HUMAN RIGHT?

Japan and Korea's Troubles with the Past

ALEXIS DUDDEN

Since the mid-twentieth century, when international war crimes tribunals established the precedent that an individual or a group acting on behalf of a nation could be found guilty of state-sponsored atrocities, victims of such violence have desired official apologies as part of the redress for the wrongs committed against them. Even so, it was not axiomatic that such apologies would become the integral part of human rights discourse that they are today. Victims and their supporters pitched themselves against their own and/or foreign governments to bring about state apologies, making official apology not simply a worthy goal, but something considered by many as a human right. When a government apologizes in some form, victims and their supporters count it as a real achievement. Such apologies, therefore, fuel an ongoing commitment for more, and official statements of sorrow and regret for past atrocities have become indispensable components in legitimating human rights issues in national histories.

In many respects, the 1990s were a decade of international apology politics. Around the world, an outpouring of national remorse for historical atrocities came to shape the language of Germany, Argentina, the United States, South Africa, and Japan. There is even a "Sorry Day" in Australia to draw attention to the country's past treatment of its aboriginal people. It has become increasingly clear, however, that presidents and prime ministers address historical atrocities to reinforce their own present claims to legitimacy. Relying on formulaic expressions for the past, world leaders describe historical events in future-oriented words that work around the content of the histories at stake. Moreover, as they apologize for wrongs considered abnormal to the international community's current collective sense of self—racial extermination, slavery, apartheid—they inscribe new histories for the pasts in question. As an historian of the Middle East, Ilan Pappe, observed, such approaches to the past can so rework the content of the historic events involved that they "eliminate" the past from history.[1]

Official apologies most often refer to events that have been muted within the larger sweep of a nation's history—the incarceration of Japanese-Americans during the Second World War, for example, before President George H. W. Bush signed the U.S. government's apology. At the same time, however, the apologies almost never refer specifically to victims' individual histories, let alone their dignity.[2] Once a national leader makes an apology, societies can incorporate the victims' past into broader, collective, forward-moving narratives, ultimately reconfiguring the same sort of progressive tale that existed before the victims' voices were heard. In anthropologist Richard Wilson's provocative phrasing, victims can, thus, lose the "human right to a human history" as the story is taken out of their hands.[3] In the early twenty-first century climate of political apology and redress, therefore, the individual stories that make up the histories of past atrocities stand precariously close to extinction because the state's narrators have massaged the histories to fit their own purposes of national narration.

The whole issue of apology is rife with contradiction. For some victims, no apology will ever suffice. However, demands for state-level apologies escalated in the late twentieth century, and many people around the world demanded apologies for the historical atrocities they survived—from former U.S. soldiers suffering the effects of Agent Orange to former sex slaves of the Japanese empire.[4] Once official statements of sorrow and regret are uttered, however, many victims and their supporters describe them as fake or lacking in real meaning, raising the problem of who should decide when an apology is real. Moreover, because apology is part of international law, the statements often come with cash compensations or reparations, leading others to say that victims are only in it for the money. Of course, only the privileged members of society—not necessarily economically privileged, but those privileged by race or gender or ethnicity as well—can find venues to say such things publicly. The ongoing debate concerning apologies and reparations to African Americans for slavery in the United States makes this abundantly clear—even mentioning the issue encourages some politicians to say things that would get others fired from their jobs.[5]

Examining apologies from the perpetrators' and the victims' perspectives—as well as that of their descendants—reveals a society's various anxieties over coming to terms with the past and also allows for the victims' voices to be heard.[6] At the same time, it is essential to notice that governments use the script of apology politics for their own purposes because the writing of history itself is disturbed as a result of this phenomenon. Official apologies now move so easily in and out of long-standing practices of apologetic history that not taking a stand on certain issues—the Rape of Nanjing, for example—can wind up aligning the historian with the state in complicating the victim's right to his or her own history.

This uncomfortable tension came into relief most clearly in East Asia during the late twentieth century, where long-quiet voices seemingly burst out of nowhere in the wake of wartime emperor Hirohito's 1989 death and demanded public recognition for their long-denied histories.[7] Widely known examples include the former sex slaves of the Japanese military, and laborers and soldiers forcibly enslaved or conscripted from throughout the empire Japan maintained during the first half of the twentieth century.

The apparent freshness of these stories in Japan during the 1990s underscores a significant difference from the post-1945 history of victims' claims and movements for redress in Germany. Although it has been persuasively and intelligently argued that too much has been made of Hitler's own responsibility in German historiography, in Japan, the leader of the wartime state—Hirohito—remained on the throne for nearly a half-century after the war ended, generating the opposite condition. Japan's postwar environment was, in effect, framed by the American government's decision not to try the emperor as a war criminal in the 1940s and, at the other end, by the 1989 death of the emperor. In between, an unusual situation existed that was known as the "chrysanthemum taboo."[8] The chrysanthemum is the symbol of the emperor and the imperial family, and the "taboo" is commonly understood as the inability of Japan's public sphere to assess the roles of the emperor and the imperial institution in and responsibility for the Japanese empire (1895–1945), Japan's wars in Asia and the Pacific (1931–1945), and the suffering therein.[9] With Hirohito's death, the silence was officially broken, touching off a public airing of the state's historical victims' narratives and placing the—now strangely irreconcilable—issue of Hirohito's responsibility for the suffering at the center of the debate, where it remains more than two decades later.

Moreover, many of the areas in Asia that Japan colonized only began to foster the conditions necessary for victims' groups to make public claims in the mid-1980s or later. Thus, the coincidence that Hirohito died just as Japan's former colonies offered new liberties to their people (North Korea and Myanmar remained wholly undemocratized in this regard)— not to mention that the Cold War was over—sparked the wave of victims' stories heard and published in the 1990s. Not insignificantly, despite the time lag in most instances, many victims were still alive to make the claims themselves.

During the past two decades, therefore, the Japanese government's response to victims of its empire and wars has made the transnational practice of national apology a centerpiece of regional and national politics.[10] There are quite literally hundreds of thousands of websites throughout Asia and North America that track and measure Japan's official statements of redress. By current estimates, the Japanese government has issued at least twenty statements of "regret" and "heartfelt apology" for the past. Such political practices now dovetail with subfields of modern history to the extent that "war responsibility studies" is a commonplace discipline in its own right and "colonial responsibility studies" is the latest development. Mainstream bookstores now devote sections to these categories, journals specialize in these topics, and the questions and controversies have generated a discourse so familiar that catch phrases stand in for entire discussions. Even the most cautious observers acknowledge that Japan's "textbook problem"—the debate over what empire and wartime events should be included in Japanese government-approved school books and how they are described—is one of the most volatile issues in the region, and the matter of apology for the past remains central to intraregional affairs.

The Rhetoric of Apology

Edwin O. Reischauer (1910–1990) was one of the world's most influential commentators on Japanese society to emerge in the post-1945 era. Reischauer's power derived from his status as an American ambassador to Tokyo during critical moments of high economic growth, his long-standing position as professor of Japanese civilization and director of the Yenching Institute at Harvard University, and his youth spent in Tokyo before the war as the child of missionaries. Regardless of why Reischauer was so commanding—or because of it—during his time as ambassador to Japan in the early 1960s, he engraved the formula for official apology into Japanese political rhetoric, the terms of which inexorably remain in play to this day, embedding him and the United States within apology discussions.

In 1964, as negotiations to establish diplomatic relations between Japan and South Korea continued, Reischauer expressed his belief that the Japanese government should do something to acknowledge Korean resentment over the era of Japanese occupation (1905–1945). In November 1964, he sent a telegram to Secretary of State Dean Rusk to report on a meeting with Japan's Foreign Minister Shiina Etsusaburo during which he urged Japan to make "some sort of apology to Koreans for colonial past."[11] Shiina's secretary responded by stating that the foreign minister's physical appearance in Seoul would come "as close to expression of apology as was feasible," to which Reischauer responded favorably and added that "some sort of forward-facing statement about turning backs on past unhappy history . . . might assuage Koreans' feelings without irritating Japanese public." Within months, Japan's foreign minister said these same words—in Japanese—on the ground in Seoul.[12]

In practical terms, Reischauer's rhetorical formula of sorrow and regret neatly froze the past into an indeterminate time period for which no one was—or is—to blame. Democratic states that rely, however, on such "forward-facing" discursive strategies at the expense of dignifying the specificity of the histories involved nonetheless humiliate survivors of atrocity—whether their own nationals or foreigners—by saying, in effect: "That was then, this is now, and your past must be swallowed for the benefit of the present at your expense." The state does not necessarily or straightforwardly deny the past, yet its victims are left with no option for protest as they run in circles in courts of the state's creation that ultimately remain indifferent to their claims.

During the 1990s, Japan's so-called miracle economy collapsed and began to be restructured, making leaders debate Japan's national interests anew in light of the country's stated aspiration to be a "normal" country in the international system, which many in Tokyo defined as a nation with a permanent UN Security Council seat and a proactive, deployable military (still technically illegal under the country's constitution). Japan's apologies to its former colonies and wartime adversaries in Asia blended into these other concerns, revealing the apologies importance to Japan's national-interests conundrum. Put simply, leaders decided it was in Japan's national interests to apologize in some measure—and so they did—because doing so maintained the status quo in terms of Japan's ties with its Asian neighbors.

Whether official apology will continue with the saliency it has had since the mid-1990s remains to be seen, but it is arguably unlikely. In August 2005, commemorating the sixtieth anniversary of Japan's defeat in World War II, then Prime Minister Koizumi Junichiro issued yet another official apology for Japan's past. Many noticed right away that Koizumi used an international setting to add weight to this apology—an aid forum in Jakarta rather than a setting in Japan. Many also noticed, though, that Koizumi did not say anything beyond what former Prime Minister Murayama Tomoichi inscribed in 1995, marking the fiftieth anniversary, regardless of the literally thousands of publications concerning atrocities and victims' claims that had appeared during the intervening decade. With many hoping for more, there was a collective sense of a step back, or worse.

Quoting the Murayama declaration (as it is known) almost to the comma breath, Koizumi stated:

> In the past, Japan, through its colonial rule and aggression, caused tremendous damage and suffering to the people of many countries, particularly those of Asian nations. Sincerely facing these facts of history, I once again express my feelings of deep remorse and heartfelt apology, and also express the feelings of mourning for all victims, both at home and abroad, in the war. I am determined not to allow the lessons of that horrible war to erode, and to contribute to the peace and prosperity of the world without ever again waging a war.[13]

These sentiments continue to be the litmus test. When former Prime Minister Hatoyama Yukio won his historic victory in 2009, bringing the party in opposition for over fifty years into the position of power, he, too, immediately vowed to "uphold the Murayama declaration." Thus these phrases—deemed safe for Japanese national interests domestically and regarded as tepid but acceptable by regional governments—hold steady at the official level while continuing to rankle those who demanded the apologies in the first place. They find the words woefully inadequate, if not disingenuous. Their frustration, anger, and sadness underscore the divide between the state's formula and what sufferers and their supporters believe constitutes a real apology for their individually lived histories. The problem continues its complex hold on the region, while the number of surviving victims, who can make claims for the history they believe is their right, quickly decreases.

The current state formula for apology has largely fallen short because its scriptwriters often find themselves so deeply ensconced within prevailing national myths that they cannot tell enough of the truth to make the apology hold. However, what those seeking apology in the first place are seeking is dignity within the narrative eliding or maligning them in the first place. In other words, they want inclusion in—not exclusion from—the history that would write them off.

When Japan's historical victims, for example the former comfort women, refused Tokyo's statements and continued their demands for what they called a real apology—or an apology they considered meaningful—critics complained that Japan had already apologized numerous times, and, there-fore, the victims were certainly in it only for the money. State narrators now openly discuss the victims' history—a history that was denied in Japan at the highest levels until the 1990s—yet none of them has to take responsi-bility for the history involved, let alone the victims' current dignity, or lack thereof. In this respect, the state is made stronger from without and within because it has displayed an amount of remorse accepted by the international community, yet it has not had to fundamentally redefine itself.

On March 1, 2007, despite years of reporting in the news, Japan's then prime minister Abe Shinzo denied the comfort women's history saying, "The fact is there is no evidence to prove there was coercion."[14] By denying "coercion," Abe denied Japanese governmental responsibility for the forced enslavement of women and girls into the notorious—and by 2007 well documented—system of sexual slavery that involved an estimated 80,000–200,000 victims from throughout Asia, particularly Korea and China. Thus, he challenged the few remaining survivors of a well-documented history to their right to claim the dignity that came as a result of telling their story and since 1993 when the government of Japan first publicly accepted responsi-bility. Many predicted that Abe would do something along those lines when he assumed office in September 2006—watching for his slip up almost became sport due to his track record regarding the contours of the Kono statement, which has provided the baseline terminology for Japan's official acceptance of the comfort women's history since 1993. It is of a piece with the Murayama declaration, yet specifically focused because its author, Kono Yohei, was a cabinet secretary, not prime minister, and thus freer to address particular histories. Abe's statements provided a swell of condem-nation around the world for Japan's recalcitrance, yet a full-page ad in the *Washington Post* in June 2007 paid for by right-wing Japanese politicians and their supporters pushed matters over the edge, at least as far as the court of global opinion was concerned.[15]

Throughout this time, the U.S. House of Representatives was consid-ering adopting a nonbinding resolution urging Japan to apologize for its wartime aggression and to the comfort women in particular. Congress regu-larly passes these opinion pieces, especially where human rights issues are concerned. Supporters of the comfort women had repeatedly asked for a resolution regarding the matter and had repeatedly failed for numerous rea-sons, not the least of which were the significance to Washington of the ability to station fifty thousand American troops on Japanese soil, or the routine payments from the Japanese Foreign Ministry to Washington lobby firms to keep issues of Japanese history off the discussion docket. However, during the summer of 2007, continuing to cover up the issue proved impossible for many U.S. congressmen because official Japanese statements were sounding eerily close to "Holocaust denial," as numerous representatives asserted. On the one hand, statements afforded some measure of dignity to the victims, on the other hand, the statements perpetuated the comfort women's challenge of trying to have their history in their terms, not forever in reference to another or for reasons of state interests.

Despite all of Japan's protests, nonbinding House Resolution 121 passed. Afterward, Japan's ambassador to Washington sent several extremely pointed letters to congressional leaders, and Japan's parliament weighed the possibility (and still does) of passing counter-resolutions—but, for the time being, nothing has really changed. In January 2010, the ever-dwindling number of surviving comfort women held their nine hundredth consecutive weekly sit-in (begun in January 1992) in front of the Japanese embassy in Seoul demanding an apology on their terms—both an imperial one and parliamentary one for most—and for their story to be credited as part of Japanese history. Without doing so, they believe, what will be lost with their ultimate deaths is what was lost during the half-century of silence that followed the Pacific War: the women themselves. Never mind how many times they have had to tell their deeply painful stories in public to gain credibility. Never mind how many times they have had to lift their shirts in public to show the scars of breasts lopped off by angry Japanese soldiers during rapes committed over a half-century ago, or to show gashes across their stomachs where army doctors cut out unborn children. Never mind those who went to their graves in silence. Japan's leaders are clear: these women and their histories are disposable.

Enduring Struggles

Although the comfort women gained the most international recognition, the disregard they face is of a piece with another group fighting for the right to tell their story. Hitting the papers on December 25, 2009, was the story of seven Korean women in their 70s and 80s who discovered 99 yen (a little less than one dollar) deposited in their bank accounts a week earlier from the Japanese government's Social Insurance Agency.[16] In 1998, the women had begun one of the many lawsuits, formed with supportive Japanese lawyers, against Japanese corporations and/or the Japanese government seeking compensation for their wartime labor. Like other plaintiffs, the women lost in court on grounds of insubstantial evidence, yet 99 yen appeared in their bank accounts when their names magically materialized on wartime government pension records. In short, the women would appear to have won their claim to telling the truth. Their compensation was so bizarrely out of touch with today's value for this money, however, that the victory seemed like a greater defeat, and worse, a further insult. Demonstrations ensued, first in front of the Japanese embassy in Seoul, where the elderly women threw their bodies on the winter ground, wailing and throwing coins in bewildered rage at the high wall surrounding the embassy. In front of the Mitsubishi Heavy Industries factory farther south in Gwangju, their support group leader, Lee Kuk-eon, cried: "During the colonial period, 99 yen covered the cost of two calves. Now it buys two packs of ramen!"[17]

From the late 1930s to 1945, millions of Korean and Chinese were physically forced, or duped, into going to Japan where they became slave labor. The women who made headlines in December 2009 were tricked in October 1944 by teachers at their middle school in Korea into going to Nagoya, where they believed they would attend high school. They found themselves instead working in wretched conditions for no pay at a Mitsubishi airplane factory until August 1945 when Japan's defeat set them free. Mitsubishi contended it had no record of these women, yet thanks to modernity's pathological obsession with recording itself, part of the pay the women never received was transferred into a national pension insurance system where their names would ultimately be remembered. The then newly established Social Insurance Agency (1942) received monthly cuts via corporations of workers' salaries, Japanese and foreign alike (as it does today), which, at the time, were often unknown to the workers (conditions not so dissimilar today), especially to the foreigners, working under what today would easily be called illegal and/or enslaved conditions.

Beginning in 2004, the South Korean government of then President Roh Moo-hyun established a Truth Commission to deal with the still lingering problem of Koreans forced into labor in wartime Japan, simultaneously establishing a domestic fund for Korean citizens in Korea making the claims. The commission made its work and demands known to the Japanese government, including the information that 40,000 of the 160,000 people who had filed claims with the commission mentioned the pension insurance payments. Although the powers that be in Japan maintained they had no records of the seven women who drew attention last year—as well as the thousands upon thousands of others—all of a sudden in mid-December 2009 the 99 yen appeared in the seven Korean women's bank accounts. Then, with even greater suddenness, back in Japan a week later, the *Asahi* newspaper reported that the government's Social Insurance Agency confirmed the names of

4,727 Koreans on its wartime roster, including the seven women who among thousands of others had worked at Mitsubishi.[18]

The Social Insurance Agency's revelation was enormous by Japanese standards, but, because the acknowledgement opens up many possibilities of tangible legal accountability, most in Japan avoid its public discussion. On top of it all, the current South Korean government of President Lee Myung-bak remained silent on the women's plight, thus bringing into stark relief the problem in South Korea of how the direction of Koreans' individual histories with Japan heavily depend on domestic politics in Seoul and ties with Japanese big business—especially when the stories revolve around those deemed relatively expendable.

In January 2008, when President Lee Myung-bak took office he announced that history—whatever it was—would not impede Korea's future. The most attention-getting of his initial remarks was that he would not ask Japan to apologize for the so-called past, unlike almost everyone else in South Korean political life since the nation's founding in 1948. President Lee wanted smooth economic relations above all and, with an eye to assuring friends in Tokyo and in his party, he declared an end to South Korea's government commissions investigating so-called collaborationist activities during the Japanese colonial era.

What Lee failed to understand at the beginning of his presidency, however, was the powerful way that South Korea's dictators from 1945 through the early 1990s had implanted Japan as a foil to legitimate themselves within South Korea on top of Koreans' lived memories of the pre-1945 era. For example, even as the former South Korean president-dictator Park Chung-hee accepted his (now documented) bags full of cash from Tokyo as part of the 1965 normalization of relations package, he and his cronies fostered anti-Japanese movements within the student protests in Seoul—which President Lee had participated in—to distract the South Korean people from the terms of the official agreement that declared the past settled between Japan and South Korea. For generations after Japan's occupation of Korea ended in 1945, creating and sustaining an "illegal" Japan made "legal" those who ruled South Korea by nefarious means, or at least that was the government's version of events.

Democratization movements in the 1980s and 1990s changed this in South Korea. Since 2008, although President Lee has derailed some of the truth-seeking commissions concerning the colonial era and has made it difficult for commissions examining more recent pasts to function freely, he and his administration have come to better understand that simply telling Koreans not to ask Japan to apologize or to seek redress from Japanese corporations will fail unless they silence the people's voices. The unre-solved legacies of the first half of the twentieth century with Japan are sim-ply too fraught to wish away in the name of business and diplomacy. Thus, although President Lee has switched course from the policies of his prede-cessors, Kim Dae-Jun and Roh Moo-hyun, and into the well-worn Cold War contours of containing history with its approved heroes and martyrs like An Jung-gun (who shot Japan's first colonial ruler in 1909) and Queen Min (whom Japanese soldiers assassinated in 1895), he and his administration will have to advocate on behalf of citizens such as the old women, however begrudgingly. The Mitsubishi women's story makes for sticky business with Tokyo because they and the other survivors of the Japanese colonial era who rail against Japan today have been abandoned by Seoul and Tokyo's Washington-orchestrated 1965 normalization agreement that launched busi-ness as usual in the first place.

In short, the women's story might once again have disappeared, as so many have since 1945, had the women not continued to fight to tell it. On January 26, 2010, the long-wronged women held yet another protest, this time in front of South Korea's Foreign Ministry in downtown Seoul, ac-cusing it and the government of President Lee Myung-bak of doing nothing as far as Korea's tortured history with Japan is concerned. Because their story of being wronged by Japan remains one of the most central strands of South Korea's national definition, however, this demonstration succeeded. The next day, the Foreign Ministry summoned the Japanese ambassador for reprimands.[19] The pattern continues. The women wait.

A New Level of Hate

During the era of apology politics, several blatantly racist and wildly xeno-phobic cartoonists became best-selling authors in Japan—the wildly pop-ular Kobayashi Yoshinori led the pack.[20] Although Kobayashi is no longer news, he continues to have mass appeal. He has, moreover, raised a genera-tion in his wake who either learned history from him, or, worse, learned to tell history the way he does because it works and it sells.

More worrisome than Kobayashi's self-aggrandizing way of telling history at the expense of those less fortunate than himself, however, is a young man named Sakurai Makoto (nom de guerre, Doronpa). Sakurai grew up under Kobayashi's cloud, and he achieved his own fame by capitalizing on Kobayas-hi's work and that of others by publishing his own series of racist rants.[21] Moreover, Doronpa aspires higher off the page than others of his crowd, demanding action on the streets. On June 9, 2007, he established the Citizens League to Deny Resident Foreigners Special Rights (the Zaitokukai).[22] Among other things, the Zaitokukai urges open violence against Koreans in Japan (and to a lesser degree Chinese and others) in an extensive set of YouTube postings and via regular demonstrations in front of government buildings, newspaper offices, the Korean embassy and consulates, as well as through neighborhoods and in front of schools. The group and its leader's significance must not be measured in terms of the ten thousand people who count themselves contributing members throughout Japan (as well as several hundred more overseas) but rather in their publicly issued orders for violent insurrection and/or military action (depending on whether the enemy is within or without), which together define the Zaitokukai as Japan's fiercest and most dangerous hate group today.

In keeping with the age-group targeted, the group gathers force on the Internet, soliciting contributions (as membership) online by direct bank deposits and by credit card (i.e., available everywhere and anytime, yet centered nowhere in particular). As of February 2011, the nearly ten thousand people listed on the group's website as members come from all over Japan, with the densest concentrations in the most populated centers: Tokyo, Osaka, and Fukuoka. The group's main web pages—as well as those to which they link—are regularly refreshed and advertise where to gather and demonstrate. The group's self-posted videos on YouTube, moreover, make clear to anyone with access to the Internet (including, for example, the police) that violent forms of protest are desirable and worthy of admiration, with postings showing Zaitokukai members openly threatening those they view as impediments to their vision of Japan.[23] Unsurprisingly, they target individuals and groups who are weak within the Japanese legal system by stalking and harassing them, and they use customary bullying tactics, for example, getting the victim to throw the first punch, knowing there will be little to no punishment for Zaitokukai members' behavior.

Recently, they most viciously zeroed in on a small group of elderly ethnic Koreans living in an enclave north of Kyoto, called Utoro. The two hundred or so remaining residents of Utoro descend from more than 1,300 Koreans brought there in 1940 by the Japanese government to build a military airstrip that was abandoned in 1945, together with those being forced to build it. The forsaken Koreans turned to the land first to sustain themselves, which the auto giant Nissan technically owned, first as a wartime airplane manufacturer then refashioned for cars, where many of Utoro's residents also worked. The company sold the land in 1987, and the new owner demanded the residents' eviction from the five-acre plot, where they had long lived, in a series of lawsuits that wound up in 2000 in Japan's supreme court. The court declared Utoro's inhabitants "illegal," squatters without rights or papers. The aging Koreans stayed on, however, vowing to honor their parents' hardship and to "die under their houses" if need be.[24] For Zaitokukai members, many of whom were not born when the lawsuits began in 1987, Utoro's residents are obvious prey, and in a December 2009 video clip, they show others what to do: to the tune of "Clap for the Killers," local Zaitokukai leaders block out the area on a map and deliver threatening leaflets into residents' mailboxes in ways shockingly evocative of the Hitler Youth brigades or the American Ku Klux Klan. This apparently proud display only builds, however, on a series of videos posted a year earlier in December 2008, in which Doronpa leads his followers, as well as some of their young children, through the residents' neighborhood armed with their constitutionally guaranteed rights to wave the national flag and speak freely, even if it is hate speech yelled through megaphones.

Consistent with the group's general belief that all things Korean are to blame for all things wrong in Japan, the Zaitokukai stands ardently opposed to an apology for any aspect of Japan's twentieth-century record. In short, any sort of apology for any past Japanese action involving Koreans or Chinese equals a "gross travesty and treachery, dishonoring our fallen forebears. Japanese like [former Prime Minister] Murayama are a disgrace to the nation and should be tried as criminals."[25] Needless to say, one could simply frown and regard all this as the ravings of a radical and insignificant fringe in Japan if only there were some hint that anti-hate speech laws were in the offing. Yet, in February 2010, the United Nations Committee on the Elimination of Racial Discrimination singled out Japan for its whole-scale absence among leading nations of such a law: "In international law," committee member Patrick Thornberry noted critically, "freedom of expression is not unlimited."[26]

Akin to human rights itself, apology can be spun in the completely opposite direction from how those seeking its inclusion in public discourse intended. No longer in Japan, for example, does it mean solely an apology to the Asian victims of Japanese imperialism as it did a decade ago. It means now—or it does so again, because it once may have done so in the immediate postwar era—official repentance also to the Japanese who suffered fighting for the state's cause. Historian Marilyn Young has demonstrated how this double valence operates with regards to human rights:

> In one way, the language of human rights can now be used to defend the reputations of those who may have committed atrocities; in the other, attention to

one past violation of human rights has led to the uncovering and discussion of tangentially related causes.[27]

While many have come to expect the latter situation as far as apology in Japan is concerned—for example, the former enslaved laborers' case initially emboldened the comfort women—the matter of the Japanese government apologizing to those who may have facilitated some of the atrocities is no longer beyond the pale.

One of the most complicated aspects of apology, the state, and Japan is, ultimately, whose apology counts. The 1947 constitution of Japan made clear that the newly redefined emperor's position would make that post subject to the Japanese parliament. Thus, many Japanese activists and liberals in favor of Japan's issuing a state apology have long argued the need for such a statement to come through parliamentary channels, thus defining it as democratically decided and the will of the Japanese people. At the same time, however, an overwhelming majority of the remaining survivors of the mid-twentieth-century atrocities committed in the name of Japan—which at the time meant in the name of the emperor—want an apology from the emperor of Japan, despite the wartime emperor now being dead for over two decades.

Precisely because history is a never-ending process during the era of apology politics, the whole issue of how to reconcile current Japan with the wartime emperor has come increasingly to the fore, and not necessarily in the way those advocating for an apology for those victimized in Emperor Hirohito's name might wish. In July 2003, Japan's best-selling literary journal, *Bungei Shunju*, included a copy of a draft of what it and the essay's author described as a recently discovered document, now referred to as Emperor Hirohito's "Imperial Edict on Apology."[28] In her essay explaining the document, journalist Kato Kyoko argued that this document holds the potential to "broadly recast a page of Showa history" (1926–1989), making quick reference to the long-standing debate over Japan and apology. Much of this document is interesting in terms of how to use it and similar materials as sources. The former emperor apologized in such a particularized form of Japanese language that the journal needed a Japanese language specialist to render the words accessible to readers. Also, as the article makes clear, Hirohito did not write the document himself; rather, it was remembered by the then head of the Imperial Household Agency, Tajima Michiji, in whose records the document surfaced. Most of all, Hirohito's "apology" is not to Japan's overseas victims who pressed to topic of apology. Instead, the document shows that Hirohito expressed "profound shame" to his noncolonial subjects—meaning Japanese—"who lost their property abroad."

The contemporary social understanding by some in Japan, however, that this document would equal Hirohito's "apology" found receptive audiences not simply with extremists of Doronpa's ilk—who oppose any statements of remorse concerning Japan's attempt to conquer Asia—but also with more mainstream Japanese who, while still committed to the Murayama declaration and the Kono statement, are tired of the rest of the world demanding that Japan do more apologizing for its past wars, especially, as its leaders routinely remind others, since Japan is the only country in the region (and including the United States) that has not waged a war since 1945.[29]

NOTES

1. Ilan Pappe, "Historophobia or the Enslavement of History: The Role of the 1948 Ethnic Cleansing in the Contemporary Israeli-Palestinian Peace Process," in *Partisan Histories: The Past in Contemporary Global Politics*, ed. Max Paul Friedman and Padraic Kenney (New York: Palgrave, 2005), 127–43.

2. See Brian A. Weiner, *Sins of the Parents: The Politics of National Apologies in the United States* (Philadelphia: Temple University Press, 2005).

3. Richard A. Wilson, *The Politics of Truth and Reconciliation in South Africa: Legitimizing the Post-Apartheid State* (New York: Cambridge University Press, 2001), 57.

4. See Elazar Barkan, *The Guilt of Nations: Restitution and Negotiating Historical Injustices* (New York: Norton, 2000).

5. See Roy L. Brooks, *Atonement and Forgiveness: A New Model for Black Reparations* (Berkeley: University of California Press, 2005).

6. Norma Field is the most eloquent writer on the subject of apology from the victims' perspective. Begin with her, "War and Apology: Japan, Asia, the Fiftieth and After," in "The Comfort Women: Colonialism, War, and Sex," special issue *Positions: East Asia Cultures Critique* 5, no. 1 (1997): 5.

7. A useful volume is T. Fujitani, Geoffrey M. White, and Lisa Yoneyama, eds., *Perilous Memories: The Asia Pacific War(s)* (Durham, NC: Duke University Press, 2011).

8. To begin see Herbert Bix's magisterial book, *Hirohito and the Making of Modern Japan* (New York: Harper Collins, 2000).

9. Norma Field, *In the Realm of a Dying Emperor: Japan at Century's End* (New York: Vintage, 1992). Such "taboos" are certainly not unique to Japan. Turkish novelist, Orham Pamuk, faced trial in Istanbul for the Turkish "taboo" of speaking out about the Armenian genocide. See Pamuk, "On Trial," in *The New Yorker*, December 19, 2005, 33–34. In it, interestingly, Pamuk mentions discussing such taboos with Japanese Nobel Prize winning novelist Oe Kenzaburo: "I heard that [Oe], too, had been attacked by nationalist extremists after stating that the ugly crimes committed by his countries' armies during the invasions of Korea and China should be openly discussed in Tokyo." P. 34.

10. See Jennifer Lind, *Sorry States: Apologies in International Politics* (Ithaca, NY: Cornell University Press, 2008).

11. Karen L. Gatz, ed., *Foreign Relations of the United States, 1964–1968: Volume XXIX, Part 1, Korea* (Washington, DC: U.S. GPO, 2000). "U.S. Efforts to Encourage Normalization of Relations Between the Republic of Korea and Japan": 745–802; See No. 349, Reischauer to Rusk, September 8, 1964, 770; and No. 353, Reischauer to Rusk, November 21, 1964, 778.

12. *Asahi Shimbun*, February 17, 1965, evening edition, 1.

13. Official translation as posted on the Japanese Ministry of Foreign Affairs website, www.mofa.go.jp (accessed February 25, 2011).

14. The comment caused a domestic and international media firestorm. Beginning with the Japanese evening papers on March 1, 2007, throughout the month each paper in Japan and Korea ran daily stories on the controversy, and the *New York Times* and the *Washington Post* had extensive coverage and editorials as well.

15. *Washington Post*, June 14, 2007.

16. *Asahi Shimbun*, December 25, 2009, evening edition.

17. *Hankyoreh*, January 5, 2010.

18. *Asahi Shimbun*, December 30, 2009.

19. *Hankyoreh*, January 27, 2010.

20. Wikipedia describes Kobayashi, author or editor of more than 200 books, as "one of the most prominent conservative authors and commentators of Japan's younger generations." See http://en.wikipedia.org/wiki/Yoshinori_Kobayashi (accessed February 27, 2011).

21. Doronpa does publish in book form, although his Internet portals are the main "action": http://ameblo.jp/doronpa01/ (accessed February 27, 2011).

22. Membership stands now at roughly ten thousand people from throughout Japan openly describing themselves as part of the group and sending money, http://www.zaitokukai.info/ (accessed February 27, 2011).

23. For example, http://www.youtube.com/watch?v=WrcBLW14P8M&feature=related.

24. For the Utoro story, see *Japan Times*, July 12, 2005.

25. By pressing a link on Doronpa's main page, one is directed to http://www.maruyamadanwa.com/.

26. Quoted in *Japan Times*, February 26, 2010. Japanese original translated by author.

27. Marilyn Young, "The State and Its Victims Remembering to Forget," in *Truth Claims: Representation and Human Rights*, ed. Mark Bradley and Patrice Petro (New York: Routledge, 2002), 11.

28. Kato Kyoko, "Fuin Sareta Shosho Soko o Yomitoku," *Bungei Shunju*, July 2003, 94–113. Author's translation.

29. Japanese poet Okunishi Ei recently published a collection of his works entitled *Nihon wa senso o shite iru* (*Japan Wages War*) (Tokyo: Doyobijutsusha, 2009). The title's eponymous poem makes the case that Japan's financing of the war on terror and assisting coalition forces is synonymous with waging war.

15

APPROACHING THE UNIVERSAL
DECLARATION OF HUMAN RIGHTS

MARK PHILIP BRADLEY

On the evening of Saturday, December 10, 1949, more than three thousand people packed into Carnegie Hall in New York City. They did so to celebrate the first anniversary of the adoption of the United Nations Universal Declaration of Human Rights at a concert performed by the Boston Symphony Orchestra with Leonard Bernstein at the podium. The crowd in the hall was largely made up of delegates to the United Nations General Assembly, which hours before had brought its fourth regular session to a close, as well as many figures, like Eleanor Roosevelt, who played central roles in the drafting of the Declaration. A larger listening public heard the event as it was broadcast on radio and televised live by the National Broadcasting Company.[1]

The program opened with a new work commissioned specifically for the event, Aaron Copland's *Preamble for a Solemn Occasion*, a short six-minute piece for orchestra and narrator. Copland took as his text for the composition this portion of the 1945 United Nations Charter:

> We the peoples of the United Nations, determined to save succeeding generations from the scourge of war, which twice in our lifetime has brought untold sorrow to mankind, and to reaffirm faith in fundamental human rights, in the dignity and worth of the human person, in the equal rights of men and women of all nations large and small, and . . . to promote social progress and better standards of life in larger freedom . . . have resolved to combine our efforts to accomplish these aims.[2]

As Sir Laurence Olivier came onto the stage, the crowd stood in silence while he read the full preamble to the Universal Declaration of Human Rights and its more specific calls for the respect and observance of individual human rights as the common standard of achievement for all peoples and nations. The Copland piece then began: initially in a dissonant vein aimed to evoke the scourge and sorrows of war, a mood that shifted in the *Preamble*'s second section toward a more triumphant sensibility supported by the liberal use of brass and percussion. Olivier then read from the UN Charter, his voice quietly underlined by an orchestral reprise of the opening segment of the piece, after which the triumphal valences of the second section returned to bring the composition to an affirmative and ringing climax.[3]

Copland's *Preamble* is not especially well known. It certainly doesn't have the same presence in the classical musical canon as his *Fanfare for the Common Man*. Copland himself dismissed it as something of a "pot boiler."[4] While critics in 1949 were considerably kinder, it remains one of his most obscure works and goes unrecorded in its original form to this day. Yet Copland's *Preamble* and its performance in 1949—both the sweep of the ambitions it conveyed and its subsequent obscurities—are a helpful way of approaching the history of the Universal Declaration and its impact on the emergent global human rights order of the late twentieth century.

On the one hand, the musical language of Copland's *Preamble for a Solemn Occasion* and its reception in Carnegie Hall capture a moment in the making of a transnational human imagination that was in fact extraordinary, if still imperfectly understood. Upon adoption in 1948 by the United Nations General Assembly, the Universal Declaration of Human Rights was the first international instrument to articulate global human rights norms and duties. Its thirty articles were hammered out over a period of two years in committees that brought together leading international figures such as Eleanor Roosevelt, René Cassin of France, Charles Malik of Lebanon, and P. C. Chang of China, along with the active participation of representatives from a variety of Latin American states, the Soviet Union, and India. The final document sought to protect not only individual civil and political rights, but economic and social rights as well. The Declaration's sweeping guarantees of their protections were as expansive as its catalog of rights. "Everyone is entitled to all the rights and freedoms set forth in the Declaration," its authors promised, "without distinction of any kind."[5] Nothing, seemingly not even state sovereignty, was to trump the individual rights enumerated in the document. Because of its concern with the individual, its capacious sensibility about what constituted human rights, and its global aspirations for their protection, there had simply never before been anything quite like the Universal Declaration.

The spirit that drove the Declaration also set into motion an unprecedented series of regional and transnational rights declarations, covenants, and conventions immediately following World War II. In Latin America, delegates at several Pan-American congresses during the war adopted a regional human rights vocabulary that anticipated the Universal Declaration and culminated in the adoption of the 1948 American Declaration of the Rights and Duties of Man. At the same time, Western European states began to draft their own rights lexicon, producing the European Convention on Human Rights in 1950. In Geneva, member societies of the International Committee of the Red Cross began discussions in 1946 to craft protections for the rights of noncombatants in times of war. Meanwhile the International Military Tribunal at Nuremberg developed the concepts of "crimes against humanity" and "crimes against the peace" that would become cornerstones of the theory and practice of universal justice in international human rights law.[6] Finally as Copland's *Preamble* was being played in Carnegie Hall, discussions at the United Nations centered on a convention to outlaw genocide; a global freedom of information covenant; protective rights of asylum for refugees; and the drafting of legally binding guarantees of the political, economic, and social rights enshrined in the Universal Declaration.[7]

In the years that followed the celebration in New York City, the Universal Declaration did not fall into quite the same deep memory hole as Copland's *Preamble*, but it was often seen at the margins of an international order shaped by the Cold War and decolonization. Even at its creation in 1948, news of the drafting and adoption of the Universal Declaration vied with events such as the Berlin blockade, the establishment of the State of Israel and war with its Arab neighbors, the communist seizure of power in Czechoslovakia, and the assassination of Mahatma Gandhi. Indeed front-page headlines the day following the commemorative concert in Carnegie Hall in 1949 trumpeted imminent Indonesian independence, the introduction of Chinese communist troops into the French war in Vietnam, and the negotiations that would lead to the establishment of the North Atlantic Treaty Organization.[8] More than twenty years would pass before the Universal Declaration's broadest aspirations began to be concretized in international human rights law and practice.

It is telling that Jeri Laber, who founded Human Rights Watch and became one of the most visible activists in the remarkable resurgence and explosion of global human rights politics in the 1970s, writes in her memoirs: "I did not use the words 'human rights' to describe our cause; it was not part of my everyday vocabulary and would have meant little to most people at that time . . . Back in the early 1970s the concept of human rights was mainly in the province of legal and academic specialists."[9] By and large historians too had forgotten the Universal Declaration and the human rights moment of the 1940s. Until 1998 the *American Historical Review* did not publish an article with the phrase "human rights" in its title, and it would be 2004 before an article appeared in the journal dealing with human rights history after 1945.[10] The first scholarly histories of the making of the Universal Declaration only emerged in the last decade.[11]

How do you write the history of a document that is both simultaneously without global or historical precedent and yet one whose very existence could seemingly be so quickly forgotten? Too often the Universal Declaration has gotten caught as a kind of stand-in for more general attitudes about the nature and significance of a global human rights order in the period after 1945. In one still influential accounting, states and peoples from ever-wider sectors of the globe inexorably seem to bring into being ever more capacious articulations of human rights and their protections in the local, national, and transnational spheres—all of this unfolding in a gradual, Whiggish progression toward an apparently soon to be realized Kantian perpetual peace. These views are usually expressed in narratives of the power of individuals—human rights heroes and heroines (most notably Eleanor Roosevelt, who is often given a star role in the making of the Universal Declaration) who collectively transform the ways in which local and global actors see the world around them.[12]

Against these evolutionary and sometimes overly celebratory narratives, others approached the very notion of global human rights with considerably more skepticism. The apparent triumphs of a human rights regime for these observers are little more than a smokescreen or illusion, what Jeremy Bentham famously called "nonsense upon stilts."[13] For many self-styled realists, the embrace of rights-talk in such normative statements as the Universal Declaration should not obscure the ways in which the more fundamental exercise and hierarchies of power within and between states and societies remains largely unchanged. Pointing to the prevalence of gross violations of human rights by liberal and illiberal states throughout the post-1945 period, they argue the voluntaristic ethos of the Universal Declaration are no match for power politics.[14] Other skeptics working in the fields of postcolonial and feminist studies have focused on how talk of universal human rights obscures its genealogies in Western imperialism and heterosocial patriarchy. Here the Universal Declaration is sometimes rendered as emblematic of how a particular set of hegemonic Euro-American norms came, unfairly in their view, to structure the global rights order.[15]

These approaches to the Universal Declaration and the broader problem of understanding the emergence of global human rights politics do important interpretive work. Accounts that center on the rise of local and global human rights movements have recovered a set of people, ideas, and processes that had been marginalized or ignored in most histories of the post-1945 world. And if realist and other skeptic perspectives too quickly remarginalize or dismiss these developments, they nonetheless remind us of the contested ground on which human rights norms stand and the enduring forces that contribute to their uneven realization in practice.

But there are dangers in collapsing our understanding of the Universal Declaration and its legacies solely into these analytical categories. Most important, they elide the questions of why the global articulation of individual human rights norms came to be *believable* through the making of the Universal Declaration in the 1940s and how those sensibilities have lingered in the more than sixty years since it was ratified by the United Nations General Assembly. To do this, we need to be willing to put aside not only some of the skepticism about the project of global human rights but also the notion of linear progress that has infused more celebratory historical accounts of its unfolding.

In their place, it may be more useful to concentrate, as Lynn Hunt urged in her study of what she termed the eighteenth-century rights revolution, on moments of "jumps and discontinuities."[16] Moments in which global rights-talk after 1945 did, in fact, become believable in a range of geographic, cultural, and gendered contexts, offering at particular times and places what transnational publics, nonstate actors, and some states saw as a powerful—if sometimes contested and contradictory—language to more fully realize human dignity and welfare in a space that transcended the local and the national.

To unpack the human rights moment of the 1940s, it is important to appreciate the liminal contours of the global environment from which the Universal Declaration emerged. The full force of the Cold War was yet to come, and to most observers the escalating pace of the move to decolonization in the global South was an unanticipated contingency. A spirit of internationalism hovered over the postwar world, most notably in the creation of the United Nations where articulations of rights and sovereignty were both in play at the intersection of the domestic and the transnational. At the San Francisco conference that brought the United Nations into being in 1945, the American delegation, under heavy pressure from domestic groups and actors in Western Europe and the global South that strongly favored international guarantees of human rights, proposed the provisions that put human rights at the center of the United Nations Charter. The language of the per-ambulatory Article 1, in which member states pledged "respect for human rights and fundamental freedoms for all," and Article 55, which guaranteed freedom from discrimination "without distinction as to race, sex, language or religion," were the product of these efforts.

Concerns about the conservative and racialist backlash that these provisions might produce in the United States and fears of the European imperial powers that the Charter's human rights language could be employed against them by anticolonial movements to hasten the end of empire, however, prompted the American delegation to introduce language in what became Article 2(7) of the Charter that promised "nothing in the Charter should authorize . . . intervention in matters that are *essentially* [emphasis added] within the domestic jurisdiction of any state."[17] But what, in fact, would "essentially" come to mean?

At the close of World War II, the relationship between the emergent global rights order outlined in the Charter, particularly its insistence that member states protect the individual rights of all their citizens, and its domestic jurisdiction clause remained open. The Charter's articulation of global rights norms, some contemporary observers believed, offered at least the possibility of remaking the bounds of sovereignty. The articulation of global rights norms in the Charter and later in the Universal Declaration appeared to these observers to offer at least the possibility of a revolutionary transformation in the relationships among the individual, the state, and the international.

This new thinking allowed the Indian delegation at the United Nations in 1946 to win the support of the General Assembly for a resolution that criticized the South African government's passage that year of the Asiatic Land Tenure and Indian Representation Act for its discriminatory treatment of the country's Indian population. The ironies here ran especially deep. South African Premier Field Marshal Jan Smuts, who had, in fact, drafted the human rights language in the preamble of the United Nations Charter—apparently never dreaming it would have any implications for his own government (or, for that matter, any substantive implications at all)—insisted that the domestic jurisdiction clause prevented discussion of or action on the treatment of Indians in South Africa at the United Nations. But after tense and sustained debate, India's argument that the General Assembly could hear and rule on cases like this one that violated the Charter's human rights language won the day by a two-thirds majority of Assembly members.[18]

Pushing on the expansive conditions of possibility in the early postwar period took place not only in the top-down elite sphere of the United Nations but emerged in more quotidian, bottom-up and local spaces as well. Daniel Cohen and Atina Grossmann's essays on the micropolitics of refugee relief policies in the aftermath of World War II in this volume can be read as instances of these more on-the-ground efforts to harness the fluidities of the postwar moment.[19] So too were a series of cases that made their way through the American courts in the late 1940s and early 1950s, which employed the then novel legal argument that the controlling authority of international human rights norms across national borders in the United Nations Charter and Universal Declaration trumped existing U.S. federal and state laws and claims of national sovereignty. Brought by Japanese American, African American, and Native American plaintiffs, these cases used a transnational frame to approach a variety of instances of domestic racial discrimination in housing, in land and fishing rights, in public accommodation, in education, and in marriage.[20]

To give just one illustrative example, *Rice v. Sioux City Memorial Park Cemetery, Inc.,* emerged in 1953 in the wake of the death of Sergeant John Rice in the Korean War. Rice's widow had entered into a contract with the Sioux City cemetery for his burial. At the graveside services, several cemetery officials noted a number of Native American mourners and suspected Rice might have been Native American. They visited his widow who told them their assumption was correct. The cemetery, with a "Caucasians only" burial policy, ordered her husband's body removed. The action drew immediate and national attention, prompting President Truman's intervention; Truman arranged for Rice to be buried at Arlington National Cemetery. Not placated by the president's symbolic gesture, Rice's widow sued in Iowa courts in part on global human rights grounds.[21] When the Iowa Supreme Court dismissed the case, she took it to the U.S. Supreme Court. In their brief for the Supreme Court, Rice and her lawyers dwelt at some length on Charter-inspired claims arguing that the Iowa court had "violated the basic and very fundamental concepts of equality not only announced but also pledged by the United Nations Charter and all of the member nations of which the United States is one."[22]

The petitioners in the Rice case and the other global rights cases in this period, along with the judges that heard them favorably, acted to harness the potentialities of international human rights guarantees and more relaxed conceptions of national sovereignty to combat racial discrimination in the United States. For them, the Universal Declaration was believable. It would, for instance, allow a California court in a Japanese land-rights case to argue in a 1950 opinion:

> Discrimination against a people of one race is contrary to both the letter and
> to the spirit of the [UN] Charter which, as a treaty, is paramount to every law
> of every state in conflict with it. [California] law must therefore yield to the
> treaty as the superior authority.[23]

The California court provided perhaps the most muscular assertion of the
domestic reach of global rights norms in the American context. Nonetheless, a substantial number of state and federal courts, and in one case several
Supreme Court justices, proved receptive to these claims. Their responses,
like those of the UN General Assembly in 1946 to the Indian case against
South Africa, reveal the horizons of possibility unleashed by the Universal
Declaration for the global protection of individual human rights.

These moves to explore the denser textures of the human rights moment
of the 1940s should not obscure its internal contradictions and limits. If the
universalizing vocabulary of the Declaration could be powerfully employed
to address local violations of human rights, it could also operate to erase
the particularities of the rights claims made in its name. In the early postwar period, for instance, the Nazi genocide against European Jewry was
drained of its specificities and a particular Jewish fate came to be represented as universal human suffering. Not only was this so at the Nuremberg
Trials, where the murder of Jews was subsumed under the label of "crimes
against humanity," the universalizing impulse resonated even more broadly
at the level of popular culture. As several scholars recently noted, the pre-
sentation and reception of Anne Frank's diary in the 1950s, when it first
became an international best seller as well as a popular stage play and film,
downplayed the centrality of the Jewish dimension of the story and the
complex richness of Anne's personality. In their place, the lives of the
Franks were rendered as an uplifting symbol of humanity and Anne a cli-
chéd figure "who possessed a seemingly never-ending optimism and hope
for mankind."[24]

The problems of human rights universalism did not go unnoticed by
some contemporary observers. The American Anthropological Association's 1947 "Statement on Human Rights," prepared at the invitation of
those drafting the Universal Declaration, rejected the notion of universal
human rights altogether, emphasizing the plurality of cultural references
and authorities for conceptions of rights.[25] Similarly UNESCO director
Julian Huxley's efforts in 1947 to find a common philosophical basis for
human rights floundered, with some interlocutors such as Gandhi questioning the whole enterprise of universal rights making.[26] The more general tendency toward absolutism for defining a universal human rights order in the

1940s, and the reticence to consider political, social, and cultural particularities, would continue to inflect human rights politics after the 1940s. They
would also pose persisting interpretative challenges for historians who were
simultaneously sympathetic to the cause of human rights but shared a disci-
plinary commitment to causality as a mode of inquiry.[27]

The moment of the Declaration turned out to be a fleeting one, with its
expansive potentialities largely closed down by the mid 1950s. For the
United States and the Soviet Union, their early postwar engagement on
human rights questions except as an extension of Cold War polemics largely
came to an end by the early 1950s. The attention of most states and peoples
in the global South was increasingly focused on collective self-determination
in the Cold War-inflected decolonization struggles of the 1950s and 1960s
rather than the individual rights claims of the Universal Declaration. For
their part, imperial powers in Western Europe, most notably Great Britain
and France, remained wary of advancing a transnational human rights agenda
that potentially undermined efforts to maintain control over their colonial
territories.[28]

In the jumps and discontinuities that shaped the trajectory of the global
rights order after 1945, the human rights norms of the Universal Declaration
became believable again in the 1970s when their spirit reemerged with a
vengeance along with a renewed appreciation of the kind of political work
the human rights frame could do. The florescence of Amnesty International
and its Nobel Prize in 1977, the claims for political and civil rights among
dissidents in the Soviet Union, the Helsinki Accords, the Charter 77 movement in Eastern Europe, the international women's conference in Mexico
City in 1975, Carter's human rights diplomacy and transnational campaigns
against human rights abuses in Latin America and South Korea and apartheid in South Africa, to name just a few, were all products of this return to
global human rights talk.

We know very little about the histories of these remarkable developments. If the history of the Universal Declaration and the human rights moment of the 1940s only began to be written a decade ago, the scale and
scope of the long 1970s have just started to come into view by historians.[29]
This exciting new work, and some of the best of it is included in this volume, suggests that global human rights politics increasingly shifted focus
from the state-dominated norm construction of the 1940s to transnational
nonstate human rights advocacy and, somewhat later, to the enforcement of
a thickening body of global rights norms by both state and nonstate juridical
actors. The rapid proliferation of nongovernmental human rights organizations, which increased ten-fold between 1961 and 1984 to more than twelve

thousand, was one critical element of the move toward transnational advocacy, as was a widening of the kinds of rights that were seen as deserving global protection and the growing ubiquity of international human rights law to enforce them. There were fewer than twenty global human rights legal instruments in force in 1950; in 2000 there were almost a hundred.[30] Moreover, beginning in the 1980s, new transnational juridical bodies such as regional courts and international tribunals—as well as the novel use of domestic courts—provided individual victims of state human rights abuses with redress and compensation. In all this, individuals mattered too. It is difficult to imagine a history of the 1970s that did not give attention to such leading figures as the Russian Andrei Sakharov, the Czech Vaclav Havel, the South African Nelson Mandela, the Argentinian group Madres de la Plazo de Mayo, the South Korean Kim Dae-jung, or the East Timorese José Ramos-Horta.

But the new human rights history of the 1970s has rightly steered away from more Whiggish conceptions of the contours of these developments and usefully foregrounds many of their tensions and contradictions. Essays in this volume by Barbara Keys, on the troubling ways in which torture came to matter to transnational publics in some instances and not others, and by Brad Simpson, on the willingness of the international community (state and nonstate actors alike) to look away from the human rights implications of genocide in East Timor, remind us that the seemingly capacious vision of human rights norms can be distressingly narrow. The violations of some rights, often political and civil and then only in particular geographic spaces, attracted Western human rights activists—who would become the gatekeepers of transnational human rights talk and practice in the 1970s and 1980s—other modes and locales of rights violations did not.

In an even larger sense that reveals the lingering potency and problematics of 1940s universalism for global rights talk, many of the nonstate actors at the forefront of the human rights campaigns of the 1970s were, consciously, indifferent to context. Political repression and its history were, building on the historian Greg Grandin's arguments about the somewhat different but related work of truth commissions, presented as moral parable rather than a causal network of political and social relations.[31] This was especially true for Amnesty International, arguably the most influential nonstate human rights actor in this period. In the organization's internal and public articulations of its self-described "impartial" mission, Amnesty continually insisted "we do not seek to explain the root causes of political repression" and that its work was based on "universally shared values, leaving all other matters to the side."[32] In leaving politics, as they are more conventionally understood, behind, Amnesty drained from many of the cases it lifted up the structural forces and local particulars that gave rise to the violations of rights in the first place. Substituting the universal for the particular brought victories and gave the movement much of its popular appeal. But it left open, and indeed ignored, the multiple and sometimes conflicting causes that had prompted the rediscovery of the lexicon of global human rights.

If pieces of the puzzle of global human rights history in the 1970s and beyond are now being put into place in an increasingly sophisticated scholarship, we still don't know where the ubiquitous presence of human rights talk in this period really came from. There are some intriguing hypotheses. In one view, the collapse of competing utopias in the 1970s—whether socialist internationalism in Europe, the liberal Cold War order in the United States, or the emancipatory discourse of Third Worldism—opened a space in which a variety of local actors from American presidents to Soviet dissidents and Latin American radicals began to see the transnational protection of human rights as a compelling form of antipolitics. A complementary though more structural explanation locates the transformations of the 1970s in the accelerating forces of globalization, most notably the emergent power of transnational finance and global civil society, that challenged the predominant political and economic statism of the postwar international order. From this perspective, the result was a world of complex interdependence in which traditional state geopolitics increasingly gave way to a new transnational politics of human rights, public health, the environment, and the global economy.[33]

In positing a fundamental break with the past, whether it be shifts in belief or in the international system (or both), these arguments begin to help us understand critical dimensions of the jumps and discontinuities represented by the moment of the long 1970s. And yet, in so forcefully drawing attention to rupture over continuity, they implicitly (and sometimes explicitly) do not attach much significance to the human rights histories of the 1940s for making sense of the 1970s and the present.[34]

That doesn't feel quite right. Let me close by offering one last case suggestive of the persisting intersections between this second global human rights moment of the late twentieth century and the larger meanings we might accord to the Universal Declaration.

On March 29, 1976, seventeen-year-old Joelito Filártiga was tortured to death by Americo Peña-Irala, the inspector general of police in the capital city of Paraguay. Joelito was the son of Joel Filártiga, a doctor and long-standing opponent of the regime that had dictatorially ruled Paraguay since 1954. Joel Filártiga unsuccessfully sought redress against Peña and the police in Paraguayan courts for the torture and murder of his son. Several years later Filártiga and his daughter came to the United States seeking permanent political asylum. When they learned that Peña was also in United States and living in Brooklyn, they filed a complaint in U.S. District Court against him claiming Peña had wrongfully caused Joelita's death by torture.[35]

The complaint rested on the Alien Tort Statute, which established U.S. federal district court jurisdiction over "all causes where an alien sues for a tort" committed "in violation of the law of nations."[36] The legal strategy was a bold one. The Alien Tort Statute, a part of the Judiciary Act of 1789, had rarely been invoked in American courts since and never before on questions dealing with human rights. Lawyers for the Filártigas argued that official torture violated an emerging norm of customary international law, in part brought into being by the prohibitions against torture in Article 5 of the Universal Declaration, and this trigged the applicability of the statute for their case against Peña.

The District Court dismissed the complaint. But in a sweeping June 1980 opinion, the U.S. Court of Appeals held that deliberate, official torture did violate universally accepted norms of international human rights law and that under the Alien Tort Statute an alien could bring an alleged torturer before federal court for actions committed outside the borders of the United States. The *Filártiga* decision foreshadowed accelerating moves after 1980—among them efforts to try the Chilean General Pinochet in Spain; the emergence of international tribunals in the Hague, Rwanda, and Cambodia; and the establishment of the International Criminal Court—aimed at global accountability in cases of torture and other gross violations of human rights.

Filártiga illustrates the revolutionary reach of human rights norms in and across the boundaries of the nation-state first set in motion by the framers of the Universal Declaration. But it also reveals some of the forces that shaped and constrained the global meanings of human rights and the legacies of the Declaration. The presiding judge in the *Filártiga* case closed his opinion this way: "In the twentieth century the international community has come to recognize the common danger posed by the flagrant disregard of basic human rights . . . The torturer has become—like the pirate or slave trader before him—*hostis humani generis*, an enemy of all mankind."[37]

Many, if not most, who read the judge's opinion (myself included) are likely to agree. In a normative sense, for most people, to enslave or torture another person is unthinkable. But, of course, in practice, it isn't. Before and after *Filártiga*, just as before and after the abolition of slavery, human rights norms and beliefs didn't necessarily govern practice. The unthinkable persists, most recently and dramatically, in American prisons in Iraq and Cuba, and in other violations of political, economic, social, sexual, and cultural rights in the United States and the rest of the world. Contemporary domestic courts, American included, have been considerably more reticent to take cases where their own nationals were accused of torture, reflecting the continuing unevenness between the universal and the particular that inflected human rights politics in the 1940s and 1970s.[38]

But the *Filártiga* case also helps us understand how the broader sensibilities of the Universal Declaration have come to make the suffering of strangers matter as much as one's own. As they do, and perhaps because they do, the history of the Universal Declaration and its meanings over the last sixty years have produced a believability in the world-shattering power of global human rights talk—no matter how contingent and situated the discourse of rights has been in historical time and however detached we ought to be from celebratory or dismissive narratives of its unfolding. If chastened by the ambiguities, contradictions, and failures of the past—and as historians by the conflicting pulls of "the cause" and causality—in the end it is the right to hope that drives us forward.

NOTES

1. "UN Code of Rights Hailed on 1st Year," *New York Times*, December 11, 1949.

2. United Nations Charter, UN website, http://www.un.org/en/documents/charter/preamble.shtml (accessed January 28, 2010).

3. Aaron Copland and Vivian Perlis, *Copland, since 1943* (New York: St. Martin's Press, 1989), 148–49; Howard Pollack, *Aaron Copland: The Life and Work of an Uncommon Man* (New York: Henry Holt and Company, 1999), 438–39.

4. Pollack, *Copland*, 439.

5. Article 2, Universal Declaration of Human Rights, UN website, http://www.un.org/en/documents/udhr/ (accessed January 28, 2010).

6. On the 1949 Geneva Conventions and Nuremberg, see William Hitchcock's and Elizabeth Borgwardt's essays in this volume. Francine Hirsch's pioneering work on the Soviet presence at Nuremberg reveals the surprising Soviet contributions to international human rights law; see her "The Soviets at Nuremberg: International Law, Propaganda and Postwar Order," *American Historical Review* 113, no. 3 (June 2008): 701–30.

7. On the Genocide Convention, see Samantha Power, *"A Problem from Hell": America and the Age of Genocide* (New York: Basic Books, 2002), chs. 2–4; and John Cooper, *Raphael Lemkin and the Struggle for the Genocide Convention* (London: Palgrave Macmillan, 2008). On the freedom of information covenant, see Kenneth Cmiel, "Human Rights, Freedom of Information, and the Origins of Third-World Solidarity" in *Truth Claims: Representation and Human Rights*, ed. Mark Philip Bradley and Patrice Petro (New Brunswick, NJ: Rutgers University Press, 2002), 107–30.

8. *New York Times*, December 11, 1949, 1; readers of the *Times* would have had to wait until page 30 to learn of the Carnegie Hall anniversary event in an article itself almost overwhelmed by a three-quarter page advertisement on the same page featuring women's rhinestone-studded "cutaway" shirts and "umbrella-pleated" dresses.

9. Jeri Laber, *The Courage of Strangers: Coming of Age with the Human Rights Movement* (New York: Public Affairs, 2002), 74.

10. Alice L. Conklin, "Colonialism and Human Rights, A Contradiction in Terms?: The Case of France and West Africa, 1995–1914," *American Historical Review* 103, no. 2 (April 1998): 419–42; and, in what continues to stand as the seminal survey of this emergent field, Kenneth Cmiel, "The Recent History of Human Rights," *American Historical Review* 109, no. 1 (February 2004): 117–35. I am grateful to Sam Moyn for drawing my attention to this indexical metric.

11. Most notably Mary Ann Glendon, *A World Made New: Eleanor Roosevelt and the Universal Declaration of Human Rights* (New York: Random House, 2001); and Johannes Morsink, *The Universal Declaration of Human Rights: Origins, Drafting and Intent* (Philadelphia: University of Pennsylvania Press, 1999).

12. See, for instance, Paul Gordon Lawrence's *The Evolution of International Human Rights: Visions Seen* (Philadelphia: University of Pennsylvania Press, 1998); and Jean H. Quataert, *Advocating Dignity: Human Rights Mobilizations in Global Politics* (Philadelphia: University of Pennsylvania Press, 2009).

13. Jeremy Bentham, "Anarchical Fallacies" in *Nonsense Upon Stilts: Bentham, Burke and Marx on the Rights of Man*, ed. Jeremy Waldron (London: Methuen, 1987), 53.

14. On the 1940s in this register, see Mark Mazower "The Strange Triumph of Human Rights, 1933–1950," *Historical Journal* 47, no. 2 (June 2004): 379–98; but also Kirsten Sellars, *The Rise and Rise of Human Rights* (London: Sutton Publishing, 2002); and, more conceptually, Stephen Krasner, "Rulers and Ruled: Human Rights" in his *Sovereignty: Organized Hypocrisy* (Princeton, NJ: Princeton University Press, 1999), 105–26.

15. For these arguments in the context of the UN Charter and Universal Declaration, see Roger Normand and Sarah Zaidi, *Human Rights at the United Nations: The Political History of Universal Justice* (Bloomington: Indiana University Press, 2007), chs. 3–6; more generally see Anthony Anghie, *Imperialism, Sovereignty and the Making of International Law* (Cambridge: Cambridge University Press, 2005); and Sally Engle Merry, *Human Rights and Gender Violence: Translating International Law into Local Justice* (Chicago: University of Chicago Press, 2006).

16. Lynn Hunt, *Inventing Human Rights: A History* (New York: W. W. Norton, 2007).

17. UN Charter, at the UN website, http://www.un.org/en/documents/charter (accessed January 28, 2010). For useful discussions of the drafting of the human rights language and the domestic jurisdiction clause of the UN Charter, see Mark Mazower, *No Enchanted Palace: The End of Empire and the Ideological Origins of*

the United Nations (Princeton, NJ: Princeton University Press, 2009), ch. 1; Carol Anderson, *Eyes Off the Prize: The United Nations and the African American Struggle for Human Rights, 1944–55* (Cambridge: Cambridge University Press, 2003), ch. 1; and Elizabeth Borgwardt, *A New Deal for the World: America's Vision for Human Rights* (Cambridge, MA: Harvard University Press, 2005), chs. 5 and 6. For concerns over implications of human rights protections for British imperial policy, especially as they emerged in deliberations over the European Convention for Human Rights, see A. W. Brian Simpson, *Human Rights and the End of Empire: Britain and the Genesis of the European Convention* (Oxford: Oxford University Press, 2001).

18. On the Indian case, see UN General Assembly, Official Records, *Plenary Meeting of the General Assembly Verbatim Records, October 23–December 16, 1946*, 1006–1061; UN General Assembly, Official Records, *Jt. Committee of the First and Sixth Committees Summary Record of Meetings, November 21–30, 1946*; Mazower, *No Enchanted Palace*: ch. 4; and Lorna Lloyd, "'A Most Auspicious Beginning': the 1946 United Nations General Assembly and the Question of the Treatment of Indians in South Africa," *Review of International Studies* 16 (1990): 131–53.

19. A similar bottom-up approach to the making of human rights norms in this period emerges in two important recent dissertations: see Stephen Mak, "Enemy Aliens in a World at War: America's Other Internment during World War II" (PhD diss., Northwestern University, 2009); and Stephen Porter, "Defining Public Responsibility in a Global Age: Refugees, NGOs and the American State" (PhD diss., University of Chicago, 2009).

20. For a fuller discussion of the American global rights cases of the 1940s see my "The Ambiguities of Sovereignty: The United States and the Global Human Rights Cases of the 1940s and 1950s," in *The State of Sovereignty: Territories, Laws, Populations*, eds. Douglas Howland and Luise White (Bloomington: Indiana University Press, 2009).

21. *Rice v. Sioux City Memorial Park Cemetery, Inc.*, 60 N.W. 2d 116–17 (1953).

22. Brief in support of petition for writ of *certiorari* to the United States Supreme Court, 18–19.

23. *Sei Fuji v. California*, Superior Court of Los Angeles County, April 24, 1950, 21: California State Archives.

24. Tony Kushner, "'I Want to Go on Living after my Death': The Memory of Anne Frank" in *War and Memory in the Twentieth Century*, eds. Martin Evans and Ken Lunn (Oxford: Berg, 1997), 17; see also Allen H. Rosenfeld, "Popularization and Memory: The Case of Anne Frank," in *Lessons and Legacies: The Meanings of the Holocaust in a Changing World*, ed. Peter Hayes (Evanston, IL: Northwestern University Press, 1991); and Daniel Levy and Natan Sznaider, *Holocaust and Memory in the Global Era* (Philadelphia: Temple University Press, 2006), 57–63. For a more general discussion of the universalizing climate that shaped Holocaust memory in the early Cold War period, and one that reads the Frank diary somewhat differently, see Peter Novick, *The Holocaust in American Life* (Boston: Houghton Mifflin, 2000), 85–123.

25. Executive Board, American Anthropological Association, "Statement on Human Rights," *American Anthropologist* 49, no. 4 (October–December 1947): 539–43. See Karen Engle, "From Skepticism to Embrace: Human Rights and the American Anthropological Association," *Human Rights Quarterly* 23, no. 3 (August 2001): 533–47.

26. UNESCO, Secretariat, *Records of the Comité sur le principes philosophiques des droits d'home, 1947–52*. For the published volume that emerged out of this project, see UNESCO, *Human Rights: Comments and Interpretations* (New York: Columbia University Press, 1949).

27. For an exceptionally thoughtful discussion of the problems of universalism for writing the history of the United Nations in this period, see Sunil Amrith and Glenda Sluga, "New Histories of the United Nations," *Journal of World History* 19, no. 3 (September 2008): 251–74.

28. For a range of the often competing interpretative perspectives in the emergent historical scholarship on the engagement in global human rights politics within the global South, see Manu Bhagavan, "A New Hope: India, the United Nations and the Making of the Universal Declaration of Human Rights," *Modern Asian Studies* (June 2008), doi:10.1017/S0026749X08003600, Cambridge University Press, http://www.cambridge.org/; Roland Burke, "From Individual Rights to National Development: The First UN Conference on Human Rights, Tehran, 1969," *Journal of World History* 19, no. 3 (September 2008): 275–96; Cmiel, "Human Rights, Freedom and the Origins of Third-World Solidarity"; and Samuel Moyn's essay in this volume.

29. For a still helpful overview of this period (and broader in its interpretative concerns than its title suggests), see Kenneth Cmiel, "The Emergence of Human Rights Politics in the United States," *Journal of American History* 86 (December 1999): 1249–50.

30. Akira Iriye's *Global Community: The Role of International Organizations in the Making of the Contemporary World* (Berkeley: University of California Press, 2002) remains foundational on the historical rise of nongovernmental organizations; see also Margaret E. Keck and Kathryn Sikkink, *Activists Beyond Borders: Advocacy Networks in International Politics* (Ithaca, NY: Cornell University Press, 1998). On human rights instruments in force, and the intersection of nongovernmental organizations, domestic policy and effectiveness of international human rights law more generally, see Beth Simmons, *Mobilizing for Human Rights: International Law in Domestic Politics* (Cambridge: Cambridge University Press, 2009), 37 and passim.

31. Greg Grandin, "The Instruction of Great Catastrophe: Truth Commissions, National History and State Formation in Argentina, Chile and Guatemala," *American Historical Review* 110, no. 1 (February 2005): 46–67.

32. *Amnesty International Report 1980* (London: Amnesty International Publications, 1980), 2, 4, 7. Like much of the history of this period, the place of Amnesty International in the global human rights politics of the 1970s is just being written;

among the most promising efforts are a series of unpublished papers by Jan Eckels in the author's possession.

33. For the more ideational argument that sees human rights in the 1970s as antipolitics, see Samuel Moyn, *The Last Utopia: Human Rights in History* (Cambridge, MA: Harvard University Press, 2010), ch. 4. The structural approach to the transformations of the 1970s emerges in Daniel Sargent, "From Internationalism to Globalism: The United States and the Transformation of International Politics in the 1970s" (PhD diss., Harvard University, 2008).

34. See Moyn, *Last Utopia*, ch. 2.

35. *Filártiga v. Peña-Irala*, 630 F.2d 876 (2d Cir. 1980), 878. The fullest discussion of the events that gave rise to the *Filártiga* case can be found in Richard Allan White, *Breaking Silence: The Case That Changed the Face of Human Rights* (Washington, DC: Georgetown University Press, 2004).

36. *Judiciary Act of 1789*, ch. 20, codified 28 U.S.C. 1350.

37. *Filártiga v. Peña-Irala*, 890.

38. See David Cole, "Getting Away with Torture," *New York Review of Books*, January 14, 2010, 39–42. For a judicious and persuasive assessment of state policy toward torture and the relative power of international legal norms, see Simmons, *Mobilizing for Human Rights*, ch. 7.

INDEX

Abe, Shinzo, 317
Abortion, 35, 60, 150
Abrams, Elliot, 234–35
Abu Ghraib prison, 14
Activism, on behalf of human rights,
  36–40, 42–43, 94, 144, 202, 214, 266,
  336; against slavery, 37–38; against
  FGM, 288, 295, 297–99, 301
Adamishin, Anatoly, 271
Afghanistan, 14, 106–8, 169
Afkhami, Mahnaz, 293
AFL–CIO, 223
African Americans, 32–33; and cold
  war, 7
African Court on Human and Peoples'
  Rights, 13
African National Congress, 10
African Women for Research and
  Development, 291
Akayesu, Jean-Paul, 14
Aleksandrov, Anatoly, 250–52
Algerian war of independence, 171
Al Qaeda, 14, 106–7
Amanpour, Christiane, 285, 298–99
American Anthropological Association,
  334
American Bar Association, 141
American Friends Service Committee,
  223–25
American Jewish Joint Distribution
  Committee, 118, 122
American Medical Association, 84
Amnesty International, 8–9, 17, 27, 28,
  39–41, 44, 181–82, 187, 190, 223,
  335–36; and Greece, 201–3, 205–11,
  214
Anan, Kofi, 53, 56
Anderson, Carol, 80
Anderson, Jack, 209
Angle, Stephen, 33–34
Angola, 170, 233
Anticolonialism, 33, 55, 159–73, 187

Anti-Semitism, 53
Apologies, as national act of redress,
  311–25
Applebaum, Anne, 43
Argentina, 28, 214
Armacost, Michael, 179
Armitage, David, 160
Arseni, Catherine, 208
"Asian values" debate, 11–12, 27
Asylum, 61
Atlantic Charter (1941), 4, 114–15, 120,
  163–65, 167
Australia, 300; and Geneva Conventions,
  97; support for Indonesia by, 181, 189,
  192
Awoonor, Kofi, 11

Baker, James, 275
Bandung Conference (1955), 7, 10, 165,
  168
Bangkok Declaration, 11
Bangladesh, 188
Barnett, Randy, 79
Baroody, Jamil, 169
Bass, Gary Jonathan, 37
Bayh, Birch, 213
Beard, Charles, 5
Becket, James, 201–2, 205–7, 213
Begtrup, Bogil, 139
Belgium, 10, 116
Belize, 190
Bemis, Samuel Flagg, 5
Benenson, Peter, 8, 205
Benhabib, Seyla, 84
Berlin, Blockade, 118
Berlin, Isaiah, 33
Bernstein, Leonard, 327
Biafra, 188
Biddle, Francis, 75, 212
Bill of Rights, American, 3, 82
Birman, Joseph, 259
B'nai Brith, 223